BRITISH POLITICS AND THE
AMERICAN REVOLUTION

BRITISH POLITICS AND THE AMERICAN REVOLUTION

The Path to War, 1773–75

BY

BERNARD DONOUGHUE

Lecturer in Politics at the London School
of Economics and Political Science

LONDON
MACMILLAN & CO LTD
NEW YORK · ST MARTIN'S PRESS

1964

MACMILLAN AND COMPANY LIMITED
St Martin's Street London WC 2
also Bombay Calcutta Madras Melbourne

THE MACMILLAN COMPANY OF CANADA LIMITED
70 Bond Street Toronto 2

ST MARTIN'S PRESS INC
175 Fifth Avenue New York 10 NY

Library of Congress Card Number 64-21438

PRINTED IN GREAT BRITAIN

TO MY FATHER
THOMAS JOSEPH DONOUGHUE

PREFACE

I WISH to express deepest appreciation to two friends : Dr. J. B. Owen, Senior Tutor of Lincoln College, Oxford, my teacher and guide for the past nine years, and Philip Williams, Fellow of Nuffield College, Oxford, who has been a constant source of help, encouragement and advice. John Brooke, of *The History of Parliament*, Ian R. Christie, Reader in Modern History at University College, London, Dr. F. R. Madden, Fellow of Nuffield College, Oxford, and Mrs. Gina Alexander, formerly tutor at Royal Holloway College, London, each read the whole work and made very many helpful improvements.

Acknowledgments are due to the Earl of Dartmouth for kind permission to reproduce documents from the Dartmouth Manuscripts belonging to him and now deposited at the William Salt Library, Stafford ; to Earl Fitzwilliam and Earl Fitzwilliam's Wentworth Estates Company for permission to publish documents from the Rockingham and Burke collections at the Sheffield Central Library ; to the Duke of Portland, the Mellish Trustees, the Newcastle Trustees and the University of Nottingham for permission to use the Portland Manuscripts, the Mellish Manuscripts and the Newcastle Manuscripts deposited in the Department of Manuscripts, Nottingham University ; to the Bodleian Library, Oxford, for permission to quote from the North Papers ; to the Trustees of the British Museum for permission to quote from several collections among the Additional Manuscripts and the Egerton Manuscripts ; and to the Controller of H.M. Stationery Office for permission to reproduce unpublished Crown-copyright material in the Public Record Office. The librarians and staffs at the William Salt Library, at the Sheffield Central Library and at the Nottingham University Department of Manuscripts gave an unfailing attention and assistance which made visits to them as pleasurable as they were rewarding.

I must express my gratitude to the Warden and Fellows of Nuffield College, Oxford, to the Ministry of Education and to the Trustees of the Charles and Julia Henry Fellowship Fund for grants to pursue the early stages of this research ; and to Professor Eliot Perkins and his colleagues at Lowell House, Harvard, who offered me friendship and hospitality beyond bounds during my stay with them.

Finally, my greatest debt is to my wife Carol. The main body of this study was written in the spare evenings, week-ends and holidays allowed by a full-time office job. Without her affection, patience and endless good humour during those three years it would never have been completed.

B. D.

20 February 1964

CONTENTS

ABBREVIATIONS

THE following abbreviations are used :

BM.	British Museum
DNB	*Dictionary of National Biography*
HMC	*Historical Manuscripts Commission*
Parl. Hist.	*The Parliamentary History of England* . . ., W. Cobbett, 36 vols., London, 1806-20
PRO.	Public Record Office
W.W.M.	Wentworth Woodhouse Muniments. The Burke papers in this Collection will be cited as W.W.M. Bk., and where they have been printed in the new Cambridge edition of Burke's correspondence the abbreviation *CEB* will be added together with the volume and page reference. The Rockingham papers in the Wentworth Woodhouse Muniments will be cited as W.W.M. R. The Rockingham papers have reference numbers and these will be given, but at the time of writing the Burke papers do not. These descriptions are those officially in use at the Sheffield City Central Library at the time the collections were examined

To facilitate reference, the title and author or editor of each printed work is given when it is cited for the first time in each chapter. Subsequent citations in a chapter contain only the author's or editor's name, except where several works by the same author are used, in which case the titles are always given, and where a published collection of original sources is known better by the author than by the editor, in which case the author's name is included in a short title — *e.g.*, *Walpole Last Journals*, *Franklin Complete Works*.

CHAPTER I

INTRODUCTION: ENGLAND AND THE AMERICAN COLONIES, 1763–1773

AFTER settling the Peace of Paris in 1763, British statesmen were able to turn to the problem of the government of America, a problem which now concerned both the thirteen Old Colonies[1] on the eastern seaboard and the vast new territories acquired in the French and Indian wars.

The root of the difficulty with the Old Colonies was the extent to which their two and a half million inhabitants had grown apart from the Mother Country.[2] A spirit of independence and the desire to escape from unwelcome authority had impelled many of the original settlers to cross three thousand miles of ocean to the New World. The Colonies which they established there had by the middle of the eighteenth century developed into mature and self-sufficient societies. The links with Great Britain remained strong, but in no sphere were the colonists dependent on her. Economically, they were growing rich from a land of boundless resources. Politically, power lay increasingly with the Provincial Assemblies which controlled the sources of revenue. Before 1763 this feeling of independence had been tempered by fear of the French in Canada, against whom British military garrisons were accepted as a necessary defence. But once the French had been removed, and the Spaniards had given up Florida, the Americans no longer felt such immediate need for military assistance and their

---

[1] In 1763, Connecticut and Rhode Island were corporate Colonies; Maryland, Pennsylvania and Delaware were proprietary; Massachusetts was chartered; and New Hampshire, New York, New Jersey, Virginia, North Carolina, South Carolina and Georgia were royal Colonies.

[2] See J. Steven Watson, *The Reign of George III, 1760–1815*, pp. 173-182. L. H. Gipson, *The Coming of the Revolution, 1763–1775*, and J. C. Miller, *Origins of the American Revolution*, also give thorough surveys of the American side of the problem and provide extensive bibliographies.

sense of equality and independence was sharpened accordingly. British attempts to regulate their industry and trade, and interference in their political affairs, seemed a reflection on their national manhood. The British Government, however, had no intention of abdicating its sovereignty; on the contrary, there was a strong conviction among many holders of Ministerial office that it was necessary to end the traditional policy of 'salutary neglect' and enforce imperial authority in order to make the colonists — who had caused great resentment by the smallness of their contribution during the war — bear at least some of the burden of defence after the war was over.[1] As part of this policy they proposed to enforce the Acts of Trade and Navigation more thoroughly than in the past, when receipts had often failed to cover the costs of collection.

The newly acquired territories stretched from Quebec in the north, down the Back Country of the Old Colonies between the Appalachian Mountains and the Mississippi river, and south to the tip of Florida. They presented three immediate problems. Were these lands to be settled? On what terms was trade to be conducted with the existing inhabitants of the Back Country, most of whom were Indians? And what military dispositions should be made against possible wars of revenge by hostile Indians, or even by the French? Many consequential difficulties also arose concerning the adaptability of the Laws of Trade and Navigation, the general status of Indian subjects, the need for religious tolerance towards Catholic Canadians, and the provision of civil government for people in areas not fully colonised. Behind these difficulties lay the urgent question of how to finance any additional administration which might be required.

Britain's colonial problems had not begun with the Seven Years' War; the question of defence costs, for instance, had vexed statesmen during the mid 1750's.[2] But war had made the difficulties more acute, and the coming of peace made it possible to reorganise the administration of the post-war Empire. In March 1763, Bute took the first step by authorising the main-

---

[1] The National Debt increased from £55 million to £133 million during the Seven Years' War. E. Robson, *The American Revolution, 1763–1783*, p. 49.   [2] *Ibid.*, pp. 13, 47-9.

tenance of ten thousand troops across the Atlantic: fifteen battalions in the mainland Colonies and five in the West Indies.[1] The expediency of Bute's measure, and the urgent need for a settlement of Indian affairs, seemed confirmed two months later by the outbreak of Pontiac's rebellion. In October a Proclamation, drafted by Shelburne and his successor Hillsborough, forbade settlement beyond a western boundary line drawn along the crest of the Alleghenies; in the following year instructions were issued regulating trade with the Indians through a system of licensed trading posts. This Western policy was modified in detail during the years ahead, but not in general design until the Quebec Act of 1774.[2]

With the military and Western policies settled, the most pressing problem for the Government — now led by George Grenville — was finance. The country gentry expected a reduction in taxation once the extraordinary war-time expenditure had been reduced. Grenville hoped to satisfy them, and he ruthlessly cut down Government spending.[3] He was unable to lower the Land Tax from its peak of four shillings in the pound, but he meant to see that the landed interest in England did not shoulder any more of the burdens of Empire and that the Americans paid for their own defence and administration. Grenville's first legislative measure to raise the American contribution was the Sugar Act of March 1764, which halved the existing duty on foreign molasses entering America, while at the same time making it quite clear that the duty would now be collected in practice as well as in theory. The Sugar Tax was raised, and new duties were imposed on foreign coffee, indigo, wines and other commodities previously free of tax. The number of 'enumerated' goods — those which, under the Navigation Acts, the Americans could export only by way of Britain — was increased. Vice-Admiralty Courts were established in America, and the navy and the customs department were strengthened in order to reduce smuggling and enforce the new legislation. The Act had several objectives, but the main aim

[1] *Ibid.*, p. 48.
[2] See below, Chapter V, for a fuller discussion of the Western Frontier question. [3] J. Steven Watson, *op. cit.*, pp. 103-5.

was, as stated in the preamble to the Act, to raise revenue, 'for defending, protecting and securing' the American Colonies. It was received with hostility in America, and some portent of the troubles ahead was given when James Otis, acting on behalf of the Massachusetts Bay House of Representatives, declared to the Governor that the Act deprived 'the colonies of some of their most essential rights as British subjects and particularly the right of assessing their own taxes'.[1]

Grenville next extended the British system of stamp duties to America and the West Indies. The Stamp Bill, which taxed legal and commercial documents, ships' and merchant papers, and pamphlets and newspapers in those Colonies, passed through the Commons with very little opposition in March 1765. The duty was expected to yield some £60,000, which was to be kept separately for imperial defence. But this time the colonists were even more enraged. A Congress of twenty-seven delegates from nine Colonies [2] assembled in New York to protest. The Americans made a distinction between internal and external taxation, and they claimed that it was unconstitutional for Britain to place internal taxes on them. At home a vigorous lobby of colonial agents and British commercial interests — openly encouraged by the new Ministry led by the Marquis of Rockingham — brought about the repeal of the Stamp Act in 1766. But few of those who in Britain supported repeal did so because they agreed with the colonists that the Act was unconstitutional. The majority merely felt that it had been inexpedient. This was clearly demonstrated when Parliament, immediately before repealing the Stamp Act, passed the Declaratory Act which asserted its *right* to bind America by legislation 'in all cases whatsoever'.

With the Stamp Act repealed the Chatham Administration of 1766 faced in its turn the unsolved problem of raising extra revenue to finance the colonial administration and defence. This problem was made worse in February 1767 when William Dowdeswell, a member of the Rockingham group, now in

[1] Quoted in L. H. Gipson, *op. cit.*, p. 68.
[2] New Hampshire, Georgia, North Carolina and Virginia did not send delegates.

opposition, proposed and carried a reduction in the Land Tax from four shillings to three shillings in the pound. The Earl of Shelburne, the Secretary of State responsible at this time for colonial affairs, suggested as a solution the setting up of an American fund, financed by quit rents, land grants and annual payments by the Provincial Assemblies. But he was unable to convince the Cabinet.[1] Charles Townshend, Chatham's Chancellor of the Exchequer, then decided to put duties on glass, lead, paper, paint and tea imported into America.[2] This proposal was put to Parliament in July 1767. It was stated that the aim of the new duties was the 'defraying the charge of the administration of justice, and the support of civil government, in such provinces where it shall be found necessary; and toward further defraying the expenses of defending, protecting, and securing the said dominions'.[3] The new measure was cleverly devised to meet the earlier American opposition to internal taxation; the duties were technically within the traditional framework of trade regulations. But the Americans once more rose in protest. They pointed out that this new financial imposition was not part of the general system of trade regulation but was an attempt to tax them solely for revenue purposes. Many colonists now began to deny, in effect, Britain's right to raise any new revenues in any form. They were further incensed by measures taken at this time to extend the power and efficiency of the British administrative system in the Colonies. The headquarters of the American Customs Commissioners was moved across the Atlantic to Boston and the penalties and powers of search of the Admiralty Courts were extended.[4]

The colonists reacted violently to Townshend's measures.

---

[1] C. W. Alvord and C. E. Carter, eds., *The New Regime, 1765–1767*, pp. 457-8, 536, 552-5.
[2] Townshend was not authorised by the Cabinet to take this step, which ran contrary to the general line of Chatham's American policy. Chatham himself had virtually retired from politics and was convalescing in the country at this time. See J. Brooke, *The Chatham Administration, 1766–1768*, pp. 94-5. Sir Lewis Namier, *Charles Townshend* (The Leslie Stephen Lecture 1959), pp. 26-9.   [3] Quoted in L. H. Gipson, *op. cit.*, p. 174.
[4] The jurisdiction of the Admiralty Courts had long been widening. In 1696 it was extended to cover all cases arising out of the Navigation Acts of that year, and in 1733, 1764 and 1765 it included the Molasses Act, Sugar Act and Stamp Act of those years. See E. Robson, *op. cit.*, pp. 31, 51, 64.

The Massachusetts Assembly had to be suspended in uproar, and there were riots in Boston, culminating in the death of five Bostonians in 1770 and the consequent withdrawal of British troops. A non-importation campaign was begun which continued until 1770. At Westminster a united Parliamentary Opposition of Chathamites, Rockinghams and Grenvilles, which was already thriving on the Middlesex election issue, exploited the colonial troubles to add to the embarrassment of the Government. In May 1769 the Ministry, which was led by the Duke of Grafton since Chatham's resignation in the previous autumn, agreed that the Townshend duties should be repealed, with the exception of that on tea, which was retained as a symbol of the undiminished right to tax the colonists. This proposal was implemented by Lord North when he replaced Grafton early in 1770. With this further attempt at compromise, and with the American extremists losing some of their impetus, Anglo-American relations entered a quieter period in the early 1770's. But a reserve of resentment remained on both sides, and none of the basic problems had been solved.[1]

The British colonial administration — which from 1768 was headed by a separate Department of State for the Colonies — was essentially conservative in its policies during these troubled years. Like all eighteenth-century Governments, the Ministers of George III were primarily concerned with administering existing law, custom and precedent. They wished to maintain due law and order in America as they would among the King's subjects elsewhere. They naturally tried to preserve the Old Colonial System — according to which imperial trade was controlled within a balanced economic community, with Britain receiving primary products from the Colonies and selling manufactures to them in return — because they believed this system was essential to the prosperity of everyone.[2] They tried to

[1] On the events summarised above see especially J. Steven Watson, *op. cit.*, pp. 102-7, 115-16, 126-8, 173-94.

[2] E. Robson, *op. cit.*, pp. 3-4. The general question of Britain's colonial policy at this time, and the changing role of America, is treated in V. T. Harlow, *The Founding of the Second British Empire, 1763–1793*, i, 1-11, 156-162, 195-222. The relation of this colonial policy to the American Revolution is most extensively covered in G. L. Beer, *The Old Colonial System*; R. L. Schuyler, *The Fall of the Old Colonial System*; and O. M. Dickerson,

defend Britain's position as a European and colonial power in competition with, and in constant danger from, other such powers. Above all, like nearly everyone in Parliament, they believed that the British Constitution was perfect, that sovereignty was indivisible, that it lay with the Crown in Parliament and that the Colonies were therefore logically and inescapably subordinate. No Ministry holding these views could allow the American Colonies to lapse into anarchy and disorder, or to trade contrary to the commercial regulations, or to refuse to help the common defence, or to deny the sovereignty implicit in all statutory legislation. These considerations formed the basis of British colonial policy.[1] Coupled with them was the hope — novel only in that a serious attempt was made to carry it out — that the colonial administration might become both cheaper and more efficient.

Unfortunately for Britain these conservative objectives were constantly frustrated by those Americans who after 1763 no longer accepted the traditional and fundamental premise of colonial subordination. As a result the whole problem of sovereignty was raised on both sides of the Atlantic. Particularly at issue was the question whether the Provincial Assemblies were separate and sovereign under the Crown, or whether they were subordinate to the British legislators at Westminster.[2] To most Englishmen the separate autonomy of the colonial Assemblies was inconceivable. Supremacy lay, as stated in the Declaratory Act, with Parliament. Governor Hutchinson tried to make this clear in his opening address to the Massachusetts Assembly in January 1773 :

> I know no line that can be drawn between the supreme
> authority of Parliament and the total independence of the

The Navigation Acts and the American Revolution. (Dickerson differs from the other two in arguing that the Navigation Acts were not an important cause of the revolution.)

[1] As late as August 1775 Dartmouth wrote hopefully that if only the Colonies would 'admit of duties for regulation of trade, and will add to that a revenue for the support of Civil Government, and such military force as they themselves shall desire to have among them, I think we may soon be agreed'. Dartmouth to Knox, 6 August 1775. *HMC, Various*, vi, *Knox MSS.*, pp. 120-1.

[2] For a discussion of the autonomy of the colonial Assemblies after 1763 see Mary P. Clarke, *Parliamentary Privilege in the American Colonies*, *passim.*

Colonies. It is impossible that there should be two independent legislatures in one and the same state, for although there
may be but one head, the King, yet two legislative bodies will
make two Governments as distinct as the kingdoms of England and Scotland before the Union.

The House of Representatives replied agreeing with the Governor that this fine distinction probably could not be drawn. But
it deduced that either 'the colonies are vassals of the Parliament,
or, that they are totally independent', and concluded that they
were independent.[1] Later Hutchinson described the process
whereby 'at first, indeed, the supreme authority seemed to be
admitted, the case of taxes only excepted ; but the exceptions
gradually extended from one case to another, until it included
all cases whatsoever. A profession of "subordination", however, still remained ; it was a word without a precise meaning
to it'.[2] To support their position the colonists introduced
abstract theories of 'natural rights' and argued that there could
be 'no taxation without representation'. In practice it was
resentment at British interference and the desire to run their
own affairs which made the existing constitutional relationship
intolerable to a growing number of them — although until the
outbreak of hostilities in 1775 it is doubtful if more than a very
small minority of them consciously sought a complete break
from the Mother Country.

Attempts were made to find a compromise, to reconcile
'indivisible sovereignty' with 'natural rights', and Britain's
practical necessity to raise revenue with the colonists' concrete
refusal to pay direct taxes of any kind imposed from Westminster. Chatham's proposal to ask for financial 'requisitions'
in the King's name,[3] Shelburne's scheme to increase quit rents
by leasing the new lands in the Mid-West, and Townshend's
trick of disguising taxes as commercial duties, were all attempts
to resolve this dilemma. But they foundered on the rock of

---

[1] Printed in the *Boston Gazette*, 11 January 1773, and quoted in L. H.
Gipson, *op. cit.*, pp. 212-13.
[2] T. Hutchinson, *The History of the Province of Massachusetts Bay from
1749-1774*, p. 256.
[3] For Chatham's views on colonial taxation see below, Chapter VI,
p. 133.

American dissatisfaction at being actively ruled by the British and having to pay for the privilege. No other political compromise seems, in retrospect, to have had any greater chance of success. The colonial demand for no taxation without representation did not, as might appear, mean that an answer lay in offering them seats in an imperial Parliament. The Assemblies of Virginia and South Carolina announced in 1764 that they would not accept representation, and Massachusetts did the same in 1768.[1] No taxation without representation meant simply no taxation except by the colonists' own Assemblies.[2] Another suggestion frequently put forward was that the Colonies should be under the sovereignty of the Crown but not of Parliament. This foreshadowed the modern Commonwealth, in which an association of self-governing States exists under a Monarch detached from the active government of its component parts. But this solution was not open to eighteenth-century British politicians. The Crown was then still active in politics. George III, a strict constitutionalist, would probably not have tried to exercise his prerogative other than through Parliament.[3] Even had he considered doing so, Parliament would have opposed such an extension of royal influence. Moreover, there is no evidence that any large body of American opinion supported such a solution.[4] One other possible compromise, which allowed England and her colonies to live at peace from 1770 to 1773, was for the Mother Country to retain a theoretical supremacy without actually exercising it. This was the general policy of the Rockinghams. But Lord North and his colleagues believed that such a compromise was neither desirable nor, in the long run, practicable. After 1770 the Ministry was increasingly prepared to take a firm stand on the issue of sovereignty. When it finally arose, over the Tea Duty, the result was a major conflict.

[1] Sir Lewis Namier, *England in the Age of the American Revolution*, (1961), p. 231.
[2] In 1778, when the British Peace Commissioners in Paris tentatively offered Westminster representation to the Americans, they were refused. E. Robson, *op. cit.*, pp. 179-82. Germain to Knox, 23 July 1778. *HMC, Various*, vi, *Knox MSS.*, pp. 144-5.
[3] Sir Lewis Namier, *op. cit.*, p. 37.
[4] E. Robson, *op. cit.*, pp. 77-81.

It is arguable that the problem facing George III and his Ministers was insoluble. They were trying to maintain a vast empire on a traditional framework of English commercial and military interests and within the limited scope of eighteenth-century finances and communications. In this endeavour they were increasingly opposed by the new political and economic aspirations of numerous colonists too strong and too far distant to be easily coerced. Yet had any solution been possible during the ten years after 1763, it is doubtful if the Government would have seen it and pursued it consistently. British politics and politicians at that time seemed particularly unsuited to settle the complex difficulties presented by the American Colonies. A succession of short-lived Ministries flickered across the political scene, and stability was not secured until Lord North settled into his long term of office. The explanation of this instability during the 'sixties, and of George III's success in restoring political equilibrium before the American crisis erupted at the end of 1773, involves a brief description of British politics at the time.[1]

Political power in eighteenth-century Britain was divided constitutionally between Parliament and the Crown. The King theoretically retained the vital prerogative of choosing and dismissing Ministers; his control of patronage was an important adjunct to this right. But the House of Commons might, according to how and where it bestowed support, limit or nullify the royal choice. Therefore Government could not proceed harmoniously unless these two institutions worked together.

Early in George III's reign there was no real party system operating in England to give a readily understandable pattern or framework to political debate. The terms 'Whig' and

---

[1] For the following see : Sir Lewis Namier, *England in the Age of the American Revolution*, especially pp. 179-228 ; *The Structure of Politics at the Accession of George III*, (1961), especially chapter i; *Personalities and Powers*, especially the essays on 'Monarchy and the Party System' and 'Country Gentlemen in Parliament, 1750–84'. Also R. Pares, *King George III and the Politicians, passim*. H. Butterfield, *George III and the Historians*, pp. 39-190. J. Brooke, *The Chatham Administration, 1766–1768*, chapter vi. I. R. Christie, *The End of North's Ministry, 1780–1782*, pp. 167-230.

'Tory' were often helpful as an indication of the political heritage of a Member, but they usually had no significance in terms of political *policies*. Toryism was finally discredited in 1745 and, though it remained for some time a general label of independence, it was dying out of the political vocabulary when George III came to the throne.[1] The denomination Whig had come by then to mean simply anybody who held or wanted public office: it defined the eighteenth-century Establishment.[2] Since George III strove from the beginning to make it clear that the politicians who served his grandfather would not automatically qualify for office under him, Whiggism lost all practical meaning during the early part of his reign.

Because of this lack of real party divisions or policies, it is more appropriate to distinguish three basic types of House of Commons Member: the politicians, the 'Court and Treasury' supporters and the independents. Many individuals inevitably defied precise classification. Even among these broad groupings it was often difficult to distinguish between a politician temporarily in the Administration and a genuine and permanent

[1] It is interesting to trace the subsequent political allegiances of the fifteen Members of Parliament described by Namier as 'Tory' in 1761 and who were still in Parliament in 1774. Eleven of them were in 1774 wholly independent. (Assheton Curzon of Clitheroe, Sir Edward Dering of New Romney, William Drake senior of Agmondesham, Samuel Egerton of Cheshire, Charles Gray of Colchester, Thomas Grovesnor of Chester, Rowland Holt of Suffolk, Thomas Knight of Kent, Thomas Noel of Rutland, Edward Southwell of Gloucestershire and Thomas Staunton of Ipswich.) The remaining four were giving independent but regular support to the Rockingham Opposition. (Richard Wilbraham Bootle of Chester, John Parker of Devon, Humphrey Sturt of Dorset and John Rolle Walter of Exeter.) John Brooke has observed that 'the Rockinghams inherited a great deal from the Tories of the first half of the eighteenth century, far more than they realised'. In this context it might also be noted that two 'radical Tories' elected in 1761, William Dowdeswell of Worcestershire and Sir William Meredith of Liverpool, subsequently joined the Rockingham squadron, though Meredith deserted to the Ministry in 1774. Dowdeswell's successor in 1775, William Lygon, also voted regularly with the Rockinghams. The other Worcestershire seat had been held in 1761 by an old Tory named Ward, who was later succeeded by Edward Foley, who actively supported the Rockinghams. See Sir Lewis Namier, *England in the Age of the American Revolution*, pp. 419-21, and J. Brooke, *op. cit.*, p. 284.

[2] There was also a relatively small number of independent country Whigs who did not seek office, and with whom in the course of the 1760's most of the remaining Tories coalesced to form the independent country gentlemen.

supporter of the King's Government; between an independent who was personally inclined to oppose the Ministry on most issues and a regular trooper in an Opposition squadron; between a genuine independent who by inclination usually supported the Ministry and one who was giving his support in the hope of exchanging his independence for a place. However, allowing for such difficulties, the three broad distinctions given above are valid and useful.

The main characteristic of the politicians was their interest in power and their ambition for high office. They sought to satisfy those desires in the 'sixties by grouping around such leaders as Grenville, Bedford and Rockingham, who had the prestige, experience and connexions necessary to force their way into Administration. The tactics of those out of office was naturally to oppose the measures of the politicians in power. Since the politicians, both 'in' and 'out', dominated the debates, these tactics frequently gave the superficial impression that the House was divided into two parties.

The 'Court and Treasury members' were not usually of sufficient calibre to qualify for the highest offices of State. But they were interested in public employment and recognition, and their existence was a reflection of the amount of patronage available to the Crown to cement support for its chosen Government. They included lawyers, military officers, Government contractors, civil servants, representatives of Treasury boroughs and Court officials. They offered their support to any Ministry which was genuinely of the King's own choosing, and through this connexion with the Monarch they hoped for some sign of favour. Some were sycophants and sinecurists, others were devoted and overworked Government servants. 'The strongest force in eighteenth-century politics', wrote John Brooke, was 'the obligation every man of goodwill had to serve the Crown to the best of his ability, and self-interest would walk hand in hand with duty'.[1] These men, who numbered roughly one-third of the Commons in 1774,[2] could not alone preserve

[1] J. Brooke, *op. cit.*, p. 22.
[2] Sir Lewis Namier, *Personalities and Powers*, p. 43. A List of Placemen in 1774 is in W. T. Laprade, ed., *Parliamentary Papers of John Robinson, 1774–84*, Royal Historical Society, 1922, pp. 14-17.

any Ministry. But they normally constituted a reliable nucleus of Commons support. However, when, as in 1742 and 1782, independent support was progressively withdrawn from a leader, the flight or abstention of a minority of the 'Court and Treasury' Members presaged the end of the long Ministries of Walpole and Lord North.

The independents were the largest section of the Commons. They included the traditional country gentry from the county seats, but some also came from urban constituencies — both from such large democratic boroughs as London and Southwark and from family-style boroughs as diverse in character as Amersham and Chester. Since they were obliged to nobody for their seats or their incomes, none of them could be called upon to vote in a certain way, or even to attend a debate. Charles Jenkinson described them as 'a sort of Flying Squadron, that you don't know where they will be in a new question'.[1] Yet they were not necessarily open-minded; prejudices and social conditioning affected these as other people. Under normal circumstances their individual political inclinations could often be predicted; some usually supported the King's Government, others adopted the traditional country role of critic of the Executive. Their duty was not to provide any part of a Government, but to support it disinterestedly until they felt it no longer deserved this support. Then, because of their numbers, they could break any Ministry. But they would do so only in extraordinary circumstances. Unless they were genuinely alarmed at the policies — or, more likely, at the failures — of a Ministry, they would hesitate to combine with the Opposition politicians to bring a Government down. Normally they were suspicious of these professional politicians and were reluctant to join with the factions at Westminster.[2]

Given the constitutional division of power between the Monarchy and Parliament, and the above composition of the

---

[1] P. O. Hutchinson, ed., *The Diary and Letters of his Excellency Thomas Hutchinson, Esq.* . . ., i, 454. (Henceforward cited as Hutchinson, *Diary and Letters*.)

[2] For example, in the votes to dismiss Walpole in February 1741, and on Dunning's second Resolution in April 1780, many independents showed their distrust of those Opposition politicians with whom they had frequently joined in opposing the Government.

House of Commons, two conditions were essential for the stability of an eighteenth-century Administration. First, it must be led by a politician who had the confidence of the King. Second, this leader must command a majority in the Commons : which meant he had to hold the support of the 'Court and Treasury' members and also not alienate a substantial number of independents. This second condition was best secured if, as well as having royal support, the leader also, as head of the Treasury, controlled patronage, and if he was personally present as a member of the House of Commons. Walpole, Pelham and Lord North met these conditions, and so began and continued the evolution of the office of Prime Minister.[1]

For the first decade of George III's reign these conditions necessary for stability were absent from British politics. George Grenville was in the Commons, but he lacked the King's confidence. Bute, Rockingham, Chatham and Grafton were all marooned in the graceful backwaters of the Upper House. Without the twin foundations of power their Ministries quickly foundered. The Bedford, Grenville and Rockingham squadrons went into Opposition in turn, and exploited the confusion, using any issue to embarrass the existing Ministry. There was nothing new in eighteenth-century politicians using this tactic. But the factions were more than usually troublesome and successful in the 'sixties because the normal stabilising conditions were not present. Colonial affairs were inevitably a victim of the disturbed state of domestic politics. One foreign observer wrote that 'Patriotism is a meer empty sound in this country, those who are out of administration want to enter, which desire is the source of all the discontent and pretended grievance. These phantoms of complaints are the cause that hitherto . . . American grievances have not been taken into consideration.'[2]

With the accession to power of Lord North in 1770, George III acquired for the first time a leader who had the confidence both of himself and of the House of Commons in which he

[1] R. R. Sedgewick, 'Sir Robert Walpole', *Times Literary Supplement*, 24 March 1945. Also J. B. Owen, *The Rise of the Pelhams*, pp. 37-40.

[2] Peter Hasenclaver to Sir William Johnson, 28 February 1770. *The Papers of Sir William Johnson*, vii, 427. Hasenclaver was an American iron manufacturer.

served. The basic conditions for political equilibrium were therefore secured. Lord North also had several personal qualifications which helped him in his twelve years of office. He was of an amiable and conciliatory disposition and, never having been the head of any faction, he had made no political enemies. Because of this he was ideal to act as common broker among his more difficult colleagues. He also felt none of the principles or ambitions which lead some politicians to resign from office. Such a man was eminently suited to restore greater stability and permanence to the King's Government. It is not surprising that George III was so insistent on retaining North, forgot his many shortcomings, forgave his lapses of memory and occasional administrative incompetence, and even paid some of his debts.

While the Government was being strengthened by the accession of Lord North, another factor was working towards political stability : the Ministry was absorbing several leading members of the Opposition, which was itself in process of decimation and collapse. Leading members of the Bedford party — Gower, Weymouth, Sandwich and Richard Rigby — had already been absorbed into the Ministry in December 1767. Another, Edward Thurlow, joined in 1770. On these occasions, in contrast with the previous Ministerial reshuffles in 1765 and 1766, no equivalent faction moved into Opposition to replace the incoming Bedfords. Chatham and Shelburne resigned in the summer of 1768, but Chatham retired to the country to nurse his sickness and 'an incalculable and disruptive force' [1] was removed from politics. The deaths of Charles Townshend, George Grenville and Bedford between 1767 and 1771 also silenced other potential troublemakers. Then, with their leader dead, the more prominent of the Grenville faction, led by Suffolk and Wedderburn, decided in 1771 to make an accommodation with the Ministry. Again no group replaced them in Opposition, which was left diminished in numbers and morale. After joining the Administration, the politicians of the Bedford and Grenville squadrons, like others before them who were gratified with office, soon lost their factious inclinations.

[1] J. Brooke, *op. cit.*, p. xi.

Consequently, when the American crisis erupted again in 1773, the Ministry was able to deal with it without any real worry about its internal stability or its majority in Parliament.

These changes in the personnel of the Ministry between 1767 and 1771 also had important implications for the future direction of English colonial policy. The accession of the Bedfords had been crucial for the Cabinet decision of May 1769 to retain the duty on tea.[1] By the end of 1771, with Gower, Sandwich and Suffolk in the Cabinet, and Thurlow and Wedderburn occupying the Law Offices, the balance of power lay heavily with those who were known to be in favour of taking strong measures against the Americans should trouble again arise. Their colleagues — North, Hillsborough, Rochford and Apsley — were certainly not opposed to the views of the Bedfords and Grenvilles, though they varied in the enthusiasm of their support. In a future crisis the Americans might expect firmer treatment from this Administration than from its predecessors.

After 1771, the only political groups left in the Parliamentary Opposition were the Rockinghams and the supporters of Chatham, and as these two followings had remained apart since their dispute over the 1771 Jury Bill their effectiveness at Westminster was greatly reduced.[2] Outside Parliament their alliances with the City politicians began to break up with the rise of Wilkes.[3] Chatham abandoned his tiny flock and retired to the country in sickness and despair; between 1771 and the beginning of 1774 he only once came up to address the Lords.[4] The Rockinghams pressed on with a little more resolution, laying claim to the Whig inheritance and accusing North's Government of high Toryism. In Edmund Burke they had a brilliant propagandist. His *Thoughts on the Cause of the Present Dis-*

---

[1] W. R. Anson, ed., *Autobiography and Political Correspondence of Augustus Henry, Third Duke of Grafton*, pp. 229-35.

[2] Among the Chatham papers in the Public Record Office there is a group of letters from Rockingham to Chatham in 1770, one letter in 1771, and then nothing more until the end of January 1775. PRO. 30/8/54, ff. 197-221. Rockingham's papers confirm this lack of contact.

[3] See below, Chapter VI.

[4] He spoke for the Dissenters Bill on 19 May 1772. Basil Williams, *William Pitt, Earl of Chatham*, ii, 294.

contents, published in 1770, rationalised their opposition into an act of party principles in defence of the traditional rights of Parliament and the Aristocracy against the alleged perversion of the Constitution by George III.[1] However, not even the genius and polemics of Burke could revive the fortunes of the Rockinghams in the early 'seventies. In December 1772 the Opposition divided with a meagre twenty-eight votes.[2] Burke commented : ' In truth, the battle for power is over ; nothing now remains but to preserve consistency and dignity. . . . My great uneasiness is about our own corps, which appears to me in great danger of dissolution.'[3] The Rockinghams even considered mass secession from Parliament, but it was not successfully pursued,[4] and during 1773, with their morale at a nadir, they suffered more crushing defeats on the East India Company Regulating Act. Their only political capital was the loyalty which had been built up during years of fruitless opposition. Their only hope seemed to lie in exploiting any crises which occurred. By 1773 such an opportunity was close at hand, for the New Englanders were again rebelling against the authority of Great Britain, and were about to bring to a head the troubles which had been festering for so long in the Atlantic Empire.

Tension in the Colonies had eased after the collapse of the non-importation campaign and with the repeal of the Townshend duties in 1770. But it was raised again at the end of 1772 when some Rhode Island patriots burned a grounded British schooner, the *Gaspee*, which had been employed in preventing smuggling in Narragansett Bay. The British Government appointed a Commission of Inquiry to examine the affair ; it discovered nothing, and once again the Mother Country seemed to have failed to exercise its sovereign authority. However, the Government had at the same time taken a positive step towards reinforcing the power of the executive in the Colonies, which further incensed the New England radicals. Late in

[1] For recent analyses of Burke's treatise, one favourable, the other critical, see H. Butterfield, *op. cit.*, pp. 54-6, and J. Brooke, *op. cit.*, pp. 232-3.
[2] On a motion to restrain the East India Company from sending out supervisors, 18 December 1772.
[3] Burke to Rockingham, 7, 10 January 1773. W.W.M. Bk., *CEB*, ii, 403, 411.   [4] Alison Olson, *The Radical Duke*, pp. 34-5.

1772 it declared its intention of setting up a Civil List in Massachusetts. The salaries of the Governor and of the judges would be paid from the revenues collected by the Commissioners of the Customs at Boston. This action threatened to break the financial hold of the Provincial Assemblies over the royal officers. In response Samuel Adams organised the Boston Committee of Correspondence and a network of similar committees spread through New England and Virginia. These were to be the nerve system of the coming revolt.

The Massachusetts Assembly and Council supported the rebellious colonists by passing early in 1773 a series of inflammatory Addresses denouncing the British supremacy.[1] The home Government did not let these pass unchallenged. In April, Lord Dartmouth, Secretary of State for the American Department since Hillsborough's resignation in the previous August, wrote to Governor Hutchinson of Massachusetts that the Addresses were 'replete with doctrines of the most dangerous nature, the latter of which does in direct terms question the authority of Parliament to make laws binding upon the subjects of that province in any case whatsoever'. Dartmouth concluded that the position of the colony

> does now require, and will have immediate and serious consideration ; but as it will be impossible for me to bring that consideration to a state of maturity before the sailing of the packet, all that I have at present in command from the King is, to recommend you to avoid any further discussion whatsoever upon these questions.[2]

During May the Cabinet continued to brood over the troubles across the Atlantic. In the end it decided to do nothing yet. Dartmouth informed Hutchinson :

> It is their unanimous opinion in which the King concurs that the authority of the supreme legislature must be supported, and that the unwarrantable declarations contained in the

---

[1] See T. Hutchinson, *History of the Province of Massachusetts Bay, 1749–1774*, pp. 370-90.
[2] Dartmouth to Hutchinson, 10 April 1773. PRO. CO. 5/765, ff. 256-7. On Hillsborough's resignation and Dartmouth's accession to the American Office, see below, p. 116.

addresses and messages of the late Council and House of Representatives, ought to be communicated to both Houses of Parliament, but it was not thought advisable to bring on the consideration of so important a matter at a time when the session was so far advanced, when so many members of Parliament were gone into the country, and the attention of those who remained, was so fully taken up with the affairs of the East Indies.

This business therefore must for the present rest as it is. . . .[1]

In the summer of 1773 the Ministers were clearly prepared to take issue with the Americans on the question of British supremacy. They sought delay only because they wanted the matter to be considered by a full Parliament — in which they could normally depend on a large majority. The Commons would not assemble in such strength until the New Year of 1774. However, before then the Government's hand was being forced by further and more serious troubles in Massachusetts. First, the publication of letters, written by Governor Hutchinson and Lieutenant-Governor Oliver, criticising the Americans, provoked the Massachusetts Assembly in June 1773 to demand the dismissal of these royal officers. Then, in the late autumn of 1773, the colonists reacted with violence to attempts to introduce cheap East India tea into America. Their resistance to the landing of this tea was only one, if the most dramatic, episode in the recent history of challenges to British authority. But it was of crucial importance because the Government at last took up the challenge, endeavouring to settle the issue of sovereignty which underlay the strong assertions by some colonists, and the growing feeling of others, that British Parliamentary supremacy was no longer acceptable to them.

This study is concerned with the British management of, and attitude towards, the colonial crisis from the Boston Tea Party in December 1773 to the opening of hostilities at Lexington and Concord in April 1775. Historians normally treat this period briefly, knowing that the English and the Americans were hurrying into war, and therefore describing the Coercive

[1] Dartmouth to Hutchinson, 2 June 1773. PRO. CO. 5/765, ff. 260-1.

Acts and the colonial opposition to them as mere stepping-stones on the way to the final collision and separation. It would be difficult to disagree with the broad lines of such an interpretation; the course of colonial history at this time seems, in retrospect, to have been charted by forces beyond the control of politicians, however wise. But, in fact, during 1774 and early 1775 the home Government sought energetically to preserve an empire in which British sovereignty was effective and recognised across the Atlantic. The attempt failed and the empire collapsed into civil war. Once war came, the whole picture changed; questions of loyalty, patriotism and national honour, of expenditure in money and blood, arose to influence the reactions of most Englishmen. The year and a half before hostilities began, however, stand as a separate period of crisis; then England was concerned simply with the colonial issues as such, with the nation's interest in those issues, and with the policies by which that interest could best be secured. It was the last time in which there was the possibility — in theory at least — of a peaceful settlement.

CHAPTER II

THE BOSTON TEA PARTY

In the spring of 1773, the Ministry added to the East India Company Regulating Bill a clause which exempted the Company from all import duties on tea brought into England and subsequently re-exported to America.[1] This was a further development in a policy of concessions begun in 1767, when all such duties were remitted providing the Company compensated the Treasury at a later date for loss of revenue, and modified in 1772, when a remission of three-fifths of the duties was granted without need to pay any compensation.[2] Now there was to be a total remission. But the threepence duty on the entry of tea into America which so enraged the colonists was retained throughout. The method of disposing of the Company's teas was also changed in 1773 : previously English merchants bought tea at the Company's auctions in London and then resold it to American merchants ; from now on the Company would work through its own export agents. These changes in tax and distribution were intended to facilitate the sale of some of the Company's seventeen million pounds of stock and so to relieve its financial crisis. By remitting the duty and eliminating the middlemen, the tea could be marketed very cheaply in America.

Not surprisingly, powerful interests in the Colonies were offended. The merchants of New England resented the fact that the East India Company could now export in its own ships,

[1] 13 George III, c. 44. The clause was proposed by Lord North in Committee and approved on 27 April, and it passed the Commons on 6 May 1773. It is difficult to assess the precise money value of the tea drawback in 1773. Contemporary politicians usually estimated it at ninepence a pound, but in fact it was composed of several percentage duties on teas which varied in grade and price. See M. Farrand, 'The Taxation of Tea, 1767–73', *American Historical Review*, III, January 1898, pp. 266-9.

[2] 12 George III, c. 60. On the parlous financial state of the Company at this time, see PRO. Treasury Minute Book, T 29/43, ff. 32-8.

employ its own chosen agents and undersell the American tea merchants ; in general they feared that this meant the establishment of a monopoly. The merchants were often pro-British in inclination, but the result of this measure was to throw them into alliance with the colonial radicals.[1] These radicals were also incensed and troubled, for the tea, being cheap, would almost certainly sell ; and since the Townshend Duty was still operating, its payment might seem to be an indirect acknowledgment of the right of Parliament to tax the Colonies. The Tea Duty had been retained in 1770 as an expression of Parliamentary supremacy ; attempts to introduce tea into America by extraordinary methods were therefore likely to bring that issue to the forefront.

The interesting question is whether the Ministers foresaw the probable consequences of their actions. It is unlikely that it was their prime intention deliberately and actively to provoke a crisis over the question of British supremacy. But there is some evidence that they may have been at least aware of the possible consequence of granting the drawback on tea and, if not keen, at least willing to face some of these consequences. During the debate on 23 January 1775 on various petitions asking for a reconciliation with America, Lord North said

it was impossible for him to have foreseen the proceedings in America respecting the tea ; that the duty had been quietly collected before ; that the great quantity of tea in the warehouses of the East India Company, as appeared by the Report of the Secret Committee, made it necessary to do something for the benefit of the Company ; that it was to serve them, that 9d. in the pound weight drawback was allowed ; that it was impossible for him to foretell the Americans would resist at being able to drink their tea at 9d. in the pound cheaper.

But Governor George Johnstone immediately rose, as he claimed,

[1] But for the tea concession to the East India Company 'the great influence of the trading classes, certainly in the northern Colonies, would have been on the side of Great Britain'. E. Robson, *op. cit.*, p. 76. See also A. M. Schlesinger, *The Colonial Merchants and the American Revolution, 1763–1776*, p. 264. On the merchant support for the Boston riots see Haldimand to Dartmouth, 5 January 1774. Dartmouth MS., D 1778, I, ii, 933. Quoted in *HMC*, II, V, *Dartmouth MSS.*, i, 346-7.

to speak a matter of fact; that he could not sit still and hear the noble lord plume himself on actions which, of all others, were the most reprehensible in this train of political absurdities. That it was unbecoming the noble lord to allege that this dangerous measure was adopted to serve the East India Company, when it was notorious the Company had requested the repeal of the 3d. per pound in America, and felt and knew the absurdity of giving a drawback here, and laying a duty there : a perfect solecism in commerce and politics. That the East India Company offered their consent, that government should retain 6d. in the pound on the exportation, if the 3d. was remitted in America. That the noble lord had been requested and intreated, by the governor himself, in his place, to remove the cause of dispute and was fortold the consequence of persevering in error. . . . I know, said he, the various intrigues, solicitations, and counter-solicitations, that were used to induce the chairman and deputy chairman of the Company, to undertake this rash and foolish business. I protested against it, as contrary to the principles of their monopoly. Yet the power of ministry prevailed, and the noble lord would now cover all those facts, which are ready, from their consequences, to convulse the empire and take credit for them as having been done with the most innocent intentions to serve the East India Company.[1]

If Johnstone was correct then the Ministry was not as naïve and innocent in 1773 as Lord North later implied. However, two factors must be borne in mind which help to explain the Ministry's position and policy when granting the tea duty concession in 1773. Firstly, the crisis in the affairs of the East India Company was then pre-eminent in the minds of all British politicians, whatever their affiliations. It was absolutely necessary to put the Company on a sound financial footing ; expansion of the tea trade to America was seen as an important means to that end. Secondly, it must be remembered that the 1773 drawback on tea was only an extension of the duty concession of the previous year. To the American radicals, of course, it was a significant policy development, especially when

[1] *Parliamentary History*, xviii, 177-8. Johnstone, M.P. for Appleby, was active in the East India Company Court of Directors. *The Annual Register 1774*, p. 47, states that many in the Company opposed the scheme.

taken together with the changes in tea distribution. But to the Ministry it was not a new and unprecedentedly dangerous step to take, certainly not so much more dangerous than the tea drawback granted in 1772 and so far without serious consequences. Clearly any act affecting the tea duty was provocative. It also appears that the Ministry was more willing at this time than earlier to risk such provocation. But historians, having the advantage of hindsight, would be harsh to condemn Lord North out of hand for not perceiving which straw among so many would break the American back.

Curiously enough it appears that none of the friends of America in the Parliamentary Opposition raised the question in the Commons at the time. Perhaps they missed the American implications of this East India Policy. On the other hand, it is just conceivable that they may have been prepared knowingly to sacrifice American interests to their own interests in the East. Burke's family, though not Edmund himself, had gambled in East India stock and had lost heavily since the crash of 1769.[1] William Burke lost further in 1773 and was subsequently forced to flee the country to escape his creditors.[2] The Duke of Richmond was also deeply involved in East India affairs, as were various other political associates of Rockingham, such as George Dempster and Robert Gregory. This might explain why the Rockinghams were quiet on the one point of the Ministry's Indian measures which promised immediately to bolster the financial position of the Company and its stockholders. But since there is no direct evidence to support such an explanation, all that can be safely concluded is that in Parliament politicians seem to have been unconcerned at, though they were not necessarily unaware of, the risks of reducing the duty on exported tea.[3]

[1] D. Wecter, *Edmund Burke and his Kinsmen*, pp. 27-48, 76-80.

[2] William Burke was probably not a kinsman, but he was regarded so and lived as one of the family. T. W. Copeland, *Edmund Burke, Six Essays*, pp. 48-62.

[3] Benjamin Franklin, who was in London at the time, was clearly in no doubt about the implications of the tea drawback. He wrote to America : '. . . the scheme is, to take off as much duty as will make the tea cheaper in America than foreigners can supply us, and continue the duty there to keep up the exercise of the right. They have no idea that any people can

Arrangements to send the tea went ahead. John Robinson, the Secretary to the Treasury, wrote to the customs at Boston in August 1773 telling them to give every assistance to the Company's agents when the cargoes arrived.[1] But the colonial radicals also pressed on with their plans to resist the landing of the tea. At the end of November the four Commissioners of the Boston custom house, and the five Company agents there, were attacked by the mob, and forced to take refuge in Castle William. Shortly after, the Company's first ships reached America. Three of them, the *Dartmouth*, the *Eleanor* and the *Beaver*, were moored in Boston harbour. On the night of 16 December, forty or fifty men disguised as Indians boarded the ships and threw some three hundred chests of tea into the sea.[2] The British troops had been alerted for trouble; but, one of their officers explained, 'the Council would not agree to the troops going to town, however it must end in that'.[3] The fleet in Boston harbour also might have prevented the riot had it been requested to do so — but, as the Admiral in charge was anxious to explain afterwards, this 'must have endangered the lives of many innocent people by firing upon the town'.[4] Thomas Pownall, a former Governor of Massachusetts, subsequently blamed Governor Hutchinson and asserted not only that the Governor could have ordered the military to prevent the riot but that it was his constitutional responsibility to do so.[5] It had not seemed so easy to Hutchinson on the spot. He wrote a week after the riot: 'I may not presume to propose measures. To enforce the duty appears beyond all comparison more difficult than I ever before imagined. . . . To concede endangers

act from any principle but that of interest ; and they believe that 3d. in a pound of tea, of which one does not drink perhaps ten lb. in a year, is sufficient to overcome all the patriotism of an American.' To Thomas Cushing, 4 June 1773. PRO. CO. 5/118, f. 119.

[1] 23 August 1773. PRO. Treasury Papers, TI/505. (The folios in this box of loose papers are not numbered.)

[2] A statement sent to Dartmouth on 23 March 1774 gave the value of the tea destroyed as £7,521. 13s. 2d. net of duties and commission. PRO. CO. 5/133, f. 101. Other ships which arrived later at Philadelphia and New York were turned away without unloading. E. Robson, *op. cit.*, p. 69.

[3] Alexander Leslie to Barrington, 6 December and 17 December 1773. BM. Add. MS. 38208, ff. 29, 31.

[4] Admiral Montagu to Philip Stephens, 17 December 1773. BM. Add. MS. 38208, f. 23.   [5] *London Magazine*, 1774, p. 182.

raising the like spirit in other cases of Parliamentary Authority.'[1]

Clearly the recipient of this letter, the Earl of Dartmouth, Secretary for the Colonies, would soon have to make the agonising choice between enforcement and concession. But it was some time before he realised it, because there followed the inevitable time lag — the first of many periods in the colonial crisis during which events in America dramatically changed the whole situation there, while England continued ignorant for the several weeks it took the news to cross the Atlantic.

First reports of the disorders in Massachusetts in the autumn of 1773 did not reach England until nearly the end of the year, and of the Tea Party not until the middle of January 1774. Members of Parliament spent their Christmas holidays unaware of the intense activity that lay ahead. During the previous session the Ministry had been chiefly concerned with East India Company affairs; but with the passing of the Regulating Act the heaviest legislative task seemed complete. Thus at the beginning of December Burke could write to New York: 'The Ministers give out that we are to have no material business before us during this Sessions'.[2]

However, on 23 December, the Chairman of the East India Company forwarded to Dartmouth the Company's latest mail from Boston (dated up to 4 November) and from New York (up to 5 November). It contained details of various preparations to resist the tea landings, and of the attacks upon officials in Boston. On Christmas Eve he sent news of the plans to resist the expected shipments of tea to Philadelphia. Between 5 and 15 January, the East India Company furnished Dartmouth with still more information about the explosive situation building up across the Atlantic.[3]

Given the bitter history of Britain's relations with her American Colonies over the previous ten years, and the conse-

---

[1] Hutchinson to Dartmouth, 21 December 1773. Dartmouth MS., D 1778, 1, ii, 921. Quoted in *HMC*, 11, V, *Dartmouth MSS.*, i, 344. For Hutchinson's version of the Tea Party see Hutchinson, *Diary and Letters*, i, 100-1.

[2] Burke to the Committee of Correspondence of the General Assembly of New York, 7 December 1773. W.W.M. Bk., printed in *CEB*, ii, 493.

[3] PRO. CO. 5/133, ff. 119 *seq.*, 138 *seq.*

quent feelings of humiliation and impatience, this fresh outbreak of trouble threatened to drive the Government quickly
to exasperation and revenge. Having prevaricated too long,
Ministers felt they could not compromise on this issue. Over
the years there had been constant complaints in Parliament
about the weight of the peace establishment, and the Parliamentary classes who paid the Land Tax were particularly irritated at
the refusal of the colonists to bear the burden of their own
administration and defence. To many, the time for temporising
was already over. During recent years no single American
issue had seemed sufficiently clear and provocative to spur the
political nation into demonstrating that the Government had
the power to enforce the law and protect officials. Now, however, the excesses perpetrated by the colonists in Massachusetts
were provoking such a demonstration of authority.

It was also at this time that the affair of Benjamin Franklin
and the Hutchinson-Oliver correspondence came to a head, and
this too played its part in pushing the Ministry towards coercion.
Some letters from Thomas Hutchinson, the Governor of
Massachusetts Bay, and his deputy, Andrew Oliver, to George
Grenville's former secretary, Thomas Whately, had come into
Franklin's possession.[1] He in turn sent them to certain Massa-
chusetts politicians, who published and distributed them.[2]
They contained statements which could easily be read as anti-
American, and the Bay radicals were incensed. The Massachu-
setts Assembly wrote a letter of complaint to Dartmouth in
June 1773, and in August they petitioned the King for the
removal of these two royal officers.[3]

[1] Andrew Oliver was appointed Lieutenant-Governor on 19 October
1770 and died in office on 3 March 1774. A. Mathews, *Notes on the Massachusetts Royal Commissions, 1681-1775*, pp. 95-6. Whateley died in 1772.
J. Brooke, *The Chatham Administration*, p. 42.
[2] Franklin's letters to America in 1773 concerning the correspondence
which he had passed on are in PRO. CO. 5/118, *passim.* Franklin's account
of the affair is in *The Complete Works of Benjamin Franklin*, ed. J. Bigelow,
v, 378-416.
[3] *The Annual Register . . . 1774*, pp. 201-2, prints the letter to Dartmouth dated 29 June 1773. George III gave his opinion of the Hutchinson
correspondence in an interview with the Governor himself on 1 June 1774.
Hutchinson's version of the King's words was: 'I remember nothing in
them to which the least exception could have been taken'. Hutchinson,
op. cit., i, 159.

Dartmouth promptly wrote to reassure Hutchinson that he need have no fear about the consequences of the petition, and he roundly condemned the petitioners for their behaviour. The petition lay unheeded for some time. At the beginning of December it was taken up again. Dartmouth told Hutchinson that 'these proceedings . . . and the applications of both Houses to the Crown in consequence of them will soon be fully examined and considered here, and I have not the least doubt that the result of such consideration will be to your honour and satisfaction'.[1] The petition was referred to the Privy Council on 3 December; but the hearing was delayed by the Christmas recess.[2] So, by the time it was finally considered, the details of the Massachusetts disorders were filtering through to London, and the political climate was becoming hostile to the Americans.

The Committee of the Privy Council for Plantation Affairs heard the petition on 11 January 1774.[3] Israel Mauduit, the agent for Governor Hutchinson, appeared before the Committee accompanied by Alexander Wedderburn, the Solicitor-General, as counsel. Franklin, acting as agent for the Massachusetts Assembly, was granted a three-week delay, and the hearing was fixed for 29 January. He already knew from common rumour that the Ministry was furious and bent on humiliating him.[4] It seems that the Ministers had been particularly shocked when they learned from Franklin's letter of 25 December to the *Public Advertiser* that he had conveyed the correspondence to Massachusetts.[5] Governor Hutchinson,

[1] Dartmouth to Hutchinson, 4 August, 17 August, 1 December 1773. PRO. CO. 5/765, ff. 265-7, 270-1, 274-5.

[2] John Pownall to Clerk of the Council in Waiting, 3 December 1773. PRO. CO. 5/133, f. 191. Dartmouth to Hutchinson, 8 January 1774. PRO. CO. 5/763, ff. 9-12. *Acts of the Privy Council of England. Colonial Series*, ed. J. Munro, v, 385. Shelburne to Chatham, 3 February 1774. E. Fitzmaurice, *Life of William, Earl of Shelburne*, ii, 297-8.

[3] *Acts of the Privy Council*, v, 385.

[4] *Memoirs of the Life and Writings of Benjamin Franklin*, ed. W. T. Franklin, ii, 396-9, especially p. 397. Mauduit's version of the hearing on 11 January is quoted by C. Van Doren, *Benjamin Franklin*, pp. 462-3. *Acts of the Privy Council*, v, 386. *The Writings of Benjamin Franklin*, ed. A. H. Smyth, vi, 185-7.

[5] *Franklin Memoirs*, ii, 395-6. Franklin to Samuel Cooper, 25 February 1774. *Franklin Complete Works*, v, 322.

when he visited Charles Jenkinson in July, was told that the Administration would not have taken such immediate and vigorous measures with the Colonies 'if it had not been for Doctor F[ranklin]'s extraordinary letter, which he published relative to your letters. This alarmed Administration, and convinced them it was high time to exert themselves when so dangerous a conspiracy was carrying on against Government.' [1]

It was into this already tense political atmosphere that the news of the Boston Tea Party was brought in late January 1774. The first official report was received on 27 January. Governor Hutchinson had written to Dartmouth on 17 December with a hasty description of what had happened during the preceding night, and the letter was sent on board the brig *Dolphin* under Captain James Scott.[2] This ship reached Dover on 26 January and Gravesend on the 28th.[3] Since the report is stamped as received on the 27 January it was probably sent post-haste either from Dover or from Falmouth.[4]

But reliable news had reached London even before Hutchinson's report. Another ship had left Boston with the *Dolphin* after the Tea Party. This was the *Hayley*, which was also commanded by a Captain Scott, and which was carrying passengers who had witnessed, or knew details of, the riotous proceedings.[5] The *Hayley* reached Dover on 19 January and Gravesend on 21 January.[6] The news it brought must have been rushed to London, either from Dover on 19 January or from Falmouth earlier. For on the evening of 19 January the

---

[1] Hutchinson, *op. cit.*, i, 185. Franklin was thought to be a liar as well as a traitor. When Hutchinson dined with the Earl of Suffolk in July the former Governor told Suffolk that he had no explanation of how Franklin acquired the Whateley correspondence 'but from the letter he published'. Suffolk replied, 'We know, that account is not true . . . we have certain evidence that it is not true ; and we know where he had the letters'. *Ibid.*, i, 192.

[2] 17 and 20 December 1773. PRO. CO. 5/763, ff. 45-6, 65.

[3] Shipping news in the *Public Advertiser*, 28 January 1774 and 31 January 1774.

[4] The American papers were normally carried in the packet between Falmouth and America. J. Pownall to A. Todd, 14 July 1773. PRO. CO. 5/250, f. 51.

[5] Hutchinson to Dartmouth, 24 December 1773. PRO. CO. 5/763, ff. 69-70.

[6] *Public Advertiser*, 20 January 1774 and 23 January 1774.

King wrote to Dartmouth : 'I am much hurt that the instigation of bad men hath again drawn the people of Boston to take such unjustifiable steps ; but I trust by degrees tea will find its way there ; for when Quebec is stocked with that commodity it will spread southward'.[1] And on 21 January the Chairman of the East India Company sent to Dartmouth a letter which had just been received from America. It was dated 17 December and began 'your tea is destroyed . . .'.[2]

Not only the Ministry and the Company received the tale of sedition. On Saturday, 22 January, the *St. James's Chronicle* printed a complete description of the Tea Party, taken from the Boston newspapers. The *Public Advertiser* carried the story on the following Monday. These Boston papers must also have been landed from the *Hayley*, together with the well-informed passengers, and consequently the whole story was popularly known in London five days before the Government had official details.

The Ministry in fact took action without waiting for Hutchinson's official confirmation. On Monday, 24 January, Dartmouth wrote to the owner of the *Hayley* and asked 'to have some conversation with the Captain of the ship whose name is Scott'. He requested that the Captain attend at his office next morning.[3] Scott then fully informed the American Secretary about the Boston riots.[4] Furthermore, that same day, 25 January, the ship *Polly* docked at Gravesend bringing back tea which the Philadelphians had refused to allow to land.[5] The following morning the East India Company sent to inform Dartmouth that their agent had returned from Philadelphia on the *Polly*, and could give him full details of what had passed there ; they also sent him their latest correspondence from the

---

[1] Dartmouth MS., D 1778, Supplementary George III. Quoted in *HMC*, 13, IV, *Dartmouth MSS.*, iv, 499.
[2] PRO. CO. 5/133, ff. 28-30.   [3] PRO. CO. 5/250, f. 67.
[4] Dartmouth MS., D 1778, 11, 808. See also Hutchinson to Dartmouth, 2 December 1773. BM. Add. MS. 38207, ff. 337-8. Hutchinson to Dartmouth, 15 December 1773. *Ibid.*, 344-5. Hutchinson to Dartmouth, 17 December 1773. *Ibid.*, 346. Hutchinson to Dartmouth, 20 December 1773. *Ibid.*, 348. Hutchinson to Dartmouth, 28 December 1775. *Ibid.*, 356.
[5] *The Annual Register* . . . *1774*, p. 84. *Public Advertiser*, 27 January 1774.

town.[1] Dartmouth immediately replied, asking to see the agent next day.[2]

So when Hutchinson's reports finally arrived on Thursday, 27 January, they can have added little to the Government's knowledge of the gravity of the situation in America — the subject which apparently preoccupied the Cabinet which met at Earl Gower's in Whitehall that evening.[3]

The effect of this news of sedition in Boston could only be to strengthen the hands of those in the Ministry who already, because of earlier disorders and because of the Franklin affair, were pushing for tougher measures towards America. That a clamour was raised by these coercionists was confirmed by an eye-witness in London who wrote on 29 January about the reception of the news: 'We do not hear of anything yet likely to be done upon it: Lord North's and Lord Dartmouth's friends do not say a great deal upon the subject, the Bedfords, and the remainder of George Grenville's friends are very loud'.[4] Now, and in the months ahead, a violent swing of public opinion against the colonists strengthened their hands.[5]

The Massachusetts petition for the dismissal of Hutchinson and Oliver was heard on 29 January, shortly after the news of the colonial crisis had arrived. Every member of the Cabinet except Lord Chancellor Apsley was present in the Privy Council for the hearing. Its proceedings thus became a strand in the tangled web of Anglo-American politics, and the wider political and colonial issues currently being discussed naturally engulfed the specific questions raised by the petition.

One of the most recent writers on the period claims that 'the hearing had been but an elaborately staged expression of imperial wrath, with Franklin as its target'.[6]

[1] PRO. CO. 5/133, f. 32.
[2] To Chairman of East India Company, 26 January 1774. PRO. CO. 5/250 f. 67. [3] *Public Advertiser*, 28 January 1774.
[4] Lord John Cavendish to Rockingham, 29 January 1774. W.W.M. R1-1479.
[5] Champion to Messrs. Willing Morris & Co., 30 September 1774 and 13 March 1775. *Letters of Richard Champion*, ed. G. H. Guttridge, pp. 32-3, 49. Franklin to Thomas Cushing, 22 March 1774. PRO. CO. 5/118, f. 72.
[6] C. R. Ritcheson, *British Politics and the American Revolution, 1763–83*, p. 160.

Contemporary witnesses support this view. Shelburne wrote to Chatham :

> Mr. Wedderburn . . . entered largely into the constitution and temper of the province, and concluded by a most scurrilous invective against Dr. Franklin ; occasioned, as Dr. Franklin says, by some matter of private animosity ; as Mr. Wedderburn says, by his attachment to his deceased friend, Mr. Whatly . . . others say, it is the opening of a new plan of American government.[1]

Burke attended the hearing with Priestley and Dr. Douglas, the future Bishop of Durham.[2] He wrote four days later to America that he felt such 'a public trial' had been unnecessary, but 'it was obviously intended to give all possible weight and solemnity to the decision'.[3] News had already spread that this would be no ordinary hearing, and some thirty-four Privy Councillors attended.[4] 'The Council was the fullest of any in our memory', wrote Burke to Charles Lee.[5] Spectators crowded to hear Wedderburn's much advertised performance, and the meeting lasted until 6 p.m.[6] The Privy Councillors

[1] Shelburne to Chatham, 3 February 1774. E. Fitzmaurice, *op. cit.*, ii, 297-8. Wedderburn's talents were always a tool to his ambition. He had gone over into the Rockingham camp in the late 'sixties when their prospects seemed good. Through his acquaintance with John Lee he became an intimate of Burke and even helped draw up the Yorkshire petition. But when the Rockingham fortunes slumped he lost his taste for opposition and in 1771 he accompanied other followers of George Grenville into North's Administration. J. Brooke, *op. cit.*, p. 267. For William Knox's hostile characterisation of Wedderburn see *HMC, Various*, vi, *Knox MSS.*, pp. 267-8.

[2] See Priestley's letter to the Editor of the *Monthly Magazine* dated 10 November 1802 and quoted in *Franklin Memoirs*, i, 356-7. In this delightful reminiscence Priestley describes how he met Burke and Douglas in Parliament Street and they went together to the Privy Council. After Burke had guided them through the scrimmage of the ante-room door, Priestley said, 'Mr. Burke, you are an excellent leader'. He claims that Burke replied, 'I wish other persons thought so too'.

[3] Burke to the Committee of Correspondence of the General Assembly of New York, 2 February 1774. W.W.M. Bk., *CEB*, ii, 522.

[4] Van Doren says there were thirty-six Privy Councillors present. C. van Doren, *op. cit.*, pp. 467-8. In a letter to Rockingham on 2 February Burke said there were only thirty-five. W.W.M. Bk., *CEB*, ii, 524. The report of the Committee names only thirty-four. 7 February 1774. PRO. CO. 5/765, ff. 287-93.

[5] Burke to Charles Lee, 1 February 1774. *CEB*, ii, 518.

[6] Mauduit's version of Wedderburn's speech is quoted in C. van Doren, *op. cit.*, pp. 469-73. Mauduit published only particular points of the

were apparently not disappointed: 'at the sallies of Mr. Wedderburn's sarcastic wit, all the members of the council, the president himself [Lord Gower] not excepted, frequently laughed outright; no one of them behaving with decent gravity, except Lord North'.[1] The newspapers — so often maligned for their alleged depravity of standards — were less impressed than the Privy Council by Wedderburn's scurrilous attack on Franklin. The *Public Advertiser* reported on 2 February:

> Mr. Solicitor General was employed on the other side, and instead of answering the learned arguments of his brethren, or refuting the allegations of the petition, contented himself with pronouncing the most severe Phillipic on the celebrated American Philosopher, in which he loaded him with all the licensed scurrility of the Bar, and decked his harangues with the choicest flowers of Billingsgate.

Franklin afterwards told his counsel, William Lee, that he took no notice of Wedderburn, but was sorry to see the Lords of the Privy Council behaving so rudely.[2] He was justifiably worried at the behaviour of the Privy Councillors since, when several of them met in the Cabinet later that day to discuss America, it is most likely that their attitudes reflected the tone of the hearing. Even Dartmouth, by disposition a moderate, was very annoyed with the colonists over the affair of the Hutchinson letters. He wrote afterwards to tell the Governor that the Privy Council report expressed 'a very just indignation at the falsehood and malevolence of the charge brought against you'.[3]

Burke was almost certainly correct in his observation that

speech, excluding the abuse. *Franklin Writings*, vi, 189-90. A version of this abuse is in *Political, Miscellaneous and Philosophical Pieces. . . . Written by Benjamin Franklin*, ed. Benjamin Vaughan, London, 1779, p. 341. See also *Public Advertiser*, 2 February 1774.

[1] Priestley to *Monthly Review*, 10 November 1802. This extract is printed in *Correspondence of William Pitt, Earl of Chatham*, ed. W. S. Taylor and J. H. Pringle, iv, 323. Franklin's opinion is in *Franklin Writings*, vi, 188-9.

[2] *Franklin Memoirs*, i, 355. In fact Franklin later took sharp revenge on Wedderburn by dedicating his treatise entitled 'Rules for Reducing a great Empire to a small one' to him — 'to a nobleman whose talents were so eminently successful in procuring the emancipation of our American brethren'. [3] 5 February 1774. PRO. CO. 5/763, ff. 57-9.

the hearing had in a general sense turned out to be a public trial. Franklin and the whole Colony of Massachusetts Bay were under prosecution. It was both a demonstration of indignation and a rally of coercionist opinion. The verdict rejecting the petition was inevitable. Franklin was sent notice of his dismissal as Deputy Postmaster in America on the Monday after the hearing — some time before the Committee reported its conclusions to the King.[1] And when the report was finally announced it was directly related to the whole American situation, indicating the trend of Ministerial opinion on the colonial problem. The petition was described as 'groundless and scandalous, and calculated only for the seditious purpose of keeping up a spirit of clamour and discontent in the said province'.[2]

On the evening of 29 January, after the Privy Council, all seven Cabinet Ministers [3] attended a Cabinet meeting at which they discussed the colonial situation in general and also a motion which the Earl of Buckinghamshire had put down in the House of Lords, asking that all papers relating to the American crisis should be laid before Parliament. As well as agreeing to accept Buckinghamshire's motion they made a crucial decision about the general lines of their future colonial policy: they agreed 'that in consequence of the present disorders in America, effectual steps to be taken to secure the Dependence of the Colonies on the Mother Country'.[4] These steps were to absorb the energies of the Government during the weeks ahead.

---

[1] Franklin was dismissed on 31 January, and the Committee did not report until 7 February. (PRO. CO. 5/765, f. 287.) Shelburne to Chatham, 3 February 1774. E. Fitzmaurice, *Life of Shelburne*, ii, 298. It was later John Yorke's opinion that had they not taken away Franklin's Post Office income he would have gone off to live quietly in Switzerland and not bothered any more with the colonial radicals. (Yorke to Hardwicke, 29 July 1775. BM. Add. MS. 35375, f. 152.) Horace Walpole was naturally sympathetic to such an interpretation. He wrote with seemingly genuine feeling : 'This place was all he had, and it was taken away'. *The Last Journals of Horace Walpole*, ed. A. F. Stuart, i, 285. These comments perhaps tell us more about Yorke and Walpole than about Franklin.

[2] Report of the Committee of Council for Plantation Affairs, 7 February 1774. PRO. CO. 5/765, f. 293.

[3] For details of the seven Ministers see below, pp. 36 *seq.*

[4] Cabinet Minute, 29 January 1774. Dartmouth MS. D 1778, ii, 799.

The year 1774 thus began with the Ministry already inclined to adopt a sterner American policy, and by the end of January the first decision had been taken in Cabinet. The Addresses from the Massachusetts Assembly and Council, the Franklin affair, the disorders in the Bay Colony during the autumn of 1773, and finally the Tea Party, served in succession to arouse and confirm the worst suspicions of the extremists within the Government. They were galvanised into action, while the ground was taken from beneath anyone who might normally have inclined towards moderation. Consequently, without exception, the Ministers viewed the problem immediately after the Boston Tea Party in terms of the same simple dilemma which Hutchinson had posed in his letter to Dartmouth in December 1773. They believed that their only choice was between effectively securing that which had previously seemed so difficult — the complete enforcement of the law in America — and doing what had hitherto proved fatal — making concessions to the colonists. It could no longer be a question of how expediently the Parliamentary sovereignty was to be exercised in America ; that sovereignty had been flagrantly resisted, and hence apparently denied. The Tea Party did not cause the colonial problem ; it was itself part of a long deteriorating situation. But it was crucial in Britain's relations with her American Colonies because, for the Government, it marked the end of vacillation and compromise. The Ministers believed they had either to make British supremacy in America effective, or else to admit that it did not exist.[1] They may have been wrong in assuming so simple a choice ; but, given that assumption, it is not surprising that they decided upon the first of these courses.

[1] William Knox wrote that the Americans had rebelled against 'no greater insult or oppression, than an adherence to a fundamental principle of the relation in which they had been first planted, and always remained, and which they had all acknowledged to be necessary to preserve the connection they had so constantly professed their satisfaction in . . .'. W. Knox, *Extra Official State Papers*, ii, 8.

CHAPTER III

DECIDING MEASURES

THERE were seven members of the British Ministry who dealt regularly in Cabinet with such political problems as that posed by the Boston Tea Party. The head of the Ministry,[1] First Lord of the Treasury and Chancellor of the Exchequer, was Frederick, Lord North. Amiable, clever, and a skilled House of Commons man, Lord North was the ideal person to preside over a departmentalised peace-time Government. But he lacked the energy, self-confidence and decisiveness necessary to a leader in times of political crisis. He drew affection from his colleagues, though rarely much respect, and he leaned heavily on his royal master for the resolution to implement policy. He often begged leave to resign, but loyalty to the King in fact kept him in office until almost the bitter end of the war. George III had spent the first decade of his reign looking for such a servant as Lord North, and he did not mean to let him go easily. He said of North to Germain in 1778, 'although he is not entirely to my mind, and there are many things about him I wish were changed, I don't know any who would do so well, and I have a good regard for him and very good opinion of him'.[2] One of his characteristics which the King might well

---

[1] Strictly North was not a 'Prime Minister' or a Premier in the modern sense. He was not the leader of a majority political party, he was not invited by the King to form a whole new Ministry and he had very little general control over the various Departments of State. Yet North's long period of power was important in the development of the office of Prime Minister. Partly because of this, but mainly for reasons of brevity, he will be described below as Prime Minister or as Premier. The more correct form 'First Minister' can be ambiguous, and any other description which was constitutionally precise would be too clumsy for constant repetition. Moreover, North was sometimes described as Prime Minister by his contemporaries : 'I had not a right idea when in America of the state of Administration. In matters of such moment the Prime Min. is much less the factotum than I imagined.' Hutchinson to Mr. Flucker, 20 January 1775. *Diary and Letters*, i, 359. [2] *HMC, Various*, vi, *Knox MSS.*, p. 267.

have wished changed was Lord North's remarkable carelessness in all his personal affairs. Though he was an experienced Chancellor of the country's Exchequer, his own domestic finances defeated him and the King had to help him pay his debts. Furthermore, North preserved scarcely any of his political correspondence, and so left one of the widest and most infuriating gaps in the documentation of eighteenth-century British history.[1]

The Secretary for the American Department had, since August 1772, been William Legge, Earl of Dartmouth, who was North's step-brother. He was a man of mild and pious temperament, and was attached to the evangelical set organised by the Countess of Huntingdon. His house at Sandwell, near Birmingham, was the resort of many preachers, and Lady Dartmouth's drawing-room at Cheltenham was opened for religious meetings. His reputation in politics was that of a moderate, particularly in his attitude towards America.[2] Hutchinson thought his 'greatest foible is an excess of humanity which makes him apt sometimes to think more favourably of some men than they deserve'.[3] The Americans hoped for much from him, and his presence in this position in the Ministry took some of the sting out of the Opposition's attacks on its American policies; particularly since he had held office under Rockingham and remained friendly with the party at least until late 1772. Dartmouth did not altogether betray their trust. Although he shared the indignation of the extremists against the Boston Tea Party, he chose first the moderate policy of punishing only the Boston ringleaders; not until that failed did he

[1] The North family papers are deposited in the Bodleian Library, Oxford, but there is very little material of any consequence for this period. Almost all the letters of value have been published by E. R. Hughes, 'Lord North's Correspondence, 1766–83', *English Historical Review*, lxii, pp. 218-238.

[2] Franklin wrote that 'No one, who knows Lord Dartmouth, can doubt the sincerity of the good wishes expressed in his letter to me'. *The Complete Works of Benjamin Franklin*, ed. J. Bigelow, v, 407. Grafton claimed that 'Lord Dartmouth . . . was the only one, who had a true desire to see lenient measures adopted towards the colonies'. *Autobiography and Political Correspondence of Augustus Henry, third Duke of Grafton*, ed. W. R. Anson, pp. 266-7.

[3] Hutchinson to unnamed friend, 1 November 1774. *Diary and Letters*, i, 285.

agree to submit the whole Massachusetts question to the wrath of the sovereign imperial Parliament. He then gave the coercive legislation his full, if not enthusiastic, support. He regretted that the issue had become a naked struggle for supremacy. But he was in no doubt that legally the sovereignty lay with Parliament.[1] As a result the colonists were bitterly disappointed in Dartmouth's conduct as American Secretary. Franklin's verdict on him reflected this bitterness, but was not without a good deal of truth: 'it is a trait of that nobleman's character, who from his office is supposed to have so great a share in American affairs, but who has in reality no will or judgement of his own, being with disposition for the best measures, easily prevailed with to join in the worst'.[2]

The basic difference of outlook between a moderate such as Dartmouth (or, to a much less extent, Lord North) and the extremists in the Cabinet became more apparent when war grew imminent early in 1775. While the question was one of Parliamentary sovereignty, and consequently of administrative coercion, Dartmouth fully supported his aggressive comrades. But war with the colonists was a different matter, and at the beginning of 1775 he began to cast about for ways of conciliation.[3] Dartmouth subsequently resigned from the Colonial Secretaryship and went to the Privy Seal in November 1775. In 1776, when Germain and the rest of the Cabinet desired an acknowledgment by the Americans of 'The supreme authority of the Legislature to make laws binding on the Colonies in all cases whatsoever' as a *sine qua non* of any peace negotiations, Dartmouth and North demurred.[4] With these two Ministers we must bear in mind this distinction between the assertion of British Parliamentary authority over the Colonies, which both at first completely supported, and the outbreak of war, which they regretted, though never to the extent of openly demanding peace.

Henry Howard, twelfth Earl of Suffolk and fifth Earl of Berkshire, was the Northern Secretary. He was an old Grenville supporter, and became leader of that connexion after

---

[1] See Dartmouth to Hutchinson, 9 March 1774. PRO. CO. 5/763, f. 109.
[2] *Franklin Complete Works*, v, 497.
[3] See below, Chapters IX, X and XI.
[4] *HMC, Various*, vi, *Knox MSS.*, p. 259.

George Grenville's death.[1] Not very much is known about him, though from the little remaining correspondence he appears as a lively and humorous personality.[2] He was of considerable importance in the Cabinet. In both 1773 and 1775 John Pownall complained that it was Suffolk who controlled American policy rather than Dartmouth.[3] In February 1778 Suffolk applied for the Garter, and North commented to the King: 'it is a matter of great consequence in the present moment to please Lord Suffolk, as there is nobody more steady, and resolute, and active, and more fit to lead the business of the Crown in the House of Lords'.[4] At the end of the year North was recommending Suffolk to be his successor as Prime Minister.[5] Shortly after this Suffolk asked to resign because of the ill health which had plagued him in recent years. He died in 1779.

The Secretary for the Southern Department was William Zuylestein, fourth Earl of Rochford. A well-known expert on Spanish affairs, Rochford changed from the Northern to the more congenial Southern post in December 1770. He was a friend of the Duke of Grafton, but voted in Cabinet against Grafton's proposal in May 1769 to repeal all the American duties. Consequently he has traditionally been blamed for much of the trouble which arose as a result of the retention of the Tea Duty. He was a supporter of coercion in 1774, but he

[1] C. W. Alvord, *The Mississippi Valley in British Politics*, ii, 39.

[2] Some letters from Suffolk to Eden are in the Auckland correspondence deposited in the British Museum, especially in Add. MSS. 34, 412. There is apparently nothing of personal or political interest for this period among the papers still in the possession of the present Earl of Suffolk and Berkshire at Charlton Park, Malmesbury. The letters in the Wiltshire County Record Office are mainly concerned with estate affairs and almost all of a later date.

[3] Pownall to Knox, 23 July 1773 and 10 October 1775. *HMC, Various*, vi, *Knox MSS.*, pp. 110, 122. For the continual feud between the American and the other Secretariats see M. M. Spector, *The American Department of the British Government*, pp. 66-76.

[4] North to King, [? 8] February 1778. J. W. Fortescue, ed. *The Correspondence of King George III from 1760 to December 1783*, iv, No. 2191.

[5] North to King, 16 November 1778. *Ibid.*, 2452. William Knox claimed Suffolk had plotted to bring down North when Hillsborough resigned in 1772, and always had this hope in mind. But Knox was jealous of the Northern Secretary's interference with the territories under the Colonial Office. *HMC, Various*, vi, *Knox MSS.*, pp. 254, 256. Also M. M. Spector, *op. cit.*, pp. 66-72.

was never an extremist. He resigned in the autumn of 1775, chiefly for reasons of ill health.[1]

Granville Leveson-Gower, second Earl Gower and later first Marquis of Stafford, had held the post of President of the Council since December 1767. His was an old Tory family, with considerable electoral power in Staffordshire. Gower was originally a member of the Bloomsbury Gang, which was led in the 'fifties by his brother-in-law the fourth Duke of Bedford. He then acquired Household office, but resigned when the Rockinghams came to power in 1765. He shared Bedford's views on coercing the Americans and gave strong support to the Punitive Acts in 1774. But he later had doubts and resigned office in 1779, though his dozen followers continued to support the Government. After the fall of Shelburne in 1783 he was offered the position of Prime Minister, but refused it. Gower was an able and important politician, whose chief talent has been described as 'an honest broker between divergent opinions'.[2] But his personality, like that of Suffolk, is not clear and it is difficult to find much original information about him.[3]

Sixth member of the Cabinet was John Montagu, fourth Earl of Sandwich. Notorious as a libertine, Sandwich was also a first-class Minister, and was responsible for many naval reforms. 'In 1771 he was, by his experience and knowledge of naval matters, better fitted to be First Lord than any other

[1] *DNB.* Also North to King, 7 November 1775. Fortescue, *op. cit.*, iii, 1743. King to North, 8 November 1775. *Ibid.*, 1745. Rochford to King, 9 November 1775. *Ibid.*, 1751. Harcourt, then Lord-Lieutenant of Ireland, praised Rochford's capacity as an administrator in a letter to Jenkinson, 24 February 1776. BM. Add. MS. 38208, f. 269. It has not been possible to trace any collection of Rochford manuscripts.

[2] E. Fitzmaurice, *The Life of Granville George Leveson-Gower, second Earl Granville*, i, 2. See also *Lord Granville Leveson-Gower (first Earl Granville) Private Correspondence, 1781–1821*, ed. C. Granville, pp. xxi-xxii; *DNB.*; I. R. Christie, *The End of North's Ministry*, pp. 206-8. For Gower's part in the political manœuvrings from 1760 to 1768 see the many references in J. Brooke, *The Chatham Administration, 1766–68.*

[3] The Gower family papers in the Sutherland MSS. were transferred from Trentham to the Staffordshire County Record Office, Stafford, at the end of 1961. They contained nothing of political interest for this study. See *HMC*, 5, Appendix I, *Sutherland MSS.* There are also some Gower papers in the Granville MSS. among the Gifts and Deposits in the PRO.

statesman in either house.' [1] Praise for his abilities came from unexpected quarters. Horace Walpole said 'No man in the administration was so much master of business, so quick or so shrewd, and no man had so many public enemies who had so few private'.[2] But as a politician he was typical of his time. 'Sandwich was the perfect type of eighteenth-century politician, accepting uncritically, exploiting skilfully, and enjoying whole-heartedly, the conventions of his age. No opportunity to extend his influence ever escaped him.' [3] Like Gower, he was an old Bedfordite, and used a part of that faction, together with his own electoral influence in Huntingdonshire, as the basis of a small personal political group. Also like Gower, he shared the Bedford views on America; though Sandwich stuck to them until finally swept from office in 1782.[4]

Finally there was Henry Bathurst, Baron Apsley, who was allegedly 'the least efficient Lord Chancellor of the eighteenth-century'. He attended Cabinet regularly during the American crisis, but this was a mere formal meeting of his responsibilities; politically he was a nonentity. He retired from the Woolsack in June 1778, but returned to the Ministry to replace Gower as Lord President of the Council in the following year.[5]

Of these seven who made policy, the two Bedfords — Gower and Sandwich — and Suffolk, a Grenvillite, were by temperament and by the inclinations of their past political conduct most likely to advocate the coercion of the Americans. The King would support this, or at least the insistence on British Parliamentary supremacy. George III cherished 'the beauty, excellence, and perfection of the British Constitution as by law established'.[6] He believed that American independence would shatter it. 'I am', he claimed, 'fighting the Battle

[1] *The Private Papers of John, Earl of Sandwich . . . 1771–1782*, ed., G. R. Barnes and J. H. Owen, i, xiii.

[2] Horace Walpole, *Memoirs of the Reign of King George the Third*, ed. G. F. Russell Barker, iv, 170-1.

[3] J. Brooke, *op. cit.*, p. 32. I. R. Christie, *op. cit.*, pp. 8, 203-6.

[4] The Sandwich Papers in the possession of Lord Sandwich at Mapperton, Dorset, were not open to inspection.

[5] I. R. Christie, *op. cit.*, p. 9. Bathurst to Hardwicke, [June] 1778. BM. Add. MS. 35614, ff. 267-8.

[6] King to North, 14 November 1778. Fortescue, *op. cit.*, iv, 2451.

of the legislature, [and] therefore have a right to expect an almost unanimous support.'[1] He also thought that severance from North America would make England a second-class power, and he told North in 1779 that it was impossible to weigh the gains in the war against the cost like a mere tradesman. His ideas were rigid, and like his Ministers he saw the choice as simple: 'I am not sorry that the line of conduct seems now chalked out ... the New England Governments are in a state of Rebellion, blows must decide whether they are to be subject to this country or independant'.[2] That was written many months before Lexington and Concord in fact initiated an explicit policy of blows.

The King had never admitted that the existing imperial relationship might be modified or compromised. 'The superiority of the mother country over her colonies must be supported', he had written to Grafton in 1768.[3] In 1774 his attitude was the same: '. . . the dye is now cast, the colonies must either submit or triumph; I do not wish to come to severer measures but we must not retreat . . . I have no objection . . . [after their submission] . . . to their seeing that there is no inclination for the present to lay fresh taxes on them, but I am clear that there must always be one tax to keep up the right, and as such I approve of the tea duty'.[4] In 1778 he wrote that 'whilst nothing short of independency will be accepted, I do not think there is a man either bold or mad enough to presume to treat for the mother country on such a basis'.[5] The next year he described the proposal that William Eden should negotiate a peace with Franklin as 'what I look upon as the destruction of the Empire'. He believed that ultimately a compromise on an economic basis was impossible because it would not satisfy the colonists: 'Independence is their object . . . which every man not willing to sacrifice every object to a momentary and inglorious peace must concur with me in thinking that this country can never submit to'.[6] On 21 June 1779 the King presided over the

---

[1] King to North, 10 September 1775. Fortescue, *op. cit.*, iii, 1709.
[2] King to North, 18 November 1774. *Ibid.*, 1556.
[3] Quoted in E. Robson, *The American Revolution, 1763–1783*, p. 82.
[4] King to North, 11 November 1774. Fortescue, *op. cit.*, iii, 1508.
[5] King to North, 11 September 1778. *Ibid.*, iv, 2161.
[6] King to North, 11 June 1779. *Ibid.*, 2649.

Cabinet for the first time during the war. He repeated his total opposition to a policy of concessions and said no politician would come to office under him unless he saw 'it signed under his hand that he is resolved to keep the Empire entire and that no troops shall be consequently withdrawn from thence, nor independence ever allowed'.[1] Even in 1782 he was protesting that 'no consideration shall ever make me in the smallest degree an Instrument in a measure that . . . would annihilate the rank in which the British Empire stands among the European States'.[2] But before long a retreat from this stand was forced upon him. 'Parliament having to my astonishment come into the ideas of granting a separation to North America,' he wrote to Townshend, 'necessity not conviction has made me subscribe to it.'[3] He was unswerving in his opinion to the end, and self-consciously so: 'this', he said of the Peace Treaty in September 1783, 'completes the downfall of the lustre of this Empire: but when religion and public spirit are quite absorbed by vice and dissipation, what has now occurred is but the natural consequence . . . I have alone tried to support the dignity of my crown'.[4]

George III was an inflexible and priggish man, who frequently mistook obstinacy for courage. As a monarch he was extremely conscious of the dignity of Crown and Parliament, and of the delicate balance of legislative and executive powers in the British Constitution. He was also completely certain that by the Constitution the American Colonies were subordinate, and he believed it was his duty to maintain that subordination. But how far was his obsession with British sovereignty the cause of the disasters and humiliations which the Mother Country suffered during the second and the third decade of his reign? Governor Tryon of New York commented rather acidly in 1773 that 'His Majesty's instructions and His Majesty's

---

[1] King to North, 22 June 1779. *Ibid.*, 2674. Germain told his Under-Secretary, William Knox, after the meeting that the King said he only reproached himself for one action in his life — for changing his Ministers in 1765 and consenting to repeal the Stamp Act. *HMC, Various*, vi, *Knox MSS.*, p. 260.

[2] King to North, 21 January 1782. Fortescue, *op. cit.*, v, 3501.

[3] King to Thomas Townshend, 19 November 1782. *Ibid.*, vi, 3984.

[4] King to North, 7 September 1783. *Ibid.*, 4470.

interests are not at all times one and the same thing, and he who in America follows implicitly the letter of the instructions will not best serve the King'.[1] Yet it is not wholly clear what other policy George III could have pursued towards America. He could not have adopted the nineteenth-century solution of slow evolution of the Colonies towards Dominion status and effective independence under the Crown. This was impossible until the Crown was completely out of politics — which could only happen when there was a party system to select the nation's governors. It was also alien to predominant English eighteenth-century thought. And in any case many Americans wanted a quick and clear solution. The best that might have been achieved, in the short run, was probably some solution of the kind suggested by Opposition leaders after 1766. This meant no direct taxation and no provocation of any kind towards the Americans; then the imperial relationship might have bumbled along, with no large-scale rejection of British sovereignty because the issue was subdued. But as a solution it would have been precarious, and the proposition was unacceptable to the many people who, after 1763, had the (administratively admirable) idea of tidying up the Empire. Certainly George III was not a man to savour mere nuances of power and inexplicit sovereignties.[2]

Suffolk, Gower and Sandwich were then the most aggressive coercionists in the Cabinet, and in the Closet they were more than matched by the King. Dartmouth and North were more moderate, and they held crucial Ministerial posts, but neither had the courage to insist on a policy against the wishes of their royal master and their Cabinet colleagues. Even more important, they could not oppose Parliamentary coercion because they supported Parliamentary sovereignty. The remaining two Ministers, Rochford and Apsley, were of no great political consequence and were happy to go along with the punitive

[1] Governor Tryon to Dartmouth, 5 May 1773. Dartmouth MS. D 1778, I, ii, 854. Quoted in *HMC*, II, V, *Dartmouth MSS.*, i, 336.
[2] See Sir Lewis Namier, 'King George III : a study of Personality', printed in *Personalities and Powers*, pp. 39-58. Also the many observations on the King's character in Sir Nathaniel Wraxall, *Historical Memoirs of My own Time*, especially pp. 229-51, 287-8.

policy. Not often in the reign of George III were his Cabinets as united as was that of Lord North in the twelve months after the Boston Tea Party.

Its inclination towards a policy of asserting British supremacy, if necessary by force, was reinforced by the subordinates whom the Ministers were accustomed to consult on colonial affairs. The two Law Officers were not in the Cabinet, but frequently gave advice on the legal implications of policy decisions. Edward Thurlow, the Attorney-General, was able, independent and intolerant by nature. He had a rigid legal mind and found it difficult to accommodate the subtle compromises which politics often demands; hence, like many of his colleagues, he could never see the American struggle as other than a simple choice between independence or subordination. He was infuriated by the weakness of Lord North, but remained wholly loyal to him as the King's chosen Minister. The King recognised Thurlow's value and wrote to Lord North: 'I think the attorney though sometimes a little too positive yet as the most to be depended upon and most firm in his present employment, who has at the same time talents for any office in his profession'.[1] Edmund Burke, though an opponent, praised him as 'intelligent, systematic, and determined'.[2] Thurlow was a firm supporter of the policies which were adopted, and it will be seen that he exercised a vital, sometimes a decisive, influence on their final form. Alexander Wedderburn, the Solicitor-General, has already been introduced with reference to the Franklin hearing. Of lesser stature than Thurlow, he shared the lawyer's instinctive concern with the constitutional powers claimed for the Government.

Two others closely concerned were the Under-Secretaries at the American Department — William Knox and John Pownall.[3] They had the civil servant's advantage of experience and continuity in office, having served under Dartmouth's predecessor, Lord Hillsborough. Moreover, Knox had previously

---

[1] King to North, 28 October 1777. Fortescue, *op. cit.*, iii, 2073.

[2] Burke to Edmund Percy, 18 July 1778. Transcript at Sheffield Central Library from the National Library of Ireland.

[3] Knox was Under-Secretary from 1770 to 1782, Pownall from 1768 to 1776.

been Provost Marshal of Georgia and Pownall was Secretary of the Board of Trade from 1761. They thus had considerable experience of colonial affairs, even though they might lack commensurate understanding. They had 'a very real influence not only in the routine business of the department but in the formulation of policies',[1] for Lord Dartmouth gave them a ready ear. Later, Knox claimed that he was in favour of meeting some of the colonial demands :

> . . . however determined we all were that the colonies should obey the sovereign authority of Parliament, we all thought that taxation ought to be given up in practise, and that the colonies should be invited to make some proposition as an equivalent. I went further, and thought there were many unjust as well as impolitic restraints on the foreign commerce of the Colonies, which ought to be taken off. . . .[2]

But there is nothing to suggest that in 1774 Knox or Pownall were other than in substantial agreement with the policies conceived and executed by the Government; indeed they played some part in shaping them.[3]

One final person who should be mentioned as exercising an influence on the Government's policy is Lord Chief Justice Mansfield.[4] In August 1774 Hutchinson included Mansfield among 'those Ministers who most concern themselves in American affairs',[5] and his concern with the Massachusetts Bay Regulating Act and the Quebec Act will be referred to below.[6] In October 1775 William Eden took a draft of the King's speech to Lord Mansfield's home and 'there, which you know is a great secret, had the kindest assistance for many hours at different times in putting it into its present form'.[7] Shortly

---

[1] M. M. Spector, *op. cit.*, pp. 37-8, 100-5.

[2] *HMC, Various*, vi, *Knox MSS.*, pp. 258, xvii-xviii. See also W. Knox, *Extra Official State Papers*, i, 18.

[3] See M. M. Spector, *op. cit.*, pp. 100-5. She describes Knox as 'the leading pamphleteer in support of Parliamentary authority over the Colonies' and asserts that he 'never understood colonial psychology'. *Ibid.*, 103, 105.

[4] William Murray, first Earl of Mansfield (1705–93), became Lord Chief Justice in 1756.   [5] Hutchinson, *op. cit.*, p. 230.

[6] See below, pp. 87, 120.

[7] Eden to Germain, 3 October 1775, *HMC, Stopford Sackville MSS.* II, 10-11.

after, Lord North consulted Mansfield on the proposal to send Peace Commissioners to America.[1] Mansfield's advisory role is interesting. As a member of the nominal Cabinet (though outside the effective Cabinet since 1763) and as a lawyer of great eminence it was perfectly respectable that the Government should consult him. But the consultation was shrouded in considerable secrecy. This may have been at the wish of Mansfield, who had a reputation for political timidity. It may also have been expediency on the part of the Government, since Mansfield was known to be a strong supporter of the royal prerogative, and his role in the prosecution of Wilkes in 1763 made him unpopular with the public and a leading victim of the pen of Junius. Mansfield's influence, though difficult to assess, seems not surprisingly to have been in favour of coercion. Dartmouth once warned Grafton that Mansfield was 'the man who will prevent your wished for ambitions on American policy from taking place'.[2]

On 1 February 1774 the Earl of Buckinghamshire introduced his motion in the Lords asking that all the correspondence relating to the riots in Boston should be laid before Parliament.[3] Buckinghamshire argued 'that the question now was, not about the liberty of North America, but whether we were to be free, or slaves to our colonies'. In reply to the motion, if not to this question, Dartmouth informed the Lords that the Ministry intended to lay these papers before both Houses; and Buckinghamshire withdrew his motion.[4] Parliament then dropped the question and devoted itself, among other matters, to proceeding against Horne Tooke for an alleged libel on the Speaker.[5] The Ministry used this breathing space to prepare its American plans.

However, the debate continued both in public and in private. General Gage, the Commander-in-Chief in America, who had been on leave in England since the summer of 1773 to report on conditions in the Colonies, wrote on 4 February to Governor

[1] North to Eden [November 1775]. BM. Add. MS. 34412, ff. 369-70.
[2] W. R. Anson, ed., *op. cit.*, p. 267.
[3] *Public Advertiser*, 2 February 1774.
[4] *Correspondence of William Pitt, Earl of Chatham*, ed. W. S. Taylor and J. H. Pringle, iv, 323-4.
[5] J. Adolphus, *The History of England*, ii, 74-5. *Parl. Hist.*, xvii, 1003-50.

Hutchinson : 'People talk more seriously than ever about America : that the crisis is come, when the Provinces must be either British Colonies, or independent and separate states. What will be done, nobody I believe can yet tell. . . . Nothing can be fixed.' [1] The newspapers, ever speculative and often well informed, were in no doubt that something very definite was going to be done. 'The affairs of America at present occupy the whole attention of Administration', claimed the *St. James's Chronicle*, 'and it is agreed on all hands to be now the most important business that has come under consideration since the accession of the present King.' [2] Shelburne tried to assess the many rumours for Chatham, who was isolated and gouty at Burton Pynsent. 'Various measures are talked of', he wrote, 'for altering the constitution of the government of New England and prosecuting individuals, all tending more or less to enforcement. The opinion here is very general that America will submit, that government was taken by surprise when they repealed the Stamp Act, and that all may be recovered.' [3]

The crux of the colonial problem now facing the Ministry was that there had occurred an open, explicit and well publicised denial of Parliament's right to impose the Tea Duty. The importance of the Boston Tea Party — why it is so much more than just a favourite children's story, with good patriots dressing up as Red Indians — is that it made the constitutional problem of England's American Colonies a stark issue of sovereignty. Before that many Americans denied certain theoretical details of British supremacy ; a few rejected it altogether. The opposition to the Stamp Act and the Townshend duties had shown the dangers of applying that supremacy in a concrete way. But while there was no particular rejection by Americans on a large scale, it could be presumed that there was a tacit acceptance of the general principle of English sovereignty. Right up to December 1773 any solution of the American problem brought forward by the Government might

[1] Gage to Hutchinson, 2 February 1774. Hutchinson, *op. cit.*, i, 100. Gage was appointed Commander-in-Chief in November 1764. E. Robson, *op. cit.*, p. 85.   [2] *St. James's Chronicle*, 1-3 February 1774.
[3] Shelburne to Chatham, 3 February 1774. E. Fitzmaurice, *Life of Shelburne*, ii, 299.

have been regarded as a modification of a seemingly accepted imperial relationship. But after the Tea Party the Ministry felt that it first had to demonstrate that the imperial relationship still remained in existence to be reformed. A few people, mainly in Opposition, argued that a relationship could continue even without the existence of a tea duty, or, indeed, even without asserting the right to enact such a duty. In retrospect these are plausible arguments. But the Ministers could not see how imperial sovereignty could allow a limitation on the sovereign's rights; they also believed that an imperial relationship certainly could not exist when a Colony could flaunt a law and could attack both the property and the persons of the executive designated to execute that law — and remain uncorrected. They felt it was no use repealing an offensive law unless the principle of respect for all laws was first restored. They insisted, as have many imperial governments since, on 'pacification before negotiation'; whereupon the Americans replied in turn that they were prepared to be peaceful and respect laws providing they were not offensive. The Ministers could not accept that the Americans should reserve judgment on their legislation and so they set out to introduce policies which would, they hoped, bring the Americans back to a due respect for the laws and supremacy of Parliament and would, thereby, make them ackknowledge the British sovereignty which seemed the keystone of the imperial structure.

The Government took its first positive steps towards both formulating and executing such policies on 4 February. General Gage was interviewed by the King and stated 'his readiness, though so lately come from America, to return at a day's notice if the conduct of the Colonies should induce the directing coercive measures'. George III was impressed by him, no doubt because the General articulated his own feelings on the problem — he said the Americans 'will be Lions, whilst we are Lambs, but if we take the resolute part they will undoubtedly prove very meek'. The King felt this was 'language . . . very consonant to his character of an honest determined man'. He begged North to see Gage and 'hear his ideas as to the mode of compelling Boston to submit to whatever may be thought necessary'.[1] Furthermore, Gage had argued that this submission could be secured without the cost of extra troops. The King decided that Gage was still the best man for the task, and within a few days it had been agreed to send him back to Boston with the annual military replacements.[2]

That evening, after Gage's visit to the King, the Cabinet met at Lord Rochford's. Dartmouth, who had earlier in the day held a conference with the Chairman of the East India Company about their financial losses in America, now proposed a measure which was the first specific step towards implementing the general principle decided in Cabinet on 29 January — 'to secure the dependence of the colonies on the mother country'.[3] He suggested, and the Cabinet agreed, 'that the Governor be directed to remove the seats of Government to such other place in the province as he shall think least likely to be influenced by the town of Boston, and that the officers of the customs do remove to such other port as shall be judged most convenient'.[4] North described this to the King as purely a punishment of the town, and this is certainly true of the proposal to shut the port of Boston. But the policy also had a faintly constructive touch : there was something to be said for getting the Bay Colony Government away from the rebellious atmosphere which infected its capital so that tempers might cool.[5]

A second decision was taken in Cabinet on 4 February. It was agreed to consult the Attorney- and Solicitor-Generals concerning the riots at Boston, and to take their opinion whether they 'do amount to the crime of High Treason, and if so against whom, and what will be the proper and legal method of proceeding against such persons'.

A noteworthy feature of the Cabinet's decisions at this stage is that legislation was not thought to be necessary. It was

---

[1] King to North, 4 February 1774. Fortescue, *op. cit.*, iii, 1379.
[2] Unsigned paper on American affairs, in Pownall's hand, early 1774. Dartmouth MS. D 1778, II, 1044. Quoted in *HMC*, 14, X, *Dartmouth MSS.*, ii, 245. [3] See above, Chapter II, p. 34.
[4] Cabinet Minute. Dartmouth MS. D 1778, II, 817. William Knox said this was first proposed by Dartmouth's Under-Secretary, John Pownall : *HMC, Various*, vi, *Knox MSS.*, p. 257.
[5] North to King, [undated : from internal evidence 5 February 1774]. Fortescue, *op. cit.*, iii, 1377.

considered that each step would be effected through royal decree, which, had it so transpired, might have raised the ghost of prerogative to haunt the sleep of English Whigs. Lord North wrote to the King that Dartmouth had suggested the removal of the custom house and the Assembly from Boston 'as a measure that could be taken immediately by the sole power of the Crown, with other propositions'.[1] And Dartmouth himself told Hutchinson that

> in the discussion of these measures the authority of the executive government, and the most effectual means of carrying them into execution, were considered with the closest attention by the Law Servants of the Crown, and every endeavour was used to establish and verify the facts by the evidence of those lately arrived from America who had been witnesses of these transactions.
>
> Unfortunately however it turned out in the result that neither the proposition of suspending the privileges of Boston as a port, nor the steps necessary to come at an immediate punishment of the offenders, could be completely effected by the sole authority of the Crown. In this situation the King has thought fit to lay the whole matter before both Houses of Parliament.[2]

Here it must be emphasised that this original policy of executive action, which was particularly supported by Dartmouth, was, in relation to the constitutional issues raised by the colonists, more moderate than the alternative course of working through Parliament. Had it been followed it would of course have provoked enraged Whig outbursts against high prerogative. But the alternative policy, ultimately pursued, was in its implications much more severe and hazardous : it meant accepting the Tea Party as a general colonial challenge to British sovereignty, putting the question before the legislative assembly of the realm, and proposing radical legislation which must deal broadly with the many sources of trouble and grievance and which would apply to all the inhabitants of Massachusetts. Dartmouth preferred to avoid this if possible. His first proposals

[1] North to King [5 February 1774]. *Ibid.*, 1377.
[2] Dartmouth to Hutchinson, 9 March 1774. PRO. CO. 5/763, f. III.

were to act within the law as it stood, to punish only those individuals who had incited and led the riots, and to suspend the statutory privileges of Boston port because, and for as long as, its citizens abused them by conniving in the destruction of the East India Company's tea. Executive action also had the attraction that it was speedy. But above all it was relatively moderate and conservative in conception, limited in object and intended to remain carefully within the lines of existing law.

No details were revealed when Dartmouth wrote to the Governor of New York on 5 February about the Government's intentions. This dispatch had been deliberately delayed from 1 February until the 5th.[1] But in the end it contained nothing beyond the general statement of principle agreed in Cabinet on 29 January: 'I have it in command from the King to acquaint you that it is His Majesty's firm resolution upon the unanimous advice of his Confidential Servants to pursue such measures as shall be effectual for securing the dependence of the colonies upon this Kingdom'.[2] Dartmouth wrote an almost identical letter to Hutchinson in Massachusetts. He added that the reports from Boston, New York and Philadelphia were 'of the most serious nature, and have induced the fullest consideration; and I shall probably in a few days receive His Majesty's command for such instructions as may be necessary to be sent to you in consequence of what has passed at Boston'.[3] The latter hope proved optimistic; nothing concrete was sent to Hutchinson until 9 March and then it was only a preliminary outline of the Boston Port Bill.[4] It was to take some time before the King's final instructions were agreed upon.

The two proposals on 4 February did sketch what must have seemed to the Ministers to be the immediate practical ways of securing American dependence. They set out to prosecute the perpetrators of the riot, to punish the town of Boston for conniv-

[1] W. Knox to A. Todd, 1 February 1774. PRO. CO. 5/250, f. 69. For details of the dispatch to South Carolina sent on 5 February see Grey Cooper to J. Pownall, 5 February 1774. PRO. CO. 5/145, f. 234.
[2] Dartmouth to Governor Tryon, 5 February 1774. PRO. CO. 5/1141, f. 128.
[3] Dartmouth to Hutchinson, 5 February 1774. PRO. CO. 5/763, f. 57.
[4] Dartmouth to Hutchinson, 9 March 1774. PRO. CO. 5/763, ff. 109-114

ing at it, and then to give the Colony's government a period away from the local passions to think about the whole situation. The Ministerial policy might be proved inadequate in the event ; or again, issue could be taken with their whole concept of the imperial relationship as one of authority on the one hand and submission on the other. But given that they held that concept, they had made a reasonable beginning. The problem of Parliamentary sovereignty seemed crucial to them — as to most people [1] — and they equated the administering of punishment with the demonstration of that supremacy. A polity which did not or could not punish breaches of its own laws was in a critical condition. The Ministers meant to prove that this did not apply to Great Britain. They were supported in the method of proof by the advice from their chief agent in Massachusetts. Hutchinson wrote :

> I see no prospect, my Lord, of the government of this province being restored to its former state without the interposition of the authority in England. . . . A conviction of this authority, or a persuasion that, at all events, the Parliament will maintain it against all opposition, will restore order.

But coming down to specific measures, Hutchinson was unable to offer any constructive suggestions.

On Saturday, 5 February, Dartmouth followed up the second Cabinet decision of the previous evening concerning the Boston riots and sent to the Attorney-General a detailed narrative of the events leading up to the Tea Party. Attached to the narrative were two 'queries', and a strong request for a prompt answer. The queries were :

1. Do the acts and proceedings stated in the foregoing case, or any of them, amount to the crime of High Treason ?

[1] In the debates on the Coercion Acts most people, Opposition as well as Administration, usually ignored the specific measures and discussed the Parliamentary *right* to tax. Also see an unsigned paper in the writing of the Earl of Buckinghamshire early in March : 'it is evident that our present situation with the Colonies is so critical that no effectual middle term can be found ; we must either insist upon their submission to the authority of the Legislature or give them up entirely to their own discretion. The first seems the lesser evil but it is by no means easy to determine the measures necessary for carrying it into execution and yet the decision upon these measures must be immediate. . . .' *HMC, Lothian MSS.*, 1905, pp. 290-1.

2. If they do, who are the persons chargeable with such crime, and what will be the proper and legal method of proceeding against them ? [1]

Not surprisingly there had been no reply by that evening, when the Ministers met again, this time at Lord Sandwich's, and once more discussed the treasonable nature of the Boston outrages.[2] For the moment they could consider only the measures they might take if the Law Officers found that there existed grounds for proceeding against the Americans concerned. In such case it was decided to give further consideration to the expediency of issuing a Commission 'under the Great Seal to certain persons [in Massachusetts] with powers of magistracy directing them to enquire concerning the said offences, and to apprehend and send over such persons as they shall find to have been guilty of the same together with the evidence against them, in order that they may be tried here'. To secure this, Dartmouth was to take the opinion of Thurlow and Wedderburn on whether the King could, by his own authority, appoint Justices of the Peace in Massachusetts Bay. But that also waited upon the Law Officers' decision on the former questions concerning High Treason.

On Monday Dartmouth saw Thurlow, who promised him that he would send an answer to the queries. But as this still had not arrived on Tuesday, Dartmouth sent the Attorney-General a polite note of reminder.[3] He received no reply ; but on Wednesday was sent more details of the rebellious happenings in Boston by the Chairman of the East India Company.[4] The next day he addressed himself once more to Thurlow, this time with a sharper rebuke :

After the expectation you gave me on Monday that I should receive the next day your opinion with that of the Solicitor General upon the questions that I had submitted to your

[1] Dartmouth to Thurlow, 5 February 1774. PRO. CO. 5/160, ff. 1-11. Attached to this is a list of the Americans mentioned, and therefore presumably to be considered as traitors.
[2] Cabinet Minute, 5 February 1774. Dartmouth MS. D 1778, II, 819.
[3] Dartmouth to Thurlow, 8 February 1774. PRO. CO. 5/250, f. 73.
[4] Chairman of East India Company to Dartmouth, 9 February 1774. PRO. CO. 5/133, ff. 67-71.

consideration, you will easily conceive the uneasiness I must be under on finding myself still unprovided with that opinion in a matter in which the interests of the public are so materially concerned and which so absolutely requires the utmost dispatch ; allow me once more to remind you of this business and to beg that no further time may be lost in conveying to me the answer to the reference that is before you.[1]

This reprimand would appear to have had effect ; for the next day Thurlow sent to Dartmouth the detailed comments of himself and the Solicitor-General upon the queries. To the first question, which asked whether the detailed acts constituted treason, they replied :

We are of opinion that the acts and proceedings, stated in the above mentioned case, do amount to the crime of High Treason ; namely to the levying of war against His Majesty.

These proceedings are an attempt, concerted with much deliberation, and made with open force, in pursuance of such concert, to obstruct the execution of an Act of Parliament of Great Britain, imposing a duty upon tea imported into America ; and to put a general restraint upon the exercise of a lawful trade, as if it were a public grievance.

The notices, to the consignees to resign their respective commissions, and to the Freemen to meet at the Liberty Tree, are connected with the meeting holden in pursuance thereof.

The conduct of Mr. Molynieux, and the committee, supposing them to be authenticated by the meeting, as their constituents, affects the last also.

The demand made on Clarke and the other consignees, and the threat if they refused, are connected with the attack, made by the same committee, on Mr. Clarke ; and make that an overt act of Treason.

The Crown's lawyers were clearly in no doubt that some of the acts were treason, and certain of the perpetrators culpable traitors. To the second query, which asked who was chargeable and how might they be proceeded against, the reply was :

We think (upon the above mentioned state of the case, supposing it to be an accurate account) that Molynieux, Denny,

[1] Dartmouth to Thurlow, 10 February 1774. PRO. CO. 5/250, f. 73.

Warren, Church, and Jonathan [?] [1] who in the characters of a committee went to the length of attacking Clarke, are chargeable with the crime of High Treason; and if it can be established in evidence, that they were so employed by the select men of Boston, Town Clerk, and members of the House of Representatives, these also are guilty of the same offence.

Williams, the moderator of the Assembly . . . the committee, and the proposers of the resolutions there taken, Adams, Molynieux, Young, and Warren, and the several persons, called a committee of correspondence, who readily accepted that commission, and acted in appointing the armed watch, and Hancock, one of the same watch, are guilty in that same degree.

The Ministry was here presented with a considerable bag of victims, and those who thirsted for Bostonian blood might at this point have hoped to have their fill. The theoretical question of how to proceed against the accused appeared simple:

The methods of proceeding against them are, either by prosecuting them for their treason, in the country, in the ordinary course of justice; or arresting them there by the justices of the peace, or some of them, and transmitting them hither to be tried in some county of England, to be assigned by the King's commission; or by sending over a warrant of a Secretary of State, grounded on sufficient information upon oath, to arrest and bring over the offenders to be tried here.

We take each of these courses to be legal; and that to be the most proper, which the circumstances of the case absolutely require. In the consideration of which we humbly submit, that a preference is due to the most ordinary course, if it be thought, in other respects, equally sufficient and effective.

The treasonable nature of the offences had, in the lawyers' eyes, been demonstrated; the offenders were named; the procedures of law defined. The only remaining difficulty was to produce witnesses against the accused whose evidence would prove conclusive in court. For the moment this proved a formidable obstacle.

[1] The script is difficult to understand. This may refer to Jonathan Williams.

Upon perusing the state of the evidence of Mr. Scott, the only person now in England who can give evidence, we think, that, as it stands, it is scarce sufficient to affect any person with the crime of High Treason; unless the resolutions, taken at the meeting which he speaks of, can be more distinctly established, and referred to the persons, he mentions.[1]

Dartmouth received this reply shortly before 4 p.m. on Friday. Later that day he wrote back to Thurlow and Wedderburn saying he had already laid their report before the King. He now wanted their opinion

whether in case His Majesty shall think fit to appoint commissioners under the Great Seal of Great Britain to make inquisition of the treasons committed within the Province of Massachusetts Bay in the months of November and December last, His Majesty can legally invest such commissioners with full powers of magistracy to be exercised by them in like manner as such powers are now exercised by the ordinary civil magistrates within the colony — by virtue of commissions granted by the Governor with the advise of his council pursuant to the authority contained in the Charter.[2]

The matter was clearly being pressed with great urgency, at least by the politicians. On Tuesday, 15 February, Dartmouth sent notes to twelve people who had lately arrived from Boston asking them to attend in his office the next day at 11 a.m.[3] He also asked Thurlow and Wedderburn to come along and assist in examining them about events in Boston.[4] Apparently the Ministry meant to remedy the deficiency of witnesses in order to proceed against the 'traitors' as soon as possible.

The witnesses were interviewed, and their information was laid before the Cabinet that evening. The Ministers decided to get this information attested before the Privy Council so that warrants could be issued for the arrest of the persons charged and they could be brought to England for trial.[5] Next

[1] Law Officers to Dartmouth, 11 February 1774. PRO. CO. 5/160, ff. 40-2. Scott's testimony makes it clear that though he knew most of the facts of the Tea Party, he did not actually see the dumping of the tea into Boston harbour. The testimony is in Dartmouth MS. D 1778, II, 807.

[2] Dartmouth to Law Officers, 11 February 1774. PRO. CO. 5/160, f. 44.

[3] A copy is in PRO. CO. 5/250, f. 74.   [4] *Ibid.*

[5] Cabinet Minute, 16 February 1774. Dartmouth MS. D 1778, II, 832.

day Dartmouth called nine of the witnesses back for a second private examination,[1] and after this all the original twelve were told to attend the meeting of the Privy Council on the 19th.[2] There Dartmouth laid before the Council the Law Officers' report; the witnesses were examined and depositions were taken on oath. These depositions were then referred to the Attorney- and Solicitor-Generals to determine whether any of the persons accused in them could be charged with High Treason on the basis of the evidence given.[3]

The Attorney- and Solicitor-Generals continued to do their homework, if not as quickly as the politicians would have liked. When the Cabinet met on the 19th, after the Privy Council, Thurlow had reported on the question concerning the King's power to send Commissioners to assist in the prosecutions in America. The King was advised to send out a proper person conversant in the law to assist in the execution of a warrant should one be issued to arrest persons guilty of treason at Boston.

It was also finally decided in Cabinet on the 19th to meet Buckinghamshire's request of nearly three weeks before and lay the American papers, together with the proceedings in the Privy Council, before Parliament. No fixed date was set for this: the Ministers merely agreed to do it 'within a few days after the ships shall be sailed with such orders and instructions as may finally be the result of the present proceedings'.[4]

However, nine days later, on 28 February, this leading prong of the Ministry's American policy was completely blunted by the decision of its own Law Officers. A Cabinet was held:

The Attorney and Solicitor General attending on the Questions referred to them by the Privy Council concerning the late disorders at Boston, gave their opinion that the charge of

---

[1] Pownall to various, 17 February 1774. PRO. CO. 5/250, f. 75.

[2] W. Knox to various, 18 February 1774. *Ibid.*

[3] Copies of the 12 depositions are in PRO. CO. 5/763, ff. 175-216. A memorandum is attached to the Privy Council report stating that the Privy Council did not consider the case again, 'the matter being taken up in Parliament'. *Acts of the Privy Council of England, Colonial Series,* ed., J. Munro, v, 391-2.

[4] Cabinet Minute, 19 February 1774. Dartmouth MS. D 1778, II, 833, 834.

High Treason cannot be maintained against any individuals on the ground of the depositions taken at the Council Board on the 19th inst.[1]

Dartmouth's efforts to muster a battalion of witnesses had failed. This punitive measure had to be abandoned after nearly a month of consideration and just as it was on the point of execution. Pownall later told Hutchinson that 'the Lords of the Privy Council actually had their pens in their hands, in order to sign the warrant . . . when Lord Mansfield diverted it by urging the other measures'. Hutchinson went to see Mansfield to check this. 'He allowed the Lords of Council had their pens prepared to sign a warrant for apprehending persons in Boston, but did not allow they desisted because another measure was thought more expedient but because the Attorney and Solicitor General were in doubt whether the evidence was sufficient to convict them.'[2] The above documentation supports Mansfield's claim. Obviously the British Government was acting with strict legality. It had tried to deal with the Boston situation within the existing law of Treason. It now gave up the attempt on purely legal grounds, because its Law Officers said that prosecution was technically impossible.

It seems probable that the opposition came mainly from Thurlow. When the Earl of Buckinghamshire spoke with Dartmouth on 2 March urging the need to press on with the prosecutions, he commented that 'the Solicitor General coincided with this, but the Attorney General objected'.[3] This perhaps throws some light on the story told by William Knox. He claimed that after a Cabinet meeting had decided to issue warrants for the arrest of the Boston ringleaders, Thurlow was instructed to prepare the warrants. The next day he and Pownall were waiting outside the Cabinet room when Thurlow

[1] Cabinet Minute, 28 February 1774. Dartmouth MS. D 1778, II, 839. This verbal report was the only statement made by the Law Officers. A note written in the margin beside the original question put to them by Dartmouth said 'no written report was made to this reference'. Dartmouth to Attorney- and Solicitor-Generals, 11 February 1774. PRO. CO. 5/250, f. 74.   [2] Hutchinson, op. cit., i, 183, 219.
[3] Minutes of conversation with Lord Dartmouth, 2 March 1774. HMC, Lothian MSS., p. 290.

emerged, and Pownall asked if everything was prepared. Thurlow is said to have replied : 'No, nothing is done. Don't you see that they want to throw the whole responsibility of the business upon the Solicitor General and me ? And who would be such damned fools as to risk themselves for such . . . fellows as these ? Now if it was George Grenville . . . there would be some sense in it.' [1] Even if this story had become garbled in Knox's memory, the impression that Thurlow was responsible for blocking the policy of treasonable prosecutions is most probably a correct one. It is to his credit that he preserved his professional integrity in judging this legal question, even though this meant the abandonment of a policy the aims of which he wholeheartedly supported.

The Law Officers' decision certainly upset both their political colleagues and their royal master : North later told Hutchinson that he personally had been convinced that the Boston proceedings were treasonable, and that only legal doubts had prevented prosecution ; [2] while the King wrote irritatedly to Dartmouth on 1 March that 'considering the time the Attorney and Solicitor General took previous to their opinion of the disturbances of Boston, I should have hoped they had so thoroughly examined the questions put to them as not to have now retracted that opinion'.[3] It was in fact unfair to accuse them of a retraction, since their position in the second report was the same as in the first — that the proceedings were treasonable, but the evidence was insufficient to warrant charges against particular persons. However, it is possible that after interrogating the witnesses with Dartmouth on 16 February, Thurlow may have given the impression that he thought their evidence might be adequate. In any case he had now made up his mind and nothing would change it.[4]

Thurlow was an independent, often even an obstinate man.

[1] *HMC, Various*, vi, *Knox MSS.*, pp. 270, xxv. Also quoted in R. Gore-Browne, *Chancellor Thurlow*, p. 82.
[2] Hutchinson's entry in his diary of 21 September 1774. Hutchinson, *op. cit.*, i, 245.
[3] King to Dartmouth, 1 March 1774. Dartmouth MS. D 1778, Supplementary George III. Quoted in *HMC*, 13, IV, *Dartmouth MSS.*, iv, 500.
[4] See I. R. Christie, *op. cit.*, pp. 8-9, for an assessment of Thurlow's stubborn character.

Originally a Bedfordite, his opinion remained that England should openly and strongly assert its authority over America. He was a great admirer of George Grenville, and once said that had he continued in power 'his firmness and wisdom would have ensured obedience without bloodshed'.[1] At another time he talked scornfully of the Opposition position on American taxation : '. . . the strange case of a right to tax America which is never to be exercised. A right to do what ? Whenever to be exercised to be wrong. But the right never to be exercised but illegally is in my opinion one of the silliest sollicisms in the [world].' [2] He was clearly for exercising English rights, and disliked the men in Boston who opposed them. Yet he refused to allow their prosecution.

Some specific reasons why Thurlow demurred and considered the evidence inadequate were given by Dartmouth in a letter to General Gage on 9 April :

> The object of the enquiry made here was to have established such a charge against the ringleaders in those violences, as might have enabled His Majesty to have proceeded against them in this Kingdom : it was found however upon the result that it would be difficult [clear and positive as the evidence was with respect to some parts of the proceedings] to establish such a connection between the acts of the body of the people, and the destruction of the tea, as to leave no doubt of the propriety and effect of bringing over the persons charged to be tried here.
>
> In this dilemma there seemed to be no other method of proceeding against them but in the ordinary courts of justice within the colony.[3]

It is worth pausing here a moment to comment upon a feature of this affair. Mr. C. R. Ritcheson, accepting the traditional simple picture of a Cabinet lashed on by the extremist Bedfordites, with Dartmouth and North as reluctant passengers, asserts that Dartmouth was responsible for blocking the

---

[1] R. Gore-Brown, *op. cit.*, p. 82.
[2] Cavendish Diary. BM. Eg. 256, f. 297. Gore-Brown quotes a more fluent expression of this opinion. 'To say that we have a right to tax America and never to exercise that right is ridiculous and a man must abuse his own understanding not to allow of that right.' R. Gore-Browne, *op. cit.*, p. 85.
[3] Dartmouth to Gage, 9 April 1774. PRO. CO. 5/763, ff. 163-4.

treasonable prosecutions.[1] In fact Dartmouth pushed Thurlow hard from the beginning, and it was the Bedfordite Attorney-General who, indirectly, shielded the Boston ringleaders from judicial proceedings.[2] Even after Thurlow's decision, Dartmouth told the King that he was still anxious to punish the offenders in some way or another.[3] And in his letter of instructions to Gage nearly a month later, Dartmouth sent details of the known offences and suspected offenders, and insisted that if he could act upon this information Gage should at least prosecute in the colonial courts. He added, however, that

> if . . . the prejudices of the people should appear to you to be such as would in all probability prevent a conviction, however clear and full the evidence might be, in that case it would be better to desist from prosecution, seeing that an ineffectual attempt would only be triumph to the faction and disgraceful to Government.[4]

The idea of the prosecutions continued to be attractive to other members of the Cabinet. In a letter to Dartmouth the Lord Chancellor stressed the need to take strong measures against the Boston ringleaders and declared that prosecution for treason was the only policy likely to be effective.[5] On 18 March Lord North said in the Commons 'with respect to the punishing individuals ; that is the object most desirable [but] . . . the nature of our law . . . the distance of places . . . make it difficult to bring to justice persons who have been guilty of disobeying the authority of this country'.[6]

In April the Prime Minister repeated his plaint :

> There is one thing I much wish, which is, the punishment of those individuals who have been the ringleaders and fore-

---

[1] C. R. Ritcheson, *British Politics and the American Revolution*, p. 161.

[2] Pownall told Hutchinson that 'the determination of the Cabinet' was '. . . to send over Adams, Molineux, and other principal Incendiaries ; try them, and if found guilty put them to death'. Hutchinson, *op. cit.*, i, 183.

[3] King to North, 14 March 1774. Fortescue, *op. cit.*, iii, 1416. Dartmouth was also by then 'very firm as to the Alteration of the Council of Massachusetts Bay' — which was enacted as the second coercionary measure.

[4] Dartmouth to Gage, 9 April 1774. Dartmouth MS. D 1778, I, ii, 965 B. Quoted in *HMC*, 11, V, *Dartmouth MSS.*, i, 351.

[5] Apsley to Dartmouth, 6 March 1774. Dartmouth MS. D 1778, II, 849. [6] Cavendish Diaries, BM. Eg. 254, f. 187.

runners of these mischiefs. Our attention will be continually active in that point. A prosecution has already been ordered against them by his Majesty's servants, but I cannot promise any very good effect until this Law shall have reached the province.[1]

In fact Dartmouth's order to Gage about prosecutions had been a qualified one, and by switching the onus to the Governor, the Ministry had admitted its incapacity to act directly on its own authority.[2]

The other punitive measure agreed by the Cabinet on 4 February — the closing of Boston harbour — was referred to the Law Officers on 10 February together with the rebuke for their slow progress with the report on the Tea Party proceedings. Dartmouth, who had made the proposal in Cabinet five days earlier, now asked for assurance on its legality: 'Can the Crown of its own authority remove the custom house [of Boston] to any other place, without the jurisdiction of such port?'[3] There was no further mention now, nor until some weeks later, of his other suggestion to move the Massachusetts Assembly out of Boston.

Next day Thurlow and Wedderburn replied: 'We think that the Lords Commissioners of His Majesty's Treasury may appoint the custom house in such ports of the province as in their discretion they think most convenient for the purpose'. They added that 'The trade of all other places wherein it is not thought necessary to appoint custom houses must resort to the

---

[1] *Parl. Hist.*, xvii, 1201. The law referred to is the Massachusetts Bay Regulating Act.

[2] The treasonable nature of the Boston Tea Party was briefly raised again in August. Samuel Dyer, who had been arrested by Gage and sent to England accused of enticing soldiers to desert, gave sworn witness before Admiral Montagu concerning the treasonable activities of the leaders in the Boston riots. Montagu wrote to the Admiralty, who in turn handed his letter over to the American Department. Poor Pownall, who could not pass it on, visited Hutchinson 'in great distress' from the prospect of the trouble involved. He had no real cause to worry; the Law Officers' February decision was repeated and the matter was dropped. So this line of Ministerial attack was finally buried, though it had been dead since the end of February. Hutchinson, *op. cit.*, i, 205. See also Admiralty to Dartmouth, 2 August 1774. PRO. CO. 5/120, f. 247.

[3] Dartmouth to Law Officers, 10 February 1774. Dartmouth MS. D 1778, II, 873.

custom houses which the Treasury shall think fit to appoint for clearances'.[1]

With this possible legal obstacle out of the way the Ministry pressed ahead with great dispatch. On this same day that he received the report Dartmouth drew up the instructions for the removal of the custom house and sent them to the Treasury. For reasons of secrecy they were enclosed in a private letter from John Pownall to Grey Cooper.[2] The instructions said that the King had decided 'for the better protection and security of the commerce of his subjects, to signify his pleasure that the Commissioners and all other officers of the customs, and such officers as are concerned in the execution of the laws respecting the plantation trade should be forthwith removed from Boston to some other port or place within the said province'. Consequently, Dartmouth told the Treasury Board, they should order the removal of these officers, and they should also decide the most suitable place to which they might go.[3] North replied on 13 February saying that he had given the orders to the Treasury Board to prepare the letters of instruction to the customs at Boston. He expected that they would be ready by the following evening.[4]

This was the high-water mark of the Government's action by executive authority in February. The treasonable prosecutions were at this time still being pressed, and now the Treasury was authorised to execute the punishment of Boston. Steps were also immediately taken to increase the military force at the disposal of the executive. On 13 February North reminded Dartmouth that Admiral Montagu must be told what to do about ships trying to enter Boston harbour once it was closed. Instructions were consequently sent to Montagu telling him to prevent any vessels whatsoever using the harbour unless they had particular authority from the custom house.[5] Furthermore,

---

[1] Law Officers to Dartmouth, 11 February 1774. PRO. CO. 5/247, f. 96.
[2] Pownall to Cooper, 11 February 1774. PRO. CO. 5/250, f. 73.
[3] Dartmouth to the Lords Commissioners of the Treasury, 11 February 1774. PRO. CO. 5/250, ff. 73-4.
[4] North to Dartmouth, 13 February 1774. Dartmouth MS. D 1778, II, 828.
[5] Undated. Dartmouth MS. D 1778, II, 1044. Quoted in HMC, 14, X, Dartmouth MSS., ii, 245.

it was decided on the 16th to send out two extra guardships to America to strengthen the Admiral's squadron there.[1]

However, by 19 February the Government had changed its intentions. In the Cabinet that evening it was decided 'that a bill be brought to remove the Port of Boston till the town of Boston or the Council appointed by the body of the people shall have indemnified the East India Company'.[2] It is difficult to discover exactly what prompted this switch from using royal decree to working through Parliament. We know that North, in his letter of 13 February to Dartmouth, expressed dissatisfaction with the form of Dartmouth's order to the Treasury Board; he sent it back together with his own draft of a suggested revision. His criticism was: 'I think as it is to be entered among our papers, it had better relate only to the removal of the Custom House officers, and be grounded upon reasoning precisely adapted to it'.[3] But lacking North's draft it is not possible to establish what modifications he suggested. Dartmouth told Hutchinson that they decided to work through Parliament simply because the policies they had in mind could not 'be completely effected by the sole authority of the Crown'[4] — a similar reason to that given later for the subsequent abandonment of the intention of prosecuting the Boston rioters for treason. This would seem to suggest that doubts had been raised about the legality of using the Crown's prerogative in cases such as this where the Colonies were concerned. Further evidence that the legality of prerogative action on colonial matters was being questioned at this time can be found in the Government's treatment of the Canadian question in 1773 and 1774.[5]

The change from prerogative to Parliamentary measures had important implications. Until now the British Government had proposed to take only specific executive actions, apparently in accordance with existing statute, against particular lawbreakers. Such steps confined the issue to the level of administration. They did not involve the whole constitutional question

---

[1] Cabinet Minute, 16 February 1774. Dartmouth MS. D 1778, II, 832.
[2] Cabinet Minute, Dartmouth MS. D 1778, II, 833.
[3] North to Dartmouth, 13 February 1774. Dartmouth MS. D 1778, II, 828.   [4] Dartmouth to Hutchinson, 9 March 1774. PRO. CO. 5/763, f. III.
[5] See below, p. 120.

of the nature of Parliament's supremacy and of the subordination of Massachusetts (and so, by implication, of the rest of the
Colonies). The Tea Party had, of course, raised that question.
But the Government's first response was to decline an explicit
constitutional struggle about the right to make law and to try
instead to concentrate on proving that England could enforce
law in the Colonies. This was sound tactics, since it implied
England's sovereignty while avoiding the open battle for supremacy which extremists on both sides wanted. It can therefore
be described as a moderate approach and not surprisingly it
was pursued mainly by Dartmouth.

But now this intended administrative action was abandoned,
first with respect to closing the port of Boston and then concerning the treasonable prosecutions. It was abandoned because
it could not be executed with strict legality. The Government
therefore had no choice but to ask Parliament to give it additional powers as quickly as possible. There, however, the issue
would inevitably be simplified into the question of constitutional right: for by passing new legislation, and particularly
punitive legislation, Parliament would prove and demonstrate
its right to legislate for the Colonies. The case for British
supremacy would then have to be spelled out, and the Government would find itself defending a less ambiguous and more
extreme position. Furthermore, as the legislation asserting and
ensuring supremacy would, directly or indirectly, apply to all
Americans, not just to individual Boston ringleaders, the
colonists had the choice of either kneeling or fighting. The
nature of the change in the Government's position was immediately illustrated in Cabinet on 19 February when, after
accepting the need to go before Parliament to close the port
of Boston, the Ministry also decided to bring in a Bill
making drastic alterations in the Constitution of Massachusetts
Bay.

During the next two weeks the business of preparing this
American legislation did not go smoothly. The Prime Minister
especially had an unhappy time. Even before Thurlow had
killed the prosecutions policy, Lord North suffered a rebuff in
the Commons. On 25 February Sir Edward Astley's motion to

make perpetual Grenville's law for trying controverted elections by a select committee was resoundingly passed. The Bill was not treated as a party question, and thirty-two place-holders together with eighty-three 'friends' of Government voted in the majority.[1] Lord North was in the minority. He alone saw this as a personal affront. He suffered one of his frequent fits of depression and as usual decided he was unfit to execute his office. The customary balms were applied. The King wrote consolingly to North on 26 February: 'I am sorry the House of Commons has yesterday been governed by a false love of popularity instead of reason'.[2] Meanwhile the Earl of Suffolk went round early in the morning to assure him that he was wanted, indeed was essential to the King's Government and was later able to report to the King:

> Lord North having walked out to breakfast I had not an opportunity of seeing him so soon as I wished, but have now the happiness to assure your Majesty that you will find him perfectly disposed to submit himself to your Majesty's pleasure: if he is not thoroughly convinced that he has abilities sufficient to carry on your Majesty's service, he is however satisfied that the event of yesterday does not lay him under an indispensable necessity to distress your Majesty, and throw this country into confusion.[3]

Within a few days North had waived his objections to the Bill.

On 28 February, having heard Thurlow's decision against the prosecutions, the Cabinet agreed to place all the American papers before Parliament on the following Monday, 7 March, and to move for an Address of support to the King in maintaining the authority of Parliament over the Colonies. Dartmouth had promised the Lords as long ago as 1 February to lay the papers before them. By the end of the month Shelburne was

---

[1] J. Adolphus, *op. cit.*, ii, 75-6. *Parl. Hist.*, xvii, 1062-77. House of Commons Division List. Fortescue, *op. cit.*, iii, 1403. The voting was 250-122. North to King, 25 February 1774. *Ibid.*, 1404.

[2] King to North, 26 February 1774. *Ibid.*, 1405. King to Dartmouth, 26 February 1774. Dartmouth MS. D 1778, Supplementary George III. Printed in *HMC*, 13, IV, *Dartmouth MSS.*, iv, 499.

[3] Suffolk to King, 26 February 1774. Fortescue, *op. cit.*, iii, 1406.

complaining to Chatham that 'There certainly is some delay about the American papers, which Lord Dartmouth told me, some time since, were to be laid before both Houses immediately, and they are not yet come'.[1] The reasons for this delay are apparent from the preceding description of the development, difficulties and changes in the Ministry's proposed measures during the month of February. The King, rather unfairly, put the whole blame on to Thurlow and Wedderburn: '. . . the seeming delay since Lord Buckinghamshire's motion arises from the Gentlemen of the Long Robe'.[2] Thurlow's stubbornness had played its part, but the Government had also considerably changed its position. Now, by the beginning of March, it had dropped the policy of taking executive action against Boston as well as the intention to institute prosecutions for high treason; and instead had resolved upon legislation both to close Boston harbour and to make major changes in the Massachusetts Charter. However, neither of these measures was ready for submission to Parliament when it met to consider the American papers on 7 March.

In Parliament the Addresses on American affairs went well, particularly in the Lords, and North and the King were in great spirits.[3] This may have increased the tempo of policy-making. On 10 March the Cabinet discussed the Boston Port Bill, which had now taken on something of its final form — for the first time the Cabinet Minute mentioned that the draft included the proposal to move the Assembly as well as the customs. It appears that North had considerable trouble drafting the Bill. Walpole says that he drew up such a bad first draft that Thurlow and Wedderburn had to make another.[4] Certainly the Prime

---

[1] Shelburne to Chatham, 27 February 1774. *Chatham Correspondence*, iv, 329.

[2] King to Dartmouth, 1 March 1774. Dartmouth MS. D 1778, Supplementary George III. Quoted in *HMC*, 13, IV, *Dartmouth MSS.*, iv, 500.

[3] King to Dartmouth, 7 March 1774. Dartmouth MS. D 1778, Supplementary George III. Quoted in *HMC*, 13, IV, *Dartmouth MSS.*, iv, 500. See below, pp. 73-6, for a description of the proceedings in Parliament.

[4] *Walpole Last Journals*, i, 324. Walpole adds that the Attorney- and Solicitor-Generals 'had never agreed before in a single point'. This is not true: they agreed to delay the grants to the Vandalia Company: C. W. Alvord, *op. cit.*, ii, 159-64. Gore-Browne suggests Thurlow himself said

Minister lost his copy of the Bill on the day on which they were to put the final touches to it, and he had to write desperately to John Pownall at the Colonial Office asking for another copy.[1] He was also forced to make some changes in the Bill that evening; but he refused to adopt all the Attorney-General's suggestions.[2] On 18 March, when the Bill went to the Commons, it was still essentially in the shape given it by Dartmouth, Pownall and himself.

The other legislative proposal which had been initiated in Cabinet on 19 February, that to alter the Charter and Constitution of Massachusetts, was also progressing slowly in the wake of the Boston Port Bill. This was not the first time such constitutional changes had been considered for the Bay Colony. After the Boston disturbances of 1768 Hillsborough, in the new post of Secretary of State for the American Department, had written of the need to regulate the government of Massachusetts Bay.[3] A committee of the Privy Council had undertaken to investigate the Colony's affairs in June 1770.[4] One of its recommendations was that the condition of the Colony should be fully discussed in Parliament with a view to legislation. The condition of civil government in Massachusetts had long been considered unsatisfactory, and its reform advocated by the officials at the American office. In the spring of 1773 the Cabinet in fact had seriously considered bringing the question before the Commons, but then decided to delay action because it was so late in the Parliamentary session.[5]

The events in Boston in December reminded the Ministry of the urgent need to act. Pownall told Hutchinson that the part acted by the Massachusetts Council in the Tea Party had so affected the Ministry 'that it was to no purpose to oppose

he had never before agreed with Wedderburn. He cites no evidence. It may be true Thurlow said it; even then it need not have been true. R. Gore-Browne, *op. cit.*, p. 86.

[1] North to Pownall, 16 March 1774. PRO. CO. 5/145, f. 238. Also in Dartmouth MS. D 1778, II, 869.

[2] North to Dartmouth, 17 March 1774. Dartmouth MS. D 1778, II, 859.

[3] Hillsborough to Gage, 24 December 1768. PRO. CO. 5/86, ff. 473-7.

[4] C. R. Ritcheson, *op. cit.*, pp. 142-3.

[5] Dartmouth to Hutchinson, 2 June 1773. PRO. CO. 5/765, ff. 260-2. Also see above, Chapter I, pp. 26-7.

the measure'.[1] Lord North described the Administration's feelings in more detail when he talked with Hutchinson on 8 July. He said that 'the behaviour of the Council and House had been such for some time past as to render it necessary there should be a change, and that it ought to have been done the last session . . .'. It had not been done, he explained, because in the past there had always been strong opposition in England to any such changes proposed for America. But since the Tea Party everyone, so he claimed, was united in the need to regulate the government of the Colony. He went on that he approved in general of giving the colonists an 'opportunity of a full defence, yet, this particular case might well be excepted from the general rule, the facts being so gross and so notorious, that he had long forbore, in hope that we should see the extravagance of our actions, and reform; but his hopes were at an end'.[2]

This is an interesting report. Very little of North's own writing remains, and in this outburst to Hutchinson he reveals his extreme impatience with the Bostonians. The Tea Party had clearly been a last straw to moderates and extremists alike in the Cabinet. North's moderate colleague in the Cabinet, Lord Dartmouth, became equally strong, at least for changing the Massachusetts Council, though he was less keen on the proposal for other alterations in the Charter. The King wrote to his Prime Minister in the middle of March, 'I have seen Lord Dartmouth this day very firm as to the alteration of the Council of the Massachusetts Bay'.[3] Thus in interpreting events at this time it is necessary to avoid drawing too clear and simple a distinction between 'moderates' like North and Dartmouth and such 'extremists' as Sandwich, Suffolk and, later, Germain. There was a clear difference in character, the one group being more pacific by nature, the other aggressive. The former first

[1] Hutchinson to his son, 6 July 1774. Hutchinson, *op. cit.*, i, 180. Hutchinson to a friend, 20 July 1774. *Ibid.*, 190-1. William Knox said Sir Francis Bernard played an important part in advocating this measure: *HMC, Various*, vi, *Knox MSS.*, p. 257.

[2] Hutchinson to an unknown friend, 8 July 1774. Hutchinson, *op. cit.*, i, 181-2.

[3] King to North, 14 March 1774. Fortescue, *op. cit.*, iii, 1416. Also see *HMC, Various*, vi, *Knox MSS.*, p. 257.

preferred moderate executive action, and when that failed required only a due recognition of the sovereign English Parliament; the latter hankered, though to varying degrees, after a more explicit and effective imperial supremacy. Dartmouth recoiled from open civil war ; his successor Germain seemed to revel in it. But these distinctions varied from person to person and from occasion to occasion, and in the early months, after the news of the Tea Party, they were completely blurred by the indignation which everyone felt. All were united in accepting the legality of an undivided British sovereignty over the Colonies.

On 1 March the Cabinet began to break down the general proposal to regulate the Massachusetts government. It decided to alter the manner of appointing Justices of the Peace.[1] On 10 March it dealt with Judges and members of the Council, and the proposed Bill was sketched into draft form. However, for the next few weeks the Ministry was wholly absorbed by the Boston Port Bill, and by Parliament's consideration of this and the American problem in general. North gave notice of the proposed Massachusetts Regulating Bill on 28 March, but its final form had then still not been agreed on. Easter brought a brief respite from the cares of government, and in fact it was well into April before the Bill was laid before the Commons. That occasion will be treated below when considering the Parliamentary proceedings on the coercive measures.

This chapter has been mainly concerned with the conception and growth of the Government's American policies before they were aired in public at Westminster. We have seen the early vigour, and sudden demise, of the proposal to prosecute the Boston rioters on charges of treason. The other initial proposal of 4 February — to move the customs house and the Assembly from Boston — survived and was produced in Parliament as the first punitive Bill. By then another legislative measure, to alter the Massachusetts Constitution, was in an advanced stage of consideration. The Ministry revealed itself as united in its opinion and minutely concerned for the technical legality of its policies. The Minister in charge of the American department

[1] Cabinet Minute, 1 March 1774. Dartmouth MS. D 1778, II, 842.

played a proper and leading role. He consulted his expert officials before making policy proposals, and when these were agreed on by the Cabinet they were submitted to the Law Officers for approbation. Once the drafting of the proposed legislation was complete, the main scene of action moved from the Ministerial offices in Whitehall to the Parliamentary forum at Westminster.

CHAPTER IV

THE MASSACHUSETTS LEGISLATION

On 7 March, the day announced for laying the American papers before Parliament, 'the House [of Commons] was much thinner than might be expected on so important an occasion. A little before 3 o'clock North presented the papers relative to America, the titles of which were severally read by the clerk.'[1] Then the Premier read the King's message to Parliament. Its conclusion was that he depended upon their zeal to 'enable his Majesty effectually to take such measures as may be most likely to put an immediate stop to the present disorders', and wished they would 'also take into their most serious consideration, what further regulations and permanent provisions may be necessary to be established, for better securing the execution of the laws, and the just dependence of the Colonies upon the Crown and Parliament of Great Britain'.[2] Thereupon George Rice, a Treasurer of the Chamber, made a motion for an Address of Thanks to the Throne.[3]

This motion produced the first of the Parliamentary session's exchanges on America. William Dowdeswell, the leader of the Rockingham group in the Commons, answered, opposing the Address.[4] He did not at this stage reject the principles and aims expounded in the King's message; in fact he went out of his way to announce his support for 'the legislative authority of this country over America'.[5] He merely objected to the moving of an Address supporting the Government's intentions towards

---

[1] *St. James's Chronicle*, 8 March 1774.   [2] *Parl. Hist.*, xvii, 1159.
[3] Cavendish Diaries, BM. Eg. 253, ff. 199-201. *Parl. Hist.*, xvii, 1159-60. *The Annual Register* . . . *1774*, pp. 58-61.
[4] Cavendish Diaries, BM. Eg. 253, ff. 202-5.
[5] Dowdeswell was M.P. for Tewkesbury 1747–54 and Worcestershire 1754–75. He was an old Tory who held office as Lord of the Treasury and Privy Councillor under Rockingham. Sir Lewis Namier, *England in the Age of the American Revolution*, pp. 53, 185, 393, Appendix A, 421.

America before Members had time to read and digest the papers relative to them. This was reasonable enough, though it was a technical rather than a political objection.

Only two Members considered the wider issues at stake in the American crisis : for the Government, Alexander Wedderburn, and for the Opposition, Edmund Burke. The Solicitor-General said that it was not yet determined what was to be done about the Colonies : whether to enforce or give up their dependence ; whether to change the degree of connexion by amending the colonial charters, or by granting new ones, or even by entering into different commercial relations with them. He posed the problems, suggested the magnitude of the task, and then pointed out that the House was not now considering measures. All that was required was Commons approval that some action be taken. To facilitate such action he asked for unanimity in Parliament. It was a reasonable request, based upon the belief that to reveal disunity to the enemy is to encourage him. But it was also a slippery, even deceitful, speech. Wishing to involve the House in American matters, Wedderburn had presented himself and the Ministry as open to advice on the colonial problems.[1] But in fact the King's Ministers were already well advanced in at least two measures — the Boston Port Bill and the Massachusetts Bay Regulating Bill — which they hoped would re-establish British control over the Colonies.

This odd deceit can be explained by the Government's concern to get the full approval of the Commons for the proposal that it should take measures against the Americans. It was an interesting little Parliamentary game, but it was also of some importance. Later the Ministry referred back to the early support it received from all sides of the House, and accused the Opposition of becoming antagonistic afterwards for purely factious reasons. The Opposition, not unjustifiably, was to point out that its initial acquiescence did not constitute a *carte blanche* for specific future policies.

---

[1] Cavendish's verbatim jottings recorded the Solicitor-General as saying :
'G[entlemen] who think [that colonial] dependence is to be given up . . . I am open to that opinion [it is a] matter to be canvassed. If [the colonies are] to be retained, I desire to know how [they are] to be retained.'
Cavendish Diaries, BM. Eg. 253, ff. 212-18.

Burke followed Wedderburn and made what amounted to a major policy statement on America. He agreed to support a war upon the Americans if they were in fact in rebellion, but pleaded with the Ministry first to make sure that this was so. 'Do not use a military proposition for a civil grievance', he urged. He suggested that the colonial civil government was at the root of the trouble : 'If . . . in all the operations, and effects, of Government . . . no man can extend them agreeable to our forms, and modes, you must change your modes . . . if such a government as this is universally discontented, no troops under Heaven [can] bring them to obedience'.[1] He then went on to review the Ministry's past misconduct in America and to fear the worst from them in the future. In so doing he ignored Wedderburn's appeal for a cosy bipartisan affirmation of the Government's good intentions. Like Dowdeswell, he refused to underwrite what he had not read, and he went even further to suggest what should be written. Burke alone in this debate voiced strong opinions on America which had a clear ring of opposition.

Ministerial men immediately complained that Rice's motion had merely expressed a general support for measures securing the supremacy of Parliament over the American Colonies, and that there was no specific commitment apart from that. They might also have pointed out that the Rockinghams fully believed in this supremacy, and it was they who introduced the Declaratory Act. The Rockinghams disapproved only of exercising the supremacy ; and since it had now been denied by the Americans, the Rockinghams might be expected to support the principle of securing its recognition.[2]

There was some justice in the criticisms of Burke's behaviour on the 7th.[3] But Burke wanted the Rockinghams to become a party which could take office. To achieve this he was prepared

[1] Cavendish Diaries, BM. Eg. 253, ff. 218-35, especially 232-3. Also *London Magazine*, 1774, pp. 165-6.

[2] Through all the discussions ahead there is a confused attempt by the Rockinghams to distinguish between *exercising* the Parliamentary supremacy and merely enforcing its *recognition*. They never managed to prove there were effective ways of securing the latter (after it had been denied) other than by the former.

[3] Barré, a Chathamite, followed Burke and severely criticised him for attempting to raise a major debate at this stage. *London Magazine*, 1774, p. 166.

to use most political tricks. He exploited any opportunity to discredit the Ministry and to inflate the virtues of the late Administration of the Marquis of Rockingham. But he did believe that his attack was justified. He knew that specific measures were imminent and he wanted both to make his position clear and to give direction to the other Rockinghams from the very start.

At the end of this surprisingly short debate on 7 March North proposed that the House should have more time to consider the American papers. He said he had intended to continue on Thursday, 10 March, but since there were now 109 papers in all he suggested that they should merely be read on the Friday, and then taken into consideration on the following Monday, the 14th.[1] With that the Address was passed without a division and Parliament's first day's work on America closed. As yet it had proved a fairly calm business. Fortunately there was then no telegraph or teleprinter in Westminster to inform members next morning that the Bostonians had enjoyed a second Tea Party during the night, dumping twenty-eight and a half chests of tea out of the brig *Fortune* into Boston harbour.[2]

The Boston Port Act

On the following Monday, 14 March, Lord North moved leave to bring in a Bill

> for the immediate removal of the officers concerned in the collection of the customs from the town of Boston in the province of Massachusetts Bay in North America, and to discontinue the landing and discharging, loading and shipping of goods, wares and merchandise at the said town of Boston or within the harbour thereof.[3]

[1] Cavendish Diaries, BM. Eg. 253, f. 242. Also *London Magazine*, 1774, pp. 165-6. The list of the 109 papers is contained in PRO. CO. 5/241, ff. 264-70. Two more papers from Boston were added on 11 March.

[2] Hutchinson to Dartmouth, 9 March 1744. PRO. CO. 5/763, f. 291. The news was received on 13 May. Mr. Ritcheson says that this second party was on 9 March, but he must have mistaken the date of Hutchinson's letter for that of the party. C. R. Ritcheson, *British Politics and the American Revolution*, p. 160. A letter from the Commissioners of the Customs at Boston to John Robinson also placed the riot conclusively on 7 March. PRO. T. I/505. (The folios in this collection are not numbered.)

[3] Two drafts of the Bill are in the Dartmouth MS. D 1778, II, 869. North's motion was made at about 4 p.m. Before this Sir Joseph Mawbey

The harbour was to be closed after 1 June 1774 (except to coastal ships carrying fuel and necessary supplies), and the custom houses were to be removed north to Salem. This punishment was intended to continue until indemnities had been paid to the East India Company for the destruction of its tea, until the injured royal officers had been compensated and until the King judged that peace was so restored that trade could continue.

In his speech introducing this Boston Port Bill the Prime Minister discussed the possibility of repealing the Tea Duty. He said that he did not oppose this in principle, but emphasised that it would not secure the desired end. The colonial agitators, he argued,

> maintained that we have as a Parliament no legislative right over them, that we are two dependent states under the same Prince . . . that such being the case, such doctrine being held we are not entering into a dispute between internal and external taxes, not between taxes laid for the purpose of revenues and taxes laid for the regulation of trade, not between representation and taxation, or legislation and taxation; but we are now to dispute the question whether we have, or have not any authority in that country. For, sir, if the town of Boston, or any persons in it can set their faces against any . . . and they might set their faces equally against all, if they were at liberty to insult our servants, if they were at liberty to obstruct our commerce, to destroy the property of those who are acting there under the protection of our laws, we have no authority.[1]

The Prime Minister was serious and pessimistic. Subsequent historians might argue that England no longer in 1774 had that political authority which he wished to maintain; or that the measures proposed would provoke the Americans to a final show of independent strength which would certainly overthrow

had presented a petition from William Bollan, agent for the Massachusetts Assembly, reminding the Commons of that Colony's traditional privileges. The House was at this time cleared of strangers for the rest of the debates on the Coercive Bills. Cavendish Diaries, BM. Eg. 254, ff. 75-85. *St. James's Chronicle*, 15 March 1774. *The Annual Register . . . 1774*, pp. 63-5, especially p. 64.   [1] Cavendish Diaries, BM. Eg. 254, ff. 109-10.

it; but not that the Ministry acted on an underestimate of the seriousness of the situation.

North explained that the Boston Port Bill had three purposes: (i) to secure a port where merchandise could safely be landed in Massachusetts; (ii) to punish Boston by preventing merchandise being landed there; and (iii) to secure indemnification for the East India Company.[1] Trade, punishment and compensation were the objects. North regretted the proposals to punish, but said that 'it must be done'. Burke thought that the Prime Minister spoke 'in a tone more languid and moderate than is usual in the expression of such ideas'.[2] Certainly the Prime Minister was too moderate for some: John Yorke wrote after the debate that North's was 'one of the coldest, and most unanimated speeches, I ever heard. Much too tender and undignified to please or satisfy my judgment of the behaviour of that Town, and without hinting at any thing more coercive than Legislative acts.'[3]

Apart from such criticisms that the Bill was too moderate, the only persons who directly condemned it were William Dowdeswell, John Sawbridge, the Wilkite alderman of London, and George Byng, a leading associate of Rockingham's ally, the Duke of Portland.[4] Dowdeswell's objections were that he thought it was unfair on Boston to single it out unheard for punishment, and that the measure would result in even worse consequences.[5] He received little support from his colleagues.[6] Rockingham's friend, Lord John Cavendish, gave a cautious approval to the Bill, while pleading that English merchants be allowed to petition if they wished — apparently shrimping for the commercial support the Rockinghams had assembled when

---

[1] For North's speech see Cavendish Diaries, BM. Eg. 254, ff. 86-111. *Parl. Hist.*, xvii, 1163-7. *The Annual Register . . . 1774*, pp. 63-4.
[2] Burke to Committee of Correspondence of the New York Assembly, 6 April 1774. W.W.M. Bk., Printed in *Edmund Burke*, ed. R. J. S. Hoffman, pp. 245-8, especially p. 246, and in *CEB*, ii, 526-30, especially 528.
[3] Yorke to Hardwicke, 14 March 1774. BM. Add. MS. 35375, f. 120.
[4] North to King, 14 March 1774. J. W. Fortescue, ed., *The Correspondence of King George III, 1760-1783*, iii, 1415.
[5] Cavendish Diaries, BM. Eg. 254, ff. 121-6. *Parl. Hist.*, xvii, 1168.
[6] Cavendish Diaries, BM. Eg. 254, ff. 131-2. See also Shelburne to Chatham, 15 March 1774. *Correspondence of William Pitt, Earl of Chatham*, ed. W. S. Taylor and J. H. Pringle, iv, 335.

they repealed the Stamp Act.[1] George Dempster was of a similarly uncommitted state of mind. The remainder of the Rockinghams had nothing more to add: some seem to have felt that the Ministry was in general acting properly, others that at least this particular measure was justified, while still others thought that it was too early, the situation too vague, for them to commit themselves. None, not even Dowdeswell, really echoed Burke's sentiments in the opening debate of the previous week. Among the followers of the Earl of Chatham, Isaac Barré spoke late at night and said of the Bill:

> I cannot help giving it my hearty, and determinate affirmative. My reasons for so doing, I believe, will not be found to impeach, or contradict any former part of my conduct. . . . I like it rash as it may appear in the eyes of some very intelligent persons in this House. I like it, adopt, and embrace it cheerfully for its moderation. . . . I think she (Boston) ought to be punished.[2]

He was later to regret this early enthusiasm for strong measures, which the Ministry did not let him forget. Governor Johnstone and Rose Fuller preferred to reserve judgment.[3] A string of Members supported the Ministry.[4] Only John Sawbridge denied England's right to tax the Americans, and he received a very noisy reception.[5]

The course of the debate gave North every assurance that the sense of the House and the country was behind his Administration. If anything, the Ministry stood on the moderate side of general opinion. Benjamin Franklin did not spare his American correspondents the true reality of this storm. He wrote: 'The violent destruction of the tea seems to have united

---

[1] *Parl. Hist.*, xvii, 1169.

[2] Cavendish Diaries, BM. Eg. 254, ff. 132-41, especially f. 133. *Parl. Hist.* xvii, 1169, has another version of the last sentence : 'Boston ought to be punished, she is your eldest son. [Here the House laughed. . . .]'

[3] For Johnstone and Fuller see below, pp. 88-9, 138.

[4] Cavendish Diaries, BM. Eg. 254, ff. 111-15. These included independents like John Rushout, M.P. for Evesham (who swung towards Opposition after 1775), and John Calvert, Hertford (who supported the Ministry till the end).

[5] Cavendish Diaries, BM. Eg. 254, ff. 117-20. *Parl. Hist.*, xvii, 1167-8. Sawbridge was M.P. for Hythe 1768-74 and for the City of London 1774-83. He voted solidly with the Opposition from 1769 to 1782.

all parties here against our province, so that the bill now brought into Parliament for shutting up Boston as a port till satisfaction is made, meets with no opposition'. And Franklin — though his English enemies would not have believed it of him — advised the Americans to pay compensation for the tea destroyed.[1]

Assured of a comfortable passage for the Boston Port Bill, and keen to bring the Ministry's policies to bear on America as soon as possible, North pushed the Bill rapidly through Parliament. On the 18th it received its first reading, and he expressed the wish that it should be 'expedited, so as to receive the Royal Assent before the holidays'.[2] He moved and secured a postponement of the proposed Committee on the American papers to facilitate this. The Bill was then read a second time on the 21st. Cavendish reported 'there was only one "No" to the reading the bill the second time, Mr. George Byng'.[3] The *St. James's Chronicle* confirms that 'After a short conversation, the bill was committed for Wednesday'.[4] There was no division.[5]

The 'conversation' had been chiefly that of Rose Fuller, who announced his intention to propose an amendment in Committee on 23 March. This he then did: he proposed that Boston should first be fined, and only if she refused to pay a sum of, say, £25,000 should the Act come into operation.[6] His suggestion received no direct support. There was, as North wrote to the King, 'some debating . . . [but] there was no division'. 'It is difficult', he observed with justice, 'to say which spoke for and which against.'[7] The Prime Minister named half a dozen, including Fuller, who spoke in some way against the Ministry in this Committee stage. Examination of the reports of their speeches proves the ragged nature of this

---

[1] Franklin to Thomas Cushing, 22 March 1774. PRO. CO. 5/118, f. 72.
[2] *St. James's Chronicle*, 19 March 1774.
[3] Cavendish Diaries, BM. Eg. 254, f. 196.
[4] *St. James's Chronicle*, 22 March 1774.
[5] *London Magazine*, 1774, p. 169.
[6] *Parl. Hist.*, xvii, 1170. Chatham agreed with Fuller that Boston should be given the chance to make reparation. But he was in Burton Pynsent. See Chatham to Shelburne, 20 March 1774. *Chatham Correspondence*, iv, 336-8.
[7] North to King, 23 March 1774. Fortescue, *op. cit.*, ii, 1422.

opposition.[1] Byng's only point was that the Bill punished English merchants, who in his opinion should be exempted from the ban on Boston commerce. George Dempster hoped that no aspersions were being cast upon the Stamp Act Repeal — and was quickly reassured by North that he had no such intention. General Conway was also relieved to learn this. Charles James Fox — lately removed at the King's behest from his lucrative post at the Treasury — made an urgent protest against leaving the fate of Boston to the arbitrary whims of royal prerogative.[2] Finally, Isaac Barré reaffirmed his initial support of the Port Bill, though he took one step back out of the Ministry's camp by expressing the fear that 'the next proposition will be a black one'.

The Prime Minister had little enough to fear from these few critics. They clearly were not as yet really opposed to his policies, though they might feel too concerned with political consistency to support him personally. Lord North's speech alone did some justice to the serious level established by Fuller's sincere and constructive amendment. But even he revealed how the Ministry, while appreciating the gravity of the situation, underestimated the courage and the resolution of the Americans. 'The good of this Act is', he said, 'that four or five frigates will do the business without any military force; but if it is necessary I should not hesitate a moment to enforce a due obedience to the laws of this country.'[3] He might well have wished that the Americans had been as easy to convince as the House of Commons. 'The feebleness and futility of the Opposition to the Boston Port Bill', wrote George III to North that evening, 'shows the rectitude of the measure.'[4]

Two days later when the Bill was read a third time the House was little over one-third full. There was an immediate test of strength over whether William Bollan, the agent for the Massachusetts Council, should be allowed to present a petition against the Bill. Only forty votes could be mustered for this

---

[1] *Parl. Hist.*, xvii, 1170-9.
[2] *The Annual Register . . . 1774*, p. 97. Fox was dismissed on 28 February 1774.
[3] *Parl. Hist.*, xvii, 1172.
[4] King to North, 23 March 1774. Fortescue, *op. cit.*, iii, 1424.

proposal and his request was refused — Burke said on the ground that 'no agent could be authorised but by the act of the whole provincial legislature', while the King described his as 'an unacknowledged Office'.[1] Yet the Commons had accepted a petition from him less than two weeks earlier. Clearly the opinion of the House was hardening against the Americans. The burden of debate on the Opposition side was chiefly carried by Burke and Dowdeswell — the only two who had previously opposed to any purpose.[2] There was no division. Burke tried to explain away this sloth on the part of the Rockingham squadron to his American employers :

> There were indeed not wanting some persons in the House of Commons who disapproved of the bill and who expressed their disapprobation in the strongest and most explicit terms. But their arguments upon this point made so little impression that it was not thought advisable to divide the house. Those who spoke in opposition did it more for the acquittal of their own honour and discharge of their own consciences . . . than from any sort of hope they entertained of bringing any considerable number to their opinion, or even of keeping in that opinion several of those who had formerly concurred in the same general line of policy with regard to the Colonies.[3]

Burke here admitted that the Opposition were split wide open at this stage. This made it very difficult for the Rockinghams to decide whether to force a division. For while those who opposed the Government's American policy wished to make their principles public, they did not want a paltry vote to advertise the Opposition's internal dissensions. Burke in this letter seems to exaggerate the strength and the explicit expression of those who did oppose — perhaps because he is chiefly talking about himself — but his summary of the Bill's presenta-

---

[1] Burke to the Committee of Correspondence of the New York Assembly, 6 April 1774. W.W.M. Bk. Printed in R. J. S. Hoffman, ed., *op. cit.*, pp. 245-8, especially p. 247, and in *CEB*, ii, 526-30, especially p. 529. King to North, 25 March 1774. Fortescue, *op. cit.*, iii, 1427. Bollan was son-in-law of Governor Shirley of Massachusetts. He had been appointed agent in 1745. In 1762 the Assembly withdrew its support, but he continued as agent for the Council until 1775. [2] *Parl. Hist.*, xvii, 1179-85.
[3] Burke to Committee of Correspondence of the New York Assembly, 6 April 1774. *Loc. cit.*

tion and reception was, from the evidence we have seen, fair. He praised the Ministry. He noted that the air of languor, which he had mentioned earlier,

> wore off in the progress of business. The Ministry seems to be better arranged than they appeared to be at first; Lord North has assumed a style of more authority and more decision; and the Bill laying Boston under a commercial interdict during the King's pleasure has been proposed and supported quite through, with expressions of the utmost firmness and resolution.[1]

Chatham also thought highly of North in March, writing that 'he serves the Crown more successfully and more sufficiently, upon the whole, than any other man now to be found could do'.[2] Probably North alone felt that he was unworthy to lead the country now; this was one of his few opinions which would ultimately prevail. But for the moment he was the Minister who was personally loved in the Commons, who was immensely skilled in Parliamentary ways, and, above all, who had finally taken decisive action in the dispute with the Colonies. 'The popular current, both within doors and without,' wrote Burke, 'at present sets strongly against America.' When the Boston Port Bill was moved, the House concurred 'not so much from any predilection, that I could observe, to the particular measure which was adopted; as from a general notion that *some act* of power was become necessary'.[3]

The Port Bill was sent up to the Lords on 25 March. The only serious debate came after the second reading on the 28th, but there was no division. The eight Opposition Lords who were present were Rockingham, Richmond, Portland, Manchester, Bessborough, Abingdon, King and Craven.[4] On the 30th, when the Bill was read a third time and approved, there

---

[1] *Loc. cit.*

[2] Chatham to Shelburne, 6 March 1774. *Chatham Correspondence*, iv, 332-3.

[3] Burke to Committee of Correspondence of New York Assembly, 6 April 1774. *Loc. cit.*

[4] *Journals of the House of Lords*, xxxiv, 96-9. Rockingham may have spoken in this debate. Among his papers there is a draft with some headings for a speech on the Port Bill. W.W.M. R. 49, 1.

was not even a debate.[1] Hardly any of the Opposition Peers were in the House — of those who later in May signed the two Protests against the American measures only Lord King was present on 30 March.

Rockingham was later aware that in retrospect this absence gave the impression of carelessness on the part of himself and his noble supporters. In the Protest of 11 May there is a direct reference to their non-attendance. Paragraph Six of the Protest objects to the statement in the Journals which describes the Boston Port Bill as having been voted 'nemine dissentiente':

> The despair of making effectual opposition to an unjust measure, has been construed into an approbation of it: an unfair advantage has been taken on the final question for passing that penal bill, of the absence of those Lords who had debated it for several hours on the second reading, that period on which it is most usual to debate the principle of a bill.[2]

One further subsidiary result of their absence from the third reading was that no Opposition peer was present that day when it was ordered that all the Lords in attendance should constitute a Committee to enquire into the proceeding in Massachusetts Bay. This Committee, or any five of the Lords constituting a quorum, was to meet from 31 March onwards. It assembled on the 31st and immediately requested a selection of all the papers laid before the House since 1764. The Committee met again a week later at Lord Dartmouth's house and asked the American Secretary for all the latest information from America.[3] Apparently the Upper Chamber, or at least some of it, meant to be well informed when it again took up the American question in May.

Lord North could go happily to his own holidays. Action had been demanded, and his Ministry had responded,[4] though

---

[1] 14, George III, c. 19.   [2] *Lords Journals*, xxxiv, 182-4.
[3] *Ibid.*, 102-4. Order of the Lords Committee, 31 March 1775, and Order of the House of Lords, 7 April 1775. Dartmouth MSS. D 1778, II, 872, 885.
[4] The Treasury Board met on 31 March and sent instructions to the customs officers in Massachusetts to proceed in accordance with the Act. PRO. CO. 5/763, ff. 171-3. Treasury Minute Book, T 29/43, f. 172. J. Robinson to J. Pownall, 8 April 1774. PRO. CO. 5/145, f. 240. Grey Cooper to J. Pownall, 1 April 1774. PRO. CO. 5/154, part I, f. 100.

whether rightly or wrongly only time could tell. In the short run judgment would be suspended; in the long run it might decide in his favour. Parliament adjourned after passing the Port Act, but the Ministry had one other executive task which it completed during the Easter recess — the dispatch of General Gage and the replacement troops [1] to North America. This was more than merely a routine return to duty for Gage, because his office and responsibilities were to be increased. Governor Hutchinson had written to England in the summer of 1773 asking for permission to leave Massachusetts.[2] This was agreed to by North.[3] Hutchinson was then delayed by a succession of events — the Tea Party, the bad weather in January, and the sickness and death of his lieutenant, Andrew Oliver. But as the Ministry were under the impression that he might already have left, they took the opportunity provided by the imminent departure of the four regiments of replacement troops for America to commission Gage to carry out Hutchinson's civil duties together with his own as Commander-in-Chief.[4]

It was an easy way to satisfy both requirements, and in the crisis there was much to be said for combining the military and executive functions. John Pownall told Thurlow that this combination, involving the immediate appointment of Gage as Governor before Hutchinson had been informed, was the idea of the American Secretary — 'Lord Dartmouth thinking that

[1] These were the 43rd Regiment of Foot from England, and the 5th and 38th Regiments previously stationed in Ireland. They were originally intended to go to Halifax, St. Augustine and New Providence, and Quebec respectively. But on 2 April Dartmouth told the Admiralty to carry them all to Boston. A fourth regiment of replacements, the 4th of Foot, was not intended to depart until June. Barrington to Dartmouth, 2 February 1774. PRO. CO. 5/247, ff. 89-90 ; Admiralty to Dartmouth, 28 March 1774. PRO. CO. 5/247, f. 98 ; Dartmouth to Admiralty, 22 February 1774 and 2 April 1774. PRO. CO. 5/250, ff. 71, 77.
[2] Hutchinson, *Diary and Letters*, i, 104-54. Also *Morning Chronicle*, 6 April 1774.
[3] Pownall to Dartmouth, 5 August 1773 and 12 August 1773. Dartmouth MSS. D 1778, 1, ii, 871, 872.
[4] This was decided in Cabinet on 10 March. Cabinet Minute. Dartmouth MS. D 1778, II, 853. The Privy Council Commission and instructions were finally issued to Gage on 31 March. His official title was 'Captain General and Governor in Chief of his Majesty's Province of the Massachusetts Bay'. PRO. CO. 5/920, ff. 425-92. *Acts of the Privy Council of England, Colonial Series*, ed. J. Munro, v, 557. Also see PRO. CO. 5/29, f. 25.

the appointment of General Gage *directly* to be Governor of Massachusetts Bay will be, under all circumstances, the Best'.[1] And in the following week, on 9 April, Dartmouth wrote and assured Gage that 'your authority as the first magistrate combined with your command over the King's troops, will, it is hoped, enable you to meet every opposition, and fully to preserve the public peace, by employing these troops with effect'.[2] On the same day he wrote to Hutchinson about his sudden replacement, comforting him that

> General Gage's continuance in the Government will most probably not be of long duration, and it is the King's intention that you should be reinstated in the Government of Massachusetts Bay (in case it shall be agreeable to you) whenever his services as Commander-in-Chief shall be required in any other station.[3]

Gage set sail on the *Lively* from Plymouth on 18 April, carrying with him the Boston Port Act. He arrived somewhat to the surprise of Boston on 13 May.[4] There had been rumours in Boston of his appointment, but the official news in Dartmouth's letter to Hutchinson on 9 April scarcely arrived before the new Governor himself. Gage rapidly had occasion to test the bellicose opinions he had expressed to his sovereign on 4 February. As he arrived in Boston Harbour a Town meeting was being held to consider the Port Act. 'The Act has staggered the most presumptuous', wrote Gage. In response they determined to appeal to the other Colonies to join in a non-importation and non-exportation agreement. Disorder spread; and soon Gage was complaining that he must immediately have vast reinforcements, while Ministers at home denounced his meekness.[5]

[1] Pownall to Thurlow, 1 April 1774. PRO. CO. 5/250, f. 77.
[2] Dartmouth to Gage, 9 April 1774. PRO. CO. 5/763, f. 161.
[3] Dartmouth to Hutchinson, 9 April 1774. PRO. CO. 5/765, f. 297.
[4] Hutchinson to Dartmouth, 17 May 1774, and Gage to Dartmouth, 19 May 1774. PRO. CO. 5/769, ff. 77, 79. These were received on 22 June 1774.
[5] Gage to Dartmouth, 2 September 1774. PRO. CO. 5/769, ff. 117-23. Printed in C. E. Carter, ed., *The Correspondence of General Thomas Gage with the Secretaries of State, 1763–1775*, i, 369-72. Pownall to Dartmouth, 18 December 1774. Dartmouth MS. D 1778, II, 1022. See above, Chapter III, pp. 49-50, for Gage's interview with the King on 4 February when he claimed that he could subdue the Americans without extra troops.

The Massachusetts Bay Regulating Act and The Impartial Administration of Justice Act

Already before the Easter Recess Parliament had been warned of another American measure — the proposal to amend the Massachusetts charter which had been before the Cabinet since 19 February.[1] On 28 March Lord North moved in the Commons for leave to bring in a Bill to this effect, and a short debate followed.[2] Lord George Germain advocated more extensive and extreme measures.[3] Thomas Pownall, a former Governor of the Bay Colony, tried to defend the character of its inhabitants. Byng and Dempster raised a slight opposition, but little else was said.

Parliament now had to wait until 15 April to learn the full details of this second coercive measure — partly because of the Easter recess, but also because of the dilatoriness of the Ministry in producing its legislation. On 13 April Lord Mansfield went to see the King to urge the need for more speedy action. George III wrote next day to impress on his Prime Minister that

the more I reflect on Lord Mansfield's opinion to you yester-day concerning the alteration of the charter the more I am confirmed in the propriety of altering the Council and I find it so much the wish of the cabinet, that I am certain [I can] not too strongly express my preferring you introducing the

---

[1] See above, Chapter III, pp. 66, 69-71.

[2] *Parl. Hist.*, xvii, 1192-7. *St. James's Chronicle*, 28 March 1774. North to King, 28 March 1774. J. W. Fortescue, ed., *The Correspondence of George III, 1760–1783*, iii, 1429.

[3] Germain's behaviour in this debate was very interesting. He had once been a follower of George Grenville, and then, like Wedderburn, had drifted towards the Rockingham squadron. By the end of 1771 he was — again like Wedderburn — beginning to tire of opposition. But he bided his time before going over to the Ministry. Horace Walpole claims that the move was negotiated by Wedderburn with North and Grey Cooper, the Secretary to the Treasury. Seemingly, Germain's part of the bargain was to speak early and strongly for the Regulating Bill — hence his speech on the 28th. (*The Last Journals of Horace Walpole*, ed., A. F. Stewart, i, 325-7.) Germain's advice that day on the appointment of juries in Massachusetts was accepted with fulsome praise by North. Later he was offered a safe seat by the Treasury at the autumn elections. He was finally brought into the Ministry to replace Dartmouth as Secretary for the Colonies on November 1775.

Bill tomorrow that is drawn up for resting the nomination of the Counsellors in the Crown.[1]

North promptly brought in for its first reading on the 15th the Bill 'for the Better Regulating the Government the Province of the Massachusetts Bay'.[2]   It had four chief propositions: the present elected Massachusetts Council should be replaced after 1 August 1774 by one nominated by the Crown;[3] the Governor should appoint, and might henceforth remove, all law officers; no town meetings were to be held without royal consent; and the traditional system of freeholders electing juries would cease from 1 September 1774.

In the brief debate that followed, Dowdeswell maintained his record of consistent opposition. 'You are not now contending for a point of honour,' he said, 'you are struggling to obtain a most ridiculous superiority.'[4]   But there was no attempt to divide the House at this stage, nor later when the Bill went smoothly through its second reading on 22 April and through Committee on the 27th.[5]

However, the Opposition had made a more determined show of strength on 19 April when Rose Fuller moved to repeal the Tea Duty.   Fuller emphasised that the proposed repeal was not intended to replace present coercive policies, but as a measure without which no policy could be effectual.   He was seconded by Richard Pennant, a relative of his with mutual West Indian interests.[6]   This was not the first time that the

---

[1] King to Lord North, 14 April 1774. Fortescue, *op. cit.*, iii, 1440.

[2] 14, George III, c. 45.

[3] This effectively revoked the charter granted to the Colony by William and Mary in 1691. The revocation was made by Statute and not, as when it was issued, by Orders in Council. This change in the constitutional balance, whereby the King no longer acted on his own account, but through Parliament, reflected the way in which a British Empire, ruled by the Crown in Parliament, had grown out of the older idea of the royal lands overseas. This constitutional nicety was relevant to the arguments of the American patriots. They persisted in appealing personally to the King against Parliament, as if the latter were now usurping the true powers of the former. They came only slowly to realise that the King and his Ministers were quite properly using Parliament to confirm each step of their policy.

[4] *Parl. Hist.*, xvii, 1198-9.

[5] North to King, 15 April 1774 and 27 April 1774. Fortescue, *op. cit.*, iii, 1443, 1451.

[6] Fuller was a Jamaican. Pennant was the grandson of the Chief Justice of Jamaica, and an owner of a plantation there. They were both related to

West Indians had defended the American colonists. When the Stamp Act was passed on 6 February 1765 it was the doyen of West Indian Members, William Beckford, who moved against the Grenville Ministry. His seconder then was Rose Fuller. The names of the minority are unknown, but Jared Ingersoll, an American agent and observer, said they were 'West Indian gentlemen and a few others connected with America'.[1] These same West Indians figured prominently in the movement in 1766 to repeal the Stamp Duty, with Rose Fuller playing a leading role.[2] *The Gentleman's Magazine* had recalled this in 1774 when it recommended electors not to vote for West Indians, since they denied British sovereignty over America.[3] This charge was not wholly true. Fuller at least never denied that supremacy, nor did the other West Indians in 1774. However, they did not want an interruption in trade between the islands and the American mainland. The Indies depended greatly on their exports of sugar and molasses to America and their imports from there of food and raw materials. Wars, blockades and non-importation agreements would threaten this trade.

The Rockinghams made preparations beforehand to exploit this opportunity to attack the Ministry. The Marquis wrote to Portland that Dowdeswell, Cavendish and Savile were going to support Fuller and he asked for 'a good attendance of our friends'.[4] Burke led the attack for them on the 19th, and *The Annual Register ... 1774* commented that 'Mr. E. Burke distinguished himself in a masterly manner'.[5] His speech on American taxation was certainly magnificent. It contained his familiar history of British policy towards America. Yet in balance of argument and style it far surpassed the previous

---

William Beckford (d. 1770), Henry Dawkins and Ed Morant, who were also members of the West Indian cousinhood in Parliament. (Sir Lewis Namier, *England in the Age of the American Revolution*, pp. 234-41.) Another factor behind Pennant's action must have been that he represented Liverpool, a port which profited from American trade and had petitioned vigorously against the Stamp Act.   [1] *Ibid.*, p. 240.

[2] See L. S. Sutherland, 'Edmund Burke and the First Rockingham Ministry', *EHR*, xlvii, 46-70, especially pp. 50, 62.

[3] *Gentleman's Magazine*, 1774, p. 404.

[4] 17 April 1774. Portland MS. Pw F 9082.   [5] P. 111.

occasions on which Burke said approximately the same things. Rhetoric is a suspicious talent. Burke's was devoted to praising some men and denouncing others, to denigrating Administration policies and to suggesting that his friends had preferable alternatives. He was aware that his arguments were dismissed and his motives questioned in many quarters.[1] In his taxation speech he said :

> The noble Lord [North] will, as usual, probably attribute the part taken by me and my friends in this business, to a desire of getting his places. Let him enjoy this happy and original idea. If I deprived him of it, I should take away most of his wit, and all his argument.[2]

Burke could never have denied that he would welcome a place. Also, despite protestations to the contrary, he was presumably conscious that his New York employers were pleased by his arguments. But it is still difficult to imagine him urging any different opinions about American taxation. The fault of Burke and the Rockinghams at this time seems to lie in that they had no immediately realistic American policies rather than that they fabricated principles; not that they misrepresented their own motives, but that they misunderstood the extreme aims of their American friends.

Burke was backed by Townshend, Barré, C. J. Fox, Frederick Montagu and Dowdeswell.[3] The latter closed for the Opposition with an appeal : 'Let us resolve to do justice, before it is too late'.[4] North again stated the Ministerial view : 'Convince your colonies that you are able, and not afraid to control them, and, depend upon it, obedience will be the result of your deliberation'.[5] The House wanted above all obedience : it did not agree that this necessarily excluded justice ; but it certainly could not conceive of justice without obedience. The House divided at 11.20 p.m., and Fuller's motion was lost 182-49.

---

[1] For a modern and extremely critical appraisal of Burke's political thinking see J. Brooke, *The Chatham Administration, 1766–1768*, pp. 232-3.

[2] For the speech see *Parl. Hist.*, xvii, 1215-69, especially 1269. The Cavendish Diaries (BM. Eg. 255, ff. 165-231) cover the whole debate. It is mostly in Cavendish's shorthand.

[3] North to King, 19 April 1774. Fortescue, *op. cit.*, iii, 1445.

[4] *Parl. Hist.*, xvii, 1273. [5] *Ibid.*

A third coercive measure had been announced to the House of Commons by Lord North on 15 April after he had successfully aired the Regulating Bill. This was a Bill

> For the Impartial Administration of Justice in the cases of persons questioned for any acts done by them in the execution of the law, or for the suppression of riots and tumults, in the province of Massachusetts Bay, in North America.[1]

Lord North said that it sought 'to give every man a fair and impartial trial',[2] but the Americans described it as a 'murder Bill'. If passed, the Act would take effect from 1 June and would last for three years. It provided that the Governor of Massachusetts should be empowered to remove trials to another Colony, or even to England, if he felt there was the danger of partial juries in the Province. This danger was particularly foreseen in two circumstances — if the officers of the colonial executive were prosecuted for carrying out the two previous coercionary Acts; and if the military were subjected to prosecution before local juries for their part in quelling disturbances.

The main problem which underlay this Bill — whether the troops ought to be used to support the civil authorities in maintaining order, and what might be the consequences of this — had been under consideration for some time.[3] After the Boston Tea Party the Lieutenant-Colonel of the 64th Regiment of Foot, Alexander Leslie, wrote to the War Office complaining that the Massachusetts Council had refused to give permission for his troops to march on Boston to suppress the riot.[4] This dispatch did not reach England until the end of January. Shortly before that, Dartmouth had again written to the Governors of New York and Massachusetts repeating that 'no requisition should be made by the civil magistrate upon a slight ground, but only in cases of absolute necessity when every other effort had failed'.[5] But the news of the Tea Party hardened the

[1] 14, George III, c. 39.   [2] Parl. Hist, xvii, 1198-9.

[3] See the letters from Knox and Pownall opposing the use of troops: Knox to Dartmouth, 6 October 1773, Pownall to Dartmouth, 6 October 1773. Dartmouth MSS. D 1778, 1, II, 887, 886.

[4] See above, Chapter II, p. 25.

[5] Dartmouth to Governor Tryon, 8 January 1774. PRO. CO. 5/1141, f. 127. Dartmouth to Governor Hutchinson, 8 January 1774. PRO. CO. 5/765, f. 277.

Government's attitude on this point, as in its other policies. And the relations between the civil authority and the military forces in Massachusetts were rationalised when it was decided in March to make General Gage both acting Governor of the Colony and Commander-in-Chief of the troops in North America.[1]

Gage and Sir Jeffrey Amherst were examined on this subject before the Cabinet on 30 March. They stated their belief that British troops who were arrested and prosecuted in the execution of their duty would have no chance of their lives before a local jury.[2] After the meeting Gage raised with Dartmouth the critical constitutional questions which would concern him in his coming task:

> Whether he might by his own authority, and without the advice of the Council of the Province of Massachusetts Bay, call out the King's troops to assist him in quelling any riots and disturbances, if any should happen within the province, and also what steps it would be advisable for him to take in case any accident should happen that might expose any persons employed in quelling such disturbances to any prosecution, and such prosecution should be commenced.[3]

Dartmouth promptly wrote to consult the Law Officers on these two points:

> (a) . . . can General Gage . . ., as the first civil magistrate, call in the military assistance without the advice and consent of the Council; and
> (b) if the Military Aid is necessary and any accident should happen that might expose General Gage, his officers or soldiers to Prosecutions and such prosecution should be commenced, either civil or criminal, what steps would it be advisable for him to take in such a case.[4]

Thurlow and Wedderburn were present when the matter was again considered in Cabinet on 7 April. They gave their

---

[1] See above, pp. 85-6.
[2] C. R. Ritcheson, *British Politics and the American Revolution*, p. 161.
[3] Cabinet Minute, 7 April 1774. Dartmouth MS. D 1778, II, 883.
[4] Dartmouth to Law Officers, 30 March 1774. Dartmouth MS. D 1778, II, 884.

opinion in favour of the extreme powers which General Gage clearly wanted. Gage was called into the Cabinet and told that

> in cases of dangerous tumult and insurrection, every man is bound to interpose for the preservation of the public peace, and that in such cases it will be the duty of the Governor of the Province to call upon all His Majesty's subjects to assist him in quelling the tumults and to repel force and violence by every means within his reach.[1]

This was not really a reversion of the previous conciliatory policy which Dartmouth had preached to the Governors before the Tea Party. Then he had said that they were not to call out the troops except in most extraordinary circumstances. After the Tea Party the Ministry had decided that such an extraordinary situation existed. Hence it now advised resolution rather than conciliation to its executive officers.

In reply to his second question, Gage was told that

> . . . in order to prevent as much as possible the effects of any unjust prosecution, the Lords present had agreed to advise the King to entrust him with the power of pardoning in cases where he should think it necessary to the due administration of justice, to interpose that power.

Thus the Government had taken the two important steps : deciding that the military could be called out at the Governor's wish, and that where his troops were concerned the processes of prosecution in the Massachusetts courts could be short-circuited by the use of the prerogative.[2]

In relation to the first of these two points it might be noted that ex-Governor Hutchinson, and possibly Wedderburn, were not completely certain that the Government had — with Wedderburn's approval — acted constitutionally. When Wedderburn visited Hutchinson in July, the latter expressed doubt whether a Governor could call out troops in case of riotous

---

[1] Cabinet Minute, 7 April 1774. Dartmouth MS. D 1778, II, 883.

[2] The Ministry also decided that the Commander of His Majesty's ships of war in Massachusetts should be directed to assist the Governor in preserving peace whenever the Governor called upon him. This should be read in connexion with Rear-Admiral Montagu's letter to the Admiralty after the Tea Party. See Chapter II, p. 25.

behaviour by the populace. Wedderburn apparently agreed : he said 'the King's Law Servants seemed generally to be of that opinion, and mentioned Lord Chancellor in particular, but, says he, I own *I am in doubt* or *not without doubt*'.[1] If this was indeed so, there is no evidence of Wedderburn having argued such an opinion in the Cabinet on 7 April — though he may then have expressed some doubts, which were over-ridden. On the other hand, with Hutchinson in July he may have been simply trimming his opinions to agree with his host.

Hutchinson's doubts were genuine. In March he had written to Dartmouth, 'I have not been satisfied that there have yet been any such rebellious insurrections as would have justified the representative of the King in bringing forward the military power in order to suppress them'.[2] But the Government did not want the resolution of its new civil and military executive undermined by any such uncertainties. Dartmouth later wrote off to Gage :

> As some doubt may possibly arise whether his Majesty's Governor can act in any case in the capacity of an ordinary civil magistrate, I think it fit to acquaint you that the King's chief Law Servants are clearly of opinion that the Governor, by his commission, is conservator of the peace in all cases whatsoever.[3]

However, by the time he received this assurance, General Gage was himself beginning to suffer from cold feet.

The early Parliamentary stages of the Justice Bill produced very little debate worthy of note. One exception was the speech by Isaac Barré on 15 April when the measure was first announced. Barré went to great lengths to explain his previous support for the Ministry's Boston policy — which he said was only given 'while they had the least colour of foundation in justice'. He said he had supported the Boston Port Bill because he disapproved of the acts of violence committed by the Americans. But 'upon the present question I am totally unprepared. The motion itself bears no sort of resemblance

---

[1] Hutchinson, *Diary and Letters*, i, 183.
[2] Hutchinson to Dartmouth, 21 March 1774. PRO. CO. 5/763, f. 315. Received by Dartmouth on 13 May 1774.
[3] Dartmouth to Gage, 3 June 1774. PRO. CO. 5/763, f. 366.

to what was formerly announced.' He went on to declare his complete disapproval of the new proposal. He suggested that they should have sent Boston the olive branch instead of the sword: 'by the olive branch I mean a repeal of all the late laws, fruitless to you and oppressive to them'. Instead the Ministry had brought in this Act, which he predicted would 'produce the rebellion you pretend to obviate'.[1] With these words Barré did a swift and complete retreat from the coercion camp, and it appeared that the Chatham group might at last become committed to active opposition.[2]

The Prime Minister moved the first reading of the Bill on 21 April to an almost empty House.[3] There was equally little discussion at the second reading on the 25th.[4] In Committee, there were 'a few short debates, but no division'.[5] Constantine Phipps suggested that the Governor should exercise his power of pardon, and so obviate the need for witnesses to travel 3,000 miles. He asked whether any Member of the Commons would lay his hand upon his heart and say 'whether any recognizance [would] induce him to go over to America'.[6] However, this common-sense argument had no effect upon the Bill.

The serious discussion on the Regulating Bill and on the Justice Bill was reserved for their third readings. The Regulating Bill was debated for the third time on Monday, 2 May. The House was fairly full, with four hundred and three members present at the division[7] — the highest attendance so far in this session. The debate began at 4 p.m. and lasted until two o'clock on Tuesday morning.[8] Thirty-six hours after, Burke

---

[1] *Parl. Hist.*, xvii, 1206.

[2] On 6 April Chatham wrote to Shelburne denouncing the Ministry's new proposals: 'by going to further severities, I fear, all is put to the hazard'. *Correspondence of William Pitt, Earl of Chatham*, ed. W. S. Taylor and J. H. Pringle, iv, 342. Horace Walpole argued that this was why Barré 'retracted his complaisance, and distinguished himself against the new regulations'. *Walpole Last Journals*, i, 338.   [3] *Parl. Hist.*, xvii, 1274-5.

[4] North to King, 25 April 1774. Fortescue, *op. cit.*, iii, 1449. *Parl. Hist.*, xvii, 1289.

[5] North to King, 29 April 1774. Fortescue, *op. cit.*, iii, 1455. *Parl. Hist.*, xvii, 1291-7.   [6] Cavendish Diaries, BM. Eg. 256, ff. 95-7, 107.

[7] North to King, 3 May 1774. Fortescue, *op. cit.*, iii, 1458.

[8] Cavendish Diaries, BM. Eg. 256, f. 110-Eg. 257, f. 37. *The Journals of the House of Commons*, xxxiv, 697, say 2.30 a.m. North told the King it was 2.15 a.m. Fortescue, *op. cit.*, iii, 1458.

was still exhausted from it — which may explain why he apparently missed some of the debates later in the week.

The Opposition led off with a two-hour speech by Dunning.[1] Dunning had been ill for some time, and he claimed that this explained his previous absence from the Opposition ranks; clearly, now that the Opposition was stirring, some had a conscience about their earlier acquiescence. Like Barré on a previous occasion, Dunning also complained of being misled; that the Ministry had implied that the Port Bill would be followed by conciliatory measures. But the Regulating Act was in no such vein. He made several points against it: that if certain persons in Boston had behaved treasonably then they should be arrested and tried; if not, then England was in fact not dealing with a rebellion necessitating the drastic Bill under consideration, but with some particular Americans who were irregularly resisting certain provocative laws; that, in this case, it should be settled by the civil government; and if the Governor could not order this without the Council, and the Council would not act with him, then the Governor should be changed rather than the Constitution. In any case, Dunning argued, this trouble could not be solved by constitutional amendments, since the discontent did not arise from constitutional defects. He discussed the Massachusetts Council in great detail, and considered the Regulating Bill's proposals very closely, clause by clause — which was almost a novelty in those debates, where most Members only talked generally about the right to tax or the need to punish the colonists. He then went on to deal even more harshly with the Impartial Administration of Justice Bill,[2] which seemed to him both partial and unjust, and also unnecessary while the Governor retained the power to pardon those officers who might be prosecuted for executing their duties. Taking the Bills together he saw 'one point of view perfectly symmetrical': the Regulating Bill was intended to provoke the colonists into rebellion by taking away their charter, while the

[1] Cavendish Diaries, BM. Eg. 256, ff. 110-65. *St. James's Chronicle*, 3 May 1774.

[2] The Opposition had decided to debate the two Bills together as part of one policy. Burke to New York Assembly, 4 May 1774. W.W.M. Bk., *CEB*, ii, 532.

Justice Bill would authorise indiscriminate throat-cutting when that rebellion occurred.

Dunning was the second follower of Chatham to make a major, unequivocal statement of opposition to the Government's scheme of American policies. Barré had taken the first steps; now it could be assumed that the Chatham group was fully and actively committed against the Government — though they still refrained from making a union with the Rockinghams.

Many of the Rockingham squadron supported Dunning in the debate. Burke, speaking from 11.45 p.m. until nearly 1 a.m., again made their leading speech, recapitulating all his arguments from preceding debates; but the general feeling of the House was expressed by the noisy and hostile reception they gave him.[1] Conway said that he had come to testify 'against what is doing. . . . I dread what is called Parliamentary spirit: it is like zeal in religion, nobody knows where it will carry them.'[2]

There was certainly plenty of zeal for the Ministry's measures. 'I say stand and deliver to the Americans', said Richard Rigby, voicing the convictions of the Bedford group.[3] And North's follower John St. John spoke for coercion in a way that was rapturously received by independents and Ministerial men alike.[4] In fact St. John was not a disinterested figure; his eyes were constantly elevated to the fruits dangling from the tree of patronage, and when he finally plucked the post as Surveyor-General of Inland Revenue, his old friend George Selwyn remarked with more truth than kindness, 'John will wallow in preferment'.[5] But St. John cogently conveyed the extreme feelings of many independent Members in the House. He said the Americans were traitors who had opposed Parliament's laws, and therefore Parliament must reassert its authority. This would be secured by pursuing the system the

---

[1] Cavendish Diaries, BM. Eg. 256, f. 303, and BM. Eg. 257, ff. 1-35. Also *St. James's Chronicle*, 3 May 1774.

[2] Cavendish Diaries, BM. Eg. 256, ff. 268-77, especially 275.

[3] *Ibid.*, f. 264.

[4] John St. John, 1746-93, was M.P. for Newport, Hants, from 1773 to 1774 and from 1780 to 1784, and for Eye from 1774 to 1780. G. P. Judd, *Members of Parliament, 1734-1832*, p. 325.

[5] George Selwyn to Carlisle, 7 November 1775. *HMC*, XV, vi, *Carlisle MSS.*, p. 301.

Ministry had begun — meting out punishment for crimes committed, establishing regulations to prevent future crimes, and finally securing protection for British officials who enforced those regulations. He warned the Ministry not to heed the Cassandras in opposition:

> Let us upon the whole be careful how we permit ourselves to be drawn aside by any mistaken ideas of levity to our fellow subjects. . . . It is said . . . that we are hurrying on into measures the consequences of which we are not able to foresee, or prepared to await. . . . 'Tis said that America will be exasperated. Will she then take arms ? 'Tis not as yet, thank God, the strength of America which we dread when put in competition with this country. She has neither army, navy, money, or men. . . . Shall we then fear the destruction of our trade ? Believe it not : while it is her interest to trade with us, so long she will in spite of her resentment. She may enter into non-importation agreements but her self-interestedness will break through all such cobweb confederacies ; her own avarice and treachery is an ample security against her combinations. . . . 'Tis an absurd supposition that the various colonies in America, separated from one another at such a distance, differing so much in the nature of their governments, in many respects in their interests, enjoying at present the benefit of the most perfect system of civil liberty, and the protection of the greatest naval power the world ever knew, should at once unite through pique.

There is much in that speech which is still familiar today : the assumption that a people will subordinate all actions to self-interest, and that material weakness means a total inferiority. St. John dismissed the constitutional claims of the American patriots because he believed economic self-interest and material strength were the only springs of action and sinews of power. Which is not to say there were no self-interested American patriots, nor that the colonists operated solely on moral righteousness ; but the belief in the justice of their cause, which St. John discounted, was one important factor in helping them to achieve the unity and success which he argued was impossible. However, in the Commons the kind of arguments voiced by

St. John prevailed and the division against reading the Bill a third time was defeated 239-64.[1]

After the passing of the Regulating Bill, the order of the day was read for receiving the report from a Committee of the whole House on the Bill for the Impartial Administration of Justice. But it was already very late and everyone was exhausted from the preceding debate; it was, therefore, decided to put off receiving the Bill until Wednesday, 4 May, when it was duly reported. On Friday, 6 May, Burke, Dempster, Barré and Sawbridge returned to the attack.[2] Barré warned the Ministry: 'You have by this law placed the Military there as the supreme power, the only power, you have made them the umpire in the business, your army has the casting voice'.[3] Two independents supported them. But when one of them, William Pulteney, began to discuss taxation 'many members called out "No, No, No", upon which he sat down'; it would seem that the House was tired of taxation and wanted to have done with the pending legislation. The second, Rose Fuller, declared he believed the present Bill to be the least harmful of the three coercive measures, though he still could not support it. He feared that 'if ever there was a nation running headlong to its ruin, it is this'. The concluding passage of his speech emphasised the political isolation of members like Pulteney and himself, and those of the Opposition who were against the American measures: 'It is not an error of the Ministry, it is an error of the nation: I see it wherever I go. People are of the opinion that these measures ought to be carried into execution.'[4] The Commons divided 127-24 on a motion that the Bill should pass.[5]

The Massachusetts Regulating Bill came up from the Commons to the Lords on 3 May. The Opposition peers prepared to take up the attack, and Rockingham gathered together several

---

[1] Cavendish Diaries, BM. Eg. 257, f. 37.
[2] *Ibid.*, ff. 123-41.   [3] *Ibid.*, f. 138.
[4] *Ibid.*, ff. 141-2. *Parl. Hist.*, xvii, 1320.
[5] *Commons Journals*, xxxiv, 712. North to King, 6 May 1774. Fortescue, *op. cit.*, iii, 1462. North's brother, the Bishop of Lichfield, wrote to their father, the Earl of Guildford, that the 'House of Commons divided again yesterday on the third American Bill 130-19 another triumph'. [7 May 1774.] North MSS. d. 24-6. There is no other evidence to support these figures.

of his noble friends to discuss what should be done.[1] They remained quiet on the first two readings. But after the second the Duke of Richmond informed North's brother, the Bishop of Lichfield, that 'he should oppose all the American Bills in every stage and protest at last'.[2] Presumably the Rockinghams had by then decided upon their tactics, for when the Bill came up for its final reading, on 11 May, they vigorously debated against it, divided the House 20-92, and finally put down a signed Protest in the Journals.[3]

The Impartial Administration of Justice Bill had followed hard on the heels of that for changing the Massachusetts charter. It was brought up from the Commons for its first reading on 8 May, had a second reading on the 13th, and went through Committee without amendments on the 16th.[4] The debate on its third reading on the 18th was chiefly remarkable for the speech by the Marquis of Rockingham : not so much for its excellence, though it seems to have been a competent effort, but because Rockingham made a major speech at all. His virtues as a leader were not inconsiderable, yet he had never been dynamic, physically or mentally, and he was certainly not over-articulate. During the whole Chatham Administration he had never uttered one public word in the House of Lords.[5] He was aware of this deficiency, confessing to Burke on one occasion 'indeed it is with difficulty that I can ever even attempt to take as much *part* in debate, as is requisite of me . . .'.[6] On 18 May he spoke late in the debate for about three-quarters of an hour. He did refer briefly to the Justice Bill which was now under consideration, but he was primarily

---

[1] The Duke of Manchester strongly dissented from joining this attack on the Regulating Bill. See Manchester to Rockingham, 20 April 1774, and Rockingham to Manchester, 20 April 1774. W.W.M. R1-1486-7.

[2] The second reading was on 6 May. Lichfield to Guildford [7 May 1774]. North MSS. d. 25, f. 1.

[3] *Lords Journals*, xxxiv, 182-4. *Parl. Hist.*, xvii, 1321-5. See below, Chapter VII, pp. 142-5, for a discussion of the Protest. A copy of Lord Camden's speech is in BM. Add. MS. 35912, ff. 221-2.

[4] *Lords Journals*, xxxiv, 171, 177, 190, 194, 198. The King had agreed that the latest letters from Hutchinson should be laid immediately before Parliament. To Dartmouth, 16 May 1774. Dartmouth MS. D 1778, Supplementary George III. Quoted in *HMC*, 13, IV, *Dartmouth MSS.*, iv, 500.　　　　　[5] J. Brooke, *op. cit.*, p. 83, note 2.

[6] Rockingham to Burke, 1 June 1774. W.W.M. Bk., *CEB*, ii, 541.

concerned with the traditional British policy towards America — as exemplified by the repeal of the Stamp Act. He claimed that the application of the Tea Duty and other succeeding measures towards America were deviations from this traditional policy. That evening Richmond wrote to congratulate him. 'I hope you feel satisfied with yourself today, I am sure all your friends must be so for you spoke as they would wish you to do oftener.'[1]

Rockingham's effort made little difference to the fate of the Impartial Administration of Justice Bill. The House of Lords was much thinner on both sides than it had been in the previous week for the Regulating Bill, and the division figures fell to 43-12 in favour of the Ministry.[2] Two days later the King gave his consent to both Bills.

The Quartering Act

A fourth emergency measure to restore the American colonists to a due obedience had been brought before the Commons three times during the heated week of 2 May, though it received slight attention and almost no opposition. This was 'a bill for the better providing suitable quarters for officers and soldiers in His Majesty's Service in North America'.[3] It was in substance an amendment of the 1765 Quartering and Mutiny Act. That had required civil authorities to furnish barracks and supplies for British troops posted in America; while in 1766 an amendment provided for their quartering in inns, ale-houses and unoccupied houses. Now it was the intention of Lord North's Ministry to broaden the scope of the previous legislation.[4] Barrington, who introduced the Bill on 3 May, said that four regiments of troops were sailing to Boston. The barracks to accommodate them were both inadequate and outside the town. The troops were needed inside the town, and so they were to be accommodated not only in uninhabited houses and inns, as was required by the 1766 Act, but also

[1] Richmond to Rockingham, 18 May 1774. W.W.M. R1-1490.
[2] *Parl. Hist.*, xvii, 1350-1. *Public Advertiser*, 14 May, 18 May 1774.
[3] 14 George III, c. 54.
[4] Dartmouth wrote to Gage that the Act was drawn up bearing in mind, and meaning to block, the artifices used in Boston in 1770 to elude the Quartering Act. Dartmouth to Gage, 3 June 1774. Dartmouth MS. D 1778, 1, ii, 982.

were to be billeted with private families if the necessity of the case required it. In view of the hostile reception given to the previous, more moderate quartering measures,[1] together with the increased antipathy of the colonists towards the British, and especially towards British troops, it might have been realised at the time that this Act could be enforced only with the greatest difficulty. But it went quickly through the Commons and was passed without a division on 9 May.[2]

The Bill went up to the Lords, and there the Earl of Chatham made one of his rare appearances for the third reading. He 'was so infirm, that he was obliged to support himself with a crutch while he was speaking'.[3] His speech was almost wholly concerned with the need to show leniency towards the Americans and the wrongness of taxing them. This strange gaunt figure, swathed in bandages, must have made an odd impression on the Lords, conscious of his past supremacy in the Lower House. He certainly added no great threat to the Government majority — which on the division was 57-16.

The Ministry lost no time in letting Gage have the texts of the Acts; they were sent on 3 June.[4] In an accompanying letter Dartmouth summarised the general purpose of the Ministry's American legislation:

> These acts close the consideration of what relates to the state of your government, and it is hoped that they will have the good effect to give vigour and activity to Civil authority; to prevent those unwarrantable assemblings of the people for factious purposes, which have been the source of so much mischief; and to secure an impartial administration of justice in all cases where the authority of this Kingdom may be in question.[5]

[1] Gage to Shelburne, 24 August 1767. PRO. CO. 5/85, ff. 309-18, and Gage to Hillsborough, 7 October 1769. PRO. CO. 5/87, ff. 347-52. Both printed in C. E. Carter, ed., *The Correspondence of General Thomas Gage, 1763-75*, i, 145-9, 238-40.

[2] *Commons Journals*, xxxiv, 695, 699, 710, 714.

[3] *Jackson's Oxford Journal*, 28 May 1774. See also Walpole's acid description of Chatham's return to Westminster in *Last Journals*, i, 347-9. *Parl. Hist.*, xvii, 1354-6. See also A. S. Turberville, *The House of Lords in the XVIIIth Century*, pp. 356-8.

[4] See J. Pownall to Admiralty, 3 June 1774. PRO. CO. 5/250, f. 80. The Boston Port Act had been sent on 18 April together with troop replacements. See above, p. 86.

[5] Dartmouth to Gage, 3 June 1774. PRO. CO. 5/763, f. 345.

However, in another letter written on the same day, Dartmouth showed that he realised how difficult it would be for Gage to execute at least one of the coercive measures. He drew Gage's attention to the Impartial Administration of Justice Act, and commented that 'it is hardly possible to conceive a situation of greater difficulty and delicacy than that which a Governor would be in, if reduced to the necessity of exercising his discretion in the case provided for; but it is a case that I trust will never occur'.[1] Dartmouth also admitted that there were deficiencies in the Official Instructions which were sent to Gage for setting up the new Massachusetts Council.[2] These Instructions contained the names of thirty-six councillors who were to be appointed by Gage. Dartmouth added that he realised that the best people had perhaps not been chosen, and that not everyone on the list would accept — 'but the case would admit of no delay, and we have been obliged to make our choice by such assistance as we could procure from those who are supposed to be the best informed'.[3] Dartmouth's misgivings were more than justified in the event, and Gage was to discover to his cost that the Council, like the Coercive Acts, looked better on paper than in practice.

Dartmouth's fourth and final letter [4] to Gage, on 3 June, sounded the note of hopeful optimism which was to prevail in Government circles throughout the rest of the summer. He told Gage that he had heard from Hutchinson about conditions in Boston up to 2 May, and that the reaction there so far had been mild. He was therefore 'willing to suppose that the people will quietly submit to the correction their ill conduct has

[1] PRO. CO. 5/763, ff. 354-5.
[2] PRO. CO. 5/765, ff. 321-6. The draught of the Instructions, drawn up by the Board of Trade on 20 May 1774, is in the Board of Trade Entry Book: PRO. CO. 5/921, ff. 17-18. Some queries concerning these, probably drawn up by Dartmouth, are in the Dartmouth MS. D 1778, II, 898.
[3] PRO. CO. 5/763, ff. 354-5.
[4] His third letter during the day asked Gage to discover the originals of Franklin's correspondence with Thomas Cushing concerning the Hutchinson/Whateley letters. PRO. CO. 5/763, f. 361. Headed 'Secret and Confidential', Gage's reply pointed out the difficulty of doing this. 25 August 1774: PRO. CO. 5/763, ff. 499-500. Printed in *The Correspondence of General Thomas Gage*, i, 364-5. The Franklin letters concerned are now in PRO. CO. 5/118, *passim*.

brought upon them, and to lay a foundation by their future behaviour for a re-establishment of their commercial privileges'.[1] The American Secretary and his colleagues in the Cabinet spent the next four months waiting and hoping for confirmation of this highly optimistic supposition.

[1] PRO. CO. 5/763, ff. 365-6

CHAPTER V

THE QUEBEC ACT

ON 2 May Dartmouth presented to the House of Lords a Bill 'making more effectual provision for the government of the province of Quebec'.[1] It was briefly debated and modified in the upper Chamber, and when it came down to the Commons it was hotly opposed by some of the Rockinghams and Chathamites.[2] Various amendments were made to the Bill by both sides of the House, and again in the Lords when it was sent up a second time for final approval.

The Quebec Act, which was passed on 16 June, contained six main provisions :

(1) The Proclamation of 1763, as far as it applied to Canada, was revoked.

(2) Legislative power, except in matters of taxation, was vested in the Governor of Quebec and a nominated, bi-racial Council. Resulting legislation was subject to royal approval. There was no mention of the Council being subject to a religious test.

(3) Roman Catholics were to enjoy free exercise of their religion, subject to the supremacy of the Crown ; and their clergy were to receive their accustomed dues and rights, but from members of their own faith only.

(4) Disputes about civil and property rights were to be settled in future in accordance with the old laws and

[1] 14 George III, c. 83. *Lords Journals*, xxxiv, 154. See Dartmouth to Crahamé, 4 May 1774. PRO. CO. 43/8, f. 69.
[2] There appear to be no reports on the Lords debate. The Public was excluded from the Chamber, and in the Commons Members protested that they knew nothing of what had passed in the Lords. *Debates of the House of Commons in the year 1774, on the Bill for making more effectual Provision for the Government of the Province of Quebec. Drawn up from the Notes of . . . Sir Henry Cavendish*, ed. J. Wright, pp. 75-94. This printed version differs in phrasing from the original manuscript diaries deposited in the British Museum. The Public was also excluded from the Commons throughout the coercive debates. *Parl. Hist.*, xvii, 1295.

customs of Canada. Provincial Assemblies might later amend this for local application.

(5) English Criminal Law was to be enforced, with some modifications — for instance the omission of Habeas Corpus.

(6) Quebec's boundary was amended. To the west it was extended up the St. Lawrence, through Lake Ontario and the Niagara River to Lake Erie, along the western edge of Pennsylvania to the Ohio River, and down the Ohio to the Mississippi.[1]

The Quebec Act was received both in England and in the Colonies as a punitive measure and has been often considered as the fifth coercive Act.[2] This was partly because it was introduced at the same time as the coercive legislation dealing with Massachusetts, and partly because its territorial, constitutional and religious provisions were open to misinterpretation by Americans, who were by now understandably suspicious about the intentions of the English Ministry towards them.

The Parliamentary Opposition frequently divided against the Bill and alleged that its design was to introduce a Stuart government, popish and despotic, into the American continent. The colonists agreed with this interpretation. Joseph Reed wrote to Dartmouth:

> The idea of bringing down the Canadians and savages upon the English Colonies is so inconsistent not only with the mercy, but even the justice and humanity of the Mother Country, that I cannot allow myself to think your Lordship would promote the Quebec Bill, or give your suffrage for it with such intentions.[3]

---

[1] A. Shortt and A. G. Doughty, eds., *Documents Relating to the Constitutional History of Canada, 1759–1791*, i, 570-6. A separate piece of legislation — The Quebec Revenue Act (14 George III, c. 88) — allowed for a revenue to be raised from duties on spirits, rum and molasses. The Revenue Act was to take effect on 5 April 1775 and the Quebec Act on 1 May 1775. The Revenue Act is not reported in Cavendish's Diary, or in the *Parliamentary History*, or in *The Annual Register . . . 1774*. See A. L. Burt, *The Old Province of Quebec*, p. 195.

[2] J. C. Miller, *Origins of the American Revolution*, pp. 369-76.

[3] J. Reed to Dartmouth, 25 September 1774. Dartmouth MS. I, ii, 1023. Quoted in *HMC*, II, V, *Dartmouth MSS.*, i, 363.

The religious communities in America were outraged at the toleration given to Canadian Catholics.[1] And the hopes of the land speculators, who had bought large claims across the Ohio, disappeared overnight when that territory was given to Quebec and so the western boundary of the Old Colonies was sealed. Joseph Reed argued that

> the Quebec Bill added fuel to the fire ; then all those deliberate measures of petitioning previous to any opposition were laid aside as inadequate to the apprehended danger and mischief, and now the people are generally ripe for the execution of any plan the Congress advises, should it be war itself . . .

These critics were wrong to interpret the Quebec Act only within the context of the Ministry's emergency American measures, though it would be equally untrue to say there was no connexion at all between the new Canadian policy and the Government's concern with events in the Old Colonies. For the incipient colonial rebellion probably precipitated the timing of the Quebec Bill. The Empire was shaking, and the Quebec Constitution had to be put on a firm foundation. It had become expedient, as well as just, to satisfy the French Canadians that British rule was benevolent, lest they were tempted to join the malcontents to the south. Furthermore, the Ministers must have realised that the clause in the Bill proposing to extend the Quebec boundary south to the Ohio would frustrate American ambitions to settle in the Far West. William Knox later wrote that one chief purpose of the Bill was 'of excluding all further settlement' in the Indian lands.[2] This step had long been considered from the viewpoint of Indian interests ; after the Boston Tea Party it must have seemed politically desirable as a means of containing the rebellious whites.

But the criticisms of the English Ministry's Canadian policy were largely unfounded. Despite its timing, its superficial similarities, and the few associations suggested above, the

---

[1] See C. H. Metzger, *The Quebec Act*, United States Catholic Historical Society, xvi, *passim*, especially pp. 191-206.

[2] W. Knox, *The Justice and Policy of the Late Act of Parliament, For Making more Effectual Provision for the Government of the Province of Quebec, Asserted and Proved*. London, 1774, p. 43.

Quebec Act was in fact very different from the previous four coercive measures. Its provisions had been debated over many years, and 'the main features of the act were determined by Canadian conditions long before the incidents which provoked the famous penal legislation with which it had been confused'.[1] Indeed, during the early months of 1774 the Ministry seems never to have discussed its Canadian policies in Cabinet at the same time as it considered the problem of the American Colonies.

The Quebec Act must be judged within the context of British policies towards Quebec and towards the western frontiers after 1763. Such an examination [2] shows that none of its clauses was framed wholly, or even mainly, as a response to the colonial crisis which broke after the Boston Tea Party. They were drafted to provide a single and acceptable civil government for two contiguous areas — for Quebec, and for the Indian reservations which were bounded by the Alleghenies, the Ohio river, the Mississippi and the Great Lakes. Both territories, which before 1763 together roughly constituted Old French Canada, had been ceded to England by the Paris Peace Treaty. The Proclamation of 1763 then severed them and made the back country into an Indian reserve.[3] But after the failure of British policies towards both the Canadians and the Indians in the next twenty years, it was decided that the two territories should be united again under a French type of Government.

The Problem of Governing Quebec Province

The first concern of the British Ministry in drafting the Quebec Act was to provide a civil government acceptable to the inhabitants of that Province. In 1763 the British had hoped that rapid immigration would anglicise Quebec. Consequently

---

[1] A. L. Burt, *The United States, Great Britain and British North America from the Revolution to the Establishment of Peace after the War of 1812*, p. 2. See also W. Knox, *Thoughts on the Act for making more Effectual Provision for the Government of the Province of Quebec*, London, 1774, *passim*, and W. Knox, *The Justice and Policy . . , passim*.

[2] There is a brief summary of this policy in the years 1763–74 among the official Quebec papers. PRO. CO. 42/14, especially ff. 138-41.

[3] The dividing line was roughly at latitude 45°. C. W. Alvord and C. E. Carter, eds., *The Critical Period, 1763–5*, pp. 39-45.

the Proclamation in that year based its government upon English laws and provided for an elected Assembly. The French Canadians were guaranteed their Roman Catholic religion by treaty, but they were entirely excluded from any share in the administration.[1]

As things turned out the French continued to be in a vast majority.[2] The result was an impossible situation. Since a great part of the populace was excluded from the Assembly, successive Governors did not call one, thus depriving the Colony both of a legislature and of a revenue.[3] The operation of English criminal law created few difficulties, but English civil law threatened the private and church property of the French Canadians. Many of the British settlers were there merely for commercial exploitation, and they were described by Governor Murray in 1766 as 'the most immoral collection of men I ever knew'.[4] The problem of blending two different races and religions, with the majority under an alien rule, seemed to grow more rather than less difficult.[5]

Successive British Ministries were confronted with the need to settle the Quebec problem. Grenville adopted a plan to show greater toleration towards the Catholic population, though the Jesuits were to be banished immediately. The Rockinghams inherited this, and implemented it in certain ways.[6] They also recalled Governor Murray early in 1766 and set up an investigation into Canadian affairs; Guy Carleton was sent out as Lieutenant-Governor, William Hey as Chief Justice and Francis Maseres as Attorney-General to assist in this investigation.[7] The Board of Trade also made recommendations in June 1766

---

[1] C. W. Alvord, 'The Genesis of the Proclamation of 1763', *Michigan Pioneer and Historical Society*, xxxvi, 20-50. A. L. Burt, *The United States, Great Britain . . .*, p. 2; and *The Old Province of Quebec*, pp. 74-101.

[2] William Knox put the proportion as high as 400-1. *Thoughts on the Act . . .*, p. 9.

[3] The only revenue coming in was from Crown lands, feudal dues and a few duties. R. Coupland, *The Quebec Act*, p. 67.

[4] Quoted in L. H. Gipson, *The Coming of the Revolution*, p. 117.

[5] See R. Coupland, *op. cit.*, pp. 6-68.

[6] C. W. Alvord, *The Mississippi Valley in British Politics*, i, 255-7. A Bishop of Quebec was consecrated, and Catholics were allowed to participate fully as jurors and attorneys in the law courts.

[7] A. L. Burt, *The Old Province of Quebec*, pp. 128-30.

to extend the tolerance of Catholics and to bring the judicial and legal system more into accord with French and Canadian needs. Most of the Rockingham Cabinet agreed with this; but Lord Chancellor Northington opposed it, and before anything more could be done George III had sent for Chatham.[1] It certainly appears that the first Rockingham Ministry was committed to many of the principles which later governed the 1774 Quebec Act. Carleton, Maseres and Hey, who were Rockingham appointments, were also among the architects of the measure. Yet in Opposition later the Rockinghams fought it bitterly.[2]

In June 1771 the English Law Officers were asked to prepare a plan for Quebec. Their reports, which conflicted in many respects, were presented separately, but all lay in the Government's hands through the summer of 1773.[3] Meanwhile, the Deputy-Governor of Quebec, Hector Theophilus Crahamé, bombarded the Government with advice. He strongly recommended that the old French laws be confirmed, that a Council be preferred to an Assembly, and that the Canadian Catholics be allowed free exercise of their religion.[4] The Government was receptive to these arguments. In August North told Maseres that he was 'fully determined to do something towards

---

[1] A. L. Burt, *The Old Province of Quebec*, p. 151. R. A. Humphreys and S. M. Scott. 'Lord Northington and the Laws of Canada', *The Canadian Historical Review*, xiv, 42-61.

[2] To be fair to the Rockinghams, they had never, in 1766, supported the idea of a nominated Council without an elected Assembly.

[3] See W. Knox, *The Justice and Policy* . . . p. 19. Wedderburn presented his report in December 1772, Thurlow his in January 1773, and the Advocate-General, Dr. Marriott, had reported by the spring. They are printed in A. Shortt and A. G. Doughty, eds., *op. cit.*, i, 424-37, 437-445, 445-83. Marriott's 141-page report is dated 3 March 1773. PRO. CO. 47/110. Also Marriott to Suffolk, 27 November 1773. PRO. State Papers Domestic, 37/10, ff. 164/34. Marriott, like Maseres, opposed certain concessions to the French Canadians which had been put forward by other advisers. Thurlow and Wedderburn also disagreed considerably. R. Coupland, *op. cit.*, pp. 89-90. For Maseres's views see his letter to Dartmouth, 4 January 1774. PRO. CO. 42/33, ff. 5-6. Wedderburn described Maseres as 'a very good man, but both in religion and politics he has a good deal of the Huguenot spirit in him'. Wedderburn to Burke, 10 June 1774. W.W.M. Bk.

[4] Crahamé to Hillsborough, 2 July 1772. PRO. CO. 43/13, ff. 19-20. Crahamé to Dartmouth, 11 November 1772. PRO. CO. 43/13, ff. 32-4. 22 June 1773. PRO. CO. 43/13, ff. 38-9. 13 December 1773. CO. 43/33, ff. 15-16. 18 January 1774. PRO. CO. 43/13, f. 59.

the settlement of that Province in the next session of parliament'. He also said he was strongly in favour of government through a Council rather than with an Assembly.[1] In November the business was held up by the loss of Marriott's report: Rochford accused Suffolk, and Suffolk Rochford, of having been the last to possess it.[2] But by 1 December all was well and Dartmouth wrote that the Quebec question was 'now actually under the immediate consideration of His Majesty's Servants, and will probably be settled in a very short time'.[3] He added that he personally would strongly urge full toleration for Catholics, and the extension of Quebec's boundaries. Carleton, Hey and Wedderburn were pressing for the restoration of French civil law. Clearly the main lines of a new Constitution for Quebec — government through Council, toleration for Catholics and the restoration of French civil law — were practically determined before the crisis broke in the American Colonies; and they were related to specific and long-standing Canadian problems.[4]

The Problem of the American Western Frontier and the Indian Reservations

The other problem dealt with in the Quebec Bill was the provision of government and the maintenance of order in the vast Indian reservations to the west of the American colonial settlements.

The alarms of the Seven Years' War, and Pontiac's Rebellion

[1] Maseres to Dartmouth, 26 August 1773, quoted in A. Shortt and A. G. Doughty, eds., *op. cit.*, i, 534. Wedderburn also supported a Council rather than an Assembly 'for a limited number of years'. Wedderburn to Burke, June 1774. W.M.M. Bk. A. L. Burt says that the idea of an Assembly had been dropped as early as 1771. A. L. Burt, *Province of Quebec*, p. 177.

[2] Marriott to Suffolk, 27 November 1773, and Suffolk to Marriott, 28 November 1773. PRO. S.P.Dom. George III, 37/10, ff. 164/35, 74.

[3] Dartmouth to Crahamé, PRO. CO. 43/8, ff. 64-5. See also J. Pownall to W. Knox, 3 December 1773. *HMC, Various*, vi, *Knox MSS.*, p. 111.

[4] An opposite view is expressed by Chester Martin, whose thesis is that the motive behind the Quebec Act was the subjugation of the colonists: 'the core of the Bill was . . . arbitrary governance, and the use which the administration proposed to make of it in America': *Empire and Commonwealth: Studies in Governance and Self-Government in Canada*, especially p. 133.

in 1763, had underlined the need to keep Britain's Red Indian subjects contented. The most immediate danger lay in the desire of American colonists to settle the lands of the Indians and to exploit their trade.[1] Shelburne and Hillsborough, successive Presidents of the Board of Trade, tried to prevent this friction between the two races when they drew up the 1763 Proclamation of policy for Britain's new possessions.

But if the prime aim of the British Government when approaching the Western problem in 1763 was the 'satisfaction of the Indians',[2] there was another motive behind it — the fear that American colonists would disappear into the back country, beyond imperial tutelage. The Southern Secretary, Egremont, wrote that

> the country called Canada is of such vast extent . . . It might . . . be necessary to fix upon some line for a western boundary to our ancient provinces beyond which our people should not at present be permitted to settle . . . planting themselves in the Heart of America, out of reach of Government and where, from the great difficulty of procuring European commodities, they would be compelled to commence manufactures to the infinite prejudice of Britain. . . .[3]

That part of the 1763 Proclamation which was devoted to Indian affairs was aimed to serve both purposes, to satisfy the Indians and to restrain the Americans.[4] The western settlement

[1] Sir William Johnson to the Lords of Trade, 25 September 1763. PRO. CO. 323/17, ff. 93-8. Johnson had been in America since 1738 and supervisor of the northern Indians since 1756. He was a dedicated official who understood and respected the natives. He was in favour of strong central regulation and of controlled expansion in the west. The southern Indians were in the charge of John Stuart. *The Papers of Sir William Johnson*, ed., J. Sullivan, A. C. Flick, M. W. Hamilton and A. W. Lanber, *passim*. Also H. L. Shaw, *British Administration of the Southern Indians, 1756–1783*, doctoral thesis presented at Bryn Mawr College, Pennsylvania, 1931, and deposited at Widener Library, Harvard.

[2] Lords of Trade to Johnson, 5 August 1763. PRO. CO. 5/1130, f. 217. See L. Gipson, *The American Revolution as an aftermath of the Seven Years' War*, p. 94.

[3] 'Hints relative to the Division and Government of the conquered and newly occupied countries in America.' PRO. CO. 323/16, ff. 194-5.

[4] C. W. Alvord, 'The Genesis of the Proclamation of 1763', *Michigan Pioneer and Historical Society*, xxxvi, 20-52. Also the author's revisions in *Mississippi Valley*, ii, 168. The Proclamation was drafted partly by Shelburne and partly by his successor, Hillsborough.

boundary of the Old Colonies was temporarily fixed at the Appalachian watershed. The new southern border of Quebec roughly coincided with latitude 45°, and the northern border of the Floridas with latitude 31°. In future the lands beyond these boundaries were to be Indian reservations. They were not, however, provided with a civil government. The cost seemed too much for the British Government to bear; [1] and it was presumably hoped that the Indians, and the Canadian communities living among them, could look after themselves providing they were left alone.[2]

Centralisation and containment were the main features of British policy towards the Western lands as outlined by the 1763 Proclamation and by the Trading Regulations which followed in the next year. But it was only partially implemented and soon ended in failure. The Regulations became a dead letter because England was never prepared to meet the full costs of a central imperial administration, and hopes of financing it across the Atlantic were never fulfilled.[3] And the inviolability of the Indian reservations, the crux of the policy, was persistently undermined by illegal white settlement: even at this early stage America's 'western destiny' could not be denied.

The next full review of British policy towards the American West — and the last before the Quebec Bill — was made during Chatham's Administration. Shelburne had returned to office

---

[1] W. Knox, *The Justice and Policy* . . . p. 40.

[2] An attempt was also made to regulate trade between whites and Indians. By a Board of Trade Ordinance issued in July 1764, the West was divided for trading purposes into two regions. These were controlled by the two superintendents of Indian affairs, who alone had the power to issue licences, and trade was to be carried on under strict regulations at specified posts. See 'Plan for the future management of Indian Affairs'. PRO. CO. 5/65, part 3, ff. 683-705. C. W. Alvord, *Mississippi Valley*, i, 180-2. B. A. Hinsdale, 'The Western Land Policy of the British Government from 1763 to 1775', *Ohio Archeological and Historical Quarterly*, i, 207-29.

[3] The Rockingham Whigs, by repealing the Stamp Act and proposing the reduction of the Land Tax, made imperial regulations nearly impossible. Shelburne had the most imaginative scheme — to set up an American fund to meet the expenses of regulation. He proposed to cut these expenses by turning the Indian trade back to colonial control, and to finance his American fund by husbanding quit rents and by making remunerative grants of land. C. W. Alvord, *Mississippi Valley*, i, 283-5. C. W. Alvord and C. E. Carter, ds., *The New Regime*, pp. 449, 454-9, 536, 552-5.

as Southern Secretary in 1766.[1] He was personally in favour of some controlled expansion, and he was now lobbied continually by American companies which were speculating in Western lands.[2] Shelburne put to the Government a scheme for founding new Colonies.[3] But he was increasingly isolated in the Cabinet, and only the most conservative of his suggestions — that the regulation of Indian trade should be returned to the American Colonies — was accepted in 1768.[4] The Indian boundary was moved further west, leaving some land technically open to settlement in the near west of New York, Pennsylvania

[1] Whether American policy before 1768 was determined by the Board of Trade or by the Southern Secretariat depended upon how far the policy was political or commercial and also upon the personalities controlling those offices. See A. H. Basye, *The Lords Commissioners of Trade and Plantations* . . . *1748–1782*, pp. 32-173.

[2] See K. P. Bailey, *The Ohio Company of Virginia and the Westward Movement, 1748–1792*, and K. P. Bailey, ed., *The Ohio Company Papers, 1753–1817*, and H. T. Leyland, 'The Ohio Company, A Colonial Corporation', *Quarterly Publication of the Historical and Philosophical Society of Ohio*, xvi, i, 1-19. The Old Ohio Company was organised in 1747 and claimed 200,000 acres on the Ohio river. The Susquehannah Company had successfully pressed the claims of Connecticut to certain Indian lands on the Susquehannah river and in 1768, when so many companies were lobbying Shelburne, hoped further to establish an independent Colony west of Connecticut: see J. P. Boyd, *The Susquehannah Company: Connecticut's Experiment in Expansion*, pp. 11-15; *The Susquehannah Company Papers, 1750–1772*, ed. J. P. Boyd, i, lxx-lxxv, iii, ii-vi. On the Loyal Company, which set up in opposition to the Old Ohio, see T. P. Abernethy, *Western Lands and the American Revolution*, p. 7. A Mississippi Company was formed in 1763 to settle the Mississippi Valley. It claimed 50,000 acres for each of its shareholders, among whom were five of the Lee family from Virginia and three Washingtons. See C. W. Alvord and C. E. Carter, eds., *The Critical Period*. pp, 19-23. The Indiana Company, which was putting most pressure on Shelburne, was set up by the colonial traders who had suffered in Pontiac's Rebellion and demanded land as compensation. Benjamin Franklin was its London representative. See Benjamin to William Franklin, 28 August 1767 and 25 November 1767. *The Complete Works of Benjamin Franklin*, ed. J. Bigelow, iv, 30-1, 53-5.

[3] For a time Shelburne was supported by Gage, Richard Jackson and Sir William Johnson. C. J. Alvord and C. E. Carter, eds., *The New Regime*, pp. 370, 422-30.

[4] For the Board of Trade's adverse comments on Shelburne's colonising schemes see PRO. CO. 5/66, ff. 367-8. Benjamin Franklin noted that 'the purpose of settling the new Colonies seems at present to be dropped'. He blamed Hillsborough for this. Franklin to William Franklin, 13 March 1768. *Franklin Complete Works*, iv, 128-33, 128. Hillsborough wrote to Gage announcing the decentralisation of the Indian trade on 15 April 1768. PRO. CO. 5/86, ff. 73-87. On Shelburne see R. A. Humphreys, 'Lord Shelburne and British Colonial Policy, 1766–1768', *English Historical Review*, l, 257-77.

and Virginia. But Hillsborough, the first occupant of the new American Secretariat, was reluctant to allow even this limited expansion. And colonisation in the Far West beyond the Indian line was ruled out of the question on political, economic and military grounds.[1]

The failure of Shelburne's scheme for controlled expansion was a triumph for conservatives in the Government. Hillsborough wrote to Gage that 'the great objects' of British policy were to reduce colonial expenses,[2] to maintain the army in America ready for quick action, and to keep the Indians contented by forbidding white expansion. It was a limited vision; but, given the poverty and weakness of the British colonial administration, it seemed a practical policy. It promised to spare Britain the troubles of Indian wars — though at the risk of provoking rebellion from land-hungry American colonists.

By 1770 the Government — and especially Hillsborough — seemed committed to support the vast Indian reservations. It was opposed to new settlements or Colonies in the West, even in the territory which became available when the Indian boundary was moved west by the Treaties of Stanwix and Lochabar. But the situation in America was far from stable. The Canadian communities settled on the reservations still lacked any form of civil government. The American colonists still caused Indian unrest by their pursuit of trade and land across the boundary line; for the restoration of Indian trade regulation to the Colonies in 1768 merely meant that there was little or no regulation at all, and the pressure to colonise the reservations gained momentum in the 'seventies, with leading Englishmen and

[1] 'Representation of the Lords of Trade on the State of Indian Affairs', 7 March 1768. PRO. CO. 5/69, ff. 119-71. C. W. Alvord, *Mississippi Valley*, ii, 30-2. C. W. Alvord and C. E. Carter, eds., *Critical Period*, p. xxiii. The new line was finally settled with the northern Indians at the Treaty of Fort Stanwix by Sir William Johnson on 5 November 1768, and by John Stuart with the southern Indians at the Treaty of Lochabar, 18 October 1770. See C. W. Alvord, 'The British Ministry and the Treaty of Fort Stanwix', *Proceedings of the State Historical Society of Wisconsin, 1908*, p. 2. See R. A. Billington, *Westward Expansion. A History of the American Frontier*, p. 148. A copy of the Stanwix Treaty is in PRO. CO. 42/14, ff. 99-103.
[2] Hillsborough told Gage that the Indian expenses must not exceed £9,000. Hillsborough to Gage, 15 July 1769. PRO. CO. 5/87, f. 251.

Americans forming companies to speculate in lands in the Near and the Far West. It was a dispute over one of these, the Grand Ohio Company, which brought about Hillsborough's fall in 1772.

The Grand Ohio Company (initially the Walpole Company) was formed by Thomas Walpole in 1769. Its ambitions expanded until it petitioned to form a new Colony of two million acres on the Ohio river.[1] But Hillsborough remained uncertain of the wisdom of western expansion.[2] The Company lined up against him an exceptionally powerful block of shareholders, including three members of the Privy Council, a group of senior administrative officials, and a whole tribe of American expansionists.[3] In July 1772 the Privy Council decided in favour of the Company's petition and on 13 August Hillsborough felt compelled to resign.[4]

It seemed at first as if the removal of Hillsborough, and the involvement of so many English politicians, would open the floodgates to settlement in the Near and even in the Far West.[5]

---

[1] Treasury Minute, 4 January 1770. PRO. CO. 5/1332, f. 150. For a history of the company's petition see L. Mulkearn, ed., *George Mercer Papers Relating to the Ohio Company of Virginia*, pp. 669-70.

[2] T. P. Abernethy, *op. cit.*, pp. 44-9, 71-2.

[3] The shareholders included : Lords Hertford (Lord Chamberlain), Gower (President of the Privy Council) and Rochford (Privy Councillor and Southern Secretary), John Robinson, Thomas Bradshaw and Grey Cooper (Under Secretaries at the Treasury), Richard Jackson (Board of Trade), Robert Wood (Under Secretary of State to Lord Weymouth), Anthony Todd (Postmaster General), Sir George Colebrooke (a director of the East India Company) and various Members of Parliament. Among the Americans were Benjamin Franklin and Joseph Galloway. See C. W. Alvord, *Mississippi Valley*, ii, 97-148. K. Bailey, ed., *Ohio Company Papers*, p. 280, and K. Bailey, *The Ohio Company of Virginia*, p. 239, and note.

[4] PRO. CO. 43/8, f. 55. For contemporary comments on Hillsborough's resignation see R. Lucas, *Lord North, second Earl of Guildford, K.G., 1732-1792*, i, 353. *HMC, Various*, vi, *Knox MSS.*, pp. 253 seq. *The last Journals of Horace Walpole*, ed. A. F. Stuart, i, 127. Benjamin to William Franklin, 17 August 1772. *The Writings of Benjamin Franklin*, ed. A. H. Smyth, v, 410. King to Suffolk, 22 July 1772. Fortescue, *op. cit.*, ii, 1100. *Memoirs of the Life and Writings of Benjamin Franklin*, ed., W. T. Franklin, i, 348, note 1.

[5] The new American Secretary, Dartmouth, seemed to support the proposed Colony, suggesting a name for it — Vandalia — and a Governor — his cousin, Major William Legge. The Privy Council actually set a committee to work on the Colony's Constitution in 1773 ; it recommended a nominated Council and not an elected Assembly — the solution which was adopted for Quebec in 1774. Dartmouth to Legge, 17 March

But soon the expansionists ran into trouble. Gage returned from America with disturbing reports from the Old Colonies and argued against any new settlements. The fur traders seem to have done some hard lobbying against settlement in their peltry reservations.[1] And, most important, Thurlow took over Hillsborough's role as the opponent of the Grand Ohio Company.[2] By the end of 1773 the proposal for the new Colony still had not passed the Law Officers' hands; and the affair of the Hutchinson/Oliver letters had put Franklin into such disrepute that he was forced to announce publicly his resignation from the Company.[3]

A final reappraisal of the British attitude to the western frontier took place in 1773–74. There were two areas which still troubled the Ministry: the Back Country east of the new 1768–70 line, which technically belonged to the Old Colonies but had not yet been officially opened to settlement, and the great Indian reservations beyond, which still lacked a civil government. In April 1773 the Privy Council took provisional steps to stabilise the situation when it ordered all officials in America to cease granting licences to purchase new land from the Indians.[4] The final policies were decided in the months after that and were declared early in 1774. Instructions issued on 2 February dealt with the first problem and laid down strict regulations under which the Back Country could be settled up

---

1773. Dartmouth MS. D 1778, 1, ii, 848. 'Propositions for the Settlement of a Colony . . .'. PRO. CO. 5/232, ff. 174-87. K. Bailey, ed. *Ohio Company Papers*, pp. 263-79. For other land companies formed in the 'seventies see C. W. Alvord, *Mississippi Valley*, ii, 199-208.

[1] See below, p. 119, *n.* 1.

[2] W. Knox, *Extra-Official State Papers*, ii, 45-8. Thurlow objected to Franklin, saying that he was 'unworthy of the Favors of the Crown'. L. Mulkearn, ed., *op. cit.*, pp. xvi-xvii. Alvord suggests that Suffolk and Gage were supporting Thurlow's obstruction tactics. C. W. Alvord, *Mississippi Valley*, ii, 159-64. See also Hutchinson, *Diary and Letters*, i, 185, and Samuel Wharton to Thomas Pitt, 25 January 1774. Dartmouth MS. D 1778, II, 795.

[3] On 12 January 1774. The Government continued to consider the new Colony, but had done nothing when the war broke out.

[4] The King's order to the colonial Governors not to grant any more lands is in PRO. CO. 5/241, ff. 233-4. Also see A. Henderson, 'A Pre-Revolutionary Revolt in the Old South West', *The Mississippi Valley Historical Review*, xvii, 2, 191-212. For Richard Jackson's description of the previous land system see BM. Add. MS. 38342, ff. 153-6.

to the Indian border.[1] Next the boundary clause attached to the proposed Quebec Bill brought all the Indian reservations north of the Ohio river into the Province of Quebec. This was aimed to solve the second — and the main — problem: it protected the Indians in the reservations from the anarchy of American or British infiltration and land grabbing, while at the same time giving their Canadian communities French civil government.

The boundary amendment was clearly not a sudden development. It had been England's policy since 1763 to keep the Indians contented and their lands inviolable. That policy had failed chiefly because the British Government had been unable to reduce colonial pressure on the Indian reservations. The boundary clause was a final attempt to do this.[2] It also threatened to bottle up the American colonists, but this was not a determining factor. Dartmouth had advocated a boundary revision before the Tea Party happened.[3] In his view it was no longer wise to limit Quebec 'to the narrow limits prescribed in the 1763 Proclamation', and he emphasised the need to attach the Indians to Britain. He was probably responding to Canadian pressures. In November a petition had arrived asking that Quebec 'be extended to its former limits'.[4] Crahamé had also written to him pointing out

> how much the interference of the Province of New York, upon the course of the St. Lawrence, may affect their commercial interests, especially in the fur trade, of which the New Yorkers have already obtained a considerable share, were the present boundaries confirmed. . . . Nature seems to point out, that the people, inhabiting the banks of this great river,

[1] Land grants were taken away from the Governors and opened to public auction. It was apparently hoped to raise more revenue from grants and quit rents — an echo of Shelburne's 1768 policy. See St. L. G. Sioussart, 'The Breakdown of the Royal Management of Lands in the Southern Provinces 1773–5', *Agricultural History*, iii, 67 *seq.*

[2] William Knox said that 'the avowed purpose' of the Bill was 'of excluding all further settlement' of Indian lands and establishing 'uniform regulations for the Indian trade'. W. Knox, *The Justice and Policy* . . . p. 43.

[3] Dartmouth to Crahamé, 1 December 1773. PRO. CO. 43/8, ff. 64-5. Also J. Pownall to W. Knox, 3 December 1773. *HMC*, *Various*, vi, *Knox MSS.*, p. 111.   [4] PRO. CO. 42/14, f. 141.

should be under the same government, and bound by the same laws and usages.[1]

A few days later Crahamé wrote again saying that the Indians were upset by rum vendors in their hunting grounds — 'these being mostly without the present limits of the Province it will not be easy to remedy, except its civil jurisdiction was to be further extended'.[2]

There was much to be said in favour of the boundary change made in 1774,[3] for the old North-West had always been connected more closely with Quebec than with the thirteen colonies. Historically the two areas were united previous to 1763, economically they were each dependent upon the fur trade, and geographically the great water system converging on the St. Lawrence made a unity out of the regions of the upper Mississippi, the Great Lakes and the St. Lawrence valley. Since the alternative policies had either failed or been rejected, the British Government had little choice other than to recognise this unity.[4] But it was open to doubt whether America's

[1] Crahamé to Dartmouth, 1 October 1773. PRO. CO. 42/32, f. 60. It would be interesting to discover how far and in precisely what ways the fur traders put pressure on the Government and so acted as a counter-lobby to the land speculators. Alvord suggested that the fur trade worked through Scottish Members of Parliament like Sir Lawrence Dundas ; but the British Government probably felt anyway that what was good for the North West Company was good for Great Britain. See C. W. Alvord, *Mississippi Valley*, ii, 242-3 ; and Gage to Hillsborough, 10 November 1770. PRO. CO. 5/88, ff. 327-43. For the extent to which the Quebec Act met the demands of the fur traders see W. E. Stevens, *The Northwest Fur Trade, 1763–1800*, pp. 33-4. Harold Innis wrote that 'the participation of American and English merchants in the fur trade immediately following the Conquest led to the rapid growth of a new organisation (the North West Company) which was instrumental in securing the Quebec Act'. H. A. Innis, *The Fur Trade in Canada*, p. 391, and also pp. 175-9, 386.

[2] Crahamé to Dartmouth, 6 October 1773. PRO. CO. 42/32, f. 67.

[3] Alvord wrote that the boundary clause was 'the last effort of the Mother Country to throw the protection of the imperial power over at least a part of the Mississippi Valley in order to prevent the disorders of that region'. *Mississippi Valley*, ii, 237. Alvord also suggests that the Ministry planned to open the South-West while closing up the old North-West, thus countenancing expansion without allowing it to threaten the Indians or the fur trade. It might also be noted that the Canadian inhabitants of the reservations had long been petitioning for civil government. C. E. Carter, *Great Britain and the Illinois Country*, pp. 145 *seq.*

[4] See Marjorie Reid : 'Canada in British Politics from 1763–1783'. Thesis deposited in Rhodes House, Bodleian Library, Oxford, particularly section II, pp. 91-5.

westward urge could have been blocked by this legislation, or any measures short of a massive occupation of North America on a scale unknown in the eighteenth century. For the Americans soon broke open the gates to the West by force — claiming to be partly provoked by the Quebec Act which was intended to keep that region in peace.[1]

The Quebec Bill in the Commons

The main lines of the Ministry's Canadian policy had been decided by the end of 1773. That the policy would be effected by a Parliamentary Statute also seems to have been formally accepted by the late summer of 1773. This was a new departure; but whether the decision was due to a new fashion in employing Parliamentary rather than prerogative authority or whether advice from legal advisers like Mansfield had cast doubts on the legality of using the royal prerogative in such cases is not clear. Certainly Mansfield's ruling a few months later in the case of *Campbell versus Hall* confirmed the necessity of a statutory settlement of the Constitution of Quebec instead of the hitherto and unbroken use of the Crown's prerogative, and several earlier cases concerning Grenada gave indications of precedent for this ruling.[2]

A great variety of minds and opinions shaped the final form of the Quebec Bill during the early months of 1774: Carleton, Maseres, Hey and Maurice Morgann [3] from Canada; the Law Officers — Thurlow, Wedderburn and Marriott — in London; Dartmouth, North, Suffolk and Rochford in the Cabinet; and Hillsborough and Mansfield as independent advisers.[4] Three drafts were drawn up, the last being towards the end of April 1774.[5] During its course through the Lords, then through the Commons, and on its return to the Lords it was often amended.

---

[1] For a discussion of how far the limitations to westward expansion may have provoked revolutionary discontent see T. P. Abernethy, *op. cit.*, *passim*; and R. B. Morris, *The American Revolution*, pp. 13-14. It will be remembered that this limitation was cited as a grievance in the Declaration of Independence.

[2] I am grateful to Dr. F. Madden of Nuffield College, Oxford, for advice on this point.   [3] Morgann was Shelburne's secretary.

[4] R. Coupland, *op. cit.*, pp. 80-90.

[5] A. Shortt and A. G. Doughty, eds., *op. cit.*, i, 535-51.

Whatever its other virtues and vices, this 'last effort of British politicians to organise the territory acquired by the Treaty of Paris' was certainly not a hasty and ill-considered step.[1]

The Bill was first introduced in the Lords on 2 May and it had its final reading there on the 17th.[2] It was brought down to the Commons on the 18th, and was debated at its second reading on the 26th.[3] North then put the main case for the Government. He apologised for bringing the Bill in so late and claimed that the business had not been delayed 'from any other desire than to be fully informed'. He said they might amend the Bill if they liked, but 'by no means leave the province of Canada in its present situation'. About the settlements in the reservations he felt that 'the least inconvenient method is to annex those spots . . . better than to leave them without government at all, or make separate governments'. He went on that 'the annexing likewise is the result of the desire of the Canadians, it is the desire of those who trade to the settlements, who think they cannot trade with safety while they remain separate.[4] He was supported by Thurlow and by Wedderburn, the latter arguing that his intention was to deter British settlement in Canada and to confine the Americans 'according to the ancient policy of this country along the line of the sea and rivers'.[5]

Opposition members used the arguments they were to maintain and elaborate throughout the debates. Dunning, Barré, Thomas Townsend (M.P. for Whitchurch) and Lord John Cavendish saw every clause in the Bill as a nail in the coffin of English liberties.[6] French law, government by nominated council, and the Roman religion, all smelled of despotism. That these were to be extended down the Back Country was evidence of the plot against the Old Colonies, the devilish conclusion to

[1] C. W. Alvord, *Mississippi Valley*, ii, 250.

[2] Its second reading was on 12 May, it went through Committee on the 13th, and was reported and engrossed on the 16th. *Lords Journals*, xxxiv, 187, 190, 193-4, 201.

[3] Cavendish Diary, BM. Eg. 260, ff. 1-146. *Commons Journals*, xxxiv, 768-85.

[4] Cavendish Diary, B.M Eg. 260, ff. 12-24, especially ff. 13-14, f. 15, ff. 16-17.

[5] *Ibid.*, f. 120.

[6] Burke was out of London for this Second Reading. *Debates of the House of Commons*, ed., J. Wright, p. 233.

the Ministry's whole punitive policy. Dunning suspected that not everything was yet revealed. 'It carries in its breast something that squints and looks dangerous to the other inhabitants of that country, our own colonies.' [1] The Opposition divided, and were defeated 105-29.[2]

When the debate was resumed on 31 May a petition was presented by William Baker on behalf of the proprietors of Pennsylvania, protesting against the boundary provisions of the Quebec Bill.[3] North immediately agreed to accept the petition. He claimed that 'it was never intended those words should intrench upon other colonies. . . . The demand is so just and so reasonable that, without hearing counsel, it may be complied with.' [4] Burke took this opportunity to speak up for New York.[5] These two States, New York and Pennsylvania, were the ones most affected by the boundary amendment. They had traditional claims to all land west of their settlements. Except for the Indian lines, which were temporary and political, no legal western border had ever been established for them. The Government, in now establishing such a border, could be accused of infringing the Old Colonies' traditional rights. But those rights were theoretical; previous to 1763 the French had the solid right of occupation, and the territory was then part of Canada — as it was to be now. The Government knew its position was sound, which probably explains why North was so accommodating on this point.

The House then discussed a question on which the Government was less helpful — the information which was used when drafting the Quebec Bill. Herbert Mackworth [6] asked for the reports of Maseres, Hey and Carleton to be made available;

[1] Cavendish Diary, BM. Eg. 260, f. 87.
[2] *Ibid.*, North to King, 26 May 1774. J. W. Fortescue, ed., *The Correspondence of George III, 1760–1782.* iii, 1467.
[3] Cavendish Diary, BM. Eg. 260, ff. 166-171. R. Coupland, *op. cit.*, p. 94, note 2.   [4] Cavendish Diary, BM. Eg. 260, f. 167.
[5] Burke wrote to the New York Assembly saying he would oppose the Quebec Bill because it allowed encroachment on New York territory. 30 May 1774. W.W.M. Bk. *CEB*, ii, 533-40. In fact the 1763 boundary between New York and Quebec had still not been completely run in 1774. See Crahamé to Dartmouth, 1 October 1773. PRO. CO. 42/32, f. 59 and ditto. 12 March 1774. PRO. CO. 42/33, f. 45.
[6] M.P. for Cardiff, 1766-90.

North replied that they would take too long to copy. Burke, Barré and William Pulteney all complained that it was impossible to form opinions about the Bill without full information.[1] Thurlow said that they could get the facts from witnesses in Committee, and Bamber Gascoyne repeated that the reports were too large to copy. The Opposition here had a genuine grievance, for the Government deliberately kept them in the dark and apparently had something to hide. This led the Opposition to read the worst possible interpretations into the Bill. On the other hand, the information which the Ministry had received was so diverse, and the opinions which were consulted were so conflicting, that it would have been impossible to reveal these and yet still to present the appearance of unity for the proposed measure.[2] The Quebec Bill was a patchwork of necessary compromises on very controversial issues; but Parliamentary tactics demanded that the Ministry's political needlework should not be obvious. The Opposition divided first on the question of laying Carleton's report before them, and then for the Law Officers' reports; they were defeated 85-46 and 85-45.[3]

The House went into Committee on 2 June and questioned Carleton and Maseres.[4] Next day, Friday the 3rd, they again examined Carleton, who was very non-committal, and William Hey and Marriott, who deftly evaded the issues. The Opposition was frustrated at every turn, and when they divided on a request to call ex-Governor Murray as a witness they were defeated 90-36.[5]

On 6 June the boundary clause was discussed in Committee.[6] Burke led the attack. He said it would put the people in the Back Country under French Government, which he equated

[1] Burke soon had less cause to complain than others. Early in June Wedderburn sent him a summary of his own recommendations and offered him Maseres's report if he wanted it. Wedderburn to Burke, 10 June 1774. W.W.M. Bk.

[2] Thurlow and Wedderburn had tried to make a joint report, but they differed so much that they had to report separately. Wedderburn to Burke, 10 June 1774. W.W.M. Bk.

[3] Cavendish Diary, BM. Eg. 260, ff. 221, 223.

[4] Ibid., ff. 234-51 ; Ibid., BM. Eg. 261, ff. 252-333.

[5] Ibid., f. 424.

[6] Ibid., BM. Eg. 259, ff. 149-240.

with tyranny. Then he accused the Ministry of amending the boundary in order to draw a 'line of circumvallation about our colonies, and establish a siege of arbitrary power'.[1] North expressed a desire to meet the wishes of the Americans but did not think it could be done now.[2] However, four days later, when the Bill was reported, he agreed to settle the boundary question there and then. Burke, William Baker, Richard Jackson and Sir Charles Whitworth went upstairs to discuss it and left the House doing nothing for half an hour; then 'at 5 o'clock Mr. Burke returned with the amendments'.[3] According to these, certain territories originally included in Quebec were now attached to upstate New York and Pennsylvania.[4] Furthermore, the last sentence of the amended clause stipulated that 'nothing herein contained, relative to the boundary of the province of Quebec, shall in anywise affect the boundaries of any other colony'.[5] Burke had done a good afternoon's work for his American employers, and he certainly could not complain that the Government had been uncooperative.

The House continued in Committee on the various clauses of the Bill on 7 and 8 June.[6] There was a very small attendance, sometimes scarcely a quorum.[7] North tried to hurry the business through, while Burke complained of 'this headlong mode of proceeding'.[8] The Bill came up for its third reading on 13 June. There was very little debate, and when the question

[1] Cavendish Diary, BM. Eg. 260, ff. 160-74, especially 160-1.
[2] *Ibid.*, ff. 174-5. William Burke described the Premier's performance that day : 'North is never at ease, when he is a little pushed, and he seems now vexed and ill at ease'. To Charles O'Hara, 6 June 1774. Transcript at Sheffield Central Library from the O'Hara MSS.
[3] Cavendish Diary, BM. Eg. 262, ff. 133-4.
[4] A. L. Burt, *The United States, Great Britain* . . . p. 21.
[5] *Debates of the House of Commons*, ed., J. Wright, p. 254.
[6] Cavendish Diary, BM. Eg. 259, ff. 240-99 ; BM. Eg. 262, ff. 1-133. On 7 June the House divided 91-31 on the clause to revoke the 1763 Proclamation, and 75-31 for Catholic toleration in Quebec. North to King, 7 June 1774. Fortescue, *op. cit.*, iii, 1473.
[7] On 8 June there were forty members present at the opening of the debates and forty-five towards the close. Cavendish Diary, BM. Eg. 262, ff. 58, 127.
[8] Despite North's impatience, he was happy to adjourn the House on 9 June to attend a grand *fête-champêtre* given in Surrey on the occasion of Lord Stanley's approaching marriage to Lady Betty Hamilton. *Debates of the House of Commons*, ed. J. Wright, pp. 233-7.

was put that the Bill pass, it was approved by 56-20.[1] It was then returned to the Lords, where a few more minor amendments were made. On 16 June Chatham came to the House and made a final attack on the despotism and the popery which he saw in the Bill. He warned that it would be a last straw for the Americans, but the Bill was passed that day.[2]

The reception of the Quebec Bill had been very noisy. Newspapers were full of protests,[3] and there were riots when the King went to give his assent to the Act and to prorogue Parliament on 22 June.[4] In the Commons the Opposition divided eight times. One interested commentator wrote :

> We have had as hard fighting and many more battles to establish government for Canada, as there were to conquer it. You would be astonished at the opposition made to the bill; ten nights the House of Commons was kept till one o'clock in the morning successively. Every inch of the ground was argued and every word disputed.[5]

But when it is looked at more closely the Opposition clearly did not amount to much. The riots were connected with Wilkes and City politics, and the Methodists were the only religious group to object to the Bill.[6] In Parliament the lateness of the season took its toll. The highest Opposition vote was 46 on 31 May; after that it slumped to 20 on the final reading. The Opposition took their stand on English laws and liberties, and the Protestant religion.[7] They accused the Government of

---

[1] Cavendish Diary, BM. Eg. 262, f. 239. North to King, 13 June 1774. Fortescue, *op. cit.*, iii, 1478. The final text of the Act is printed in A. Shortt and A. G. Doughty, eds., *op. cit.*, i, 570-76.

[2] R. Coupland, *op. cit.*, pp. 96-105.

[3] *Jackson's Oxford Journal*, 25 June 1774, said 'the Quebec Act is the only Statute which has been passed these 200 years to establish Popery and arbitrary power in the British Dominions'.

[4] *Walpole Last Journals*, i, 358-9.

[5] Sir Thomas Mills to Haldimand, 14 June 1774. Quoted in V. Coffin, *The Province of Quebec and the Early American Revolution*, p. 395. Mills was Receiver-General of Quebec. He was guilty of some exaggeration : the House debated the Bill on nine (unsuccessive) days, and not always till one in the morning.

[6] *Walpole Last Journals*, i, 356. See also *Jackson's Oxford Journal*, 25 June 1775.

[7] There were differences among the Opposition : Burke was in favour of Catholic toleration, but Barré showed himself a strong anti-papist in this

expanding the prerogative and encircling the Americans with a French despotism. But they were not really attacking the details of the Bill so much as the motives of those who drafted it. They were thinking more about America than Canada. They read it in the context of the other coercive measures. Yet it was quite different from those — even though it played a role in the slide towards revolution — and its boundary clause was made more attractive to the Government by the behaviour of the old colonists. It was meant to solve the problems of the Indian reservations and of Quebec. Had the Parliamentary Opposition been in power, and dealing with these problems, it seems probable that they would have adopted a similar approach. The Government was sensible not to apply the familiar Irish formula of racial ascendancy and religious intolerance.[1] Burke above all should have realised this.[2] The task of the imperial Government was to reconcile the Canadians to their new rulers. The effect on the Americans was unfortunate, and the Government was partly responsible for this, because had it dealt with Quebec earlier the Bill would not have become tangled with the punitive legislation. Yet there was no point in delaying further just because of the Boston crisis.[3] As one historian has argued, 'without the Quebec Act they [North and his colleagues] would still have lost the thirteen colonies. With it Canada was at least saved'.[4]

session. The Rockinghams had accepted many of the principles which governed the 1774 Act when they considered the Quebec problem in 1765–1766. See above, pp. 109-10.

[1] Wedderburn wrote to Burke 'The present Bill tho' it does not come up to my wishes yet with a few alterations would I think be a great benefit to the Canadians, and I trust to your real public spirit that you will rather consider how it is to be corrected than how it is to be opposed.' Wedderburn to Burke, ?10 June 1774. W.W.M. Bk.

[2] On Burke's antipathy to the English and Protestant ascendancy in Ireland see T. H. D. Mahoney, *Edmund Burke and Ireland*, pp. 189-90.

[3] Dartmouth had, however, told Crahamé that such a delay might occur for this reason. 6 April 1774. PRO. CO. 42/33, f. 29.

[4] R. Coupland, *op. cit.*, p. 122.

CHAPTER VI

THE FRIENDS OF AMERICA

The Opposition to the Coercive Policies in the House of Commons

IN retrospect Lord North's Ministry, its Parliamentary majority, and the mass of British opinion, appear to have been often misguided in the American policies which they prosecuted and supported between 1773 and 1775. Consequently considerable interest attaches to the minority who opposed these measures, and who in the end profited politically from their failure. It is apparent from the debates reported above that this minority did not function as predictably as does Her Majesty's Opposition in the twentieth century. It is therefore worth examining more closely the composition of the Opposition to Lord North, its political morale during the coercive debates, the attitudes it normally brought to the American problem, and, particularly, its reactions to the Government's measures in 1774.

The main Opposition groups — the Rockingham confederation and the supporters of the Earl of Chatham — were disillusioned and disunited during the early 'seventies.[1] But even had they been reunited and revivified by the crises which followed the Boston Tea Party they would have found it difficult on their own to make an impression on the Ministry's coercive policies; for at the beginning of 1774 they constituted only a small proportion — certainly not much more than one-tenth — of the House of Commons. And even if supported by sympathetic independents, they would still be far from a majority.

It is impossible to set out with finality the membership of the Rockingham squadron. It was not a party in any modern sense, and to establish the degree and nature of attachment to it of various so-called supporters is extremely difficult. There is

[1] See above, Chapter I, pp. 16-17.

127

also particular difficulty in distinguishing between Members who were apparently on the fringe of the squadron and those independents who frequently voted with it. Fortunately, there is no need to delay over these fine distinctions. All that is required here is a rough estimate of the squadron's numbers in order to assess the potential voting strength of the Opposition in the House of Commons when it was considering the Government's measures to coerce the Americans.

The core of the Rockingham party — those attached to the Marquis himself — probably totalled something over twenty members at the time of the coercive debates. By 1774, Rockingham had been in the political wilderness for eight years. He had shed his fair-weather followers, and most of his remaining personal supporters had been attached to him at least since 1767. They were drawn mainly from a coalition of Yorkshire families. But a few, such as William Baker, George Dempster or Robert Gregory, were attracted by personal friendship or political conviction. Some depended on Lord Rockingham's influence for their Parliamentary seats ; others were well able to run their own electoral affairs. In addition to this central body of Rockingham's personal followers, there were also several small groups of Members who followed particular politicians — the Duke of Richmond, the Duke of Portland, and the Cavendish and Fox families — and yet usually accepted the general or nominal leadership of the Marquis. These political associates numbered about another dozen in the Commons : which means that altogether the Rockingham confederation certainly totalled less than fifty, and probably less than forty, in the spring of 1774.[1]

Even with so few members, the Rockingham squadron was, by eighteenth-century standards, a connexion of considerable potential strength if it were given a controversial issue and if its members could be brought to act together. But the immediate prospect of its overthrowing the Ministry in 1774 was remote, for the confederation was of the loosest kind and it lacked dynamic leadership. Charles Watson-Wentworth, second Mar-

---

[1] For a list of Members who were connected with Rockingham see the Appendix, pp.291-2.

quis of Rockingham, had no striking abilities as a politician. He was ambitious, but was timorous and a poor speaker in Parliament. According to a modern historian of the period, 'Rockingham has shone in history with the reflected light of other men: the friend of Savile, the patron of Burke, the ally of Fox. . . . He raised his prejudices to the dignity of principles. . . . Defeat in America, not Rockingham's leadership, brought his party back into power in 1782. Rockingham triumphed only when other men failed.'[1] His contemporary, Horace Walpole, wrote harshly of 'a weak, childish and ignorant man, by no means fit for the head of an Administration'.[2] Yet one virtue which Rockingham possessed was his ability to conciliate. The members of the squadron often disliked, distrusted or disagreed with one another; but they coincided in their affection for this kind, loyal and otherwise mediocre man. Burke wrote in 1775: 'We fall into confusion the moment you turn your back; and though you have the happiness of many friends of very great ability and industry, and of unshakeable fidelity to the cause, nobody but yourself has the means of rightly managing the different characters and reconciling the different interests that make up the corps of opposition'.[3]

The other segment of the organised political Opposition was the Chatham-Shelburne group. Chatham despised 'party', and consequently his connexions were bound to be small in number. He had at one time or another attracted rebels, patriots, City radicals and old-style Tories because he appeared to stand against party, the Government and the oligarchic Whigs. But he never bothered to organise them into a political squadron, and after 1767 his withdrawal from London to play the oracle at Hayes or at Burton Pynsent was a disadvantage to them as a Parliamentary group.

When he left office in 1768 Chatham was still supported by various individuals in the Commons. But after 1771 he did not

---

[1] J. Brooke, *The Chatham Administration, 1766–8*, pp. 25-6.
[2] *Memoirs of the Reign of George III, by Horace Walpole*, ed. G. F. Russell Barker, ii, 222.
[3] Burke to Rockingham, 7, 10 January 1775. W.W.M. Bk., *CEB*, iii, 408. Also see *ibid.*, ii, xi-xiv, for Miss Sutherland's estimate of Burke's own role in the Rockingham squadron.

cultivate this support, and by the beginning of 1774, out of his old followers only Sir George Yonge, Sir Piercy Brett, Robert Pratt (Camden's nephew) and Thomas Calcraft were still in Parliament and they had no direct connexion with the Earl.[1] Yonge alone returned after the elections in the autumn of that year. Consequently Chatham's political power in the House of Commons was based chiefly on the patronage of his lieutenant, Shelburne, who brought in Isaac Barré, John Dunning and his own brother Thomas Fitzmaurice. Shelburne also received frequent political support from John Aubrey, who was elected on Lord Abingdon's interest, and from James Townsend, who was electorally independent, and can be termed a City radical, but whose political sentiments grew increasingly closer to those of Shelburne.[2] The three members of the Rutland Group might also be considered as sympathetic towards Chatham.[3] The sum of Chatham's and Shelburne's supporters in the Commons during the coercive debates was therefore at most a dozen, and no more than half of these were given any sort of active leadership. Although their debating strength often belied their numbers, the Chathamites added little to the voting potential of the Opposition to Lord North.

The numbers of the potential Opposition can be increased, probably more than doubled, if to the supporters of Rockingham and Chatham are added all those Members who were personally independent but who usually inclined to support Opposition. There were at least sixty of these in Parliament in 1773–1774.[4] They ranged from the county magnates like Thomas Skipwith, Richard Hippesley Coxe and Ambrose Goddard to the radical businessmen returned from the metropolitan constituencies, such as John Sawbridge, Richard Oliver, Frederick Bull and Sir Joseph Mawbey. It is almost impossible to distinguish some of them — for instance, Joseph Bullock, Paul

---

[1] In 1773–4 they were M.P.s for Honiton, Queenborough, Horsham and Poole respectively. Of Chatham's other followers, George Cooke had died in 1768, William Beckford in 1770 and John Calcraft in 1772. Chatham's relative James Grenville left Parliament in 1770. See J. Brooke, *op. cit.*, pp. 249-55.

[2] M.P.s for Chipping Wycombe, Calne, also Calne, Wallingford and West Looe.

[3] See Appendix I, p. 292.   [4] See Appendix I, pp. 292-3.

Feilde, Sir John Griffin and Sir James Pennyman — from the fringe members of the Rockingham confederation. Any independent might at one time or another vote with the Opposition; it is the distinction of these sixty or so Members that personal and political considerations often determined them to do so. However, during the American debates in 1774 few of them opposed the Ministry's measures.

The Opposition was numerically in a poor position to launch an offensive when the spring session of the 1774 Parliament opened. Its subsequent performance showed that its morale — and particularly the morale of the Rockingham squadron — was also low. Rockingham did write to Burke on 8 January that he thought 'there were matters enough to make the ensuing session of Parliament, not an idle one, I do believe there are *points* which *we* might take up to advantage and be of some service in'.[1] But he did not specify the points. He felt sick and was busy and could not see himself leaving Yorkshire for London before late January. In fact he did not arrive there until 4 February, more than a fortnight after the Boston news arrived. Lord John Cavendish sent a mild reproof to his leader: 'as to you I could have wished you had found it convenient to have been in town rather earlier; not that I know any good that you could have done, but I suspect some fools have been surprised at your absence'.[2] Cavendish made no bones about the condition in which Rockingham would find his flock: 'it is a comical state that we are in, but though I think our inaction much better than a frivolous bustle, yet I think we make a very silly figure'. Nine days later, after the party had suffered final defeat at India House over the implementation of the Regulating Act of 1773, he repeated that 'we are in that sort of state that I see nothing to be wished for but an honourable retreat'.[3] Richmond had already conveyed this impression to Rockingham, and possibly thereby neutralised his own appeals for his leader's immediate attendance in London. He reported that 'our friends here have agreed to be very silent in Parliament till some matter of

---

[1] Rockingham to Burke, 8 January 1774. W.W.M. Bk., *CEB*, ii, 511.
[2] Cavendish to Rockingham, 20 January 1774. W.W.M. R1-1478.
[3] Cavendish to Rockingham, 29 January 1774. W.W.M. R1-1479.

great consequence calls them forth which seems to be very wise'.[1]

The matter of great consequence called a few days later when the news arrived of the Boston Tea Party. 'The American business', wrote Cavendish to Rockingham, 'at present engrosses the whole talk of the town'.[2] But what would be the Opposition's reaction ? What was its American policy ? The attitude of the Rockinghams to the American problem in the 1770's was founded upon the twin pillars of the Declaratory Act and the repeal of the Stamp Act : the one established their support for the absolute supremacy of the British Parliament over the Colonies, the other pointed out the inexpediency of exercising that supremacy.[3] This policy contained the subtle idea of a sleeping sovereignty, a supremacy that is tacitly accepted without being tested and demonstrated. But in its political origins the idea cast no great credit on the Rockinghams, for they had executed the measures of 1766 mainly out of expediency, were sometimes false to them in the years immediately after, and only subsequently elevated them to the level of consistent principles.[4] When they later looked back to that time and claimed that they had always held a consistent American policy, they were guilty of some misrepresentation. But this does not mean that they were charlatans when they took up the American cause in the 'seventies. They had certainly never been coercionists : [5] in 1765 they offered the

[1] Richmond to Rockingham, 15 January 1774. W.W.M. R1-1476.
[2] 29 January 1774. W.W.M. R1-1479.
[3] See especially G. H. Guttridge, *English Whiggism and the American Revolution*, pp. 65-9.
[4] Mr. Brooke has argued that the Marquis of Rockingham did not oppose the American measures *per se* in the 'sixties, but only because they were supported by George Grenville. He shows that Rockingham intended to join in Administration with the Bedfords, who had strong coercionist views ; that he and his followers said nothing when Charles Townshend announced his intention to tax the Americans in January 1767, and, furthermore, that they always intended to have Townshend in high office in any Administration of theirs ; that the Rockinghams voted for the reduction of the land tax in February 1767, which made American taxes nearly inevitable ; and he concludes, that 'the pro-Americanism of the Rockinghams was rather accidental than conscious, a shibboleth in British party politics rather than a serious factor in imperial affairs'. *Op. cit.*, pp. 61-2, 96-8, 105-10, 206-8, and especially p. 96.
[5] Sir Lewis Namier, however, claimed that the Rockinghams' ideas 'were no less hierarchical and authoritarian than those of George III and Lord North'. *England in the Age of the American Revolution*, p. 39.

administration of American affairs at the Board of Trade to Lord Shelburne, and when he refused they gave it to another reputed moderate, Lord Dartmouth.[1] During their long opposition these 'liberal' tendencies became predominant and were reinforced by a desire, which they shared with the colonists, to return to the golden age before the accession of the present interfering Monarch; an age when the colonists contentedly ran their own affairs and the Whig oligarchy ruled England. The Rockinghams saw the Americans suffering, like themselves, from the oppressive authority of the royal prerogative as lately exercised. They could, therefore, with genuine conviction take up the cause of the discontented Americans. But what they would not do was support any diminution in British sovereignty.[2] Here the Rockinghams differed from Chatham. He believed that the supremacy of Parliament was constitutionally limited — because it did not have the right to impose internal taxation or to maintain a standing army in the Colonies against their will. Consequently the Declaratory Act was always anathema to him.[3] Where Chatham and the Rockinghams agreed, at least in the mid-seventies, was in the impossibility of admitting American independence. Richard Champion put their position to his transatlantic grain supplier in November 1775:

> The Whigs in England are the only body which the Whigs in America have to trust to, if they do not mean independence; for if they have any such views, the Whigs in England must equally be her enemies with the Tories who are now in power. Though they love the liberty of America upon Principle, because they would have all men possess liberty as well as themselves, yet they have a strong predilection, even a stronger to the interest of their own country than the Tories,

[1] C. W. Alvord, 'The British Ministry and the Treaty of Fort Stanwix', *Proceedings of the State Historical Society of Wisconsin*, 1908, pp. 171-2. The American Colonies were then under the political direction of the Southern Secretary, at this time General H. S. Conway.

[2] The Rockinghams began to divide on this point in 1777, when Richmond and Abingdon both came out for the repeal of the Declaratory Act. See Richmond to Rockingham, 2 November 1777. W.W.M. R1-1739.

[3] G. H. Guttridge, *English Whiggism and the American Revolution*, pp. 77-8. See also K. Hotblack, *Chatham's Colonial Policy*, pp. 184-5.

and never will abandon or give it up. They are willing to make concessions . . . and trust for a grateful return to the duty and affection of America . . . but must require that America on her side should abandon, or at least not insist on some claims that tend to weaken or rather take away the rest of the general, superintending legislative authority.[1]

Given these beliefs it is easy to understand the dilemma of the Opposition after hearing the news of the Tea Party. At first they naturally joined in condemning the riots. Chatham described the colonial behaviour as 'criminal' and said they 'violate the most indispensible ties of civil society'.[2] Lord John Cavendish stated bluntly that 'the Bostonians' behaviour is indefensible'.[3] He thought that the Rockinghams should not participate in the coming debate on Buckinghamshire's motion for the American papers. There was only one circumstance in which Cavendish believed they should take up active opposition. 'It is most probable', he wrote, 'that the repeal of the Stamp Act will be arraigned, in the course of the proceedings, in which case we must defend ourselves.'

Richmond, Fitzwilliam and Dowdeswell all — according to Burke — agreed with Cavendish. Burke told Rockingham they felt they ought

> not to countenance the interested petulance of those paltry discontented people, who, without embracing your principles, or giving you any sort of support, think to make use of your weight to give consequence to every occasional spirit of opposition they think proper to make, in order to put the Ministry in mind, that they are to be bought by private contract, as unconnected individuals. When you mean opposition, you are able to take it up on your own grounds, and at your own time.[4]

---

[1] Champion to American friends [probably Messrs. Willing, Morris & Co.], November 1775. *Letters of Richard Champion*, ed. G. H. Guttridge, pp. 63-4.

[2] Chatham to Shelburne, 20 March 1774. *Chatham Correspondence*, iv, 336.

[3] Cavendish to Rockingham, 21 January 1774. W.W.M. R1-1479.

[4] Burke to Rockingham, 2 February 1774. W.W.M. Bk., *CEB*, ii, 523-4. This reads much like many other letters by Burke, stating his

Rockingham's own reaction was consistent with the traditional colonial principles of his squadron. 'The conduct of the Americans can not be justified', he said, 'but the folly and impolicy of the provocation deserves the fullest arraignments, and notwithstanding all that has passed, I can never give my assent to proceeding to actual force against the Colonies.'[1]

In January and February 1774 the Opposition groups did not know whether the Ministry would take any action in response to the Boston riots. Nor, if the Ministry acted, did they know whether it would work through Parliament or depend solely upon royal prerogative.[2] They were not left in any more doubt after the Parliamentary Addresses of 7 March. Then the fragile unity they had shown in condemning the riots was broken, and the Government's subsequent proposals for America split them asunder. Edmund Burke spoke out against coercion from the beginning; he carried with him George Byng and, more cautiously, William Dowdeswell. But the other followers of Rockingham and Chatham clearly approved of the Boston Port Bill as a necessary punishment for the rioters.[3] The next two measures, the Massachusetts Regulating Bill and the Justice Bill, upset more of the Rockinghams; at that stage a tardy clarion call from the gouty Earl at Burton Pynsent also brought the Chatham group into the fray. But there was still little cohesion among them. The Parliamentary Opposition was foundering on the complexity of its own American principles and policies; those Members who placed most emphasis on securing colonial recognition of English sovereignty were much slower to swing into Opposition than those who emphasised the need to conciliate the colonists and were averse to any form of military coercion.

In summary, the Opposition to the American measures of Lord North's Ministry was small in potential numbers. Its

general theory of party and trying to fit the reluctant Rockinghams into it. See Burke to Rockingham, 5 January 1775. W.W.M. Bk., *CEB*, iii, 87-90, and Burke to Rockingham, 6 January 1777. W.W.M. R1-1701, *CEB*, iii, 308-15.

[1] Rockingham to Burke, 30 January 1774. W.W.M. Bk., *CEB*, ii, 516.

[2] Dempster to Fergusson, 31 January 1774. *Letters of George Dempster to Sir Adam Fergusson, 1756–1813*, ed. J. Fergusson, p. 81.

[3] For example, Lord John Cavendish and Isaac Barré.

morale had for a long time been low and its fortunes on the ebb. The heart of this Opposition was the Rockingham confederation, itself a loose alliance of independent and often conflicting personalities. Its general policy towards America was based upon a delicate and, in the circumstances of 1774, seemingly untenable compromise between supporting English supremacy and advocating conciliation towards the colonists. The Chatham group was as strongly opposed to the Rockingham Declaratory Act as it was to the Ministry's coercive measures, and was headed by a sick old man who gave little or no active leadership. It is therefore not surprising that during the Parliamentary debates on the American measures in the spring of 1774 the members of the Opposition are seen to find difficulty in working with one another, or to any purpose, or, especially, with any effect.

To illustrate convincingly the ineffectiveness of the Opposition at this time it would be extremely helpful to analyse the divisions on the coercive measures, thereby showing who did and did not vote against the Government. Unfortunately only one minority list has been located — that for the division on the third reading of the Impartial Administration of Justice Bill on Friday, 6 May.[1] This vote came at the end of a week during which the Parliamentary Opposition made its greatest effort of the session. On Monday 2 May, it polled its highest vote, sixty-four against the Massachusetts Bay Regulating Act — although this was still only one-ninth of the membership of the Commons. By Friday the number in attendance had dropped and the minority fell to twenty-four; even so, the list is an interesting and useful piece of evidence.

Of the twenty-four dissenters on 6 May, and out of an aggregate division of 151, only four were regular supporters of the Rockingham squadron: Nathaniel Cholmley, George Dempster, Frederick Montagu and Samuel Salt.[2] Dempster

---

[1] It was published in the *St. James's Chronicle* on 9 May 1774 and may not be completely accurate, though it can be treated as broadly reliable.

[2] M.P.s for Boroughbridge, Perth Burghs, Higham Ferrars and Liskeard respectively in 1774. The exact degree of Salt's attachment is not clear, but he voted regularly with the Rockinghams after 1771. On these and all other Members of Parliament at this time the definitive authority is *The*

and Montagu alone of these could be said to be of consequence among Opposition politicians. The other main Opposition group, led by Chatham and Shelburne, provided two voters in the minority, Isaac Barré and Sir George Yonge.[1] To these half-dozen might be added Stephen Fox and George Manners Sutton, who gave frequent support to the Opposition politicians.[2] Three others of the minority were what have been termed 'City radicals'. Frederick Bull was Lord Mayor of London at this time ; he had been elected to one of the City seats in 1773 and voted consistently with Opposition until 1783. James Townsend (West Looe) was an experienced City of London politician, an alderman, a former Lord Mayor, and a radical leader of talent and integrity. He had supported the cause of John Wilkes, but he disliked Wilkes and gave the casting vote which allowed Bull to defeat Wilkes for the Mayoralty in November 1773. His Parliamentary position, in sentiment if not explicitly in party tie, was with Shelburne. They were old friends, and when Dunning was elevated to the Peerage in 1782, Shelburne gave Dunning's seat at Calne to Townsend, who held it till his death in 1787.[3] The third City member was Richard Oliver, who was a close friend of Townsend's, also acted often with Shelburne, and voted with Opposition while holding a seat for the City between 1770–80.[4] Thus, in all, eleven Members from the various political and radical groups registered dissenting votes on 6 May.

Twelve of the remaining minority voters can be described as more or less independent : which meant they were free of ties

History of Parliament: The House of Commons, 1754–1790, by Sir Lewis Namier and John Brooke.

[1] See above p. 130. Barré, born, like Burke, of a Dublin family, had served in America as a Lieutenant-Colonel and was very knowledgeable on American affairs. On 14 March 1774 he had supported the Boston Port Bill. See above p. 79.

[2] Sutton (M.P. for Grantham 1754–80, and for Newark 1780–83) was in the Rutland group. Rutland was probably closest to Chatham and Shelburne and later took office in Shelburne's Ministry. Fox, M.P. for Salisbury since 1768, died later in 1774.

[3] L. S. Sutherland, *The City of London and the Opposition to Government, 1768–1774*, The Creighton Lecture, 1958, pp. 20, 21. *Notes and Queries*, 11 series, v, 2–4. *Gentlemen's Magazine*, 1787, p. 640. E. Fitzmaurice, *Life of William, Earl of Shelburne*, ii, 287–92.

[4] On the City politicians see below pp. 146–56.

of patronage or office, or patent hopes of these.[1] It is worth looking a moment at these, for out of such material the Rockinghams must hope to fashion the Government's downfall in the House. 'There were many eccentric men who would not belong to a party', Chatham remarked to Richmond in 1771, 'they were the real strength of opposition.' [2]

Six of these twelve independents might be loosely grouped together because they seem to have disapproved specifically of the American measures. William Pulteney was one of the greatest land owners and richest men in England. His independence in politics was never questioned, and John Sinclair wrote of him : 'I believe that he never gave a vote in parliament without a thorough conviction that it was right'.[3] He was deeply concerned with American affairs, and wrote one of the best treatises to come out of the ferment of the Revolution.[4] In December 1777 he offered to go to Paris to negotiate with the Americans, and he was sent in March 1778 ; in March 1782 he voted with the Administration so as not to embarrass them should peace negotiations with the Americans begin.[5] Alongside him may be placed his brother George Johnstone, though he was of much inferior quality.[6] He was a strange and often violent man, who had once been appointed Governor of Pensacola and West Florida, and posed as an expert on American affairs. He was appointed to the Peace Commission in 1778, but served only to sabotage it by apparently treating behind the Commission's back. From the Wilkes affair until 1778 he had often voted with Opposition, but afterwards he took a naval command and supported the Ministry in the Commons.[6] Rose Fuller was a Jamaican, and as such was particularly concerned

---

[1] The City radicals were also independent in many ways, as were the Rutland group, but both through their committed opposition and their tendency to work in groups they can be separated from the individual and uncommitted independents described here.

[2] Richmond to Rockingham, 12 February 1771. Quoted in J. Brooke, *op. cit.*, p. 239.

[3] M.P. for Cromartyshire 1768–74, and for Shrewsbury 1775–1805. See I. R. Christie, *op. cit.*, pp. 22, 179, and especially p. 228.

[4] W. Pulteney, *Thoughts on the Present State of Affairs with America and the Means of Conciliation*, London, 1778.   [5] I. R. Christie, *op. cit.*, p. 349.

[6] M.P. for Cockermouth 1768–74, for Appleby 1774–80, and for Lostwithiel 1780–84.

for the state of trade — and consequently of imperial relations—
between England, America and the West Indies.[1] He had
opposed the Stamp Act in 1765, and had taken a leading part
among the merchants and politicians who worked for its repeal
in 1766. In 1774 he proposed to repeal the Tea Duty. On 25
February 1774 North described him to the King as a 'Friend',
and Burke called him 'a ministerial man' even on 20 May, after
he had voted against the Government on the 6th. But on
colonial matters he could not support the Government in a
policy which threatened to disrupt the Empire and cut the West
Indies off from their source of food and raw materials in the
mainland Colonies.[2] The three other independents in this
group were much lesser political figures. Sir Thomas Frankland was an admiral who had seen a considerable amount of
service in North America and the West Indies; he did not
usually take a very active part in Parliamentary affairs, but
occasionally voted with Opposition on American matters down
to 1780. Richard Fuller and Joseph Martin were successful
City bankers who had undoubtedly been exposed to radical
City opinions; Martin often supported the Opposition, especially on American questions.[3]

Four of the independents were country gentry: Richard
Wilbraham Bootle,[4] John Parker,[5] Thomas Skipwith[6] and
Thomas Whitmore.[7] Parker and Skipwith were both county
Members who had voted with Opposition for some time: the
former at least since 1768, and the latter since coming into
Parliament in 1769. Bootle had been a Member for twenty-
three years in what Sir Lewis Namier called 'a quasi-feudal'
constituency: which did not mean that it was in any way
corrupt, but that good will and the local family tradition secured

---

[1] M.P. for Rye, 1768–77.
[2] See 'House of Commons, Division List of 25 February 1774'. J. W.
Fortescue, ed., *The Correspondence of King George III, 1760–1783*, iii,
1404. Sir Lewis Namier, *England in the Age of the American Revolution*, pp.
237-40.
[3] M.P.s for Thirsk, Stockbridge and Gatton respectively in 1774.
Richard Fuller was no relation of Rose Fuller.
[4] M.P. for Chester 1761–90.
[5] M.P. for Bodmin 1761–62 and for Devon 1762–84.
[6] M.P. for Warwickshire 1769–80 and for Steyning 1780–84.
[7] M.P. for Bridgnorth 1771–95.

the seat for Bootle, assured him considerable independence —
at least from Ministerial influences — and gave it some of the
aspects of a county seat. He had a touch and colouring of
Opposition temperament — Namier described him as being a
'Tory' in 1761 — though this would never fall into a party
mould.[1] He was also a lawyer, and so might have objected to
the technicalities of the Justice Bill, particularly with reference
to the appeal for murder in the Colonies. Whitmore was of a
similar electoral background, being more involved in politics
in Shropshire than in London. Bridgnorth gave him the same
quasi-feudal independence, and he used it generally to support
Opposition in the eleven years between his coming into Parliament and the end of the American war. There were two other
independents in the minority. Crisp Molineux was a country
gentleman with radical leanings who voted regularly against the
Government; he was more consistent in his opposition than
the Members in the first of the above two groups of independents, perhaps more involved in Westminster politics than
those in the second.[2] John Damer was an eccentric member of
the Milton family and had voted with the Opposition during the
whole Parliament.[3]

The final dissenter of the twenty-four was John Skynner,
who was normally a solid supporter of the Administration.
There is no evidence that he opposed the political direction of
the Ministry's American measures, but he apparently demurred
on a technical point of the law.[4] He was a prominent lawyer,
having been made a King's Counsel and Attorney-General of
the Duchy of Lancaster in 1771. The Ministry clearly did not
hold this aberration on 6 May against him, for he was knighted
and made a Baron of the Exchequer in 1777. He had a special
knowledge and legal interest in this particular issue; Ministers
would respect this, and the Opposition could draw little comfort
from his vote.

---

[1] Sir Lewis Namier, *Structure of Politics*, pp. 84, 143. Also *Personalities and Powers*, pp. 60-1. I. R. Christie, *op. cit.*, p. 176.
[2] M.P. for Castle Rising 1771–74, and for Kings Lynn 1774–90.
[3] M.P. for Dorchester 1762–80.
[4] M.P. for New Woodstock 1771–77. The *DNB* states that 'he protested against the introduction of appeal for murder into America'.

The minority on 6 May has been investigated at some length in order to identify the Members voting against the Ministry on this occasion, to assess their affiliations, if any, and, if possible, to discover why they voted in that way. There are dangers in generalising from any one division list, and clearly this division on the Impartial Justice Bill was in itself far from ideal. The main Opposition effort came at the beginning of the week; by Friday many of their leaders were exhausted, their followings had dispersed into the country for the week-end, and less than one-third of the House was in attendance. Yet this list does support the conclusion, which is in accordance with evidence provided elsewhere in this study, that the leaders of the political groups in Opposition, and especially the Rockinghams, found it difficult to convince and to muster their regular supporters to vote against the Government's American policies. Even including the radicals, they were a minority of a small minority on 6 May. Compared to these professional Opposition politicians, a relatively high proportion of the minority list were independents. But many of these had a long record of individual opposition to the Administration. There was little sign of discontent among the normally uncommitted independents. In any case, the number of independent Members who were prepared to oppose the Government in May 1774 was still only a very small fraction of the total independent vote in the Commons, and a small minority even among those independents who usually sided with the Opposition. This impression of a weak Opposition, drawn from the vote on 6 May, can be further substantiated from the other minority divisions on American affairs during this session of Parliament. These were: forty for Bollan's petition on 25 March; forty-nine for Rose Fuller's motion to repeal the Tea Duty on 19 April; thirty-two for Bollan's petition on 28 April; sixty-four against the Regulating Bill on 2–3 May; and on the Quebec Bill the Opposition divided eight times with votes varying from twenty to forty-six. The Opposition did not even try to divide the Commons against the Boston Port Bill and the Quartering Bill. While this situation continued, Lord North's Ministry was unlikely to be seriously troubled in its efforts to maintain a Parliamentary majority for its American policies.

The Opposition to the American Policies in the House of Lords

In the House of Lords, as in the Commons, the opposition to the coercive measures was directed chiefly against the Massachusetts Bay Regulating Bill and the Impartial Administration of Justice Bill. Votes of twenty and of twelve were registered against the third readings on 11 May and 18 May respectively. The composition of these minority votes is discussed in Appendix II at the end of the book. Two main impressions emerge from these divisions : firstly that the Government's majority in the Lords, at this time at least, was impregnable, and, secondly, that the regular Opposition in the Upper House could hope for little support outside the central nucleus of Rockingham, Richmond, Portland, occasionally Chatham, and their immediate friends and relations. It seems unlikely that any Peer was persuaded to go into the Opposition lobby against his normal habit ; among the aristocracy there was apparently no independent equivalent of William Pulteney or John Skynner.[1] The Bishops were also strongly behind the Government. Only Shipley of St. Asaph, sometimes supported by Hinchcliffe of Peterborough, voiced opposition in 1774, whereas in 1767 there had been as many as seven Bishops in the minority.

More interesting than the votes recorded are the Protests which were placed in the *Lords Journals* after the two divisions on 11 and 18 May, for they attempt to spell out the official Rockingham position on the American question. The squadron had been caught unawares by the Tea Party and had met the Boston Port Bill with a confused and disunited front. During March, and later, as was seen in the discussion of the Commons debates, the Rockinghams were clearly still a divided force.

[1] A list of some fifty Peers and Bishops considered to be usually in sympathy with the Opposition is published in Debrett's *History, Debates and Proceedings of both Houses of Parliament*, vii, 18. It may not be completely accurate or comprehensive — for instance it does not include Chatham. It might be noted here that because of his American sympathies the Earl of Stair was omitted in November 1774 from the Government's list of sixteen recommended Scottish Peers to sit in the House of Lords. He was not re-elected. *DNB.*

Even in May they could not muster anywhere near a full complement of loyal troops to make a last stand against the policy of coercion. But at least by then the inner core of the party had had time and occasion to mull over their attitudes to the American situation. In so far as they agreed to oppose the Act for the Better Regulation of the Government of Massachusetts Bay, their opinions, both with specific reference to that Act, and more generally towards the American Colonies as a whole, were contained in the seven points of the first Protest.

The protesting Peers first recorded particular criticisms of the procedure by which the Bill was rushed through the Lords. It was pointed out that the House had not been asked to discuss the original Charter, nor the ways in which it was deficient; and it was asserted that certain constitutional rights were being taken away from the people of Massachusetts without proving their guilt, indeed without even giving them an opportunity to present their defence. Proceeding to the provisions of the Act, they protested that the clause placing the power to appoint all members of the Council in the hands of the Governor invested him, and, indirectly, the Ministers of the Crown, with too much power; that it could only destroy the spirit of the colonial Assemblies. They also objected to the clause making the officers of the judiciary responsible only to the Governor: again claiming that this inflated the power of the executive in a manner contrary to the nature of the British Constitution. 'We see in this bill', they went on, with more than a little hindsight, 'the same scheme of strengthening the authority of the officers and Ministers of State, at the expense of the rights and liberties of the subject, which was indicated by the inauspicious Act for shutting up the port of Boston.' They also felt that if the British troops could not restore order then certainly a change of Charter would make little difference. The final paragraph of the Protest was a restatement of the Rockingham American policy, as proclaimed by the Declaratory Act and the Repeal of the Stamp Act, and as vindicated by recent events. The Lords claimed that the change in the charter was intended to support a scheme for taxing the colonies in a manner new and unsuitable to their situation and circumstances. Parliament has asserted the authority of the legislature of this Kingdom supreme and unlimited over all the members of the British Empire. But the legal extent of this authority furnishes no argument in favour of an unwarrantable use of it.

Here was the appeal to the Declaratory Act as the premise of imperial policy, together with the injunction to use caution in asserting it — which meant in fact that any explicit exercise of authority was unwarrantable, because it would provoke disturbance and was therefore inexpedient.

The protesters went on to quote the repeal of the Stamp Act as the true signpost to a wise policy:

This principle of repeal was nothing more than a return to the ancient standing policy of this Empire. The unhappy departure from it has led to that course of shifting and contradictory measures which have since given rise to such continued distractions. . . . To render the colonies permanently advantageous, they must be satisfied with their condition: that satisfaction we see no chance of restoring, whatever measures may be pursued, except by recurring, in the whole, to the wise and salutory principles on which the Stamp Act was repealed.

The essence of the Rockingham American policy can be distilled from this statement: the unquestioned supremacy of the English Parliament over the Colonies; the inexpediency of ever explicitly asserting that authority; the passing of the Declaratory Act and the repeal of Stamp Act to illustrate this policy in operation; the belief that the Rockinghams stood for the traditional British imperial position, learned over many generations and proved by common experience; the accusation that the 'Tory' Ministries of George III (excluding Chatham's and their own) had introduced a new system of despotic control, exercised through the officers of the executive, civil and military, based upon the royal prerogative, and aiming at direct taxation of the Colonies and the destruction of constitutional liberties, firstly in America and subsequently in England; the assertion that this new system had caused all the troubles in America; and a reminder, as is stated elsewhere in the paragraph quoted, that the permanent advantages of the Colonies were chiefly, perhaps wholly, derived 'from a flourishing and increasing trade'.

On 18 May Rockingham again entered a Protest in the *Lords Journals*. This time only eight Peers signed. Richmond wrote to tell the Marquis that 'you may save yourself the trouble of sending to Lords Shelburne and Camden as they told me they would not sign it'.[1] And yet, oddly enough, Lady Chatham wrote to Rockingham shortly afterwards that 'the Protests are both of them such, for matter and form as it must be a grief to Lord Chatham not to have the honour of his name, enrolled among those, who have signed them'.[2]

The second Protest was shorter than that of a week before. Its first point specifically related to the Justice Bill: it stated, with some reason, that there was no evidence that officers of the executive indicted for murder would not receive a fair trial in America. The rest was general. 'The Bill', said the second clause, 'amounts to a declaration that the house knows no means of retaining the colonies in due obedience, but by an army rendered independent of the ordinary course of law.' The third maintained that 'a military force, sufficient for governing upon this plan, cannot be maintained without the inevitable ruin of the nation'. Lastly it complained again of the 'introduction of essential innovations into the government of this empire'.[3]

In retrospect it would be difficult to quibble with many of these observations. At the time they had another, though not necessarily more effective, virtue apart from justice. Taken together the two protests did constitute a declaration of Rockingham colonial policy. But how realistic or relevant was this policy? Clearly the Rockinghams were right to suspect that a new effort to centralise the administration of the Colonies had been attempted, if spasmodically, under George III. Yet they

---

[1] Richmond to Rockingham, 18 May 1774. W.W.M. R1-1490.
[2] Hester Chatham to Rockingham, May 1774. W.W.M. R1-1491.
[3] *Lords Journals*, xxxiv, 205-6. *The Annual Register . . . 1774*, pp. 271-6, especially p. 275.

did not seem to realise that this had been made imperative by the legacy of the Peace of Paris and was not the whim of a prerogative-minded monarch. Further, while it is possible that the traditional British imperial policy of absent-mindedness might have provoked fewer riots in America by 1774, it would have led just as certainly to American independence in the end — though by lapse rather than revolution. Another weakness in Rockingham policy was that it had not yet been adjusted to the fact that the Americans were already in virtual rebellion. The doctrine of a non-exercised sovereignty contains much political subtlety : many people will give allegiance and obedience to an authority provided they are not forced to think about it too closely. But since 16 December 1773 certain Americans had rejected British sovereignty. There is no evidence in the Protests that the significance of the new situation had been grasped. For the Rockinghams time had stopped in 1766.

The Friends of America 'Without Doors'

During the Stamp Act crisis of 1765–66, American interests were served in England by a combination of Parliamentary and extra-Parliamentary forces. The Rockingham Ministry worked with the English mercantile classes and with American and West Indian colonial agents to secure the repeal of the Stamp Duty. A similar conjunction of interests assisted the Americans in their opposition to Townshend's duties in 1769–70. Various provincial trading towns — especially Liverpool, Manchester, Bristol, Leeds and Glasgow — played a part each time in the agitation, but the great focal point for these various lobbies was the City of London. Strategically placed at the doors of Parliament, the City was the centre of mercantile interests and also had a long civic tradition of political activity. It was internally divided between the aristocracy of aldermen, rich merchants and financiers on the one hand, and the 'middling' class of merchants, tradesmen, craftsmen, etc., on the other. The former usually supported the Government of the day ; but the latter were the great majority and during much of the eighteenth century they were in alliance with the Opposition politicians at

Westminster.[1] The important question for the purpose of this study is why was the alliance of political and economic forces which worked so effectively in the American interests during the 1760's so little in evidence during the American crisis of 1774–1775 ? The answer can probably be best explained through a brief description of the nature of the original alliance and of the changes which effected it in the years before 1774.

The alliance between the City and successive groups in Opposition at Westminster was based upon two main common interests. First was the general desire to oppose the Government; for the politicians this was often simply a method of forcing a way into the Administration, but to the City it represented a more permanent state of social attitude and political opinion. Second was a common concern for the mercantile classes : the City wished to have the mercantile point of view powerfully represented at Westminster, and the politicians wanted to use the merchant Members and the trading communities to strengthen their Parliamentary position. This alliance was brought to its zenith in the late 'fifties and in the 'sixties when two of the most prominent Opposition politicians, the elder Pitt and Rockingham, continued to cultivate the City both when in Opposition and in office.[2] Among its greatest triumphs were the repeal of the Stamp Act and the repeal of all but one of Townshend's duties. In each case the American colonists were the major beneficiaries, but the individual parts of the alliance in England were naturally more concerned with their own interests than with colonial contentment for its own sake. In 1766, the merchants wanted America pacified for the sake of trade, and the Rockinghams wanted it for the sake of their own peace of mind — and for the merchant support it brought them. During 1769–70 the mercantile classes again felt, though with less unanimity than in 1766, that a compromise with the colonists was necessary for trade. The City politicians

---

[1] See L. S. Sutherland, *The City of London and the Opposition to Government, 1768–1774*, The Creighton Lecture, 1958, pp. 6-7. Also 'The City of London in Eighteenth Century Politics', in *Essays presented to Sir Lewis Namier*, ed. R. Pares and A. J. P. Taylor, pp. 49-74, especially pp. 54-6.

[2] See L. S. Sutherland, 'Edmund Burke and the First Rockingham Ministry', *EHR*, xlvii, 46-70, especially p. 59.

were also at this time deeply committed in Wilkes' cause against the Administration. The Parliamentary Opposition, though genuinely in sympathy with the Americans, took the opportunity to exploit the City and mercantile agitation in order to embarrass Grafton's Ministry.

But even at this period of its greatest success, two influences were already at work to undermine the roots of the alliance: the growth of radicalism in the Metropolis made it increasingly difficult for the Rockinghams and the Chathams to work with the City politicians against the Administration; and the relative importance of American trade to English mercantile interests was declining, with the result that English merchants were less willing to demand capitulation to the American point of view. A third change was in the political position of the colonists themselves; growing every year more extreme in their constitutional demands, they alienated an increasing number of the Parliamentary and mercantile forces which had previously defended them. These developments, which had taken effect by 1774, together provide an important explanation of the weakness of the Opposition to Lord North's Ministry and its American policies after the Boston Tea Party.

Miss Sutherland has described how in London in the 1760's, 'at this time in the metropolitan area alone, there existed the predisposing conditions for the development of Radicalism as a political force'.[1] The important point for this study is that the traditional City position of general opposition to Administration evolved during 1764–70 into a positive radical programme which criticised the whole existing system of government. Men of education among the rising professional classes met at the various political clubs to discuss constitutional rights and political representation. Such radical Members of Parliament as James Townsend and John Sawbridge were the true products of this movement. John Wilkes gave it leadership and publicity, though he was less worthy of its deepest aspirations. These aspirations were summed up in their slogan, 'Annual Parliaments, Equal Representation, Place and Pension Bill',

[1] See her writings cited above, especially *The City of London and the Opposition to Government*, p. 5.

and were set out at greater length in the instructions given to the City of London Members in 1769.[1]

One of these City Members, William Beckford,[2] played an important role in drawing up the 1769 instructions and in trying to build up a nation-wide radical organisation. For a short time the various Parliamentary groups worked with the City radicals : Chatham and Shelburne through Beckford,[3] James Townsend, and Richard Oliver, while the Rockinghams worked through Barlow Trecothick. In 1770 Beckford dined the Parliamentary leaders at the Mansion House in the hope of winning them over to a programme of Parliamentary reform. But the Rockinghams could not reconcile this new radicalism with their traditionally aristocratic view of Government. 'All direction of public humour and opinion', wrote Burke, 'must originate in a few.'[4] Of the common people he said : 'God and nature never made them to think or to act without guidance and direction'.[5] More often he would refer to them in stronger terms — to 'the unprincipled behaviour of a corrupt and licentious people'.[6] The new democratic movements troubled the Rockingham leaders, who opposed the idea of mandating Members and had a vested interest in Rotten Boroughs. They feared the mob

[1] The instructions given to Ladbroke, Beckford, Harley and Trecothick provide a fair *resumé* of radical policies at this time towards various questions including America. The Members were to give full attention to questions of promoting trade, and therefore should support measures for reconciliation with America ; to prevent all future, and enquire into all late uses of military force by the civil magistrates ; to oppose payments of Civil List debts without a full enquiry ; to promote Bills to limit the number of pensioners and place-men ; to prevent peers from interfering in elections ; to promote a Bill for shorter Parliaments ; and to change the method of election to ballot, as 'the most likely method of procuring a return of members on the genuine and uncorrupt sense of the People'. *Broadsides 1702–80*, in Bodleian Library, Oxford.

[2] Beckford (1709–70) was M.P. for Shaftesbury 1747–54, and for London 1754–70. He was Lord Mayor of London in 1762–63 and 1769–70.

[3] Chatham's correspondence from Beckford is in the Chatham Papers, PRO. 30/8/19, and from Townsend in *ibid.*, 30/8/64.

[4] Burke to Rockingham, [22] 23 August 1775. W.W.M. Bk., *CEB*, iii, 190.

[5] Burke to Richmond, 26 September 1775. W.W.M., Bk. *CEB*, iii, 218.

[6] Burke to John Bourke, 11 July 1776. W.W.M. Bk., *CEB*, iii, 281. In 1769 Burke argued in favour of *reducing* the English franchise (and against American representation in the British Parliament) in his 'Observations on a Late Publication entitled The Present State of the Nation'. Quoted in Thomas D. Mahoney, *Burke and Ireland*, p. 45.

beating on the doors of Parliament; to them it was a small and select club, not a national assembly, and its doors should be kept closed.

Chatham was less upset by the political policies of the radicals, and while his friend Beckford was alive he maintained his alliance with the City. But Beckford died in 1770, and the City became increasingly an independent political force, divided from the Parliamentary Opposition groups, and embodied in the person of John Wilkes, with whom Chatham could not work. Early in 1772 Chatham, now in virtual retirement at Burton Pynsent, wrote: 'A headlong self-willed spirit has sunk the city into nothing; attempting powers it has no colour of right to, it has lost the weight to which it is entitled'.[1]   In October 1774, when Chatham was asked to intervene in the City elections to dissuade a friend of Wilkes from standing, he replied that he could do nothing, and added sadly, 'I do not understand the times'.[2]

By 1772 the recent alliance between the City and the Opposition groups had fallen apart. The Rockinghams had reacted against the radicalism of the Metropolis; Chatham could not work with Wilkes; many of the City radicals themselves included the Parliamentary Opposition in the system of vested interests which they wished to destroy.[3] There was still nothing to prevent them in future from condemning the Ministry's American policies in similar terms — as they did to some extent in 1774–75 — but it was no longer possible for them to work together politically as they had between 1766 and 1770. And when it came to positive solutions, it was certainly inconceivable that the radicals, who believed that it was not only expedient but right to meet the colonists' constitutional de-

---

[1] Chatham to Shelburne, 10 January 1772. *Chatham Correspondence*, iv, 187.

[2] Chatham to Stephen Sayre, 8 October 1774. *Ibid.*, 366-7. Sayre, an American by birth, was a City alderman and banker, and was Sheriff of London in 1773–74.

[3] Burke later complained: 'We were put out of the question of Patriots; stripped of all support from the multitude; and the alternative wildly and wickedly put between those, who disclaimed all employments, and the mere creatures of the Court. They would hear of nobody else.' To John Bourke, 11 July 1776. *CEB*, iii, 280-1.

mands, could ally with the Rockinghams, who stood by the Declaratory Act. The effects of these developments were clearly apparent after the Boston Tea Party, when there was very little cooperation between the Rockinghams and the City politicians.[1] Indeed, when Burke ventured into Westminster in search of a seat in the elections of October 1774, he met with a sharp rebuff from Wilkes.[2] Not until 1775 did the Rockinghams swallow their distaste and make a serious attempt to recreate the alliance with the City. In August Burke wrote to his leader : 'I hope I am as little awed out of my senses by the fear of vulgar opinion as most of my acquaintance. . . . But speaking of the prudential consideration, we know that all opposition is absolutely crippled, if we can obtain no kind of support without doors.' He proposed a scheme 'for reviving the importance of the City of London by separating the sound from the rotten contract-hunting part of the mercantile interest, uniting it with the Corporation, and joining it with your lordship'.[3] Three weeks later Burke spent a whole day canvassing for support in the City.[4] He subsequently explained that his 'sole motive . . . was to keep the City, now and for ever, out of the hands of Wilkes's, Olivers, and Hornes . . .'.[5] But by then England was at war with the colonists. During the critical period between the Tea Party and Lexington and Concord there was no political alliance between the City and the Parliamentary Opposition to deflect the Ministry from its chosen course of action against the Americans.

The second root of the alliance in the 'sixties was economic. The mercantile classes wanted to influence colonial policies in their interests, and in return these mercantile classes, in the provinces as well as in the City, offered to the Parliamentary Opposition substantial support from among the fifty or so [6]

---

[1] Another factor was the illness of Trecothick, who suffered a palsy in January 1774 and was incapacitated until his death in 1775. But this was not decisive, since the relations between the Rockinghams and the City were not such that an active representative there could have made much difference. [2] *CEB*, iii, 53.

[3] Burke to Rockingham, [22] 23 August 1775. W.W.M. Bk., *CEB*, iii, 192. [4] Burke to Rockingham, 14 September 1775. *Ibid.*, 211.

[5] Burke to Rockingham, 1 October 1775. *Ibid.*, 224.

[6] Sir Lewis Namier, *England in the Age of the American Revolution*, pp. 241-56, especially p. 254.

merchants in the Commons and from the trading communities in the country at large. The Government contractors among them usually refused to combine with the Opposition, but the remainder were potentially a strong lobby, and had greatly influenced colonial policies in America's favour during 1766–70. Why did this not happen again in 1774–75 ?

The first reason lies in the changed objectives of the Americans. Once the colonists began to deny Britain's Parliamentary supremacy and to question the Mother Country's right to regulate their trade, many British merchants were driven to support coercive policies designed to restore the Americans to their proper subordination. For even when most active in their support for the Americans, few British merchants had accepted the more radical colonial demands for changes in their constitutional status.

The second reason lay in the changed interests of the mercantile classes themselves. During the 1760's it had seemed to them essential that the Americans' trade should be maintained uninterrupted. Fear of the effects of the American non-importation movement stimulated most of the petitions demanding reconciliation with the Americans which were presented in 1769–70. But trading experience in the early 'seventies modified the merchants' attitude to the Colonies. One short-term factor was the business depression in 1772–73, when credit collapsed and a number of merchants trading to the Colonies got into serious financial difficulties. Many businessmen were then disenchanted with the American market and came to feel that it would not be satisfactory again until the colonial political situation was permanently stabilised.[1] Partly as a result of this collapse in the colonial market, but mainly because of other much wider economic forces, British trade was at this time in any case swinging away from the Colonies and towards Europe.[2]

[1] For an elaboration of this point see Dora M. Clark, *British Opinion and the American Revolution*, p. 72.

[2] During 1771–75 exports to the mainland American Colonies from England and Wales fell to less than one quarter of their average level in the previous few years. But exports to Russia rose by 300 per cent, to Africa, Sweden and Flanders by over 100 per cent, to France, Italy, Canada, Denmark and Norway by more than 30 per cent. See Elizabeth Boody Schumpeter, *English Overseas Trade Statistics, 1697–1808*, pp. 16–17, tables III and V.

These developments influenced the general approach of the English mercantile classes to colonial questions in the early 'seventies. Certain other particular factors also worked to make them less concerned than earlier to bring about immediate reconciliation with America after the actual crisis had arisen in 1774. For instance, the merchants were not so worried by the threat of non-importation because they had survived the previous bans.[1] On the contrary, the Americans themselves stepped up their imports from England during 1774 in order to stockpile for the future. The orders for clothing and arms to furnish the soldiers going to America in 1775 also provided a great deal of work. These circumstances made poor prospects for a Parliamentary Opposition seeking for support 'without doors' against Lord North's coercive measures.

The Rockinghams were well aware that the economic situation in 1774 and 1775 was very different from that which rallied merchant support to them on American questions in the 'sixties. In September 1774 Rockingham went to the Sheffield cutlers' feast and 'enquired particularly whether as yet there had been any stop in the American trade', and was assured 'there had been none'.[2] A certain Mr. Dixon wrote to Rockingham in January 1775 pointing out that 'the representation of the distressed state of manufactures in this part of the country is not justly true. There are but 2 or 3 merchants in Leeds whose sole trade lies to America. . . . Their other exports in these manufactures being to Italy, Germany, Holland, Spain, Portugal, Russia, etc.' This correspondent added that even the merchants whose main trade was with America were preparing a petition to Parliament supporting coercive measures 'as the best means of promoting trade'.[3] In March 1775 Richard Champion wrote to America : 'The manufactories of the Kingdom have not been affected in any degree to excite a clamour by the non-importation agreement. The trade of Yorkshire,

---

[1] On the Bristol merchants stocking up in anticipation of the collapse of the non-importation agreement, see Burke to Rockingham, 14 September 1774. *CEB*, iii, 209.

[2] Rockingham to Burke, 13 September 1774. W.W.M. Bk., *CEB*, iii, 25.

[3] Mr. Dixon to Rockingham, 30 January 1775. W.W.M. R-1542.

Manchester, Norwich and the clothing counties near this town continues very brisk, even Birmingham is not greatly affected.'[1] In July 1775 Colonel John Maunsell wrote that 'England was never in a more flourishing state — new doors opened to commerce; manufacturers fully employed; stocks as high as before the dispute'[2] and in August Burke analysed England's prosperity to his leader:

> War indeed is become a sort of substitute for commerce. The freighting business never was so lively on account of the prodigious taking up for Transport Service. Great orders for provisions and stores of all kinds. New clothing for the troops . . . puts life into the woollen manufacture; and the number of men of war ordered to be equipped, has given a pretence for such a quantity of nails and other iron work as to keep the midland parts tolerably quiet. All this with the incredible increase of the Northern market since the peace between Russia and the Port, keeps up the spirits of the mercantile world and induces them to consider the American war not so much as their calamity as their resource in an inevitable distress. This is the state of most — not of all the merchants.[3]

During much of 1774 the Rockinghams did nothing to arouse the mercantile spirit other than to lament its absence. 'The insensibility of the Merchants of London', wrote Burke in September 1774, 'is of a degree and kind scarcely to be conceived. Even those who are the most likely to be overwhelmed by any real American confusion are amongst the most sanguine.'[4] But at the end of the year, and in preparation for the new Parliament, they made their first serious efforts to start a petitioning movement in the style of five years earlier. A series of meetings of London merchants were called and a petition was drawn up. At first the merchants refused to make any reference to politics: Burke complained that there was

[1] Champion to Messrs. Willing, Morris & Co., 13 March 1775. *Letters of Richard Champion*, ed. G. Guttridge, p. 51.
[2] Quoted in Sir Lewis Namier, *England in the Age of the American Revolution*, p. 255.
[3] Burke to Rockingham, [22] 23 August 1775. *CEB*, iii, 191.
[4] Burke to Rockingham, 18, 25 September 1774. W.W.M. Bk., *CEB*, iii, 31.

'Not a word purporting the least dislike to the proceedings of the last Parliament. Not a syllable that indicated a preference of one system of American government over another.' But William Baker, who was acting for the Rockinghams among the merchants, 'with great address and perseverance' managed to carry 'some distant reflection on the American laws, and some compliment on the beneficial effects of the repeal of the Stamp Act'.[1] Meanwhile Burke himself had arranged through Champion for a petition to be sent from the citizens of Bristol and another from the Society of Merchant Venturers. These petitions, which asked that the petitioners should be heard in the proposed Committee on the American papers, were presented and refused by the Commons on 23 January 1775.[2] On 26 January Alderman Hayley presented another petition from the London merchants requesting that no Resolutions concerning America be passed without first hearing the petitions, but this was again defeated.[3] Burke and Baker continued in liaison with the London merchants and with leaders of the West Indian group, though the West Indians proved particularly uncooperative.[4] Various trading towns followed London's example and a dozen or so petitions were presented during January and February.[5] But the mercantile classes were obviously not too enthusiastic for the American cause. For example, Rockingham had considerable difficulty in raising support even in his home territory of Yorkshire, and several counter-petitions supporting

---

[1] Burke to Rockingham, 12 January 1775. *CEB*, iii, 97-8. See also William Baker to Rockingham, January 1774. W.W.M. R1-1541. On the Ministry's vigorous efforts to counter the petitioning movement see two letters from William Molleson to Dartmouth, December 1774. Dartmouth MSS. D 1778, 11, 1028, 1037 ; and Mr. Blackburn to Dartmouth, December 1774. *Ibid.*, 1025.

[2] *CEB*, iii, 101. *Parl. Hist.*, xviii, 168-81.

[3] By 250-89. *Ibid.*, 184-94.

[4] Baker was working closely with David Barclay and John Sargeant — two merchant friends of Benjamin Franklin — and with John Ellis, who was now leading the opposition among the West Indians. See Rockingham to Burke, 9 February 1775. W.W.M. Bk., *CEB*, iii, 113. On the difficulties in persuading the West Indians, and especially Rose Fuller, to support the Rockingham line, see Burke to Rockingham, 12 January 1775. *Ibid.*, 98. On the West Indian lobby in general see L. Penson, *The Colonial Agents of the British West Indies*, especially pp. 203-4.

[5] On Parliament's reception of these petitions, see below Chapter XI, p. 238.

the Ministry were drawn up.[1] In July 1775 the Court of Common Council of the City of London received a letter from New York, dated 5 May, asking London's help 'to restore union, mutual confidence, and peace to the whole Empire'. After long debates the City fathers agreed to present an Address to the King asking him 'to suspend hostilities against our fellow subjects in America'. The King replied that, while the Americans continued to resist constitutional authority he was bound 'to continue and enforce these measures by which alone their rights and interests can be asserted and maintained'. There was strong sympathy for the King's arguments, and afterwards, the Common Council voted not to send a copy of their Address to New York.[2]

The petitioning movement petered out with no effect on Government policy. In the summer Burke remarked : 'We look to the merchants in vain. They are gone from us, and from themselves. They consider America as lost and look to administration for an indemnity.'[3] Richard Champion told his American grain supplier 'it is a truth, though a melancholy one, that the generality of the American merchants are not your best friends'.[4] Many of the mercantile classes, in the City of London and in the provinces, had, like the American colonists themselves, changed considerably in their attitude to colonial questions since 1766; the Rockinghams alone continued to treasure the glories and to lament the ruins of the great alliance 'without doors' which had once given them a brief taste of popularity and power.

The remaining element in the successful alliance of the 1760's was the group of colonial agents, who worked to rally the mercantile interests in and outside the City and the Westminster

---

[1] See Rockingham to Mr. Pemberton, 15 February 1775. W.W.M. R1-1553. See also the letter from William Lee to Thomas Adams on 10 March 1775, stating that '. . . the Ministry knew well enough the merchants, except 2 or 3 of us, were not all serious ; hence it is, that our petitions are almost all . . . little else than milk and water'. Quoted in Sir Lewis Namier, *England in the Age of the American Revolution*, p. 255.

[2] *London Chronicle*, 8 July 1775.

[3] Burke to Rockingham, 23 August 1775. *CEB*, iii, 191.

[4] Champion to Messrs. Willing, Morris & Co., 26 August 1775 : *Letters of Richard Champion*, p. 60.

politicians behind the American cause.[1] In the seventeenth century the American colonial agents were special ambassadors sent to London on particular occasions to secure or preserve specific rights and interests. During the eighteenth century, however, a new type of agency evolved: held by a regular official of the Colony, preferably an American but sometimes an Englishman, who was resident in London and drew a fixed salary from the colonial treasury. His task was to watch carefully all that went on at Court and in Parliament, to canvass M.P.s and Ministers, to present the colonial point of view, to work to prevent obnoxious legislation — in fact, to further the interests of his Province in every way possible. The qualities required were influence, ability, knowledge of colonial conditions and sympathy with their aspirations; legal training was also valued because of the importance of boundary disputes. At some periods a Colony had no agent in London, at other times it might have several. Proliferation of agencies occurred especially when a Colony was involved in internal constitutional struggles between the legislature and the executive, and each side wished to have an instrument in England working for it. Virginia and Massachusetts, for example, had periods of dual representation, with both the Assembly and the Governor and Council sending men to London.[2] By the eve of the Revolution, however, most agents were working in the interests of the popular Assemblies against the Executives, and the practice was growing of combining the agencies of several Colonies into one man.[3]

A striking feature of the crisis which followed the Boston Tea Party is that these agents appeared to have played only a minor and ineffective role in English politics. Apart from the two petitions by William Bollan in March 1774,[4] there is little

---

[1] See especially L. B. Namier, 'Charles Garth and his Connections', *EHR*, liv, 639-41, 646-52. Also J. J. Burns, *The Colonial Agents of New England*, pp. 135-6.

[2] During 1768–72 Edward Montagu represented the Virginia Assembly and James Abercrombie the Council. During 1768–75, William Bollan was agent for the Massachusetts Council, and first De Berdt and then Franklin for the Assembly.

[3] See E. P. Tanner, 'Colonial Agencies in England during the Eighteenth Century', *Political Science Quarterly*, xvi, 24-49.

[4] See above, Chapter IV, pp. 76 *n* 1, 81-2.

sign of their activity until the end of the year. Then William Lee [1] and Burke worked in London and in Bristol to encourage support for the merchant petitions, and Franklin made a series of visits to Chatham, who was preparing his American motions for the coming session of Parliament.[2] Franklin also made a last bid for reconciliation early in 1775.[3] But there is little evidence of the organised vigour shown by the agents a few years earlier. This weakness was particularly illustrated when the petition from the first Continental Congress to the King setting out the various colonial grievances arrived in London in December 1774. It came to Franklin but was also addressed to the other American agents. Franklin wrote to them to try to arrange a meeting to discuss how best to present the petition. Burke, Thomas Life and Paul Wentworth [4] declined on the grounds that they had received no instructions from America relating to it. Wentworth told John Pownall that he considered the claims made in the petition, and the tone of expression, highly offensive.[5] Only William Bollan and Arthur Lee were prepared to work with Franklin. They presented the petition to Dartmouth before Christmas [6] and he passed it on to the King, who, he said, would recommend it to the consideration of Parliament. But when it was put before the Commons on 19 January 1775 it was 'among a heap of letters of intelligence from Governors and officers in America, newspapers, pamphlets, handbills, etc., from that country, the last in the list, and was laid upon the table with them, undistinguished by any

[1] William Lee was a merchant, American by birth, and was Joint Sheriff of London with Stephen Sayre in 1773–74. He was acting as agent at large in 1774 and also worked with his brother, Arthur, for Virginia.
[2] Chatham first entertained Franklin in August 1774, and again on 27, 29 and 31 January 1775. It appears that Franklin had almost no influence on Chatham's proposals, though he approved of most of them anyway. A. von Ruville, *Chatham*, iii, 283-94. There are some letters from William Bollan to Chatham in the Chatham Papers, PRO. 30/8/20 and from Arthur and William Lee in *ibid.* 30/8/48.
[3] See below, Chapters X and XI, for details of Franklin's abortive negotiations with David Barclay and Dr. John Fothergill.
[4] Agents respectively for the New York Assembly, for Connecticut, and for New Hampshire.
[5] Pownall to Dartmouth, 20 December 1774. *HMC*, xi, v, *Dartmouth MSS.*, i, 372.
[6] See Dartmouth to Bollan, 23 December 1774. PRO. CO. 5/250, f. 91.

particular recommendation of it to the notice of either House'.[1]
On 26 January 1775, Franklin, Bollan and Lee petitioned
through Sir George Savile to be heard on the subject of the
Congress petition laid before the House on 19 January, but this
was rejected by 218-68.[2]

One explanation of the ineffectiveness of the colonial agents
may lie in the condition of the agencies themselves at the time of
crisis. During the period between the Tea Party and Lexington
there were altogether only nine colonial agents in England.
These were: William Bollan (agent for the Massachusetts
Council, 1745–75); Benjamin Franklin (agent for the Massa-
chusetts Assembly since 1770, for Pennsylvania since 1767, for
Georgia since 1768 and for New Jersey since 1769); Arthur
Lee (agent for Virginia and Maryland, 1767–76 and agent for
the Massachusetts Assembly in 1775); Thomas Life (agent for
Connecticut, 1760–76); Charles Garth (agent for South Caro-
lina, 1762–75 and for the Maryland Assembly, 1767–75);
Edmund Burke (agent for the New York Assembly, 1771–75);
James Abercrombie (agent for the Governor and Council of
Virginia, 1761–74); Paul Wentworth (agent for New Hamp-
shire, 1774–75); and Denis De Berdt, junior (agent for New
Jersey, 1775).[3]

Only the first six of these were in England during the whole
of the crucial policy-making period between January 1774 and
February 1775. Moreover, not all of these six were active in

[1] Franklin to Charles Thomson, Secretary to the Congress, 5 February
1774. *Franklin Complete Works*, v, 427-8.
[2] *Parl. Hist.*, xviii, 193-4. Franklin's conclusion was that 'from the
constant refusal, neglect, or discouragement of American petitions, these
many years past, our country will at least be convinced that petitions are
odious here, and that petitioning is far from being a profitable means of
obtaining redress. A firm, steady and faithful adherence to the non-
consumptive agreement is the only thing to be depended upon.' *Franklin
Complete Works*, v, 428.
[3] To these might be added William Lee, who acted with his brother
Arthur as an 'agent at large'. Details of these agencies are contained in:
Marguerite Appleton, 'The Agents of the New England Colonies in the
Revolutionary period', *The New England Quarterly*, vi, 2, especially 372-87.
J. J. Burns, *op. cit.*, p. 136. E. Lilly, *The Colonial Agents of New York and
New Jersey*, passim. E. Lonn, *The Colonial Agents of the Southern Colonies*,
appendix I. B. W. Bond, 'The Colonial Agent', *Political Science Quarterly*,
xxxv, 372-92. On William Lee see W. C. Ford, ed., *Letters of William Lee,
1766–1783*, i, 1-68.

the colonial cause. Charles Garth, one of the most distinguished among their number, was by then inclining towards, if not already associated with, the Administration. Garth, the Member for Devizes since 1765, was by instincts and family tradition an independent in politics. He also had family connexions with America and had voted against the Stamp Act in February 1765. In the early 'seventies he was still voting occasionally with the Opposition, but he seems to have swung towards the Ministry some time around 1774. He was definitely receiving a pension from 1777, and possibly earlier. Whether because of a change of convictions or because of financial exigencies, Charles Garth ceased to work for the colonists at the time when they needed him most, and in January 1775 was advising the use of military force against them.[1]

Of the other five, two — Burke and Life (a London barrister) — were Englishmen whose loyalties naturally became strained after the Tea Party when the colonial case was increasingly directed against England and for independence. Burke was expecially conscious of the delicate balance between his role as a Member of Parliament and as a paid agent of one of the colonies. After the Tea Party he wrote to his employers: 'I should be glad of your instructions relative to my conduct with regard to office, if you think any be necessary. I shall as religiously obey your orders in this respect, as in my parliamentary capacity I shall always steadily retain my own freedom, and deliver my own opinion only in what I shall think the good of the publick.'[2] But he left them in no doubt that the public good, in his view, lay in 'the proper subordination of America, as a fundamental, incontrovertible maxim, in the government of this Empire'.[3] As for Franklin, who should have been the spearhead of the colonial lobby, he was in disgrace after January

[1] L. B. Namier, 'Charles Garth and his Connections', *EHR*, iv, 443-70, 632-62. Also J. W. Barnwell, 'Charles Garth, the last Colonial Agent of South Carolina in England, and some of his work', *South Carolina Historical and Genealogical Magazine*, xxvi, 67-92, and 'Garth Correspondence', *ibid.*, xxviii, 33 *seq.* See also below, Chapter X, p. 220.

[2] Burke to Committee of Correspondents of the General Assembly of New York, 2 February 1774. *CEB*, ii, 522.

[3] Burke to Committee of Correspondence of the General Assembly of New York, 6 April 1774. *CEB*, ii, 528-9.

1774 because of his part in the affair of the Hutchinson–Oliver letters. Although he continued to work for his compatriots, he could exercise little personal influence over English politics. In the autumn of 1774 he told a correspondent that he had 'seen no Minister since January, nor had the least communication with them'.[1]

Yet of much greater importance than the weakness and divisions of the American agents was the magnitude, perhaps the impossibility, of their task. The colonial lobby could only succeed if, as in 1766–70, domestic interests were prepared to support them, and if the Ministers were willing, and events capable of being influenced in the desired direction. But in 1774 and 1775 the merchant and City alliance with the Opposition in Parliament was dead. The agents therefore lacked a substantial and rooted interest in the Community and in Parliament ; and without it they became an isolated band of agitators. Moreover, the British Government which they hoped to influence was at this time totally and inflexibly committed to its policy of coercion. The imperial relationship had in 1774 probably passed the point at which there could be further compromises and reversals of policy in London. To attempt to restore harmonious relations between the Colonies and the Mother Country, on terms acceptable to both sides, was apparently, as Franklin observed, like 'trying to hinder the setting of the sun'.

[1] Franklin to Mrs. Jane Mecom, 26 September 1774. *Franklin Writings*, vi, 247.

CHAPTER VII

A SUMMER WAITING FOR RESULTS

PARLIAMENT was prorogued on 22 June 1774 when the King
went to Westminster to give his consent to the Quebec Act.
During the next few weeks the Ministers relaxed and waited for
their American legislation to cross the Atlantic and then take
effect. Many politicians dispersed to the country, though it
was a sad and wet summer and most of their rural pleasures
were spoilt.[1] However, they were at least given time to reflect
upon the colonial problem and the steps which had been taken
to solve it. One very interested observer, Thomas Hutchinson,
arrived in England at this time and recorded the many views
which he solicited during his intensive social rounds. Consequently his diary and letters are a valuable aid in assessing the
state of opinion on this side of the Atlantic immediately after
the decisive steps had been taken towards a policy of coercion.[2]

Hutchinson had sailed from Boston for England on 1 June
and his boat docked at Dover on the 29th. He reached London
on the following evening and immediately contacted Dartmouth,
who told him to come to his home the next day at noon.[3] When
he arrived there, he was hurried off to an audience with the King.

George III immediately plunged into serious conversation
about Massachusetts and asked Hutchinson how the Bostonians
had received the news of the coercive measures. Hutchinson,
according to his diary, replied that the reports of the Port Bill,
which were all that had reached Boston when he left, were

[1] Mr. Jeffrys to Hardwicke, 28 July 1774. BM. Add. MS. 35612, f. 24,
and Thomas St. George to Hardwicke, 17 August 1774. *Ibid.*, f. 35.
[2] Hutchinson's opinions were not unbiased, since he had suffered from
attacks by the Massachusetts patriots and he was well received by the home
Ministry. But he brought a fresh eye to the English scene, he had ready
access into the highest social and political circles, and he was himself keen
to assess the position here in England and to relate it to the American
situation. [3] Hutchinson, *Diary and Letters*, i, 155.

'extremely alarming to the people'.[1] In a later letter to General Gage, Hutchinson reaffirmed that he made this point to the King.[2] He also then claimed that at the same time he had asked the King to offer some relief to the Boston merchants, and that he had pointed out how difficult it was for the Bostonians to show their willingness to pay the requisite duties when no goods were allowed into the port — unless, as he hoped was not the case, the King required an explicit declaration of submission.

Yet after this conversation the King wrote to Lord North claiming that Hutchinson had told him 'the people of Boston seemed much dispirited' and that 'the Boston Port Bill was the only wise and effectual method'. The King added that he was 'now well convinced that they will soon submit'.[3] Now assuming that Hutchinson and the King were honest in their reporting, it does seem that there was a basic misunderstanding of what Hutchinson actually said. One possible explanation is that the King was looking to the Massachusetts Governor for expert approval of his Government's measures towards that Colony and that he read such approval into Hutchinson's presumably guarded words. If so, it throws an interesting light on the King's state of mind at this time — of hope, but not of confidence that he had done the right thing.[4]

Apart from this misunderstanding, Hutchinson was astonished by the King's 'knowledge of so many facts' and his grasp of the colonial situation.[5] This is borne out by his diary notes on the two-hour interview, which suggest that George had a close acquaintanceship with the names of people and recent events in Massachusetts. Hutchinson was led to comment that George 'is more his own Minister than is generally imagined'.[6]

[1] *Ibid.*, 157.

[2] Hutchinson to Gage, 4 July 1774. Printed in *ibid.*, 175-7.

[3] King to North, 1 July 1774. J. W. Fortescue, ed., *The Correspondence of George III, 1760–1782*, iii, 1486.

[4] This optimistic interpretation of Hutchinson's views was readily passed on by Dartmouth to Hardwicke, who promptly congratulated him on 'so happy a beginning of your American plan'. 3 July 1774. Dartmouth MS. D 1778, 11, 919.

[5] Hutchinson to Gage, 4 July 1774, and to an unnamed friend, 11 July 1774. Hutchinson, *op. cit.*, i, 175, 195, note.

[6] Hutchinson to his son, 6 July 1774. *Ibid.*, 179.

In the week after his meeting with the King, Hutchinson looked more closely into the Government's American policy. On 4 July he was shown copies of the Massachusetts Regulating Act and the Impartial Administration of Justice Act. He commented, with some astonishment, that these two Acts were 'quite unexpected to me. . . . I think it a most fortunate circumstance for me, that I have never had the least share in promoting or suggesting any part of them.' [1] He was also critical of the list of nominees for the new Massachusetts Council, which Dartmouth had sent to him, though he was 'pleased to see some good men among them'.[2]

Hutchinson's most interesting and important activity was to try to find an answer to the crucial question of what specific settlement by the Americans would be acceptable to the Ministry. He had touched upon this in his interview with the King on 1 July, when it had been agreed that what was required was some form of 'abstention from opposition to the supreme authority of the Empire' as evidence of American submission.[3] But they did not discuss how this abstention would be registered and recognised. Yet in raising the point Hutchinson apparently made the Government briefly aware of the need for clarity if they were to avoid a misunderstanding with the Americans. For on 6 July Dartmouth wrote to Gage: [4]

We are to look forward to the execution of these measures for a test of the people's obedience and of their submission to the execution of the law, which is all that Parliament requires . . . and I rather mention this as I find from Governor Hutchinson, that what I have said upon that subject, has been taken in too large a sense, and understood to imply an absolute Declaration from the people in the terms of the Declaratory Act.[5] Such a Declaration will not, I conceive, be either

[1] Hutchinson to Gage, 4 July 1774. Hutchinson, *op. cit.*, i, 177.
[2] Hutchinson to Dartmouth, 3 July 1774. Dartmouth MS. D 1778, II, 920.   [3] Hutchinson, *op. cit.*, i, 155.
[4] In answer to Gage's letter of 30 May 1774 which arrived on 5 July and which pointed out that 'no means are yet adopted to comply with the [Boston Port] Act'. PRO. CO. 5/769, f. 82. Printed in C. E. Carter, ed., *The Correspondence of General Thomas Gage, 1763–1775*, i, 355-6.
[5] When North met Hutchinson on 7 July the Premier said that he had been told that Hutchinson had interpreted the Boston Port Act as saying that an explicit submission was required from the Americans. Hutchinson

required or expected; and whenever it shall be certified, that
compensation has been made to the East India Company by
the Town of Boston, and it shall appear by your report of the
state of that town, that the King's duties may be safely
collected there, His Majesty will no doubt restore it to its
privileges as a port; and more especially if the principal
inhabitants should think fit, by any public act, to declare
their resolution effectively to prosecute and bring to justice
all such as should by force or violence interrupt the commerce
of the King's subjects.[1]

Since these dispatches to North America were held up for a day
while Dartmouth consulted with the King on certain matters,
it is possible that George III specifically authorised him to
stress this point.[2]

Such clarification was a prerequisite to any settlement, and
the Government, in seeming not to demand an explicit submission, had made a settlement slightly more possible — though
it was still very unlikely that the Bostonians would prosecute
their own patriot leaders. Hutchinson later claimed the credit
for having thus modified the Government's position. He wrote
to a friend in Boston:

> I am fully satisfied that such an acquiescence as I have
> pointed out, without any explicit declaration, will obtain the
> relief we wish for, though I am as well satisfied, that if it had
> not been for the opportunities I have had with the King and
> with his Ministers, the idea of the necessity or propriety of
> such a submission would have remained with a great part of
> those concerned with promoting the Act, and I believe with
> the General [Gage] also, who would have received nothing
> from Administration to explain the first instructions given
> to him.[3]

denied this, and presumed that the King was responsible for this misunderstanding. Hutchinson to unknown friend, 8 July 1774. Hutchinson, *op. cit.*,
i, 181-2.
  [1] PRO. CO. 5/763, ff. 394-6.
  [2] W. Knox to A. Todd, 6 July 1774. PRO. CO. 5/250, f. 82.
  [3] Hutchinson to a friend, 20 July 1774. Hutchinson, *op. cit.*, i, 189-90.
Hardwicke had written to Dartmouth advising that 'a general recognition
of the legislative power is no more than appears to me necessary from those
assemblies which have denied it — and particularly from the Bostonians'.
3 July 1774. Dartmouth MS. D 1778, 11, 919.

Hutchinson was probably exaggerating when he claimed to have changed British policy, since there is little evidence that the Government was previously united or clear in its own mind about the nature of the submission which was required from the Americans. Furthermore, later events suggest that the other Ministers were not united behind Dartmouth in his assertion that no explicit declaration was required from the colonists. In August Hutchinson himself said that he was still trying to persuade them to agree to this. But it is to his credit that he was raising this vital question and that he was trying to influence the British Government towards a more moderate position.

However, Hutchinson admitted there was little hope that the Ministry would retreat from coercion unless the Americans did submit, whether implicitly or explicitly. 'They have gone too far here to recede', he wrote, 'let the opposition in America be what it will.' [1] This impression was confirmed when he spent the evening of 7 July with Lord North in Downing Street. It was the first time Hutchinson had seen the Premier, who had been out of Town since he arrived. Lord North was quite adamant that the Americans deserved correction, and his only regret was that it had not been applied earlier. He said that the time of temporising was over and that the Mother Country was 'at last fixed and determined'. Hutchinson commented afterwards that he knew 'several gentlemen of character, who had their doubts at the time of passing the Act, some of whose sentiments I knew from my correspondence with them, but they say now there is no going back'.[2] For instance, he visited Hardwicke on 9 July and this former supporter of Rockingham admitted he had been 'very active in promoting the late measures in Parliament. He often repeated that he had no apprehensions of rebellion, or forcible opposition to the King's troops.' [3] On 16 July Hutchinson talked with Lord Chancellor Apsley, and the following day with Lord Mansfield.[4] 'They both', he reported afterwards, 'say that the Government

[1] Hutchinson to his son, 6 July 1774. Hutchinson, *op. cit.*, i, 179.
[2] Same to an unknown friend, 8 July 1774. *Ibid.*, 181.
[3] *Ibid.*, 185-6.   [4] *Ibid.*, 192-3.

will never recede from its present resolution to maintain the supremacy of Parliament.' [1]

This determination was common to the whole Ministry, including the 'moderates'.[2] When Dartmouth sent the Coercive Acts to Gage he accompanied them with a letter exhorting Gage to be firm in dealing with the Americans, who, he claimed, had brought the whole British Empire to a point of crisis. He said:

> The constitutional authority of the Kingdom over its colonies must be vindicated, and its laws obeyed throughout the whole Empire. It is not only its dignity and reputation, but its power — nay its very existence depends upon the present moment; for should those ideas of independence, which some dangerous and ill-designing persons here are artfully endeavouring to instil into the minds of the King's American subjects once take root, that relation between this kingdom and its colonies which is the bond of peace and power will soon cease to exist, and destruction must follow disunion.

Dartmouth was fully in favour of asserting British sovereignty over America. He looked to the military commander in America actively to secure that sovereignty. He asserted that

> it is actual disobedience and open resistance that have compelled coercive measures; and I have no longer any other confidence in the hopes I had entertained, that the public peace and tranquility would be restored, but that which I derive from your abilities, and the reliance I have on your prudence for a wise and discreet exercise of the authorities given to you by the Acts I now send you.[3]

During July the Ministry was clearly quite firm in its intentions and fairly optimistic in its outlook. But this attitude was

---

[1] Hutchinson to a Boston friend, 20 July 1774. *Ibid.*, 191. For repetitions of this opinion see Hutchinson to Chief Justice Oliver, 19 July 1774; to Gage, 1 August 1774; to Thomas Hutchinson, 3 August 1774. *Ibid.*, 202, 204, 201.

[2] Burke wrote to America in May: 'That you may not be deceived by any idle or flattering report, be assured, that the determination to enforce obedience from the Colonies to the laws of revenue, by the most powerful means, seems as firm as possible, and that the Ministry appears stronger than ever I have known them'. Burke to the Committee of Correspondence of the General Assembly of New York, 4 May 1774. W.W.M. Bk., *CEB*, ii, 534. [3] Dartmouth to Gage, 3 June 1774. PRO. CO. 5/763, f. 534.

based more upon hope than on evidence. The Ministers believed that the Americans would submit quietly to the first assertions of British supremacy. And yet they must have realised that the colonists might resist, that the coercive measures would then be extremely difficult to enforce, and that if they failed the existence of the Empire would be at stake. From the British point of view all depended directly upon General Gage. To the Ministry, and to most Members of Parliament, the coercive measures were hurried and well-meaning attempts to solve a crisis three thousand miles away : having devised and passed them, the Ministry sat, waited and hoped. But to General Gage these measures were orders which had to be executed immediately and in a practical manner despite the local situation ; having received them, he had to act.

In America the situation was not propitious for Gage successfully to meet his Government's expectations. Disorder was spreading throughout Massachusetts and, more ominous, its Committee of Correspondence began to call the other Colonies to its side.[1] The Ministry was aware of this possibility ; Dartmouth had often received letters from Joseph Reed in Philadelphia like the one posted on 30 May which said that 'if the Boston Port Bill and the other proceedings against the Province have been founded on a supposition that the other Colonies would leave them to struggle alone, I do assure your Lordship there never was a greater mistake'.[2] Nevertheless the Government had been forced to take a calculated risk that Massachusetts would be isolated and subdued. At the beginning of August Dartmouth received the first intimations that the gamble might not succeed. On the 2nd, dispatches arrived from Boston in which Gage informed the American Secretary that he had dissolved the Massachusetts Assembly which had met at Salem, and he included the rebellious Resolutions which had been passed during the session.[3] He also said that preparations were being made to resist the three Coercive Acts when

[1] J. C. Miller, *Origins of the American Revolution*, p. 370.
[2] Reed to Dartmouth, 30 May 1774. Dartmouth MS. D 1778, 1, ii, 980. Quoted in *HMC*, 11, V, *Dartmouth MSS.*, i, 353–4.
[3] Gage to Dartmouth, 26 June 1774. PRO. CO. 5/763, ff. 403–8. Printed in *The Correspondence of General Thomas Gage, 1763–1775*, i, 357–8.

they arrived.[1]   Still worse, in one of the last-dated dispatches in this packet, Gage reported that the attempt by a loyalist minority in a town meeting at Boston to pass a Resolution calling for the payment of compensation to the East India Company had been heavily defeated.   He added that it had proved impossible for him to secure any punishment of the tea rioters.[2]   Thus two of the Ministry's suggested conditions of conciliation had been rejected.   The prospect of military repression therefore loomed closer — and the troop replacements, the future instruments of such repression, had just arrived at Boston.

Dartmouth was very upset by these developments.   He called at Hutchinson's lodgings on the following day, and 'spoke with great emotion, that he was not one who thirsted for blood; but he could not help saying that he wished to see H[ancoc]k and A[da]ms brought to the punishment they deserved : and he feared peace would not be restored until some examples were made, which would deter others'.[3]   But at this very time any remaining hope of prosecuting the Boston victors was finally dashed as Thurlow reported that some depositions made by Samuel Dyer against the rebels were inadequate grounds for prosecution.[4]   All that Dartmouth could do at this stage was to write a letter of encouragement to Gage.   He said he realised that it might be some time before the Americans submitted, but he took comfort from the fact that prominent people in Boston had proposed compensation to the East India Company, and he felt that 'the hour of distress must soon come that will, I hope, awaken the people to a right sense of their situation'.[5]

This forced optimism was echoed when Hutchinson attended Court that day.   The King said to Richard Jackson : 'Well :

---

[1] Apparently rough drafts of the three Acts had been published in Boston on 4 June.

[2] Gage to Dartmouth, 5 July 1774. PRO. CO. 5/763, f. 438.   Printed in *The Correspondence of General Thomas Gage, 1763–1775*, i, 358-60.

[3] Hutchinson, *op. cit.*, i, 203.

[4] See above Chapter III, p. 63 *n* 2.   Also J. Pownall to Dartmouth, 4 August 1774. Dartmouth MS. D 1778, 11, 938.   Dartmouth to Admiralty, 4 August 1774. PRO. CO. 5/250, f. 83.

[5] Dartmouth to Gage, 3 August 1774. PRO. CO. 5/763, ff. 453-6.

matters go on well in America : they are coming right'. Jackson answered, 'I hope, Sir, they will come right, but it may require some time'. Yet Jackson, from his long experience at the Board of Trade, knew too much about American affairs to share completely his sovereign's cheerful interpretation of affairs. He said to Lord Dudley shortly afterwards, 'I don't see how we can go back ; but I hope we shall take the first opportunity to close with them, as soon as it can be done with honour'.[1]

On 6 August the long expected Coercive Acts reached Boston.[2] They forced the Bay Colony radicals into even more resolute opposition, and this attitude spread through the other Colonies as they approached the Continental Congress which was to be held at Philadelphia in September. Similar feelings of resolution continued to prevail in England. Hutchinson wrote to a correspondent in Massachusetts on 8 August : 'I have not met with one person in the Kingdom — and I have seen flaming patriots, as well as fawning courtiers — who thinks the avowed principles, either of the House or Council, admissible'.[3] To another American friend on the same day he emphasised that colonial intransigence would not bring the English Ministry to terms. 'The present Ministry seem determined not to yield,' he said. 'The body of the people seems to be of the same mind ; and if there should be a change of Ministry, of which there is not the least prospect, what can tempt them to new measures ?'[4] He recommended the Massachusetts patriots to stop pursuing 'a phantom' — that Parliament should renounce its right to tax. Meanwhile, he claimed that he was still trying to persuade the Ministry to abandon the pursuit of its own phantom — that of forcing the Americans to acknowledge Parliament's right to tax.[5] In this way he hoped the issues

---

[1] Hutchinson, *op. cit.*, i, 204-5.

[2] Gage to Dartmouth, 27 August 1774. PRO. CO. 5/769, f. 106. Printed in *The Correspondence of General Thomas Gage*, i, 365-8.

[3] Hutchinson, *op. cit.*, i, 213. He instanced Governor Thomas Pownall as one of those 'that formerly espoused your cause, (but) are now as forward as any in condemning you'. To an unknown friend, 9 August 1774. *Ibid.*, 220. He later said he had found similar sentiments 'in travelling about the country'. To J. Green, 27 August 1774. *Ibid.*, 230.   [4] *Ibid.*, 230.

[5] Hutchinson to an unknown friend, 8 August 1774. *Ibid.*, 214. Hutchinson later claimed that all the Ministers had at least recognised the

could be blurred and everyone satisfied : for there would then be no part of the Empire with *acknowledged* exemption from Parliament's sovereignty, and yet no British supremacy would be *exercised* in America. To this extent his ideas corresponded fairly closely with those of the Rockingham party. Hutchinson, however, also faced a fact which the Rockinghams ignored — that British sovereignty had already been explicitly denied. His answer was to suggest that the colonists should petition the King, expressing apologies for past misdemeanours, and asking for a guarantee that in future taxation would never be raised in America — not as a question of constitutional right but on grounds of long-usage and customary privileges. He added that if the colonists were not willing to do this there was no possible solution, and they should secede immediately from Great Britain.[1]

Hutchinson's assessment of the situation was realistic, and his proposals for a settlement were sensible. The possibility of such a settlement, however, presupposed one factor — that the two sides would be prepared to compromise and allow the basic issue of rights to be blurred. But the mood of most Americans at this time held out little hope of compromise on their part. And the British Ministry, as Hutchinson so often noted, was not prepared to yield an inch. On 11 August Lord North visited Hutchinson before leaving for the country.[2] 'He said he did not expect less from the late Acts than what has happened' and he did not 'conceive them less necessary than he did before'. Furthermore, 'he was not apprehensive of any great matters

inexpediency of taxing the Colonies. (To G. Erving, 31 August 1774. *Ibid.*, 233.) Hutchinson apparently saw himself in the role of a conciliator. He wrote to Isaac Winslow that 'the payment for the Tea, and a little further advance towards an orderly state than what had been made before I came away, would most infallibly have enabled me to obtain the desired relief for the Bostonians'. Undated. *Ibid.*, 231.

[1] Hutchinson to unnamed friend in America, 8 August 1774. *Ibid.*, 213-217.

[2] On 15 August Hutchinson dined with Dartmouth at Blackheath and was asked if he would accept a baronetcy. He declined on the grounds that his fortune was insufficient, and Dartmouth said he would not wish him to take anything less. This offer fulfilled a promise made to Hutchinson in April that he would be rewarded by an early mark of the King's favour. Dartmouth to Hutchinson, 9 April 1774. Dartmouth MS. D 1778, 11, 887. Hutchinson, *op. cit.*, i, 126-8, 221.

from the proposed Congress'.[1] The longer the two sides stood so firmly apart, the more the width of the gulf between them became apparent, and the more that gulf was recognised, the less was the chance of bridging it. The inevitable outcome of intransigence, as Hutchinson realised, was secession.

In the middle of August the English Government machine came to its seasonal halt. Lord North left for Somerset on the 17th and the Treasury Board was adjourned till September. Not a single Minister remained to spend the dog days of summer in London.[2] There was a small alarm towards the end of the month when Suffolk sent news to the Prime Minister and to Dartmouth that large quantities of gunpowder were being purchased in Holland and shipped to North America.[3] Dartmouth even returned to his house in St. James's Square.[4] But the Government remained inactive. John Pownall told his fellow Under-Secretary at the American office: 'I have done nothing but play truant since you left us, for I found nobody would do anything, and I begin to have as much contempt as my betters for that solicitude for the public welfare you have so often laughed at me for cherishing'. He reported that no letters of any importance had arrived from America for some time. 'I do not wonder', he added, 'that the state of our Colonies is an object of speculation in other countries. Our interests there grow more and more serious; but though the seeds of disunion begin to germinate, it must be our own fault if they ripen into maturity in the present generation.'[5] On 7 September Dartmouth himself, back at the office, was complaining of 'the want of that assistance from the rest of the King's servants — which

[1] Hutchinson, *op. cit.*, i, 211-12. Elsewhere Hutchinson wrote 'nobody seems to give themselves the least concern about the consequences of the projected Congress, supposing it can do no hurt to the Kingdom'. To his son, August 1774. *Ibid.*, 221.

[2] Langton to Hardwicke, 17 August 1774. BM. Add. MS. 35612, f. 37. Ten days later Hutchinson wrote: 'The cessation from all sorts of public business cannot well be greater than at present; every person being out of town who is at the head of the Boards'. Hutchinson, *op. cit.*, i, 228.

[3] Suffolk to Dartmouth, 31 August 1774. PRO. CO. 5/138 (part II), f. 392.   [4] Hutchinson, *op. cit.*, i, 232.

[5] J. Pownall to W. Knox, 31 August 1774. *HMC, Various*, vi, *Knox MSS.*, pp. 114-15.

it is impossible to engage at this season of the year'.[1] As late as 20 September Rochford remarked to the King that 'a Cabinet cannot be conveniently held at this time of the year . . .'.[2]

In fact, as Dartmouth admitted to Hutchinson, there was nothing the Government in England could do until details were received of the reception given by the Americans to the Coercive Acts and of the outcome of the Philadelphia Congress.[3] This Continental Congress was instigated by the Virginia Committee of Correspondence. It met in September with delegates from twelve Colonies present. An immediate cleavage was apparent between those members, like Joseph Galloway, whose main aim was to restore complete harmony with England, those, like Patrick Henry, who already had their eyes on independence, and the large body in the middle who hoped for some compromise between the two extremes. These divisions continued for some time ahead, and not until 1776 was independence considered desirable by a majority of colonial leaders.[4] But the first Congress advertised the growing strength of radical feeling. In October it announced the Continental Association, which laid down that no British goods were to be imported after 1 December 1774, and no colonial goods exported to Britain after 10 September 1775. Machinery was set up to enforce the boycott. This provided a network of committees which were the sinews of the coming revolution. A petition was drawn up to be sent to the King and Addresses to the people of Great Britain and Canada. The first Continental Congress was many things: it was a clearing house for discontent and a united voice for the member Colonies; it was an act of rebellion against the old Empire and the seedbed of a federal union in the

[1] Dartmouth to Governor Carleton, 7 September 1774. PRO. CO. 42/33, f. 63. [2] Fortescue, op. cit., iii, 1509.
[3] Hutchinson, op. cit., i, 232. Hutchinson received personal letters from America on 20 August, which he forwarded to Dartmouth, but there was nothing official. Dartmouth MS. D 1778, 11, 968. Some dispatches from Gage written on 27 July did arrive on 7 September, but since the Coercive Acts had then not yet reached Boston they contained nothing new apart from a note of increased pessimism. Dartmouth could only reply expressing the hope that the Congress would make no rash decisions. To Gage, 8 September 1774. PRO. CO. 5/763, ff. 487-9. Also Gower to Dartmouth, 5 September 1774. Dartmouth MS. D 1778, 11, 957.
[4] E. Robson, The American Revolution, 1763–1783, pp. 70-1.

New World. Above all it was a challenge to George III and his Ministers, for it set America against Great Britain.

But what was the Ministry's attitude to the Congress ? Hutchinson reported that the Government was quite untroubled and felt it could leave the Americans to stew in their own juice. He concluded that 'nobody seems to give themselves the least concern about the consequences of the projected Congress, supposing it can do no hurt to the Kingdom'.[1] Lord Dartmouth, who as American Secretary was most directly concerned, expressed his feelings about the Congress at great length in a private letter to Hardwicke :

> Such a meeting is undoubtedly illegal [he said] but as it has been adopted with too much precipitation to be prevented . . . and will certainly take place, I am not without hopes that some good may arise out of it, and illegal as it is, if it should chalk out any reasonable tone of accommodation, or make any moderate or temperate proposal, I should in my own private opinion think it wise in government to overlook the irregularity of the proceedings, and catch at the opportunity of putting our unhappy differences into some mode of discussion that might save those disagreeable consequences which must arise to everyone of us either from open rupture and hostility with our fellow subjects, or from the no less calamitous interruption of our commercial intercourse with them.

Dartmouth was here clearly inclining to moderate treatment of the Americans — unlike his feelings on 3 August, when bad news had made him almost bloodthirsty. But he knew his sentiments might not be shared by his colleagues. He went on :

> This your Lordship perceives I throw out as my own private opinion only, and therefore you will have the goodness to keep it to yourself as such. I can easily admit that it might be very doubtful whether I should find many opinions to concur with mine.[2]

[1] Hutchinson to his eldest son, Thomas, August 1774. Hutchinson, *op. cit.*, i, 221.
[2] Dartmouth to Hardwicke, 29 August 1774. BM. Add. MS. 35612, f. 43.

One opinion which did not concur was that of the King. George III was in a less conciliatory frame of mind. He wrote to his Prime Minister:

> The dye is now cast, the colonies must either submit or triumph; I do not wish to come to severer measures but we must not retreat; by coolness and an unremitted pursuit of the measures that have been adopted I trust they will come to submit; I have no objection afterwards to their seeing that there is no inclination for the present to lay fresh taxes on them, but I am clear that there must always be one tax to keep up the right, and as such I approve of the tea duty.[1]

North accepted his monarch's opinions, and was breathing coercion when Hutchinson met him on 21 September. He insisted that some way must still be found to punish the Boston rioters for their treason, and added that if the American Congress decided on a non-importation movement then 'Great Britain would take care they should trade nowhere else'.[2]

From this survey of the state of opinion and morale in governing circles after the enactment of coercive measures and the prorogation of Parliament in June 1774, it appears that the King and his Ministers were still united in their unqualified resolution to enforce the recognition of England's complete supremacy over the Colonies. Dartmouth and North were as convinced as Mansfield and the King that the issue of sovereignty could no longer be avoided as it was in the 1760's. They had high hopes that the coercive measures would resolve the problem in England's favour, though the Government had never agreed on what should be recognised as a suitable submission. This optimism continued through the summer while they waited for official reports from Gage on the effect of the coercive measures. When some early news arrived indicating that the colonial reaction was one of defiance, the Ministry's

---

[1] 11 September 1774. Fortescue, *op. cit.*, iii, 1508. The King was discussing the contents of a letter from some American Quakers which had been conveyed to him by North. It expressed loyalty to the King but suggested England should make some concessions to the Americans.

[2] Hutchinson, *op. cit.*, i, 245-6. This may be an early hint of the Bills passed in March and April 1775 which barred trade between the Colonies and other States.

resolution hardened and the first indications were given that they might be prepared to meet force with force.

The first of Gage's material reports, full of bad omen, arrived on 1 October, and created a small flurry of activity among the few Ministers still in London. But ironically, after waiting so long, the majority of English politicians now no longer had time for American matters. For, the day before the reports reached London, the Ministry had announced its decision to dissolve Parliament and hold new elections.[1] These elections dominated the nation's affairs for some weeks ahead.

[1] The arrival of Gage's dispatches and the announcement of the dissolution were so nearly simultaneous that some people thought the one caused the other. See Franklin to Cushing, 6 October 1774. *The Writings of Benjamin Franklin*, ed. A. H. Smythe, vi, 249. The Bishop of Lichfield, Lord North's brother, wrote to their father (Lord Guildford) that the dissolution was 'universally well spoken of in this county [Trentham, Staffs] and I believe indeed it was very necessary, for Lord Gower showed me *in confidence* General Gage's letter and his account of the proceedings of the people of Boston is worse than I possibly could have conceived'. E. R. Hughes, 'Lord North's Correspondence, 1766-83', *English Historical Review*, lxii, 224-5. In fact, as will be seen, the timing of the two events was coincidental, although the general situation in America was one factor behind the dissolution.

CHAPTER VIII

THE 1774 ELECTIONS

The Dissolution

THE Parliament which had been elected in 1768 was not due to expire until March 1775. But on 24 August 1774 George III wrote to his Prime Minister 'a few lines on the calling a new Parliament' and suggested that an immediate dissolution be arranged. He argued:

> The general Congress now assembled in America; the Peace of Russia with the Turks and unsettled state of the French Ministry are very additional reasons to show the prosperity of the measure; [1] besides I trust it will fill the House with more Gentlemen of landed property as the Nabobs, Planters and other Volunteers are not ready for the battle; as soon as you can fix on a proper day for the dissolution I desire you will write to the Chancellor and Lord President, but not above a week before the measure is to be into execution.[2]

[1] Louis XV died of smallpox on 10 May 1774. He was considered to be a friend to England and some observers thought his death would mean hostility between the two countries renewed, and possibly war. (See Dowdeswell to Rockingham, 25 May 1774. Dowdeswell Papers. Transcripts in possession of The History of Parliament.) It is interesting to see George III express concern over Continental affairs. Like many of the younger generation of English politicians, George III was usually opposed to involvement in Europe. 'The Politics of the Continent', wrote Burke, 'which used to engage your attention so much, attract no part of ours.' (To Charles Lee, 1 February 1774. *CEB*, ii, 518. See also Sir Lewis Namier, *England in the Age of the American Revolution*, pp. 303 *seq*.) Of course, the King in his letter on 24 August might have been producing just another plausible reason for dissolving Parliament. But it is possible that he was genuinely worried about the position of France in the summer of 1774. Here it might be noted that Lord Mansfield had (according to Horace Walpole) been sent to Paris in July to visit his nephew Lord Stormont, who was Ambassador there, 'to persuade the French Court not to interfere with our differences with America'. *The Last Journals of Horace Walpole*, ed. A. F. Steuart, i, 373.

[2] King to North, 24 August 1774. J. W. Fortescue, ed., *The Correspondence of King George III, 1760–1783*, iii, 1501. It was probably Suffolk who originally suggested the idea of a dissolution to the King. In a debate

The King's intention was to keep the plan secret and then to spring the dissolution suddenly. But little could be done at this time of year, when the Prime Minister and his colleagues were so scattered. There was no more mention of the matter until well into September. Then North went off to Sion Hill to see his Secretary to the Treasury, John Robinson, who was already apprenticed as the Government's election manager. The Prime Minister reported back gloomily that if an election were to be held immediately every Member for Middlesex would be 'a determined opposer of the Government'.[1] Two days later North was still with Robinson when he wrote to the King:

> As a premature dissolution of Parliament renders the necessary preparation almost impossible Government can not expect to be so strong in the next House of Commons, as if we were at the natural end of the Parliament, Lord North hopes that his Majesty will not think him to blame if some important elections succeed contrary to his wishes; Many good consequences will result from a sudden dissolution, but some seats in the House of Commons will probably be lost by it.[2]

The King immediately replied to his timorous Minister, admitting it was 'not unlikely but that a premature dissolution may in some few places be disadvantageous', but reassuring him that he was 'thoroughly convinced that with temper, firmness and due activity, that by degrees the hands of Government will be as strong as before the many untoward events that have of late years risen'.[3] It appears that North had doubts about the wisdom of a sudden dissolution; though he was probably most worried by the thought of the effort required to conduct an election.[4] But he swallowed his misgivings as usual, and began

on 20 January 1775 Suffolk claimed in the Lords that he had been 'one of the principal advisers' and he openly avowed that his reason was to get the election over before the influence of the Philadelphia Congress was felt. *Parl. Hist.*, xviii, 161, and see also *Walpole Last Journals*, i, 421. *HMC, Various*, vi, *Knox MSS.*, p. 257.

[1] North to King, 25 September 1774. Fortescue, *op. cit.*, iii, 1511.
[2] North to King, 27 September 1774. *Ibid.*, 1513.
[3] King to North, 27 September 1774. *Ibid.*, 1514.
[4] On 14 May 1774, *Jackson's Oxford Journal* reported that 'the greatest part of the Ministry are for the Dissolution of Parliament this summer, but that the Premier is against it'.

to chase noble patrons and to make preparations to fight the metropolitan elections.[1]

In the meanwhile North had discussed the whole matter with Gower, Suffolk and Rochford, who 'had all given him their opinions for an immediate dissolution of the present administration'.[2] None of these was in London when the Cabinet met on 29 September, but the other four Ministers — Apsley, Dartmouth, North and Sandwich — attended and agreed 'to submit their opinion to his Majesty that it would be advisable to dissolve the present Parliament and call a new one'.[3] The following day the dissolution was announced.[4]

Although the Ministry's decision was unexpected, and meant to be secret, it inevitably leaked out before the official announcement.[5] The newspapers were soon full of analyses of the Government's motives. They were often very accurate, and some sounded almost as if they had read the King's letter to North on 24 August.[6] The consensus of opinion was, rightly, that the step was taken for two chief reasons: firstly to catch the Opposition unawares and so to secure a result favourable to the Administration; secondly because the Government feared that it might soon have more American business on its hands, which it neither wanted to deal with in the dying sessions of Parliament nor have interrupted by weeks of elections in the following spring. The importance of this second point was

---

[1] North to King, 29 September 1774. Fortescue, *op. cit.*, iii, 1515.

[2] Cabinet Minute, 29 September 1774. Dartmouth MS. D 1778, 11, 972.

[3] *Ibid.* See also J. Robinson to C. Jenkinson, 29 September 1774. BM. Add. MS. 38208, f. 105. Suffolk was ill at Hampton Court from 26 September and for most of October. He had returned from the country to London on 24 September to discuss the dissolution question. Suffolk to W. Eden, 22 September 1774. BM. Add. MS. 34412, ff. 294-5. See also Suffolk to King, 26 September 1774. Fortescue, *op. cit.*, iii, 1512. King to North, 29 September 1774. *Ibid.*, 1516.

[4] This was the first premature dissolution since 1747.

[5] Portland to Burke, 29 September 1774. W.W.M. Bk. G. Cressener to W. Knox, 10 November 1774. *HMC, Various*, vi, *Knox MSS.*, p. 116. Also *Walpole Last Journals*, i, 375. North himself leaked the news prematurely to the Duke of Newcastle. North to Newcastle, 25 September 1774. Newcastle MSS., NEC 2843.

[6] See a feature signed 'Candour' in *London Chronicle*, 5 October 1774. There is a summary of public reactions in *Town and Country Magazine*, October 1774.

emphasised by Lord North on 19 November 1774 when he told Hutchinson: 'I will venture to tell you that Parliament was dissolved on this account — that we might, at the beginning of a Parliament take such measures as we could depend upon a Parliament to prosecute to effect'.[1]

The suddenness of the dissolution certainly caught many people unprepared. Even Lord North and John Robinson, who were given a month to prepare before the decision was publicly announced, found this quite insufficient and, particularly in the metropolitan constituencies, were unable to organise their forces properly.

For the Opposition the difficulties were in general even greater.[2] Rockingham complained to Portland on 1 October that 'this manœuvre of the Ministry has taken me very much unaware, and I am not a little perplexed by it'.[3] He was troubled by doubts about whether Sir George Savile, Edmund Burke and William Baker would find seats, and he had not begun to sort out how he would dispose his own boroughs. Next day he told Burke: 'I did not believe that it would happen, till after the 16th of November, and I had relied on being in London and of having conversation with you and several of our friends previous to the event'.[4] During the following week he became sick and was unable to go to York where he would have discussed various electoral problems with his supporters.[5] Richmond alone was happy about the dissolution. 'It suits mine [interests] perfectly', he wrote to Portland. 'But I confess I think we should in general have done still better next spring, by which time I believe the American affairs would have made the Ministry generally as odious as they deserve.'[6] The advantages of timing gave consolation to Government supporters. John Yorke, a minor placeman, wrote to his brother, Lord Hardwicke, that the dissolution came 'much to our surprise'

[1] Hutchinson, *Diary and Letters*, i, 298.
[2] The Government repeated the device of a sudden summer dissolution six years later and, oddly enough, again caught everyone apparently unprepared. I. R. Christie, *The End of North's Ministry*, pp. 41-5, 118.
[3] Portland MS., PW F 9084.
[4] Rockingham to Burke, 2 October 1774. W.W.M. Bk., *CEB*, iii, 48.
[5] Rockingham to Portland, 7 October 1774. Portland MS. PW F 9085.
[6] 30 September 1774. Portland MS. PW F 6318.

but he felt 'that in a public light I very much applaud the measure, as it will from the secrecy and suddenness of it confound the schemes of a vast number of those who start on the popular line, and prevent a deal of riot, confusion and extravagance'.[1]

The Election Campaign

The great complexity of the eighteenth-century electoral structure and the variety of local and personal pressures which operated in determining results have been described in extensive and penetrating investigations by modern historians.[2] The county seats had a very wide franchise; yet sometimes local nobility made their influence felt in one or even both seats. County Members traditionally represented the landed interests, but there were also a number who had connexions with commerce, banking and industry. The boroughs were, in general, subject to greater influence, about half of them being under some form of patronage. However, the power of many of these local patrons was based upon willing acceptance by the local voters. Furthermore, the larger boroughs were probably the most democratic of all constituencies. It is impossible to draw a brief, clear and comprehensive picture of the election proceedings which were quickly under way in October 1774. There was no broad battle between Government and Opposition, between Whig and Tory, between Influence and Democracy, or between Landed and Commercial interests — although numbers of contests might exhibit one, some or all of these features. There was an enormous variety of local struggles, compromises and agreements which reflected the various social forces of eighteenth-century England. Contemporaries expressed this diversity quite simply when they often referred to 'the elections' rather than to the General Election.

The Government

Although the electorate of 1774 was not being asked to give a vote of confidence in Lord North's Government, nor in its

---

[1] Yorke to Hardwicke, 3 October 1774. BM. Add. MS. 35375, f. 132.
[2] Particularly see Sir Lewis Namier, *The Structure of Politics at the Accession of George III*, pp. 1-157. I. R. Christie, *op. cit.*, pp. 46-163.

measures, the Ministry did play an active role. It interfered, directly or indirectly, to try to secure the election of Members who might be relied upon to support the King's Administration. Two men were officially responsible for promoting the Government's interest — Lord North, as First Lord of the Treasury, and his secretary, John Robinson. Robinson knew where interests friendly to the Government could be stimulated or supported, and North, acting as the King's manager, distributed about £50,000 to help various Government supporters with their expenses.[1] Now that the elections were upon them, North was overwhelmed with the immediate tasks of electoral management — finding candidates, negotiating with constituency patrons, writing to influential local notables, and settling accounts. In briefly looking at these operations it should be possible to compare how the Government machine worked in 1774 with the intensive organisation which went on for the electoral campaign six years later.[2]

As usual the twenty-odd seats in 'Government boroughs' were distributed for the most part to men of business who were valuable to the Government in an administrative capacity. The Treasury seat at Winchelsea went to Charles Cornwall, who was a Commissioner of the Treasury.[3] At Harwich one seat (formerly Charles Jenkinson's) was given to Edward Harvey, Adjutant-General of the Forces and Governor of Portsmouth.[4] John Robinson reserved the other for himself. Jenkinson moved across to Hastings to take Samuel Martin's place; the other seat there had been arranged during the summer for Henry Temple (Viscount Palmerston), who was a Commissioner of the Admiralty.[5] The Admiralty seat at Queenborough went

[1] North to King, 10 April 1782. Fortescue, *op. cit.*, v, 3674. I. R. Christie, *op. cit.*, pp. 98-107.

[2] For an exhaustive coverage of the Government's campaign in 1780, see *ibid.*, pp. 69-107.

[3] Cornwall had swung to Opposition in 1768. He returned to the Government in 1774 and was given a place at the Treasury. In 1780 he became Speaker of the House. J. Brooke, *The Chatham Administration, 1766–68*, p. 352; I. R. Christie, *op. cit.*, pp. 89, 236-7.

[4] When Harvey died in 1778 he was replaced by George North, the Premier's eldest son.

[5] E. Millward to J. Robinson, 4 October 1774, and Samuel Martin to Jenkinson, 5 October 1774. BM. Add. MS. 38458, ff. 110, 112-13. North

to Sir Walter Rawlinson, a supporter of the Earl of Sandwich,[1] and the other place at Queenborough was retained by Sir Charles Frederick, the Surveyor-General of the Ordnance.[2] The Secretary at War, Viscount Barrington, and Admiral Sir Charles Hardy remained in the two Admiralty seats at Plymouth, and those at Saltash went to Grey Cooper, a joint Secretary at the Treasury, and Thomas Bradshaw, a Lord of the Admiralty.

Even in Government boroughs, however, the Ministry had some trouble. At Seaford opposition was raised against the sitting Administration Members (Lord Gage and George Medley) by Stephen Sayre and A. J. C. Chetwood. The latter were strongly supported by the poor, but these had no qualification to vote and in the poll Sayre and Chetwood secured only one legal vote each.[3] There was also a contest at Portsmouth,[4] and at Dover the Ministry was defeated in its attempt to nominate to both seats.[5] One of the old Members at Dover, Joseph Yorke, had written to the Earl of Hardwicke in March that he wished 'to avoid Dover if possible, and to procure a more quiet and independent seat. I see very plainly that prices are high, but one must take them as they run, or give up the point, for I cannot flatter myself that things are circumstanced at Dover to come off cheaper, and it may cost a great deal more, over and above all the disagreeable scenes one must go through.'[6] In September Lord North told Yorke that he would prefer him to remain at Dover; but if he insisted on moving, then North could find him a seat in the West Country, and the Ministry would run two new candidates at Dover. Yorke did insist, and so John Henniker and Sir Charles Whitworth (chairman of the

to Robinson, 5 October 1774. Robinson Papers, BM. MS. Facs. 340 (i), f. II.   [1] I. R. Christie, *op. cit.*, pp. 204, 206, 279.

    [2] R. Beatson, *A Political Index to the Histories of Great Britain and Ireland . . .*, i, 393. Sir Lewis Namier, *England in the Age of the American Revolution*, p. 226.

    [3] H. Stooks Smith, *The Register of Parliamentary Contested Elections*, p. 116. *Jackson's Oxford Journal*, 15 October 1774. *St. James's Chronicle*, 17 October 1774.   [4] *Jackson's Oxford Journal*, 15 October 1774.

    [5] Dover was a 'mixed' borough, where Government influence was strong but depended on local initiative. I. R. Christie, *op. cit.*, pp. 65, 80.

    [6] Yorke to Hardwicke, 7 March 1774. BM. Add. MS. 35370, f. 205. The other old Member, T. Barrett, retired in 1774. He was also a Government supporter.

Committee of Ways and Means) were put up. However, one of the local patrons declared against Whitworth and announced he would propose John Trevanion, a patriot and a Wilkite. North agreed to a compromise in order to avoid a costly and perhaps unsuccessful contest.[1] Henniker and Trevanion were returned unopposed and remained the Members for Dover, respectively voting for and against the Ministry, until the fall of Lord North's Government.

The electoral weight of patronage and influence was certainly still considerable in the 'seventies. But the direct influence of the Government, which controlled less than thirty seats, was small compared to — and declining before — such private empire-builders as Lords Falmouth, Edgcumbe, and Northumberland, Humphrey Morice, Edward Eliot and the Buller family. Each controlled several seats, and so could do a 'package deal' with the Government; many other lesser patrons were also prepared to be wooed by the Treasury. Altogether they had influence in about sixty seats, and it was from these private patrons that North and Robinson drew their secondary line of electoral support.[2] The disposal of some of these borough seats had been long arranged, privately or with the Government; but others, particularly in the West Country, remained open for quick negotiation and they provided the Ministry with a reserve of seats for any important supporters who found themselves stranded.

At the dissolution, Lord North had immediately on his hands Joseph Yorke, Sir Charles Whitworth, Thomas Graves, John Pownall, Henry Conway and Bamber Gascoyne. He did his best to satisfy them all. In September he wrote to Yorke, 'you may suddenly hear you are duly elected for a Borough you do not think of'.[3] The Prime Minister then negotiated with Edward Eliot for a seat for him at Grampound at a price of £2,500.[4]

---

[1] J. Yorke to Hardwicke, 18 October 1774. BM. Add. MS. 35370, ff. 286 seq.

[2] A detailed description of Lord North's dealings with the private patrons in 1780 is in I. R. Christie, op. cit., pp. 90-4.

[3] North to Yorke, 19 September 1774. BM. Add. MS. 35370, f. 275.

[4] For the activities of Eliot as a patron see I. R. Christie, op. cit., pp. 56, 90-2, 108-10, and J. Brooke, op. cit., pp. 240-1. Eliot's seats at Liskeard went to Edward Gibbon and Samuel Salt; those at St. Germans were taken

Yorke never heard a word from Eliot and he only learned that he had been elected when he read it in the *Morning Chronicle*.[1] When Whitworth was rejected at Dover, North decided to send him to one of John Buller's seats at East Looe.[2] He soon changed his mind, however, and decided to bring in Thomas Graves[3] there as soon as an alternative seat could be found for Whitworth.[4] This situation was not finally cleared up until 1775, when the Admiralty seat made vacant at Saltash by the death of Thomas Bradshaw was given to Whitworth, and Graves then took Whitworth's place at East Looe. North did similar juggling with his other commitments. He decided first to send John Pownall to take one of Lord Edgcumbe's seats at Lostwithiel; but this fell through, and in the end Lord Fairford, son of the Earl of Hillsborough, was elected there. Pownall did not find a place in this election, but North secured for him Edward Eliot's seat at St. Germans when Eliot moved to the Cornwall county seat in 1775.[5] Henry Seymour Conway was at first intended for Lostwithiel and then for one of Lord Falmouth's seats at Tregony.[6] But in the end he was fitted in at Midhurst, where the patron (Lord Montagu) was a pensioner and where the original candidate, Herbert Mackworth, preferred to stand for Cardiff. Another seat controlled by Falmouth — at Truro — was allocated to Bamber Gascoyne, a Commissioner of Trade and Plantations.[7]

The Government interfered in other elections as well as those where its own influence was decisive or where patrons were cooperative. Before leaving for the country on the 5th North told Grey Cooper to consult Robinson and Richard

by Benjamin Langlois (a placeholder) and by Eliot himself. The other seat at Grampound went to Richard Neville, a newcomer to Parliament.

[1] Yorke to Hardwicke, 8 November 1774. BM. Add. MS. 35370, f. 292.

[2] North to Grey Cooper, 5 October 1774. Robinson Papers, BM. MS. Facs., 340 (i), f. 4.   [3] Formerly M.P. for West Looe.

[4] North to J. Robinson, 5 October 1774. BM. Add. MS. Facs., 340 (i), f. 10.

[5] As Pownall was made an Excise Commissioner shortly after, North asked Eliot to return his £2,500 because Pownall had held the seat for only five months.

[6] North to Cooper, 5 October 1774. *Loc. cit.*, North to Robinson, 5 October 1774. *Loc. cit.*

[7] *St. James's Chronicle*, 29 October 1774.

Rigby about getting two Ministerial candidates for Westminster.[1] In fact the Government could do nothing at this stage,[2] for the Duke of Northumberland had his own two candidates — his son, Lord Percy, who was serving in America, and Lord Thomas Pelham Clinton. But its help became valuable when three radicals stood against Northumberland — two of them formally approved by John Wilkes.[3] The King ordered the Horse and Grenadier Guards to turn out to vote for Percy and Clinton.[4] The Opposition not surprisingly complained that royal servants had interfered in the election and that various Peers canvassed, entertained and corrupted the electorate.[5] The poll was long and riotous, but when it closed at the end of October Percy and Clinton had overwhelming majorities.[6]

Elsewhere in the Metropolis the efforts of Government supporters failed dismally. North and Robinson sought desperately for candidates to contest Middlesex, but the ill-feeling engendered by the Ministry's role in the Wilkes-Luttrell affair, and the popularity of Wilkes and John Glynn, the declared candidates, were too much for them. Wilkes and Glynn were running on a strong radical programme and Ministerial men blenched at the prospect of challenging them. North reported how one possible candidate finally decided to decline 'notwithstanding a most pressing letter from Mr. Robinson'.[7] The King described this retreat as 'disgraceful'[8] but there was nothing that

---

[1] North, 5 October 1774, BM. Add. MS. Facs., 340 (i), f. 2.

[2] Edmund Burke, who was also trying to get one of the Westminster seats, offered himself to run with Percy, but Northumberland refused. Burke to Portland, 7 October 1774. *CEB*, iii, 59.

[3] They were Lords Mahon and Mountmorres, the official radical candidates, and Humphrey Cotes, who was blamed for splitting the Opposition vote. They all signed a radical declaration similar to that at Middlesex (see below, p. 196). *London Chronicle*, 5 October 1774.

[4] King to North, 10 October 1774. Fortescue, *op. cit.*, iii, 1529.

[5] *Jackson's Oxford Journal*, 3 December and 17 December 1774. Horace Walpole wrote that 'the Duchess of Northumberland sat daily at a window in Covent Garden making interest for her son'. *Walpole's Last Journals*, i, 405.

[6] *Jackson's Oxford Journal*, 15 October and 29 October 1774. See North to Newcastle 25, 28, 30 September, 2, 26 October 1774. Newcastle MSS., NEC 2, 845, 851, 847, 844, 843. (The Newcastle MSS. are deposited in the Nottingham University Library.)

[7] North to King, 9 October 1774. Fortescue, *op. cit.*, iii, 1528.

[8] King to J. Robinson, 8 October 1774. BM. Add. MS. 37833, f. 4.

could be done. Wilkes and Glynn were duly elected unopposed. In the City the Court at least managed to produce a candidate, John Roberts, but he finished bottom of seven candidates at the poll.[1]

The Ministry made other, less direct, interventions with varying degrees of success. In Bedfordshire a contest was suddenly raised when Thomas Hampden, a former Member for Lewes who was inclined to the Opposition, declared against the sitting Members Lord Ossory and Robert Ongley. North promptly wrote to Sir George Osborn, his kinsman, and asked him to withdraw his support for Hampden. He does not appear to have succeeded in this, though Hampden was beaten at the poll. Yet the final twist came in November 1775 when Ossory was won over to the Opposition by his brother-in-law, C. J. Fox, and he voted against North until the end of the American war.[2] At Southampton North and Dartmouth tried vigorously to persuade Lord Charles Montagu, an Administration pensioner, to withdraw his opposition to two Ministerial candidates. Montagu, encouraged by the Duke of Cumberland, the King's brother, stood despite them, but was beaten.[3] In Sussex Sir James Peachy, with strong Government backing, intervened unsuccessfully against Thomas Spenser Wilson.[4]

The Government's electoral activities were certainly greater than those outlined above. Much work was done by word of mouth and in other cases the documents have not come to light. Yet the general impression remains that the 1774 elections were not organised by the Government as intensively or as extensively as those in 1780.[5] A major reason for this was that in 1774 political issues were not as sharp and the Government majority was not in such danger as it was in 1780. But a further factor

[1] On the efforts to get Roberts nominated see Robinson to King, 7 October 1774. *Ibid.*, f. 3.
[2] Hadley Coxe to Hardwicke, 15, 21 and 27 October 1774. BM. Add. MSS. 35693, ff. 240-1, 245-6, 248-9.
[3] North to Dartmouth, 2 October 1774, and Hans Stanley to Dartmouth, 9 October 1774. Dartmouth MSS. D 1778, L ii, 1035-6, 1041.
[4] *London Chronicle*, 18 November 1774. A seat was found for Peachy in 1774 when he took John Pownall's place at Lostwithiel.
[5] See I. R. Christie, *op. cit.*, pp. 46-163.

may have been the ill health of John Robinson, the Government's election manager. Robinson had fallen sick before the dissolution.[1] He was at work again by 8 October.[2] But he suffered a relapse, and Grey Cooper, who saw Robinson at Bath in the Christmas recess, reported that 'my hopes are almost gone' of his ever recovering.[3] Not until the following spring was his health restored.[4] During his absence much of his work was handed to other officials — particularly to William Eden — and much fell on the shoulders of Lord North. The incapacity of such a skilled and industrious public servant undoubtedly rendered the Ministry's electoral campaigning less effective.

Opposition

The dissolution caught the Rockingham squadron unprepared and in considerable disarray. Its leaders in both Houses of Parliament, Rockingham and Dowdeswell, were sick ; trouble in Buckinghamshire between the Verney and Grenville families put Verney's seat in jeopardy ; the two Burkes and William Baker had to find new seats elsewhere ; Portland was having electoral troubles in Nottingham and in Cumberland ; and Rockingham himself had problems in his home territory of Yorkshire. The suddenness of the dissolution gave the Opposition even less time than the Ministry to settle these troubles, but the flood of letters in the Burke, Rockingham and Portland collections indicates the efforts they made.

The most immediate difficulty for Rockingham was the threatened retirement of Sir George Savile, who had held a Yorkshire county seat since 1758. Savile was a man of extremely independent character, who had always supported the Marquis, but was never tied to the Rockingham squadron. His value to Rockingham, as a personal friend and as a Commons member

---

[1] Robinson to C. Jenkinson, 23 September 1774. BM. Add. MS. 38208, f. 102.

[2] North to King, 9 October 1774. Fortescue, *op. cit.*, iii, 1528. King to North, 10 October 1774. *Ibid.*, 1529.

[3] Grey Cooper to William Eden, 4 January 1775. BM. Add. MS. 34, 412, f. 326. At one time in October Robinson was rumoured to be dead. Germain to General Irwin, 17 October 1774. *HMC, Stopford-Sackville MSS.*, i, 134.   [4] Hutchinson, *op. cit.*, i, 446.

who was widely respected for the sincerity of his principles, was considerable.[1] On 9 August Rockingham begged Savile not to retire because this would force him to give up all his plans for both the county and the country.[2] But Savile was quite adamant, and told Lady Rockingham next day that he could face neither the prospect nor the physical strain of another seven years in Parliament and would announce his retirement publicly within a week.[3] She conveyed this news to her husband, who was away from home, and commented 'I should scarce have thought Sir George with his tender feelings could have been so hard hearted and have wrote so dry upon what works you to death'.[4] During September Savile continued firm in his intention to retire, although he still did not announce it publicly, and he was being pressed by Portland to continue for one more Parliament.[5] However, the sudden dissolution which precipitated Rockingham's other difficulties ended this particular worry. Since his resignation at this stage would cause great confusion, Savile gracefully agreed to stand again, and was returned unopposed.[6]

No sooner had Rockingham settled the county, however, than he was in trouble with the city of York, normally a safe stronghold for his supporters. The sitting Members were Lord John Cavendish and Charles Turner. Cavendish had held office in the first Rockingham Administration and had since become a prominent figure in the Opposition, leading them in the Commons when Dowdeswell was ill.[7] Turner, a former

---

[1] J. Brooke, *op. cit.*, p. 278. For a contemporary and similar view see James Harris to Hardwicke, 16 May 1778. BM. Add. MS. 35614, f. 222. Burke said 'much of the strength of our cause has arisen from its having his support'. Burke to Rockingham, 7–10 January 1773. W.W.M. Bk., *CEB*, ii, 408.

[2] W.W.M. R1-1497.

[3] 10 August 1774. W.W.M. R1-1498. Lady Rockingham wrote separately to plead with Savile. 10 August 1774. W.W.M. R1-1499.

[4] 11 August 1774. W.W.M. R1-1500.

[5] Rockingham to Burke, 13 September 1774. Burke to Rockingham, 18–25 September 1774. W.W.M. Bk., *CEB*, iii, 23-4, 28.

[6] Savile to Portland, 2 October 1774. Portland MS. PW F 2081. Savile stayed in Parliament until 1783.

[7] Burke accused Cavendish of being dilatory in his duties, and of spending more time hunting foxes than in Parliament. Burke to Rockingham, 5 January 1775. W.W.M. Bk., *CEB*, iii, 88-9.

Lord Mayor of York, normally voted with the Rockinghams, though he was an extremely independent man.[1] A group of aldermen nominated Martin Hawke [2] to oppose Cavendish and Turner, and during the poll Rockingham was kept up half the night dealing with mail to and from York.[3] The trouble apparently lay in Turner's eccentricities. Cavendish reported on 5 October that

> the town is yet perfectly quiet, but the vulgar begin to be rather discontented for want of drink and Charles' manner and conversation does not mend the matter. He yesterday objected to taking any steps towards treating the town after the election was over, and wanted to give all his money to some public work but he has come to rights this morning, and has consented to appoint a committee, with full powers to manage for us.[4]

Hawke pressed Turner and Cavendish closely, and was in the lead early in the poll, but he later slipped back and was forced to concede them the victory.[5]

At Hull another friend of Rockingham encountered difficulties. The previous Member, William Weddell, was retiring due to ill health,[6] and David Hartley was nominated in his place.[7] But opposition was raised by an independent, Captain Shirley.[8] Rockingham again became very concerned at the prospect of a defeat, for this was a seat over which he had influence, though no certain control.[9] The contest was very close, but Hartley squeezed home by sixty-six votes.[1] A third Yorkshire consti-

---

[1] J. Brooke, op. cit., pp. 347-50.
[2] Son of Sir Edward Hawke, First Lord of the Admiralty, 1766–71.
[3] Rockingham to Burke, 11 October 1744. W.W.M. Bk., CEB, iii, 64.
[4] Cavendish to Rockingham, 5 October 1774. W.W.M. R1-1512.
[5] London Chronicle, 14 October 1774.
[6] Rockingham to Savile, 9 August 1774. W.W.M. R1-1497. Rockingham to William Hammond, 9 August 1774. W.W.M. R1-1496. The other seat was held by Lord Robert Manners, a Ministerial supporter.
[7] In fact William Weddell did return to Parliament — at Malton, when Burke preferred Bristol.
[8] Shirley was the brother of Earl Ferrers, who was executed for murder in 1760.
[9] Rockingham to Portland, 7 October 1774. Portland MS. PW F 9085.
[1] London Chronicle, 18 October 1774. W. W. Bean gives slightly different figures: The Parliamentary Representation of the Six Northern Counties of England, p. 849.

tuency to cause worry to Rockingham was Hedon. The sitting Members, Sir Charles Saunders and Beilby Thompson, were solid supporters of the squadron. Opposition was declared by John Frederick, who was backed by the Ministry. Again the attack was repulsed, and Rockingham maintained his influence in Yorkshire.[1]

Elsewhere in the country more of the Marquis's friends ran into trouble. The chief difficulty was caused by a struggle for influence in Buckinghamshire between Earl Verney (a Rockingham supporter) and Earl Temple. In the last Parliament Verney took one county seat himself and secured the other for his friend Lowndes. But in September 1774 Temple began to canvass for his nephew, George Grenville.[2] Temple first proposed that Lowndes should retire to make way for Grenville, and then that the two of them unite to oust Verney. He 'sticks at no artifice to gain his point, let it be ever so low mean and dirty', complained Verney, ''tis his wish and desire to command the county'.[3] Edmund Burke, who had sat for Wendover on Verney's interest, immediately campaigned for his patron. He wrote to Rockingham, Portland, Richmond, Abingdon and William Baker urging them to help Verney.[4] He received sympathy, but there was little that could be done, and the penurious Verney was in no position to repel Temple's attack. George Grenville took one seat with Verney, and to avoid a contest Lowndes retired from the county representation.[5]

Verney could now no longer afford to bring in Edmund

[1] Frederick took Humphrey Morice's seat at Newport (Cornwall) when Morice preferred Launceston.

[2] Burke to Rockingham, 18–25 September 1774. W.W.M. Bk., *CEB*, 28-9.

[3] Verney to Burke, 25 September 1774. W.W.M. Bk.

[4] Burke to Rockingham, 18–25 September 1774. W.W.M. Bk., *CEB*, iii, 32-41. Burke to Richmond [post 26 September 1774]. W.W.M. Bk., *CEB*, iii, 38-9. Burke to Portland, 28 September 1774. Portland MS. PW F 2078. *CEB*, iii, 40-1. Richmond to Burke, 26 September 1774. W.W.M. Bk., *CEB*, iii, 37. W. Baker to Burke, 30 September 1774. W.W.M. Bk. Portland to Burke, 1 October 1774. W.W.M. Bk. Abingdon to Burke, 2 October 1774. W.W.M. Bk. Rockingham to Burke, 2 October 1774. W.W.M. Bk., *CEB*, iii, 55-6.

[5] Abingdon to Burke, 4 October. W.W.M. Bk. *Jackson's Oxford Journal*, 8 October 1774.

Burke gratis at Wendover.[1]   Burke immediately made enquiries at Westminster, but the sole possibility — that of standing as a Wilkite candidate, in any case unpalatable to him — was vetoed by Wilkes.[2]   Meanwhile Rockingham wrote to Burke to say that he could have one of his seats in Yorkshire.[3]   But by then Burke had decided to reach for a richer prize — the city of Bristol.   He had first been approached in June by some Bristol merchants who were dissatisfied with the sitting Members, Matthew Brickdale and Lord Clare.   He accepted their proposal to stand, while insisting he could not afford the expense of a contest.[4]   However, when Burke's name was put forward there was insufficient support, and the merchants had to be content with one pro-American nominee — Henry Cruger.[5] Even so, one of Burke's Bristol admirers, Richard Champion, who was a Quaker and a merchant engaged in the American trade, summoned him to the electoral battlefield.[6]

Burke received Champion's letter at 3 p.m. on 4 October; he left London an hour and a half afterwards.   But by the 7th he was convinced he had no hope of nomination there, and so he set out on the long trek north to secure his seat at Malton, where he arrived on the 9th.[7]   In the meantime, however, the situation had changed dramatically at Bristol.   Lord Clare,

[1] Previously Verney had brought in both Burke and John Bullock without charge. Burke to Rockingham, 18–25 September 1774. W.W.M. Bk., *CEB*, iii, 33. Richard Burke (Senior) to Joseph Bullock, 5 October 1774. W.W.M. Bk., *CEB*, iii, 55-6.

[2] Burke to Rockingham, 18–25 September 1774. W.W.M. Bk., *CEB*, iii, 32. Portland to Burke, 1 October 1774. W.W.M. Bk. Portland to Burke, 2 October 1774. W.W.M. Bk., *CEB*, iii, 51-3. Portland to Burke, 2 October 1774. W.W.M. Bk. Rockingham to Burke, 2 October 1774. W.W.M. Bk., *CEB*, iii, 49-50. Keppel to Burke, 3 October 1774. W.W.M. Bk. Burke to Portland, 7 October 1774. *CEB*, iii, 58-9.

[3] Rockingham to Burke, 2 October 1774. W.W.M. Bk., *CEB*, iii, 48.

[4] Rev. Thomas Wilson to Burke, 28 June 1774, 11 July 1774. W.W.M. Bk. Burke to Wilson, 1 July 1774. W.W.M. Bk., *CEB*, iii, 3-4.

[5] Cruger, a native of New York, was the son-in-law of Samuel Peach, a leading Bristol merchant. See P. T. Underdown, 'Henry Cruger and Edmund Burke : Colleagues and Rivals at the Bristol Election of 1774', *William and Mary Quarterly*, xv, 14-34.

[6] On Champion's role in Burke's election see also *CEB*, iii, xi-xiv.

[7] Richard Champion to Burke, 1 October 1774. W.W.M. Bk., *CEB*, iii, 43-7. Champion to Burke, 3 October 1774, and Champion to Burke, 3 October 1774. Champion Letter Book (transcripts at Sheffield). Burke to Champion, 5 October 1774. *CEB*, iii, 54. Burke to Champion, 7

lacking the stomach for a fight with Cruger, had retired at the end of the first day's poll.[1] Burke was immediately nominated and Champion once again called him to Bristol,[2] where he arrived breathless on the 13th. He plunged straight into a vigorous campaign which, after 27 days of polling, brought him victory over Brickdale.[3]

The Opposition was less successful at Nottingham, where the Duke of Portland tried to secure a seat for his brother, Lord Edward Bentinck. A Rockingham supporter, John Plumptre, was retiring at Nottingham and Portland hoped that Bentinck would rally the support of the 'old Whig interests'.[4] But Sir Charles Sedley had already declared his intention of standing, and he had local 'Tory' support. Rockingham joined with Portland in trying to make Sedley either withdraw or join with Bentinck against the other old Member, William Howe.[5] But Sedley, while assuring them of his personal sympathy, claimed to be the prisoner of his supporters.[6] At the poll Sedley won easily and Bentinck trailed in third place behind Howe.[7]

Another Rockingham supporter in trouble was William Baker. As his patron, Lord Edgcumbe, had engaged his place at Plympton to the Ministry, Baker wrote to Rockingham in September asking for a seat.[8] Rockingham eventually offered him the possibility of a seat at £3,500 but Baker felt that this was a little too high.[9] Meanwhile he entered the contest for the City of London. However, he refused to join with Wilkes in

October 1774. *Ibid.*, 60-1. Burke to Rockingham, 9 October 1774. W.W.M. Bk., *CEB*, iii, 62-3. Rockingham to Burke, 9 October 1774. W.W.M. Bk., *CEB*, iii, 63-4.

[1] *Jackson's Oxford Journal*, 15 October 1774.
[2] Champion to Burke, 8 October 1774. Champion Letter Book. (Transcript at Sheffield.)
[3] *Jackson's Oxford Journal*, 5 November 1774.
[4] Portland to Rockingham, 8 October 1774. W.W.M. R1-1514.
[5] Rockingham to Sedley, 8 October 1774. W.W.M. R1-1515.
[6] Rockingham to Portland, 9 October 1774. Portland MS. PW F 9087. Sedley to Rockingham, 9 October 1774. W.W.M., R1-1517.
[7] H. Stooks Smith, *op. cit.*, p. 116. Bentinck secured the county seat in 1775 when Thomas Willoughby was elevated to be Lord Middleton. Then he was supported by Lord Howe. Howe to Portland, 21 December 1774. Portland MS. PW F 5542.
[8] Baker to Rockingham, 14 September 1774. W.W.M. R1-1505.
[9] Baker to Rockingham, 3 November 1774. W.W.M. R1-1526.

signing the radical manifesto, and finished fifth in the poll.[1] As a result, Baker was out of Parliament until 1777, when he found a seat at Aldborough (Yorkshire).

Edmund Burke's relative, William, suffered a similar fate. Formerly at Great Bedwyn, he was forced to vacate his seat, and Edmund made desperate efforts to find him a place. But these were unavailing; Rockingham wrote, 'yourself being in Parliament, is the principal thing necessary', and Portland was also unable to help.[2] William finally contested Haslemere, though in the end his defeat mattered little since personal and financial difficulties drove him to leave the country.[3] Charles James Fox and Nathaniel Bayley, who had both gone over into opposition during the course of the year, were also defeated, at Poole and at Abingdon, but each was returned elsewhere (at Malmesbury and at Westbury). Thomas Skipwith, James Scawen, Robert Gregory and Sir John Griffin (independent friends of Rockingham), Lord George Lennox (follower of the Duke of Richmond), and Alexander Popham (a Shelburne supporter), were also involved in contests for Warwickshire, Surrey, Rochester, Andover, Sussex and Taunton, but all survived unscathed. The Rockinghams also gained a seat at Lincoln, where George Sanderson, Lord Lumley, was elected.

The Opposition emerged from the elections with little change in numbers. The chief impression which emerges is of the piecemeal way in which various Opposition magnates and candidates arranged their elections. There was some consultation to try to help stranded supporters. But there was really no organised Opposition electoral campaign.

National Politics and the 1774 Elections

A question which must be considered in this study is how far national issues, and particularly the American crisis, were reflected in the elections of 1774. Too much should not be read into the fact that there were considerably more contests in

---

[1] *Jackson's Oxford Journal*, 15 October 1774.
[2] Rockingham to Burke, 2 October 1774. W.W.M. Bk., *CEB*, iii, 48. Burke to Portland, 4 October 1774. *CEB*, iii, 53.
[3] *London Chronicle*, 14 October 1774. D. Wecter, *Edmund Burke and his Kinsmen*, p. 79, and note II.

England in 1774 than in 1780, and nearly twice as many as in 1761,[1] since there were very few contests in 1774 which could be directly related to national politics. Among the few were the victories of Burke at Bristol and of Robert Gregory — an independent but solid supporter of Rockingham — at Rochester, which were won over sitting Members who had given North unwavering support in the last Parliament. At Southwark the radicals defeated a Government supporter, Sir Abraham Hume, and in the City of London they pushed the Court candidate to the bottom of the poll. The Ministry in its turn beat off the radical challenge at Westminster.

Much more common were contests over purely local affairs. In 1774 there were contests at Bedford, at Coventry and at Abingdon in which the decisive factor was whether the Member should be chosen by the Corporation or by independent interests. In Westmorland, Cumberland and Carlisle the empire-building of Sir James Lowther caused friction with Lord Portland and Lord Carlisle and with the local gentry; their efforts to avoid contests failed. Elsewhere members of leading families tried to mark their social status by acquiring a local Parliamentary seat — Mark Milbanke in the city of Durham, Denis Rolle at Barnstaple, and Thomas Harley, who retired from his seat in the City of London to try to win his native county of Hereford. At Tamworth and at Newcastle-under-Lyme the established families of Gower and Weymouth successfully defended their domains against independent intruders. Contests of these kinds, both local and personal, were the norm of mid-eighteenth-century election politics. Their number might vary considerably for particular reasons which were of little consequence to the national political scene; and in 1774 there happened to be more than usual.

Perhaps the most interesting political feature of the elections was the effort made by the radicals — because they almost alone raised the American issue. They concentrated their attack

---

[1] Reports of at least eighty contested elections in England in 1774, six in Wales and over a dozen in Scotland are contained in contemporary sources and later secondary works. In England there were sixty-eight contests in 1780 and forty-two in 1761. See I. R. Christie, *op. cit.*, p. 119. The definitive authority on these elections is *The History of Parliament: The House of Commons 1754–1790*.

on open constituencies, chiefly in the metropolitan area and in the ports.[1] John Wilkes remained their guiding spirit. The Declaration which he announced to a meeting of five hundred freeholders at Mile End on 26 September provided the radicals with the outline of something that no other grouping in England considered — political objectives. He swore to work for: (i) shorter Parliaments; (ii) 'free and equal representation of the people'; (iii) freedom of elections; and (iv) repeal of the Coercive Acts.[2] At the nomination meeting early in October, Wilkes and John Glynn stepped up the bidding, signing resolutions to lower the price of porter and to reduce taxes on various consumer goods. (A proposal to tax all travellers to France three guineas was negatived.[3]) Much of this was blatant and unoriginal vote-catching; but it had the virtue of containing some specific proposals — the most interesting of which is the clause demanding the repeal of the Coercive Acts.[4]

The radical Declaration was introduced into several other constituencies apart from Middlesex. Wilkes's personal influence was decisive in the City of London, where three of the successful candidates had signed his Declaration.[5] At Southwark, Nathaniel Polehill signed it, Henry Thrale announced that he agreed with some but not all of its provisions, and Sir Abraham Hume refused to have anything to do with it. At the poll they finished in that order, with Hume a very long way behind.[6] But the radicals had less luck at Westminster (the abortive radical campaign there by Mahon, Mountmorres and Cotes has already been described above); at Worcester, where Sir Watkin Lewes waged a popular, but unsuccessful, contest based on the principles of the Declaration; at Cambridge, where Thomas Plumer

---

[1] Of the eight boroughs with the largest electorates the radicals contested four — Westminster (11,000), London (7,000), Newcastle-on-Tyne (2,500), Worcester (2,000). [2] *Jackson's Oxford Journal*, 1 October 1774.

[3] *London Chronicle*, 7 October 1774.

[4] For other examples of radical programmes see the list of instructions to the Members of Parliament for Newcastle-on-Tyne in 1769, contained in *The Freeman's Magazine, or the Constitutional Repository* (Newcastle, 1776), and a similar list to the City of London members in a collection called *Broadsides, 1702–80* (both are deposited in the Bodleian Library, Oxford).

[5] John Sawbridge, Frederick Bull and George Hayley. The fourth Member, Richard Oliver, refused.

[6] *Jackson's Oxford Journal*, 8 October and 15 October 1774.

Byde and Samuel Meeke, the unsuccessful candidates against
the sitting Government Members, signed the Declaration; and
at Southampton, where Lord Montagu failed in his attempt to
press the candidates to subscribe to the Declaration.[1] Radicals
also contested seats in Surrey, Essex, Seaford, Great Yarmouth
and Dover; and at Newcastle-on-Tyne and Milburne Port there
was a strong radical flavour to the campaigns, but it is not
certain whether any of the candidates publicly signed the
Declaration, and Dover provided their only success.[2] In Kent,
although there was no contest, there was certainly a lively
radical campaign. John Sawbridge and Lord Mahon both
canvassed vigorously, and at the nomination meeting in August
Mahon made a resounding speech preaching radical ideals and
demanding either the abolition of Pocket Boroughs or the
doubling of county representation. He told one candidate that
his 'saying he would act on Revolutionary Principles was saying
nothing, unless he would declare what he meant thereby' — a
rebuke which would have silenced many an old Whig.[3]

As far as can be judged, the American issue was raised in
some sixteen, possibly in less than a dozen, constituencies in
1774 — in those where the Wilkes Declaration was certainly
introduced, together with those where popular candidates stood
and may have raised points from the Declaration, and at Bristol.[4]
Everywhere except Bristol the colonial question was introduced
only as part of the general radical campaign, and it was certainly
considered less important than Parliamentary reform. Only at
Bristol did America seem to matter much in the electors' minds.
The American merchants there were very concerned about the

[1] *London Chronicle*, 12 October 1774.

[2] The candidates were: Sir Joseph Mawbey in Surrey, Lord Waltham
in Essex, Stephen Sayre and J. Chetwood at Seaford, William Beckford and
Sir Charles Saunders at Great Yarmouth, John Trevanion at Dover, Constantine Phipps and Thomas Delaval at Newcastle, and Temple Luttrell at
Milburne Port. (Delaval was a very doubtful radical and Phipps certainly
not one, and their campaign was mainly concerned with local grievances,
but they stood with the backing of a strong local radical organisation.)
Since Sayre was American by birth and a well-known City radical it is highly
probable that he took a stand against the coercive measures.

[3] *St. James's Chronicle*, 26 and 30 August 1774.

[4] For a description of the activities of Wilkes and his supporters in the
election see I. R. Christie, 'The Wilkites and the General Election of 1774',
The Guildhall Miscellany, II, 4, 155-64.

effect of coercion upon trade with the Colonies, and when they asked Burke to stand they explicitly said that they did so in view of his position on America.[1]

In the spring of 1774 Richard Henry Lee had predicted that the prospect of elections ahead of them would deter the English Government from using coercion against the colonists. 'The wise and good in Britain', he wrote, 'are too well convinced of the unmerited abuse we have received for 10 or 12 years past not to produce consequences from a dispute with America, fatal to the views of Ministry at a General Election.'[2] But the Ministry pressed on with its American measures. And it had cause not to be deterred by the prospect of elections; for the American issue was clearly not yet an important electoral factor.

There were two main reasons for this lack of concern with the state of affairs in the Colonies. Firstly, and primarily, national politics played little part in most eighteenth-century elections. The Government did interfere in a number of constituencies to secure the return of its supporters to Parliament. Rockingham, Portland and lesser lights in the Opposition also strove hard to keep their various regional influences and so maintain the strength of their voices in national business. But national party politics, with its concomitants of alternative party policies and alternating governments, did not yet exist. In fact, the very concept of policy, as distinct from administration, was scarcely recognised. And, as for party,

> the unenfranchised classes, not yet herded into towns, were hardly aware that political action might be a remedy for their grievances, economic rather than political in their nature. There was no mass electorate, and no need for party programmes. The story of party in the eighteenth-century centres in Parliament rather than in the constituencies.[3]

[1] Rev. Dr. Thomas Wilson to Burke, 28 June 1774. W.W.M. Bk.
[2] To Samuel Adams, 24 April 1774. *The Letters of Richard Henry Lee*, ed. J. C. Ballagh, i, 107.
[3] J. Brooke, *op. cit.*, p. 220. For an interesting contemporary discussion on the decline of party, and how 'the names of Whig and Tory have been some time laid aside, and that of the Court and Country party substituted in their room', see *London Chronicle*, 1 September 1774.

The activities of a few political radicals were already beginning to change this picture (and military defeats accelerated the process by 1780). But it was still generally true in 1774. As yet there was no war in America; the problem there appeared to be still one of administration rather than of policy. How little the mass of the English electorate felt called upon to judge such issues was lamented by Burke: 'Until I knew it, both by my own particular experience, and by my observations of what has happened to others, I could not have believed how very little the local constituent attends to the general public line of conduct observed by their member'.[1] Although he had learned about it from experience, Burke could not reconcile himself to this apparent apathy. In February 1774 he remarked on 'the supineness of the public. Any remarkable highway robbery on Hounslow Heath would make more conversation than all the disturbances of America.' And in September he said that

> in the present temper of the nation, and with the character of the present administration, the disorder and discontent of all America and the more remote future mischiefs, which may arise from these causes, operate as little as the division of Poland. . . . The character of the Ministry, either produces, or perfectly coincides with the disposition of the public.

Burke's Celtic temperament could not accept, or appreciate, the Anglo-Saxon docility: 'they bear their calamities', he said, 'as they bear the seasons; not as arising from the faults of those who rule them, but as dispositions of providence'.[2]

In the second place it is doubtful if many of the British electorate, even had they been more concerned with national issues, would have been sympathetic with the American position of Burke and his colleagues. As the American challenge to British sovereignty became more open, so to most people of political awareness the need to enforce that supremacy became

---

[1] Burke to Richard Champion, 26 June 1777. W.W.M. Bk.
[2] Burke to Rockingham, 2 February 1774. W.W.M. Bk., *CEB*, ii, 524. Burke to Rockingham, 18–25 September 1774. W.W.M. Bk., *CEB*, iii, 31.

more apparent.[1]   This was particularly true of the commercial classes.   It is significant that whereas in 1766 these groups had risen up against the Stamp Act and forced the Government's hand, during 1774 they were almost silent.[2]   Although the industrial and trading towns were already the seedbeds of radicalism, the manufacturing and commercial classes who lived and voted in them in 1774 did not in general feel that their vital interests were deeply threatened by the American situation.   To them, with just a few exceptions, the elections were, perhaps for the last time, ordinary matters of local interest.

The Results of the Elections

On 14 November Lord North sent to the King 'a state of the supposed numbers in the new Parliament', informing him : 'This state has been formed with as much caution as possible, and every member left out of the list of pros, whose sentiments are not perfectly known, and of whose conduct the least doubt can be entertained'.[3]   The list of Members who he thought would support the Government numbered 321, including about fifty who might be sick, absent or abroad.   This left 237 divided among the other two lists — of Opposition and of doubtfuls. A number of these doubtfuls, if they voted at all, could be expected to vote sometimes, even most often, for the Administration.   And the remaining Opposition list contained its own proportion of sick and absent friends.   It is clear that Lord North's Ministry had maintained its nominal majority in the House of Commons.   How long it would retain this in the new Parliament would very much depend on events in America.

[1] See Burke to the Committee of Correspondence of the General Assembly of New York, 6 April 1774. W.W.M. Bk., *CEB*, ii, 528. Hutchinson came to the same conclusion when touring East Anglia in the autumn. Hutchinson, *op. cit.*, i, 237, 253, 258.
[2] See above, Chapter VI, pp. 146-56.
[3] North to King, 14 November 1774. Fortescue, *op. cit.*, iii, 1554.

CHAPTER IX

THE COLLAPSE OF THE
GOVERNMENT'S POLICY

THE first of General Gage's long-awaited reports describing the reaction in Massachusetts to the Coercive Acts had been sent on board the *Scarborough*, which reached Spithead on Friday evening, 30 September.[1] The Ministry did not receive his two letters until the next day, 1 October,[2] although there were rumours in London on Friday 'that advice had been received of there having been some commotions at Boston'.[3] The first letter, written on 27 August, reported that the official copies of the three Coercive Acts had reached Boston on the 6th. Gage had immediately contacted the nominees to the new Council and arranged the first meeting for the 16th; twenty-four had accepted, seven refused, three were still wavering and one was already dead.[4] This still held out grounds for optimism. But the second letter, dated 2 September, announced a grave deterioration in the Massachusetts situation.[5] Gage wrote that

[1] According to the *St. James's Chronicle*, the *Scarborough* 'had dispatched her letters to Town that were for the Government a day or two before she arrived at Spithead'. *St. James's Chronicle*, 4 October 1774. None of the newspaper 'shipping news' columns give details of the *Scarborough*'s movements. The *Public Advertiser*, usually a good source, merely reported on 4 October that she had arrived at Portsmouth.

[2] Cabinet Minute, 3 October 1774. Dartmouth MS. D 1778, II, 975.

[3] *St. James's Chronicle*, 1 October 1774. These rumours may be connected with the introduction to the King on 28 September of Sir James Perrot, who brought secret intelligence relating to America. Mr. Fraser to Dartmouth, 27 September 1774. Dartmouth MS. D 1778, I, ii, 1027. See also *St. James's Chronicle*, 1 October 1774.

[4] Gage to Dartmouth, 27 August 1774. PRO. CO. 5/763, ff. 503-10. Printed in C. E. Carter, ed., *The Correspondence of General Thomas Gage, 1763-1775*, i, 365-8. Lieutenant-Governor Oliver was the thirty-sixth nominee to the Council.

[5] Gage to Dartmouth, 2 September 1774. PRO. CO. 5/763, ff. 543-8. Printed in *The Correspondence of General Thomas Gage, 1763-1775*, i, 369-372. Gage's reports were accompanied, and his impressions confirmed, by two letters from Admiral Graves to the Admiralty describing the violent

intimidation of the nominees to the Council had forced several to resign, and people were refusing to serve on juries. The Bostonians had also found a loophole in the clause of the Massachusetts Regulating Act forbidding public meetings; they had called a meeting before the Act arrived and then deliberately adjourned it so that henceforward they were able to reconvene and claim they were continuing an old meeting and not calling a new one. Gage described the Colony as being in an uproar, and declared : 'civil government is near its end'. He pointed out that the rebels were 'not a Boston rabble, but the Freeholders and farmers of the country.' He pleaded for more military reinforcements because 'nothing that is said at present can palliate. Conciliating, moderation, reasoning is over. Nothing can be done but by forcible means.' He concluded that 'the whole is now at stake' and the only hope lay in striking an immediate and decisive blow.

The tone of Gage's letter was frantic and he had clearly lost confidence in his own capacity to restore order in the Bay Colony.[1] The measures which he immediately took to acquire troop reinforcements showed how gravely he now interpreted the situation. He sent transports to Quebec to collect the 10th and 52nd Regiments, and wrote to Carleton 'as I must look forward to the worst from the apparent disposition of the people here, I am to ask your opinion whether a body of Canadians and Indians might be collected and confided in for the service in this country should matters come to extremities'.[2] It was still only

---

attacks on various officers of the executive in Massachusetts. Admiralty to Dartmouth, 1 October 1774. PRO. CO. 5/247, f. 107. Vice-Admiral Graves had taken over from Montagu as C.-in-C. North America in April 1774.

[1] Although Gage was only now prepared to admit his pessimism officially, he had privately confided in June how much he disliked his task in Boston. Hutchinson, who saw the letter when he stayed with Lord Gage in August, said then that it 'discovers greater anxiety and distress of mind that what appears from all the accounts we have received concerning him'. Hutchinson, *Diary and Letters*, i, 223-4.

[2] Gage to Carleton, 4 September 1774. PRO. CO. 5/7 (part 2), f. 309. Carleton replied on 20 September that a Canadian regiment might be a good idea, and the Indians were in good humour — 'but you know what sort of people they are'. *Ibid.*, f. 310. Two companies of the 65th Regiment were sent from Newfoundland to Boston at the beginning of October. Molyneux Shuldham to the Admiralty, 4 October 1774. PRO. CO. 5/120, ff. 296-7.

a few months since the Ministry had sworn — and with justice — that the Quebec Act was never devised as a means to use the savages against the old colonists. But General Gage was being forced to clutch at any straw, and obviously he was already contemplating extreme military measures.

In London the American news was received with equal seriousness. When it arrived on Saturday, 1 October, a majority of the Ministry were away from the capital — because of the season, on electoral business, or for reasons of health.[1] But the remainder, Apsley, North and Dartmouth, gathered for a Cabinet meeting on Monday at the Prime Minister's house and took an immediate decision. The American Secretary

> communicated the Dispatches received on Saturday last from General Gage and Admiral Graves and it was agreed by the Lords present that the state of His Majesty's affairs in New England should be further considered and another meeting to be held as soon as the rest of the King's servants can attend, and that in the meantime it will be advisable that the Admiralty should be consulted whether two or three ships of war with as large a detachment from the marines as can be convincingly accomodated, may be sent to Boston immediately without any material hazard or difficulty.[2]

Next day the King wrote to Dartmouth suggesting that two regiments of infantry from Ireland be sent together with the marines.[3] But when Dartmouth wrote in turn to Sandwich he was not wholly convinced that it was a good idea to send troops.[4]

---

[1] Gower was at Trentham, Rochford at St. Osyth, and Sandwich at Hinchingbrooke. (See the Bishop of Lichfield's letter to Guildford from Gower's home, above Chapter VII, p. 176 *n* 1. Rochford to Dartmouth, 5 October 1774. Dartmouth MS. D 1778, I, 1038, quoted in *HMC*, II, v, *Dartmouth MSS.*, i, 364. Sandwich to Dartmouth, 5 October 1774. PRO. CO. 5/120, f. 278.) Suffolk was ill with gout. Suffolk to Lovell Stanhope, 11 October 1774. PRO. S.P. Dom. George III, 37/10, f. 87/15.

[2] Cabinet Minute, 3 October 1774. Dartmouth MS. D 1778, II, 975.

[3] King to Dartmouth, 4 October 1774. Dartmouth MS. D 1778, Supplementary George III.

[4] It was probably around this time that North wrote an undated letter to Dartmouth admitting that Gage's dispatches gave grounds for reinforcements, but that England could not provide these in less than twelve months. Furthermore he doubted the strategic wisdom of using a land army in North America. North to Dartmouth (undated), 1774. Dartmouth MS. D 1778, II, 1073.

He enclosed Gage's dispatches and said they revealed that civil government was nearly at an end in Massachusetts and that 'the people seem resolved at all events to oppose by force the execution of the late Acts of Parliament regarding that province'. He pointed out that Gage's fear

> that even with all the troops in North America that can be collected he may still be exposed to great risk and hazard is a very embarrassing consideration for us [.] on the one hand it seems highly dangerous to trust to any additional forces that can be now levied there, so on the other hand the season of the year and many other considerations of general policy subject the proposition of sending troops from here or from any other place to great objection.

Consequently, he concluded, the Cabinet had decided 'that the best that could be done for the present would be to send two or three ships to Boston immediately with as large a number of Marines as can be conveniently accommodated if in your Lordship's opinion it may be done at this season of the year without any material hazard and difficulty . . .'.[1]

The Cabinet's decision to increase the naval force in American waters was very necessary. When Admiral Graves had taken over the North American Command in the spring of 1774, he found there was only one warship, a few small frigates, and a dozen sloops and schooners, and he promptly requested reinforcements.[2] Now this deficiency appeared in a new and critical light. On 5 October Sandwich replied to Dartmouth: 'I have thoroughly considered the practicability of sending a reinforcement of ships and Marines to North America, and am satisfied that measure may be executed without any material inconvenience'. He had written to tell the Admiralty to fit out three guardships immediately 'with as many Marines from the several quarters as can possibly be spared; and as there may be a probability of their landing, to order a Major to command

---

[1] Dartmouth to Sandwich, 4 October 1774. PRO. CO. 5/120, f. 276. Sandwich was at Hinchingbrooke.
[2] 'Disposition of His Majesty's ships and vessels in North America under the command of Admiral Graves.' 30 October 1774. PRO. CO. 5/120, f. 8. Seven of these ships were in Boston executing the Port Act.

them'. He pointed out that it was rather late in the year to expect a good Atlantic crossing, but added with pride that 'English men of war, especially single ships, are very likely to make their passage at any time of the year . . .'.[1] Dartmouth received this letter on the 6th, and on the 7th he formally instructed the Admiralty to send three extra ships of the line to the American Command.[2] The Admiralty complied, using guardships from the home ports, and they were filled with ten companies of Marines.[3] These three ships reached Boston at the beginning of December.[4]

The Ministry was put into a great bustle by the need to settle simultaneously American policies in London and election business in the country.[5] But slowly the various Ministers registered their reactions to Gage's dispatches. Sandwich took swift decisions at Hinchingbrooke. Rochford wrote comfortingly from St. Osyth that 'I do not yet despair of the American business turning out right, for if I understand Gage right, the Bostonian rebels will not meet with assistance from the other colonies'.[6] Gower, on the other hand, was extremely depressed when he received the American news at Trentham. 'I think it of a very alarming nature, and big with mischief to the two countries, for I am sure they may properly be called two now. I think the servants of the Crown who were in town have done wisely to advise his Majesty to give all the support possible to

---

[1] Sandwich to Dartmouth, 5 October 1774. PRO. CO. 5/120, f. 278.

[2] *Ibid.*, f. 286.

[3] The Marines were formed into a single battalion, under the command of Major-General Pitcairn, and they later featured in the skirmishes at Lexington and Concord.

[4] The *Scarborough* arrived on 3 December and was later sent to Piscatagua. The *Asia* and the *Boyne*, which reached Boston on the 5th and the 9th, remained stationed there. PRO. CO. 5/121, ff. 21-3, 133.

[5] 'Both the Secretaries were out of town, and Lord North in a hurry that I wish your Lordship may be able to imagine. I am not able to give you any notion of it.' Marchmont to Hardwicke, 6 October 1774. BM. Add. MS. 35612, f. 98. After holding the Cabinet on the 3rd, Lord North set off for Oxfordshire, was robbed by a highwayman *en route*, and returned by way of his home at Bushey, reaching London again on Sunday 9 October. North to Cooper, 5 October 1774. Robinson Papers, BM. MS. Facs. 340 (i). North to King, 9 October 1774. J. W. Fortescue ed., *The Correspondence of King George III, 1760–1783*, iii, 1528.

[6] Rochford to Dartmouth, 5 October 1774. Dartmouth MS. D 1778, I, ii, 1038. Quoted in *HMC*, II, V, *Dartmouth MSS.*, i, 362.

General Gage in the alarming crisis.'[1]   Only Suffolk — sick with gout — apparently remained silent.[2]

In London Dartmouth was working on his reply to Gage, and when Hutchinson saw him at this time he reported that 'now he seems to despair'.[3] When Dartmouth submitted his draft reply, George III approved its 'great candour', but suggested that adding 'an additional paragraph assuring him that, though the conflict is unpleasant, Great Britain cannot retract, might do good as it [would] give him resolution, and without it I should fear he would think that there was some wavering which the present moment I am sure cannot allow to be the case with the most gentle minds'.[4] The King clearly did not intend to allow Dartmouth, the most gentle of his Ministers, to waver at this crucial moment.   Yet Dartmouth was not the only Minister who was worried by the turn of events.   Hutchinson saw Charles Jenkinson on 13 October and reported that 'he [Jenkinson] wishes something could be done to satisfy the Colonies . . . but is at a loss in what it can be done'.   Next day Hutchinson encountered Thurlow, the Attorney-General, and found him 'strongly inclined to relinquish all claim to taxation . . . but in what way or manner this could be done without giving up all, he was utterly at a loss'.[5]

On 17 October Dartmouth sent his reply to Gage, and from the letter it appears that nothing more had been decided since the Cabinet meeting on the 3rd.   He wrote that the Government realised that there was near anarchy in Massachusetts and that Gage needed troops.   But

the state of this Kingdom will not admit of our sending more troops from Great Britain.   Considerations of general safety forbid our sending any from our distant stations, and though *perhaps some* might be spared from Ireland, yet the advanced

---

[1] Gower to Dartmouth, 6 October 1774. Dartmouth MS. D 1778, I, ii, 1038. Quoted in *HMC*, II, V, *Dartmouth MSS.*, i, 364.

[2] Suffolk to Lovel Stanhope, 11 October 1774. PRO. S.P. Dom. George III, 37/10, f. 87/15.

[3] Hutchinson to Mr. Foster, 10 October 1774. Hutchinson, *op. cit.*, i, 262.

[4] King to Dartmouth, 10 October 1774. Dartmouth MS D. 1778, Supplementary George III.

[5] Hutchinson, *op. cit.*, i, 260-1.

season of the year making it next to impossible for transports to secure a passage to North America, their departure must be postponed until the spring.

He informed Gage that the three guardships were to be sent, and closed with the hope that the friends of Government in America would remain loyal.[1] In a separate and secret letter Dartmouth pressed Gage to keep the Government more closely informed of events in Boston and told him to take action against a certain Lieut.-Colonel Lee who was seditiously supporting the rebels there.[2]

During the time since Gage's dispatches had arrived, and while it considered them, the Government had also been increasingly concerned with another, though related, problem — the smuggling of arms from Europe to North America. General reports of this had first arrived at the end of August, and Dartmouth promptly wrote to Lieut.-Governor Colden at New York telling him to stop any contraband into the port.[3] But the extent of the traffic in arms was not fully realised until October. Then the news of the critical political situation in Boston was rapidly followed by details of several smuggling ventures which were already under way. The Commissioners of Customs at Boston wrote to ask for extra ships to prevent illicit smuggling from Holland to New York.[4] The Secretary at War, Viscount Barrington, informed Dartmouth that a ship was sailing from Plymouth to North America with a cargo of gunpowder.[5] Suffolk sent news that the English brig *Smack* had arrived at Amsterdam from Rhode Island and taken on board forty pieces of cannon, and, shortly after, he reported that arms were being shipped from Hamburg.[6]

[1] Dartmouth to Gage, 17 October 1774. PRO. CO. 5/763, ff. 619-26.
[2] PRO. CO. 5/763, f. 615. Headed 'Separate and Secret'.
[3] Suffolk to Dartmouth, 31 August 1774. PRO. CO. 5/138 (Part II), f. 392. And Dartmouth to Colden, 7 September 1774. PRO. CO. 5/1141, ff. 133-4.
[4] Commissioners of Customs at Boston to the Treasury, 10 August 1774. (Received 3 October.) PRO. T. 1/505. (The folios in this box are not numbered.)
[5] Barrington to Dartmouth, 14 October 1774. Dartmouth MS. D 1778, II, 979.
[6] Suffolk to Dartmouth, 24 October 1774. PRO. CO. 5/138 (Part II), ff. 404, 408.

The Government acted with unaccustomed speed. On 18 October Dartmouth told the Admiralty to send a ship to Amsterdam, where it should wait for the *Smack* to sail and then arrest her.[1] At the same time Suffolk instructed Sir Joseph Yorke, the English diplomatic representative in Holland, to ask the Dutch to seize the smugglers.[2] A meeting of the Privy Council was also arranged for the following day, when the King issued an Order in Council prohibiting the export of arms or gunpowder from Great Britain except under licence from the Privy Council.[3] The measures had quick effect. The cutter *Wells* went to Amsterdam and forced the *Smack* to discharge both its cargo and crew.[4] A ship was also dispatched to intercept a sloop shipping arms from the Elbe.[5] But the Government's efforts did not stamp out the gunrunning. Letters continued to arrive from the Continent reporting arms shipments.[6] From New York, Colden wrote that 'the contraband trade carried on between this place and Holland . . . prevails to an enormous degree', and that his son, a customs officer, had been offered a bribe of £1,500 'if he would not be officious in his duty . . .'.[7]

Towards the end of October reports began to filter through of the final proceedings at the Philadelphia Congress.[8] Hutchin-

[1] Dartmouth to Admiralty, 18 October 1774. PRO. CO. 5/250, ff. 86-7. Also Admiralty to Dartmouth, 9 December 1774. PRO. CO. 5/247, f. 111. Yorke had suggested that a vessel should be sent. Dartmouth to Admiralty (October), 1774. Dartmouth MS. D 1778, II, 990 (draft).
[2] Pownall to Dartmouth, 18 October 1774. Dartmouth MS. D 1778, II, 984. Suffolk to King, 17 October 1774. Fortescue, *op. cit.*, iii, 1541.
[3] Dartmouth to Admiralty, 19 October 1774. PRO. CO. 5/250, f. 87. Also Dartmouth to Gage, 19 October 1774. PRO. CO. 5/763, f. 629. The papers concerning smuggling were passed among Ministers on 20 October because 'there is not a sufficient time to make a separate copy for each member of the Cabinet'. Dartmouth MS. D 1778, I, ii, 1051.
[4] Lieutenant Walton to Admiralty, 1 November, 11 November, 6 December 1774. PRO. CO. 5/120, ff. 308 *et seq.*
[5] Dartmouth to Admiralty, 1 November 1774. PRO. CO. 5/250, f. 88.
[6] PRO. CO. 5/138 (Part II). The Dutch also warned the English that no more British warships were to enter Dutch harbours. Sir Joseph Yorke to Suffolk, 15 November 1774. PRO. CO. 5/138 (Part II), f. 434. Will Eden to J. Pownall, 9 January 1774. PRO. S.P. Dom. Naval, 42/49, f. 17.
[7] Lieutenant-Governor Colden to Dartmouth, 2 November 1774 (arrived 13 December). PRO. CO. 5/1139, ff. 180-6.
[8] North told Hutchinson that the Government had a private correspondent in Philadelphia who kept them informed. Hutchinson, *op. cit.*, i, 296.

son, on his endless social rounds, recorded the reactions of various Ministers to the way matters were developing. On 31 October he noted that he found

> Mr. Knox much altered by the late news: he supposes now that all Treaty is over. The first thing, he says, will be to let America know, that Britain will support its authority; and then concede what shall be thought fit.[1]

Next morning he called on Dartmouth and John Pownall at the American office. 'Both seemed thunderstruck with American news: at present seem to suppose it impossible to give way.' In the evening he saw Lord Chancellor Apsley, who 'seemed much struck: could answer for himself he should not recede'.[2] On 5 November Hutchinson dined with Suffolk, who announced he saw no solution other than 'settling the authority over them', and on the 10th he visited Lord President Gower, who 'expressed his sense of the necessity of effectual measures with respect to America'.[3]

The Ministry had reacted violently against the seditious happenings in the Colonies. Hutchinson admitted that now 'it is out of my power any longer to promote a plan of conciliation'.[4] The situation rapidly deteriorated. News was received by the New York packet on the 10th that the Congress had recommended an immediate non-importation agreement, to be effective until their decisions were reached. Two days later Lord North told Hutchinson that 'now the case seemed desperate, Parliament would not — could not — concede. For aught he could see it must come to violence'.[5]

The activities of the patriots in Massachusetts further enraged the Premier. It had proved impossible to enforce the Boston Port Act and Gage had been forced to withdraw his troops from Salem. As a result the Commissioners of the Customs had 'found it necessary immediately to come to Boston for our own personal security . . . we could not carry on the service any longer at Salem'.[6] Gage's dispatches revealed that

---

[1] *Ibid.*, 272-3.   [2] *Ibid.*, 273.   [3] *Ibid.*, 279, 291.
[4] *Ibid.*, 284.   [5] *Ibid.*, 292-3.
[6] Commissioners of Customs at Boston to Treasury, 20 September 1774. PRO. T. 1/505. Admiralty to Dartmouth, 15 November 1774. PRO. CO.

the Commander-in-Chief's morale was ebbing. He partly blamed the Coercive Acts. 'The enfeebled state in which I found every branch of Government astonished me', he asserted, 'and my first object was to give it force, in which I hoped to have made some progress when the arrival of the late Acts overset the whole, and the flame blazed out in all parts at once beyond the conception of everybody.'[1] He offered only one solution: 'there is no prospect of putting the late Acts in force but by making a conquest of the New England Provinces'.[2] He wrote telling Hutchinson how this conquest might be secured:

> I think it would be policy to temporize a while by suspending the execution of the Acts for a time and the province might send home Deputies and in the meanwhile to prepare for the worst. Hanoverians [and] Hessians may be hired and other steps taken necessary to ensure success for by all appearances these provinces must be first totally subdued before they will obey and a powerful force must in that case be employed.[3]

The Government reacted more sharply to these than to Gage's earlier dispatches. When Hutchinson saw the Premier on the 19th, the day after Gage's dispatches, North exclaimed 'it was to no purpose any longer to think of expedients: the Province was in actual rebellion and must be subdued. . . . As for Hessians and Hanoverians, they could be employed if necessary: but he was of opinion there was no need of foreign force.' North also roundly denounced General Gage for talking of suspending the Coercive Acts and insisted that 'the Acts must and should be carried into execution'.[4] In this he was echoing the words and sentiments of his royal master. The day before the King had declared that Gage's

> idea of suspending the Acts appears to me the most absurd that can be suggested . . . this must suggest to the Colonies a

---

5/247, f. 110. Knox to Dartmouth, 15 November 1774. Dartmouth MS. D 1778, II, 994.   [1] 20 September 1774. PRO. CO. 5/769, f. 134.
    [2] Gage to Dartmouth, 25 September 1774. PRO. CO. 5/763, f. 684. Printed in *The Correspondence of General Thomas Gage, 1763–1775*, i, 376-7.
    [3] Gage to Hutchinson, 17 September 1774. Dartmouth MS. D 1778, II, 967. (Extract in Knox's hand.)
    [4] Hutchinson, *op. cit.*, i, 296-8, especially 297.

fear that alone prompts them to their present violence; we must either master them or totally leave them to themselves and treat them as aliens; I do not by this mean to insinuate that I am for advising new measures; but I am for supporting those already undertaken.

The King was almost relieved that the die was cast. 'I am not sorry that the line of conduct seems now chalked out . . . the New England Governments are in a state of Rebellion, blows must decide whether they are to be subject to this country or independent.'[1] George III had never appreciated the refinements of constitutional wrangles. His mind was simple and puritanical. Those who were not for him were against him; and the sooner the people made up their minds the happier was the King. It appears from his letter that the King almost welcomed the prospect of a decision by blows. It was a form of contest which he understood and which he felt that England was certain to win.

Whether General Gage was the man to wage the contest, however, now began to be doubted, and his prestige with the Government started to wane.[2] Pownall suggested that Sir Jeffrey Amherst and two Major-Generals be sent out to America to share the responsibilities with Gage, perhaps even to supersede him.[3] Lord North agreed that Gage needed capable assistants. The King and, with some reservations, Dartmouth, concurred. Suffolk, however, thought this was a quite inadequate remedy:

[1] King to North, 18 November 1774 (two letters). Fortescue, *op. cit.*, iii, 1556, 1557.

[2] *HMC, Various*, vi, *Knox MSS.*, p. 257. Franklin had already noted that 'General Gage, who when going was talked of as a cool prudent man, and therefore fit for that service, is now spoken of as peevish, passionate and indiscreet'. Franklin to Cushing, 10 October 1774. *The Writings of Benjamin Franklin*, ed., A. H. Smyth, vi, 252. William Knox said it was these letters written in September which 'turned us all so much against Gage . . .'.

[3] *HMC, Various*, vi, *Knox MSS.*, p. 257. Also King to North, 18 November 1774. Fortescue, *op. cit.*, iii, 1556. Hutchinson visited Dartmouth's Office on 21 November. He reported that Pownall 'has a plan in his head for an act of Parliament to suspend all the Militia Laws of Massachusetts Bay. He said Sir J[effery] A[mherst] would be sent, and suspend Gage in his military command until the Province is reduced to order.' Hutchinson, *op. cit.*, 1, 299.

I have reflected much on Mr. Gage's conduct and I am thoroughly persuaded that it is not to be rectified by sending a couple of subordinate officers to him. He is too far gone to be recovered. It is therefore much better to supersede him at once. In a case of so much importance nothing should stand in the way of the most wise and expedient measure. Gage should be removed and the fittest person, whoever he is, appointed to succeed him, I think not only in the command of the army but in government also. It is idle to do things by halves. . . .[1]

Suffolk was unable to convert the Cabinet to his extreme views, and the Government decided to retain its trust in Gage, at least for the time being;[2] but the American Commander was obviously already cast for the role of scapegoat, and his months of command were numbered.[3]

A full Cabinet met at Lord Rochford's office on Thursday evening, 1 December.[4] It discussed Gage's dispatches and decided to consult the Attorney- and Solicitor-Generals as to whether the outrages in Massachusetts constituted acts of overt treason and rebellion. If so, Dartmouth was asked to direct them 'to prepare the draft of a Proclamation requiring all persons who have been guilty of the same, except such as shall be therein excepted, to surrender themselves before a certain day, and to declare that such as shall not surrender themselves shall be treated as rebels and traitors'.[5] By this time both North and Dartmouth at any rate considered Massachusetts to be in rebellion.[6] When the next Cabinet was held on 10 December at Lord North's it was agreed that nothing could be decided about

---

[1] Suffolk to Dartmouth, 22 November 1774. Dartmouth MS. D 1778, I, ii, 1078. Quoted in *HMC*, II, V, *Dartmouth MSS.*, i, 370.

[2] *HMC, Various*, vi, *Knox MSS.*, p. 257.

[3] Gage was recalled in August 1775 and arrived in England in November. Hutchinson saw Charles Jenkinson on 26 November 1774 and Thurlow and Richard Jackson on 1 December and they all blamed Gage 'for not suppressing the late riots with his troops'. Hutchinson, *op. cit.*, i, 306, 312.

[4] Sir Stanier Porten to J. Pownall, 30 November 1774. Dartmouth MS. D 1778, II, 1003.

[5] Cabinet Minute, 1 December 1774. Dartmouth MS. D 1778, I, ii, 1084. Quoted in *HMC*, II, V, *Dartmouth MSS.*, i, 371. Amongst the Dartmouth papers there is a note headed 'Propositions', which discusses the proposed Proclamation. Dartmouth MS. D 1778, II, 1047.

[6] See Hutchinson, *op. cit.*, i, 302.

America until the Government heard from Gage — his last letters were dated in September. There was some dissatisfaction at Dartmouth's reluctance to act. Rochford afterwards confided to Sandwich: 'What surprises me, between you and I, is that the Minister of the department, Lord Dartmouth, does not come with some plan to cabinet. I should think it only duty to do so, was there any dispute with France and Spain.' He also thought that if the Americans 'would propose a fair accomodation, it would be listened to, but in my opinion they have thrown away the scabard; in that case the ultima ratio regum must try its strength'.[1] First the King, then North, Suffolk and Gower, and now Rochford, had openly stated that blows would and must decide the issue in America. The Government was being conditioned to receive the news of Lexington and Concord, which were barely four months ahead. But when Dartmouth wrote to Gage that evening there was as yet no decision to report. He informed Gage that the condition of Massachusetts was still under consideration and a sloop was lying ready at Spithead to convey any further orders.[2]

Three days later, on the 13th, Thurlow and Wedderburn replied to the Cabinet directive of 1 December. This had asked them to consider 'whether the Acts of the people of the province of Massachusetts Bay [described in the dispatches from Gage and Graves] are overt acts of treason and rebellion?' The Law Officers were adamant in their reply:

> ... we are of opinion, that the letters above mentioned contain the history of an open rebellion and war in the Province of Massachusetts Bay. J. Bigelow, E. Rawson, T. Denny, J. Goulding and J. Gilbert are charged therein with an act of overt treason, in levying war against His Majesty, on the 26th day of August ... and several others at different times.

[1] Rochford to Sandwich, 10 December 1774: *Sandwich Papers*, pp. 55-7. Copies of letters describing riots at Piscatagua had reached the Treasury on 8 December. Governor Wentworth to Dartmouth, 13 September 1774. PRO. T. 1/509. (The folios in this Treasury box are not numbered.)

[2] Dartmouth to Gage, 10 December 1774. PRO. CO. 5/763, f. 703. The packet to America was delayed until 14 December because the Address of the House of Commons to the King was not yet ready. Hutchinson, *op. cit.*, i, 320.

But the acts of treason imputed to them are the leading the rebel forces; which, as we collect from those letters, possess the whole of the open country, and every part of the Province, except the town of Boston; wholly prohibiting the exercise of His Majesty's authority, and suppressing the execution of his laws : insomuch, that there exists no internal legislature, or court of justice within the limits of the colony.[1]

Thurlow and Wedderburn now asked for instructions toward drawing up a proclamation of rebellion, what terms of surrender should be offered, and who was to be excepted. The question of treason was once again in the forefront of Ministerial thinking. The Law Officers were not this time — as in February — proving a stumbling block, and the procedure of issuing a Proclamation of treason was pursued in the months ahead.[2]

Meanwhile other less extreme policies were being aired. An important development in early December 1774 was that for the first time since the beginning of the American crisis the difference of outlook between Dartmouth and the more extreme members of the Cabinet began to be reflected in conflicting lines of policy. Probably inspired by the failure of the coercive legislation and by the critical situation which was developing in the Colonies, Dartmouth began to say that 'something should be held out to the Colonies'.[3] He was encouraged in this by the personal pressure of some of his moderate friends who wanted an accommodation with America, and who privately initiated a fascinating series of negotiations with Benjamin Franklin. These negotiations formed a sort of undercurrent pulling at the Government's policy during the months ahead.

The negotiations began at the end of November 1774, when Lord Hyde,[4] the Chancellor of the Duchy of Lancaster, suggested to David Barclay [5] that Barclay and his friend, Dr. John

---

[1] Law Officers to Dartmouth, 13 December 1774. PRO. CO. 5/159, f. 3.
[2] See below, Chapter XI, pp. 238-43, 247-51.
[3] HMC, Various, vi, Knox MSS., p. 258.
[4] Thomas Villiers, 1st Baron Hyde, later 1st Earl of Clarendon (1709–86).
[5] Barclay was a Quaker of Scottish noble descent. He was a banker and a merchant to North America.

Fothergill,[1] should try to arrange a reconciliation with the Colonies through Benjamin Franklin.[2] It seems unlikely that Hyde had any official authority for his action, though his friend Dartmouth might have intimated that some attempt at reconciliation would be welcome to him personally. In any case, the two Quakers plunged enthusiastically — and perhaps too optimistically — into their assignment. They met Franklin at Doctor Fothergill's house in Harpur Street on 4 December 1774 and asked him to draw up a list of terms which he believed would satisfy the colonists.[3] Franklin agreed, and when they met again on the 6th he brought with him his 'Hints for Conversations upon the Subject of Terms that may probably produce a *Durable* union between Great Britain and her Colonies'. The three men made some alterations, and then Barclay took one fair copy to Lord Hyde and Fothergill another to Dartmouth, whom he was visiting daily in his medical capacity.[4] Hyde and Dartmouth discussed the drafts together and made many critical comments and corrections.[5] In the end they decided that the terms were too high and Hyde wrote to Barclay on 13 December that they 'should be moderated'.[6]

There the matter rested for a few more weeks, and the subsequent negotiations are described below. But the trend towards reconciliation was quickly echoed in the Cabinet, where Dartmouth, on John Pownall's suggestion, put forward the idea that English Commissioners should be appointed to meet colonial delegates 'to discuss and settle all claims, and Parliament to confirm, if approved what they should agree upon'.[7] The King did not receive this suggestion happily. On 13 December the New York mail had arrived with details of the

---

[1] Fothergill was an eminent physician and also a leading Quaker. He had already been in contact with Franklin over their common scientific interests. R. Hingston Fox, *Dr. John Fothergill and his friends*, p. 28.

[2] *Ibid.*, p. 326.

[3] Franklin's description — 'An Account of Negotiations in London for effecting a reconciliation between Great Britain and the American Colonies' — written to his son on board the Pennsylvania Packet in March 1775, is in *Franklin Complete Works*, v, 440-523.

[4] R. Hingston Fox, *op. cit.*, p. 327.

[5] Their originals are in Dartmouth MS. D 1778, II, 1007.

[6] Printed in R. Hingston Fox, *op. cit.*, Appendix A, p. 395.

[7] *HMC, Various*, vi, *Knox MSS.*, p. 258.

Philadelphia Congress's plans to interrupt British trade with the Colonies.[1] On the 15th the King informed North that he was

> not so fond of the sending Commissioners to examine into the disputes; this looks so like the Mother Country being more afraid of the continuance of the dispute than the Colonies and I cannot think it likely to make them reasonable, I do not want to drive them to despair but to submission which nothing but feeling the inconvenience of their situation can bring their pride to submit to.[2]

George III had little sympathy for Dartmouth's and Pownall's proposition, or for any other conciliatory schemes. He had always believed that submission rather than conciliation was the right object of Government policy, and that coercion was the way to achieve it; each mail from America seemed to confirm him in this opinion. 'Nothing can be more provoking', he told Dartmouth, 'than the conduct of the inhabitants of Massachusetts Bay. Some measures must undoubtedly be adopted after Christmas to curb them, and by degrees bring them to a due obedience to the Mother Country, but reason not passion must point out the proper measures.'[3] Till after Christmas nothing could be done. In the first place the Ministry had not yet evolved any new policy to put before the Commons. The realisation was growing that the measures of the previous spring had proved a failure, but time — which the holiday provided — was needed to think out new approaches to the problem. In the second, any measures which were put forward would require the full support of Parliament. But by mid-December many Members had gone home for the vacation and no full attendance could be expected till Parliament reassembled at the end of January.[4]

Meanwhile on 18 December another dispatch from Gage

---

[1] Hutchinson, *op. cit.*, i, 323. W. Molleson to Dartmouth, 15 December 1774. Dartmouth MS. D 1778, II, 1403.

[2] King to North, 15 December 1774. Fortescue, *op. cit.*, iii, 1563.

[3] 15 December 1774. Dartmouth MS. D 1778, Supplementary George III. Quoted in *HMC*, II, V, *Dartmouth MSS.*, i, 439.

[4] See Hutchinson, *op. cit.*, i, 325.

brought further shocks for the Ministers.[1] The details of the proceedings in the Philadelphia Congress were not surprising, since these had already been conveyed in the New York Mail two days earlier. What astonished them was the feeble tone in which Gage expressed himself, and what seemed to them to be criminal inactivity on his part. John Pownall reported that

> Lord North thinks that some other person must be immediately sent out either to supersede or advise and assist General Gage. The King concurs and I have given orders for a ship that will be ready to sail on Wednesday. . . . Indeed, my Dear Lord things seem to be in a desperate situation, and I am totally at a loss to account for the strange conduct of General Gage which seems devoid both of sense and spirit.[2]

There had been a similar outburst against Gage in November. But then the extreme view of Suffolk that Gage ought to be removed had not been supported by the King and Lord North. By now they had apparently been converted. The name of Sir Jeffrey Amherst was again mentioned as Gage's most likely successor. Lord North also wanted to send a Major-General immediately to America to serve under Gage and stiffen his morale.[3] But the King advised him to wait:

> The sending a Major General to America will [be] very proper ; but as a general plan is necessary to be formed for that Country would it not be right not to act by detail but have the whole digested before any step is taken : should it be thought right to give the command of the forces in America to Sir Jeffrey Amherst it would be right he should be consulted as to the Generals to serve with him ; therefore if yet you wish a Major General should be sent prior to the formation of a plan of future conduct, I think he ought to be consulted who will suit best this kind of service which requires as much prudence as firmness.[4]

Since October Gage had reported the virtual collapse of the Government's first coercive policy, and details of the Philadelphia

[1] Gage to Dartmouth, 3 October 1774. PRO. CO. 5/763, ff. 709-10. Printed in *The Correspondence of General Thomas Gage, 1763–1775*, i, 377-8.
[2] Pownall to Dartmouth, 18 December 1774. Dartmouth MS. D 1778, II, 1022.
[3] North to King, 17 December 1774. Fortescue, *op. cit.*, iii, 1564.
[4] King to North, 18 December 1774. *Ibid.* 1565.

Congress revealed how wide and how deep was the colonial discontent. But the proposed reappraisal of policy did not mean that there was much more likelihood of compromise by the Government. It has been shown in this chapter that during the autumn every Minister except Dartmouth spoke privately of the need to take firmer measures against the Americans, and the King, North, Suffolk, Gower and Rochford all talked of using military force. Such reinforcements as were available had been sent across the Atlantic. Gage was being criticised, and his replacement discussed, because he seemed dilatory in suppressing the colonists. Legal processes had been started to declare Massachusetts in open rebellion and some of its inhabitants to be traitors. Dartmouth's attempts to secure a reconciliation, which in December reflected the first division in the Cabinet since the crisis began, formed a lone exception to the prevailing trend.

The Ministers considered possible new measures during the Christmas holiday. Lord North went off to Banbury, Rochford to his country seat, and many others went to Bath.[1] In London there was 'the appearance of all the tranquility which might be expected if America was perfectly quiet'.[2] When the Ministers returned and gathered together again in January they were ready with fresh ideas to put before the new Parliament.

[1] Grey Cooper to W. Eden, 4 January 1775. BM. Add. MS. 34412, f. 326. [2] Hutchinson, *op. cit.*, i, 336.

CHAPTER X

DEVISING NEW MEASURES

In the first week of 1775 still worse reports reached England from North America, confirming that the Ministry needed fresh measures to deal with the unruly colonists. Gage stated outright that the Coercive Acts had only made matters worse. 'Nobody here, or at home,' he remarked, 'could have conceived that the Acts made for the Massachusetts Bay could have created such a ferment throughout the continent, and united the whole in one common cause.' He sent more resolutions from the Philadelphia Congress [1] together with some passed by a Provincial Congress held in Massachusetts. He felt that 'affairs are gone to so great a length, that Great Britain cannot yield without giving up all her authority over this country', but feared that he personally could do little and had to proceed with great caution 'Lest all the continent should unite against us . . .'. He was convinced that in the end the issue would be decided by military force, and pointed out that his own troops, numbering only some 3,000, 'will encourage resistance, and not terrify'. He told Dartmouth that 'foreign troops must be hired' and that, when war came, 'to begin with an army of 20,000 strong will save Great Britain both blood and treasure'.[2]

This was not the first time Gage had written home in a pessimistic vein, though rarely had his language been so blunt.

---

[1] On 14 October 1774, the Congress signed the Declaration of Rights, which listed the colonial grievances against the British Parliament and asserted the rights of Americans. On 26 October a Petition to the King and an Address to the British people were agreed upon. Each restated the grievances and asked for redress. Also on the 26th, a Continental Association was formed to enforce non-importation, non-exportation and non-consumption agreements.

[2] Gage to Dartmouth, 30 October 1774, received 2 January 1775. Dartmouth MS. D 1778, II, 989, printed in C. E. Carter, ed., *The Correspondence of General Thomas Gage, 1763–1775*, i, 380-1. Also Gage to Barrington, 1 November 1774. PRO. CO. 5/769, f. 146.

Furthermore, his interpretation of the situation was confirmed by a letter received four days later from Lieutenant-Governor Colden of New York. Colden had previously played down the seriousness of affairs in New York by assuring the Ministry that the respectable citizens and men of property there were solidly behind the Government. Now he wrote 'it is a dreadful situation. If we are not rescued from it by the wisdom and firmness of Parliament, the colonies must soon fall into distraction, and every calamity annexed to a total annihilation of government.'[1] Dartmouth in his reply to Colden commented: 'it cannot but be the wish of every candid and unprejudiced person, that the proceedings of the General Congress had been of such colour and complexion, as to have invited accommodation without provoking the vengeance of the mother country'.[2]

Dartmouth had genuinely hoped that accommodation would be possible with the Congress[3] and was still concerned in the negotiations with Franklin which had begun at the end of November 1774. Now he realised that the line of vengeance and coercion, begun at the end of the old Parliament, would have to be taken up again in the new.[4] He was confirmed in this opinion when he took advice from informed — if not unprejudiced — people. For instance, he sent for three New Englanders, Messrs. Blowers, Ingersoll and Bill, who had arrived on the December packet. They visited his office on 4 January and advised the use of military force against the colonists. Similar opinions were being expressed by Charles Garth, a colonial agent and a respected expert on America, when he dined with members of the Government.[5]

At a Cabinet meeting held at Lord Rochford's office on Friday, 13 January,[6] the Ministers plotted the main lines of the strategy that they were to follow in the months ahead. Firstly

---

[1] Colden to Dartmouth, 7 December 1774. PRO. CO. 5/1139, f. 190.
[2] Dartmouth to Colden, 7 January 1775. PRO. CO. 5/1141, ff. 136-7.
[3] See Dartmouth to Hardwicke, 29 August 1774. BM. Add. MS. 35612, ff. 48-9.
[4] Hutchinson said that Suffolk and Thurlow had also swung to more extreme views since the Resolutions of the Congress arrived. Hutchinson, *Diary and Letters*, i, 364-5.   [5] *Ibid.*, pp. 341-2, 396.
[6] See Suffolk to Dartmouth, 9 January 1775. Dartmouth MS. D 1778, V, 875.

it was decided 'that the army under General Gage should be reinforced by sending as soon as possible two Regiments of Infantry and one of Light Cavalry from Ireland and also a further detachment of 600 marines'. It was also decided to recommend that Gage should raise a corps of loyalist irregulars in America.[1]

Secondly, as a riposte to the Colonial Association formed at Philadelphia, 'it was agreed that it would be proper to propose in Parliament that the associated colonies should be prohibited for a limited time from trading to any other ports than those of Great Britain, Ireland and the Islands in the West Indies, and also restrained from carrying on the fishery'. This proposal received strong support, and possibly originated, from the Secretary at War, Viscount Barrington, for in December he had written to Dartmouth suggesting that the best way to deal with the Americans was by a naval blockade 'totally interrupting all commerce and fishery'.[2]

The third measure which was discussed was Dartmouth's suggestion to send Commissioners to America to consider ways to effect 'a nearer union with the Colonies for the immediate interest of both parts of the Empire'. The question of sending Commissioners had already been considered before Christmas, and it then received a poor reception from the King.[3] But the Colonial Secretary still clung to the hope of reconciling America by this means and so kept alive the negotiations with Franklin which had continued in London during the Christmas recess.[4] At Hyde's instigation, Franklin had been introduced to Admiral Lord Howe, who, on 28 December, assured him that 'there was a sincere disposition in Lord North and Lord Dartmouth to accommodate the differences with America, and to listen

---

[1] Cabinet Minute. Dartmouth MS. D 1778, II, 1102. This idea had been proposed by a Colonel Ruggles, and was forwarded to the Ministry on the packet which arrived in England on 2 January. Hutchinson, *op. cit.*, i, 343.
[2] Barrington to Dartmouth, 24 December 1774. Dartmouth MS. D 1775, II, 1035.
[3] See above, Chapter IX, p. 216. The King later referred to 'Your original idea of a commission'. To Dartmouth, 28 January 1775. Dartmouth MS. D 1778, Supplementary George III. Quoted in *HMC*, 13, IV, *Dartmouth MSS.*, iv, 501. [4] See above, Chapter IX, pp. 214-15.

favourably to any proposition that might have a probable tendency to answer that salutary purpose'.[1] Howe asked Franklin whether he thought it might be helpful if Commissioners were sent to America to enquire into grievances and to try to reach a settlement. Franklin approved of the idea, and he also agreed to draw up another list of propositions for peace with the colonists which might be more acceptable to the Ministry than his earlier paper presented at the beginning of December. This second list was sent to Howe early in the New Year. It was very similar to the Petition of the First Continental Congress, stating that if British troops were withdrawn, the Coercive Acts repealed, Congress recognised, and other grievances met, then the Colonies would consider the British requests. Howe replied that the propositions seemed to him unlikely to be acceptable, but he undertook to forward them to the Ministry. There were no more developments before the Cabinet meeting on 13 January. Dartmouth had by then presumably learned of Franklin's approval at least of the suggestion for sending Commissioners to America, and he put the idea formally to the Cabinet. But it does not seem to have drawn a more favourable reaction from his colleagues in January than it did from the King in the middle of December. Two weeks later Dartmouth told Hutchinson that he wished the measures agreed on 'could have been accompanied with other measures which he had proposed, particularly the appointment of Commissioners to go to America', and he hoped this might yet be done, though he added 'when I proposed it, it was scouted at'.[2] At the end of 1775 the idea was in fact raised again, and soon after was adopted, but by then Dartmouth was out of office and the problem was no longer to halt the slide towards war but to end a war already begun. In January 1775 the Ministry was not prepared to make such a gesture of conciliation.

On the 16th the Cabinet resumed its deliberations.[3] No dated Minute exists for this next meeting. There is among

---

[1] *Franklin Complete Works*, v, 479. See also Sir John Barrow, *The Life of Richard Earl Howe*, pp. 85-9.   [2] Hutchinson, *op. cit.*, i, 363.
[3] North to King, 16 January 1775. J. W. Fortescue, ed., *The Correspondence of King George III, 1760–1783*, iii, 1576.

the Dartmouth papers an undated note, with the heading 'To be added to the minute', which might possibly refer to the discussions on the 16th.[1] But its form and contents seem to connect more naturally with a later Cabinet.[2] A more certain guide to the proceedings on the 16th is the contents of two letters written two days later by Lord Rochford, who was host to the meeting. He wrote to the Admiralty saying that it had been decided to send out ships and a further six hundred marines to reinforce Admiral Graves.[3] This was merely an extension of the measures agreed on the 13th for building up the military forces in America. Much more interesting is the letter which he wrote to the King stating that 'Lord North's plan which he partly opened was thought not only feasible but the wisest that could be pursued'.[4] There is nothing in this letter to explain what Lord North had suggested. But it is probable that he then sketched for the first time the plan which was fully discussed at the next Cabinet meeting five days later — that the British should promise not to exercise the right of taxation over the colonists, and that the Americans in return should pay for their own administration and so tacitly accept British supremacy.

This next Cabinet, held at Lord Sandwich's house on 21 January, agreed that

an address be proposed to the two Houses of Parliament to declare that if the Colonies shall make sufficient and permanent provision for the support of the civil government and administration of justice and for the defence and protection of the said Colonies, and in time of war contribute extraordinary supplies, in a reasonable proportion to what is raised by Great Britain, we will in that case desist from the exercise of the power of taxation, except for commercial purposes only, and that whenever a proposition of this kind shall be made by any of the Colonies we will enter into the consideration of proper laws for that purpose, and in the meanwhile to entreat

[1] Dartmouth MS. D 1778, II, 1076.
[2] *I.e.* that on 21 January. See below, p. 224.
[3] Rochford to Admiralty, 18 January 1775. PRO. State Papers Naval, 42/49, f. 10.
[4] Rochford to King, 18 January 1775. Fortescue, *op. cit.*, iii, 1579.

his Majesty to take the most effectual methods to enforce due obedience to the laws and authority of the supreme legislature of Great Britain.[1]

There is no other writing on this Minute, but the undated paper mentioned above seems to follow on in perfect sequence and it probably refers to the meeting on the 21st.[2] It begins: 'That in order to effect that object the army under General Gage to be reinforced by 3 Regiments of Infantry[3] and one of light Dragoons augmented 10 men a troop from Ireland and that a further reinforcement of 600 marines be sent to Ireland'. The remaining paragraph repeats the intention of introducing into Parliament a Bill to restrain American commerce and fisheries.

At these three Cabinet meetings on 13, 16 and 21 January, a fresh plan for America had been marked out. It can be divided into three parts: the Bill to blockade New England, which was merely another coercive measure, an act of punishment on the colonists for their misbehaviour in New England and at Philadelphia; the reinforcement of General Gage and Admiral Graves, which was necessary to enforce British supremacy and stamp out sedition in New England; and the moves towards reconciliation, first by the abortive idea of sending out Commissioners, and then through the offer to desist from taxation providing the Colonies came to heel.

In making this fresh approach to the colonial problem the Government had tacitly admitted that the dose of coercion prescribed in 1774 had not succeeded. Yet the new prescription was not, except for its third part, very different from the old. As in February 1774, coercive legislation and military reinforcement were the heart of the policy. The novel features were the proposals to send Commissioners to America and to desist, if certain conditions were fulfilled, from imposing taxes for revenue. In the event, since the first suggestion remained for long a dead letter, the second became the Government's single

---

[1] Cabinet Minute, 21 January 1775. Dartmouth MS. D 1778, I, ii, 1093. Quoted in *HMC*, 11, V, *Dartmouth MSS.*, i, 372-3.

[2] Note headed 'To be added to the Minute', undated. Dartmouth MS. D 1778, II, 1076.

[3] This had been increased by one regiment since the Cabinet on 13 January.

conciliatory proposition.[1] It was important for several reasons.
It possibly reflected some effort on the part of Lord North to
compromise with the terms communicated by Franklin, though
in fact Franklin's second list of proposals, sent to Howe in the
New Year, had been rejected by Dartmouth as 'inadmissible
and impractable'.[2] It certainly revealed a willingness on the
part of the Ministry to work for reconciliation, which was not
evident in April 1774 when the Government totally opposed
Rose Fuller's motion to repeal the Tea Duty. It showed that
the Government was to some extent aware that, if a settlement
was ever to be reached, it must make some effort to define what
concessions it was prepared to make and what it expected from
the colonists.[3] It also reflected the conflicting sentiments which
were beginning to emerge in the Cabinet. But it would be
wrong to exaggerate the amount of pressure for conciliation at
this stage; the only supporters of conciliation were North and
Dartmouth, and even they were divided by desires to punish
and to assert Parliament's authority, as well as to reconcile the
colonists. Governor Tryon referred to this combination of
intentions in a letter to Dartmouth on 19 January, and he
commented that he could not agree with the idea of 'holding
out the olive branch in one hand and the rod of chastisement in
the other'.[4] In fact such a policy appealed to Lord North, who
always wanted the best of all worlds, and Dartmouth himself
expressed the hope that a combination of firmness and indulgence would restore peace.[5] In any case, if it failed to produce
peace, the conciliatory motion promised some political advantages. It would be a bait to any Colony which was reluctant to

[1] It has been argued that North's proposition was suggested to him
by William Knox. See M. M. Spector, *The American Department of the
British Government*, p. 139. In any case it was already in the air by the New
Year. Grey Cooper wrote to William Eden on 4 January that he had
'expected to have heard of Lord North's motions'. BM. Add. MS. 34,
412, f. 327.

[2] Dartmouth said so to Fothergill. *Franklin Complete Works*, v. 487.

[3] When Dartmouth wrote to Gage in February about North's conciliatory resolution he said it was meant to explain to the colonists 'what is
ultimately expected from them'. 22 February 1775. PRO. CO. 5/765, f. 372.

[4] Tryon to Dartmouth, 19 January 1775. Dartmouth MS. D 1778, II,
1112.

[5] Dartmouth to Legge, 22 February 1775. Dartmouth MS. D 1778,
II, 1157.

risk war or was unwilling to suffer the threatened naval blockade. Breaches might thus be made in the Continental Association proclaimed by the Philadelphia Congress. This was clever tactics and was essential to the success of the Government's new plan. That plan, taken as a whole, was repressive. Despite the conciliatory gestures, the predominant aim was still to reduce the Americans to submission and the new policies conceded very little of substance to colonial ambitions.

The trend towards repression in Ministerial thinking was underlined when Dartmouth wrote to Gage on 27 January informing him of the Government's new intentions.[1] Dartmouth began by observing:

> Your dispatches . . . relate to facts and state proceedings that amount to actual revolt, and shew a determination in the people to commit themselves, at all events, in open rebellion. The King's dignity and the honour and safety of the Empire require, that in such a situation, force should be repelled by force. . . .

He informed Gage that the necessary force, marines, infantry and dragoons, was being organised to go to America, and he instructed him to go ahead with the plan to raise a corps of irregulars in New England. He also encouraged Gage to take the offensive against the colonists.

> It appears that your object has hitherto been to act upon the defensive, and to avoid the hazard of weakening your force by sending out detachments of your troops on any occasion whatsoever; and I should do injustice to your prudence and discretion if I could suppose that such precaution was not necessary. It is hoped however that this large reinforcement to your army will enable you to take a more active and determined part.

Dartmouth then referred to the statement in Gage's letter received at the New Year to the effect that the only solution was to conquer New England with 20,000 men. He pointed out

[1] Dartmouth to Gage, 27 January 1775. PRO. CO. 5/765, ff. 349-65. These instructions to Gage were long delayed — it is not clear why — and they did not reach him until the middle of April, a few days before his troops set out from Boston for Lexington and Concord. See below, p. 267.

that 'you must be aware that such a force cannot be collected without augmenting our army in general to a war establishment' and he was 'unwilling to believe that matters are as yet come to that issue'. In any case, Dartmouth argued, since the rebels were only 'a rude rabble', he felt that 'a smaller force now, if put to the test, would be able to encounter them with greater probability of success than might be expected from a greater army . . .'.

The important point here, which Dartmouth reiterated throughout this long letter, was that Gage must be prepared to use the military against the colonists. He admitted that such an action might, as Gage had warned, be 'a signal for hostilities, yet, for the reasons I have already given, it will surely be better that the conflict should be brought on, upon such a ground, than in a riper state of rebellion'. This cannot be read to mean anything other than that the Ministry, or, at least, Dartmouth, had considered the risk of starting a civil war and had decided that it was better to take that risk than to allow disorder to spread.[1] This risk, and the fact that it was the most pacific English Minister who was forced to take it, points the tragic dilemma of the Anglo-American relationship at this time. Unless the Government enforced law and order and stamped out sedition, then the Colonies would slide into anarchy and lapse from British dominion by default of government. Yet any act of enforcement which was firm enough to warrant success might also be provocative enough to start a civil war.

Now, as after the Tea Party, the general choice before the English Ministry was fundamentally quite simple: either Britain should abdicate its sovereignty voluntarily, or it must make every effort to secure the recognition of that sovereignty. There was no possibility of accepting the status quo, and leaving things to settle down, because acts of defiance had already been committed and were still continuing. A political sovereignty only exists while it is acknowledged. This acknowledgment can, in normal circumstances, be implicit. But once the sovereignty has been denied it must be re-established. This can be

[1] 'Some of the chief say they had rather hear of an action.' Hutchinson to Lieutenant-Governor Oliver, 18 January 1775. Hutchinson, *op. cit.*, i, 356.

done peaceably, either by a statement of explicit acknowledgment by the subjects concerned, or by their dissociating themselves, explicitly or implicitly, from the acts of defiance. Failing such a peaceable settlement, the sovereignty must be restored, if necessarily by force of arms. At this time, in January 1775, Dartmouth realised that the Americans showed few signs of willingly making amends to Great Britain and that military force might therefore have to be used; for British supremacy must not only exist, but must be seen to exist. Consequently, the main object of this letter was to point out to Gage 'with precision the idea entertained here of the manner in which the military force under your command may be employed with effect'. In conclusion he reminded Gage that he could make use of martial law in time of rebellion, and he enclosed an opinion of the Law Officers that the facts described in Gage's earlier letters constituted such rebellion.

Throughout this letter to Gage there is a current of submerged criticism. Dartmouth never openly said that Gage had been too restrained, that he had failed to exercise his power and authority. But he repeatedly touched upon the need to be more resolute and aggressive in the future. This reflected the trend of English opinion about its Commander-in-Chief in America. The question of his removal had been brought before the Cabinet in November, and though it was then rejected there was support for it, especially from Suffolk.[1] Now the matter was raised again. The general criticism which was implicit in the letter was rapidly translated into another concrete proposal to replace Gage.

On 28 January, after reflecting upon the matter for some days, the King wrote to Dartmouth about Gage.[2] He informed him that he had already discussed with Lord North 'the opinion of the troops in America and of the General Officers in this Kingdom, that should matters become serious in that part of the globe, more activity and decision would be requisite than they

[1] See above, pp. 211-12.
[2] 28 January 1775. Dartmouth MS. D 1778, Supplementary George III. Quoted in *HMC*, 13, IV, *Dartmouth MSS.*, iv, 501. See also Rochford to King, 24 January 1775. Fortescue, *op. cit.*, iii, 1581.

esteem the present commander possessed of'. George III wished the matter to be treated 'with all imaginable tenderness' and suggested that Gage should keep his pay as Commander-in-Chief. But he wanted Gage to be replaced by Sir Jeffrey Amherst.

> I am [of this opinion] not only from the consideration that troops never conduct themselves so well as under the command of a General they have an opinion of, but also from the political one of the necessity of having someone in America, unattached to any particular Province, ready to transmit the sentiments of those who wish well to English Government . . . for as he [Amherst] is respected by the Colonies they will give more credit to his assertions than those of any other person.

However, Amherst, to whom he immediately put the proposition, declined it. 'I stated very fully the intention to send him with an olive branch on one hand, whilst the other should be prepared to obtain submission', reported the King afterwards.[1] But his efforts went unrewarded: Amherst declared stubbornly that 'nothing but retreat would bring him to go again to America'. George III, greatly annoyed, had to abandon a scheme which he thought 'bore a prosperous aspect of bringing those deluded people to due obedience without putting the dagger to their throats'.

General Gage had been saved again, though it was clearly only a question of time before the Ministry found a replacement and so would be able to make a scapegoat of him. For the time being, the Ministry made the best of such officers as were available. 'We must do what next is best,' continued the King to Dartmouth, 'leave the command to Gage, send the best Generals that can be thought of to his assistance, and give him private instructions to insinuate to New York and such other provinces as are not guided by the madness of the times what the other would have been entrusted to negotiate.' Three

---

[1] King to Dartmouth, 31 January 1775. Dartmouth MS. D 1778, Supplementary George III. Quoted in *HMC*, 13, IV, *Dartmouth MSS.*, iv, 501.

days later, Howe, Clinton and Burgoyne were appointed to go to America and serve under Gage.[1]

By the end of January the new lines of the Government's American policy were virtually complete. Within the space of less than a fortnight it had decided on three main measures: first, to send out large reinforcements of infantry, cavalry and marines; second, to blockade colonial trade with foreign nations; and third, to promise not to exercise the right of taxation over the colonists, provided they in turn recognised that right and offered to pay for their own defence and administration. This policy was in general repressive. Admittedly, North's conciliatory proposal was the first positive step towards conciliation taken by the Government since the beginning of the crisis, but it did not truly reflect the weight of opinion in the Cabinet, which was better shown by the rejection of Dartmouth's suggestion that Commissioners should be sent to America to try to make peace. Dartmouth himself seems to have played a curiously ambiguous role. On the one hand he was still working for reconciliation, both in the Cabinet and secretly through the Franklin negotiations. On the other hand his orders to General Gage insisted in no uncertain terms that the Commander-in-Chief must use military force against the colonists, and that immediate hostilities might be preferable to an outbreak later when the Americans were better prepared. It is hard to escape the conclusion that the 'moderate' elements in the Cabinet, in the persons of Dartmouth, and, to a less extent, North, were divided in their own minds over whether to be conciliatory or repressive, or to what extent to balance one with the other. At bottom they shared with the rest of the Cabinet the common desire for colonial submission. In as much as they recognised that this would most likely entail the use of troops, they were already prepared psychologically for the outbreak of hostilities at Lexington and Concord.

[1] Skene to North, 23 January 1775; Barrington to Dartmouth, 3 February 1775. Dartmouth MSS. D 1778, II, 1116, 1131.

CHAPTER XI

THE NEW POLICY ENACTED

PARLIAMENT had already reassembled to discuss colonial matters before the Ministry completed the design of its new American policy at the end of January. America was mentioned in the King's speech at the opening of the new Parliament on 30 November 1774,[1] though only in terms of persevering with the measures effected in the previous session.[2] The Commons Address of Thanks to the King, promising him full support in any actions he felt compelled to take in the Colonies, was debated on 5 December and passed by 264-73.[3] During the next two weeks the news from America grew more serious, and the Opposition in the Commons pressed for a full debate on the colonial situation. In response to this pressure Lord North promised them on 16 December that he would lay information before the House shortly after the holidays and that he would also set up a Committee of the House to consider American affairs.[4]

In accordance with this promise the American papers were put before Parliament on 19 January 1775. There was a full selection of letters received from colonial officers, though they

---

[1] On 23 November 1774, Lord Rochford had summoned to a meeting at his house one hundred and fifty Lords and Bishops who normally inclined to support the Government. On 2 December Rochford reminded forty-four of them to attend at the House for business in the following week. 'List of Peers etc'. 23 November 1774. Dartmouth MS. D 1778, II, 1000. Rochford to various Peers, 2 December 1774. PRO. State Papers Domestic, 37/10, f. 87/18. The Opposition also had a pre-campaign meeting, though they found many of their troops still out of Town. Rockingham to Burke, 29 November 1774. W.W.M. R.153-4, CEB, iii, 80.

[2] This paragraph on America was written by the two Under-Secretaries, Knox and Pownall. 'This speech was the only one we were ever consulted upon.' HMC, Various, vi, Knox MSS., p. 258.

[3] Parl. Hist., xviii, 45. King to North, 27 November 1774 and 7 December 1774. J. W. Fortescue, ed., The Correspondence of George III, 1760–1783, iii, 1558, 1561.   [4] Parl. Hist., xviii, 59.

had often been carefully pruned — little remained, for instance, of Gage's pessimism or his reflections on the wisdom of the Coercive Acts.[1] The Parliamentary considerations of the American situation set on foot with the presentation of these papers continued almost until the end of March.

The first important business was Lord Chatham's motion to withdraw all British troops from Boston, which he put to the Lords on 20 January. Chatham said this motion was part of his plan 'to establish for the American an unequivocal, express right of not having his property taken from him but by his own assembly'. He protested that he was 'not to be understood as meaning a naked, unconditional repeal; no, I would maintain the superiority of this country at all events'. But the Americans, like all true Whigs, had the right to defend their property from expropriation and not to pay taxes unless represented. He accused the Ministry of acting vindictively and making the error of using troops against the Americans when 'troops and violence were ill means to answer the ends of peace'. He therefore made this first motion as a proof of goodwill, because there could be no satisfactory solution in America without first establishing the goodwill of both sides. The motion suggested that an Address be sent to the King begging

that, in order to open the ways towards a happy settlement of the dangerous troubles in America, by beginning to allay ferments and soften animosities there; and, above all, for preventing in the meantime, any sudden and fatal catastrophe at Boston, now suffering under the daily irritation of an army before their eyes, posted in their town, it may graciously please his Majesty, that immediate orders may be dispatched to General Gage for removing his Majesty's forces from the town of Boston, as soon as the rigour of the season, and other circumstances indispensable to the safety and accommodation of the said troops may render the same practicable.[2]

Lords Suffolk, Rochford and Gower answered strongly for the Ministry. Suffolk insisted that 'the Mother Country should

---

[1] On 15 December Knox had told Hutchinson he hoped Parliament would not ask for the American papers 'especially Gage's letters, which he speaks of as not proper to be shown'. Hutchinson, *Diary and Letters*, i, 325.   [2] *Parl. Hist.*, xviii, 149-60, especially 157, 158, 160.

never relax till America confessed her supremacy . . . any concession on our parts, till the right on which all our pretensions were founded, was allowed, would be to the last degree impolitic, pusillanimous, and absurd'. He thought it 'high time for the Mother Country to exert her authority, or forever relinquish it. . . . I should scorn to continue one of his Majesty's Ministers, and not advise coercive measures, when I was so firmly and fully convinced of their necessity; and I take a particular pride in avowing those sentiments; and mean steadily to abide by them at all events.' He finished by declaring 'the ministerial resolution of enforcing obedience by arms'.[1]

The Rockinghams were very wary in the support they gave to Chatham. Rockingham and Richmond spoke in favour of withdrawing troops, and they and other members of the squadron were in the minority of eighteen who voted for the motion.[2] But they were annoyed because Chatham had not told them that he intended to introduce it. Burke claimed that 'more would have been in the minority if Lord Chatham had thought proper to give notice of his motion to the proper people'.[3] Above all, the Rockinghams feared that Chatham would propose the repeal of their precious Declaratory Act. Chatham had visited Rockingham on 7 January, and during an hour-long discussion about America he said that the Declaratory Act had been the cause of all the troubles in the Colonies and that early in the session he would move to have it amended.[4] This caused trepidation in the Rockingham ranks. The Duke of Manchester advised that the squadron would have to defend their Act, but they must try to do so without openly disputing with Chatham. He said:

nothing can be so advantageous to administration, nothing so ruinous to opposition, nothing so fatal to American Liberty, as disunion among the leaders of opposition, a breach with Lord Chatham and his friends. I do not mean to overrate his abilities, or to dispair of our cause, though he no longer

[1] *Ibid.*, 161-2.   [2] It was defeated 68-18. *Ibid.*, 168.
[3] Burke to the citizens of Bristol, 20 January 1775. W.W.M. Bk., *CEB*, iii, 103.
[4] Rockingham to Burke, 7, 8, January 1775. W.W.M. R1-1536, *CEB*, iii, 91-2.

existed, but while the man treads this earth, his success, his eloquence, the cry of the many, must exhalt him into a consequence, perhaps far above his station . . . on our part, it may be prudent on this occasion not to enter the lists with Lord Chatham.[1]

In fact, since Chatham on the 20th did not deal seriously with the question of sovereignty, the division in the ranks of the Opposition was not made too evident. But while the American problem continued to be Parliament's chief concern, the Rockinghams had to be ready to deal either with suggestions from Chatham on the one side or the Ministerial propositions on the other. Before the session Burke had impressed on his chief the need to take up America 'as a Business'. Three weeks later he repeated that 'the question then is, whether your Lordship chooses to lead, or to be led . . .'.[2] But it was decided by the group 'not to get the start of Lord Chatham or run races with him as to motions'. Richmond reminded Rockingham of this after Chatham's proposal on the 20th, when the Marquis suggested that they should meet to discuss possible motions on American matters.[3] The problem of relations with Chatham, like most other issues, divided the Rockinghams. Burke thought that they should press on regardless of him, Richmond that they should try to consult with him on joint action, Manchester that they should dissociate from his opinions without fighting him, and Rockingham agreed with whomsoever advised him last. But Chatham was too big to ignore and too egocentric for an alliance. The Rockinghams were forced to watch him setting the pace while they carefully avoided making an issue on the critical question of British sovereignty.[4]

On Tuesday, 31 January, Chatham informed Rockingham of his intention to put his main conciliatory plan before the House of Lords on the next day. 'Being on the eve of the doom

[1] Manchester to Rockingham, 18 January 1775. W.W.M. R1-1539.

[2] Burke to Rockingham, 5 January 1775 and 24 January 1774. W.W.M. Bk., *CEB*, iii, 88, 107.

[3] Richmond to Rockingham, 28 January 1775. W.W.M. R1-1540. Also Rockingham to Burke, 22 January 1775. W.W.M. Bk., *CEB*, iii, 105. Burke to Rockingham, 24 January 1775. W.W.M. Bk., *CEB*, iii, 106-8.

[4] Richmond, who pressed most for an alliance with Chatham, was the least attached to the Declaratory Act.

to be pronounced against America,' he announced, 'there is not a moment to lose for whoever has anything to propose for preventing a civil war going in a few days to be inevitably fixed.'[1] Rockingham immediately wrote off to Shelburne asking if he knew what Chatham had in mind, but Shelburne denied having seen the final plan, though he had discussed the outlines of it with Chatham. Shelburne assured Rockingham that since it was 'founded on liberty and right commercial views, I presume [it] will meet your Lordship's approbation'.[2] So the Opposition went to the Lords with no more idea than the Ministry of what would be proposed.[3]

Chatham presented his plan to the Lords in the form of a Bill entitled 'A Provisional Act for settling the troubles in America, and for asserting the Supreme Legislative authority and superintending power of Great Britain over the Colonies'. It had ten main proposals. (i) Parliament should continue to have the supreme legislative authority and superintending power over the Colonies. (ii) But 'no tallage, tax, or other charge for his Majesty's revenue, shall be commanded or levied, from British freemen in America, without common consent, by act of provincial assembly there, duly convened for that purpose'. (iii) Although the Crown had the right to keep a standing army in America, 'no military force . . . can ever be lawfully employed to violate and destroy the just rights of the people'. (iv) The Philadelphia Congress should be recognised as a lawful assembly with the authority to make recognition of the sovereignty of the British Parliament. (v) The Colonies assembled at Philadelphia should grant the King a perpetual revenue to alleviate the British National Debt. (vi) The Admiralty courts in America would be returned to their ancient limitations. (vii) Trial by jury in civil cases was to be restored, and criminal

[1] Chatham to Rockingham, 31 January 1775. W.W.M. R1-1543. Rockingham to Chatham, 31 January 1775. Chatham Papers, PRO. 30/8/54, f. 221. See also Shelburne to Chatham, 31 January 1775. *Ibid.*, 30/8/56, ff. 162-5.
[2] Rockingham to Shelburne, 31 January 1775, unfinished draft. W.W.M. R1-1545; and Shelburne to Rockingham, 1 February 1775. W.W.M. R1-1546.
[3] Rockingham to Portland, 30 January and 31 January 1775. Portland MS., PW F 9089.

cases were not to be sent to other Colonies or abroad for trial. (viii) Various Statutes complained of by the colonists were to be suspended, particularly the Coercive Acts. (ix) Judges in the Colonies were to hold their office subject to good behaviour. (x) Colonial charters and Constitutions could be violated only on grounds of legal forfeiture.[1]

These sweeping proposals, taken together with Chatham's motion to withdraw the troops from Boston, represented the most radical and comprehensive attempt so far to solve the American problem. Burke might later brush aside 'as ridiculous the Chathamite attempt to limit sovereignty as regards money with some vague line'.[2] But it was not much more ridiculous than Burke's belief in a sovereign right which was never exercised — at a time when much of the dispute was about rights which had been exercised and denied.[3] What Chatham tried to do was to remove many particular grievances raised by the colonists, to grant recognition, and therefore responsibility, to their leaders gathered at Philadelphia, and, above all, to yield the British rights of taxation to the colonists without completely destroying British legislative sovereignty, without harming the Navigation Acts and without removing the whole American revenue.

Chatham's plan was doomed to failure in Britain because no one but he could take such an Olympian view of the colonial struggle. He proposed to suspend parts of a dozen or so Statutes at one sweep, to concede the American demands on nearly every point, and to reorganise the legislative and fiscal arrangements in the Colonies. His sole object was to preserve and reanimate the mighty British Empire and he made no concessions to the pride or prejudices of British politicians. The Bill was introduced without any attempt to convince the Opposition or to convert the Administration. From the British

---

[1] *Parl. Hist.*, xviii, 198-203, especially 198-200.

[2] J. Steven Watson, *The Reign of George III, 1760–1815*, p. 200.

[3] Franklin, who had been consulted beforehand, praised Chatham's plan and said it 'would have prevented present mischief' and with some modifications might have led to 'a perfect union', which is probably true — had Chatham introduced it seven years earlier. Franklin to Charles Thomson, 5 February 1774. *The Complete Works of Benjamin Franklin*, ed. J. Bigelow, v, 432.

point of view, it was an act of pure statesmanship, unrelieved by any touch of political awareness, and therefore without a hope of being passed and put into practice. Parliament was momentarily stunned, then protested at the way in which such a great project was suddenly put before them, and then passed on to smaller matters more within its narrow vision. Even had the Bill passed, however, it may be questioned whether it would have satisfied enough of the Americans who were leading the dispute against Britain. For its main intention was to preserve the material sovereignty — Britain's control over imperial industry and commerce — and it is far from certain that the American radicals would have accepted this. But the essential point is that Chatham's proposal was impractical, because it had no chance of passing through Parliament and because it depended upon goodwill between England and America, which did not exist and which probably could not be created by Act of Parliament.

In the debate on the Bill Dartmouth spoke first for the Government. He said the proposals were too complex for an immediate decision and he suggested that the Bill should lie on the table until all the American papers were taken into consideration. But Sandwich, who followed Dartmouth, opposed this suggestion and insisted that to make any concessions would mean the end of all authority in the Colonies. He therefore moved that the Bill be rejected, and was strongly supported by Gower. Lord Camden spoke first for the Opposition and pledged himself

> to prove every leading proposition on which the Bill rests, particularly the main one, which in a great measure includes all the rest, the rescinding the Declaratory Law asserting that the British Parliament can bind the colonies in all cases whatsoever. On that ground I am ready to meet my antagonists.

But Rockingham and his friends, who might have been expected to rise to this challenge, kept silent on that point. They gave support to Chatham's general object of reconciliation and they voted with him in the lobby when Sandwich's motion to reject was passed 61-32.[1] Richard Champion later explained that Chatham's proposals were 'in several respects contrary to their [Rockinghams'] sentiments, and were supported by them in the House of Lords only that the Ministry might not derive any appearance of triumph from any disunion among them'.[2]

While the House of Lords considered Chatham's proposals, the Commons was receiving various petitions on the subject of America. On 23 January Alderman Hayley presented a petition from the Merchants of London demanding an immediate reconciliation with the Americans. This was killed together with two petitions from Bristol by referring them to what Burke called 'a committee of oblivion'. On the 24th a similar petition from Glasgow, and on the 25th two others from Norwich and Dudley shared the same fate. The London Merchants presented a second petition on the 26th, and it was followed by petitions from the American colonists, the merchants of Liverpool, the manufacturers of Manchester and the traders of Wolverhampton. These were all, as Burke predicted, buried in the committee which considered them on the 27th and the 31st, and the Rockinghams' efforts to rouse the English mercantile classes petered out feebly.[3]

On 2 February the whole House resolved into Committee to consider the American papers which had lain before it for the previous twelve days. The prevailing mood was perhaps reflected in a remark made by Edmund Gibbon two days earlier: 'We are now arrived at the decisive moment of preserving or of losing for ever both our trade and Empire'.[4] Lord North opened for the Government.[5] He proposed that an Address be made to the King noting that an actual state of rebellion existed

---

[1] For the speeches see *Parl. Hist.*, xviii, 203-15, especially 209. Apparently the reason for the large minority was that 'many Lords were in favour of *receiving* the Bill, since it was from a member of their House, even though they would have been opposed to passing it'. Hutchinson, *op. cit.*, i, 366-7.

[2] Champion to American correspondents (probably Messrs. Willing Morris & Co.), November 1775. *Letters of Richard Champion*, ed., G. H. Guttridge, p. 64.

[3] For a fuller discussion of the merchant question, including the background to these petitions, see above, Chapter VI, pp. 154-6.

[4] Gibbon to J. B. Holyrod (Lord Sheffield), 31 January 1774, *The Letters of Edward Gibbon*, ed., J. E. Norton, ii, 56.

[5] *Parl. Hist.*, xviii, 222-4.

in Massachusetts Bay, that various other Colonies had encouraged this and begging the King to take immediate action to ensure obedience to the laws and sovereignty of England. The Premier also gave a hint of the measures the Government had in mind — the proposals to send more military forces and to blockade New England which had been made in the Cabinet on 16 and 21 January.

The form of the Address differed considerably from what had been decided on 21 January.[1] Then the Cabinet had agreed that it would offer not to tax the Americans in return for payments raised by the colonists themselves towards administrative expenses. Now it made only one general reference to the willingness of the Government to show the Americans 'every just and reasonable indulgence' should they 'make a proper application'. The main emphasis was on the misbehaviour of the colonists and the need to take every measure necessary to restore law and order. And the most interesting point was the assertion that Massachusetts was in a state of rebellion — another critical step towards the use of force in the Colonies. This decision was reached after full consideration by the Law Officers, and, given the circumstances, was technically correct. The Law Officers had already on 13 December 1774 given the Cabinet their opinion that the proceedings of the Provincial Congress in Massachusetts,[2] reported in Gage's letters received in the middle of December, constituted an act of treason. But it had then been decided to wait for more details.[3] When fuller reports arrived they were submitted on 20 January to the Law Officers with the question 'whether the said Resolutions and Proceedings are Acts of Treason and Rebellion, and whether the persons present and acting in such Congress may not be arrested and imprisoned as Traitors and rebels'.[4] On

[1] Hutchinson read the Address on 30 January and again on 4 February and observed that on the second occasion it 'appeared stronger expressed'. The changes were presumably made between 30 January and 2 February when the Address was presented. Hutchinson, *op. cit.*, i, 364, 369.
[2] J. C. Miller, *Origins of the American Revolution*, pp. 398-9.
[3] Pownall to Dartmouth, 18 December 1774. Dartmouth MS. D 1778, II, 1022.
[4] Dartmouth to Attorney- and Solicitor-Generals, 20 January 1775. PRO. CO. 5/159, f. 46.

2 February — the day of the debate — the Law Officers reported back :

> We are of opinion that the seizing public money, and new officering and disciplining the militia, for the purpose avowed, and insisted upon, in the resolutions of the Provincial Congress, amount to High Treason, and the several resolutions above mentioned, ordering the same, are overt acts, by which to prove the same, and the being present at a meeting, where such resolutions were taken, is *prima facie* evidence of the crime of Treason.[1]

In the Commons debate on the Address on 2 February, John Dunning, for the Opposition, concentrated on the question of rebellion, and denied that Massachusetts was in any such condition. 'I insist', he said, 'that every appearance of riot, disorder, tumult and sedition . . . arises not from disobedience, treason or rebellion, but is created by the conduct of those, who are anxious to establish despotism.' [2] But Thurlow and Wedderburn were ready with strong arguments. The Attorney-General pointed out that several Provinces had organised and armed their militia ready for active service against the King's Government and that they had already seized Gage's stores and munitions. 'Now, Sir,' asked Thurlow, 'if this is not rebellion, I desire the learned gentleman will explain what is rebellion.' [3] The Opposition had little else to say. Burke, normally its leading voice, was sick. North's motion was passed by 296 to 106 — and although this was by far the highest division secured by the Opposition on an American question since the start of the colonial crisis in 1774, the Government vote was also at a peak and the Ministry drew its customary encouragement from having a substantial majority of Parliament behind it.[4]

---

[1] PRO. CO. 5/74, f. 121.   [2] *Parl. Hist.*, xviii, 225.
[3] *Ibid.* 225-33, especially 226.
[4] Pownall to Gage, 3 February 1775. PRO. CO. 5/154 (Part I), f. 126. On the question of majorities, Burke told the Americans : 'There are certainly some Members in both houses, who earnestly desire, that measures of another complexion and tendency might be adopted. But these men . . . are not apparently much more numerous, or much more considerable in this Parliament than in the last. It is true, that the numbers, which have divided in the Minority against some of the strong measures, are somewhat higher

The Address was reported back to the Commons on Monday, 6 February. A long debate followed in which it was clear that Members realised that this was a crucial stage in England's colonial policy. John Wilkes made his first major speech on American affairs in this Parliament, describing the Address as 'unfounded, rash, and sanguinary'. He praised Chatham's conciliation plan as the best way to peace yet proposed and declared that, in contrast, the Ministry's plan would drive the colonists not just to rebellion but to revolution. Burke reminded the House that if Britain resorted to force she would be dealing with the whole of America and he pressed the independent Members particularly to consider the consequences of such widespread action. Some independents took heed. William Jolliffe, often a supporter of the Government, said he 'could not give his assent to measures his soul shuddered at. He disapproved of the plan, and was for considering it in every light, lest resistance should be made justifiable.' Governor Johnstone described the Address as 'this dreadful sentence upon a meritorious, sober, and industrious people' and said it 'hurries us into that situation, from which there is no retreating. It obliges the Americans immediately to act. By declaring them in rebellion, they must have recourse to arms.' But others, like William Mayne, felt that

> so very violent has been, and still is, the conduct of the Americans, that there is scarce an opening left for British justice and British humanity . . . if, after all, conciliating measures shall fail, this country has no alternative left, but to make use of that power they enjoy, under heaven, for the protection of the whole Empire ; and to shew the Americans that as our ancestors deluged this country with their blood, to gain this constitution for us, we . . . are determined, in glorious emulation of their example, to transmit it perfect and unimpaired to posterity, or perish in the attempt.

The Government supporters continued firm in their intentions, and the debate lasted until after two o'clock on Tuesday

than those which divided on similar questions in the last Parliament. But the majority is also greater.' Burke to the Committee of Correspondence of the New York Assembly, 14 March 1775. W.W.M. Bk., *CEB*, iii, 135.

morning. At the end Barré reminded the House 'you are this night to decide, whether you are to make war on your colonies'. But the Government carried its question by 288-105, and the Address was sent to the Lords for discussion later that day.[1] The debate in the Lords was a long and curious affair. The Duke of Richmond was almost the only peer to discuss the merits and implications of the Address. For the rest, Shelburne spent much time accusing Mansfield of being the secret hand behind the coercive measures, and Mansfield even longer in denying this. Camden began by discussing the vital legal questions of rebellion and treason, but was soon embroiled in a personal argument with Lord Lyttelton. Sandwich made a long speech praising his own work at the Admiralty. It was nearly two o'clock in the morning when the Address was passed by 104-29.[2] Thereupon the Opposition put down a Protest

> against an Address amounting to a declaration of war, which is founded upon no proper parliamentary information . . . which followed the rejection of every mode of conciliation ; which holds out no substantial offer of redress of grievances ; and which promises support to those Ministers who have inflamed America, and grossly misconducted the affairs of Great Britain.[3]

Despite the fact that the Opposition numbers were higher than at any time since the American crisis began, the King was happy to see the Address passed with such majorities. He told North and Rochford to make sure that a large number of Members and peers came with the Speaker to present the Address to him at St. James's. He also believed that the Royal Answer he would then give to Parliament 'ought to open the eyes of the deluded Americans but if it does not, it must set every delicate man at liberty to avow the propriety of the most

---

[1] *Parl. Hist.*, xviii, 233-65, especially 234, 244, 247, 248, 253, 260, 263, 264. King to North, 7 February 1775. Fortescue, *op. cit.*, iii, 1586. After the debate on the Address Edward Gibbon wrote 'I am more and more convinced that with firmness all may go well ; yet I sometimes doubt Lord N.'. To J. B. Holroyd, 8 February 1775. *Letters of Edward Gibbon*, ii, 59.
[2] There is a list of the minority in W.W.M. R1-1551.
[3] *Parl. Hist.*, xviii, 265-96, especially 296. See also Richmond to Burke, 8 February 1775. W.W.M. Bk., *CEB*, iii, 110.

coercive measures'.[1] Not for the first time, the King gives the impression that he relished the idea of being released to pursue the most coercive measures. He was aware that 'delicate' men had scruples, but there is little evidence that he shared them, at least not on this issue.

Having now secured in form the general support of Parliament, the Government proceeded to introduce the various measures which had been decided in January. On Friday, 10 February, Lord North moved for leave to bring in

> a Bill to restrain the trade and commerce of the Provinces of Massachusetts Bay, and New Hampshire; the colonies of Connecticut and Rhode Island, and Providence Plantation in North America, to Great Britain, Ireland, and the British Islands in the West Indies; and to prohibit such provinces and colonies from carrying on any fishery on the banks of Newfoundland, or other places therein to be mentioned, under certain conditions, and for a time to be limited.[2]

The Bill was to be temporary, either until the end of 1775 or to the end of the next session of Parliament. The Premier justified it on the grounds that there was rebellion in New England and also with the argument that since the Americans had refused to trade with Britain 'it was but just that we should not suffer them to trade with any other nation'. After a thin debate, leave was given to bring in the Bill by 261-85.[3] On 13 February the Commons voted an additional two thousand seamen for 1775, and on the 15th Barrington asked for grants to increase the land forces by four thousand men. He said these were necessary to make up the force at Boston to some ten thousand troops. The Government's measures thus progressed very satisfactorily. The Address had given it the full approval of Parliament. The Trade and Fisheries Bill was ready to come before the Commons, and the Government now had all the extra force that it felt

---

[1] King to North, 8 February 1775. Fortescue, *op. cit.*, iii, 1588, 1589.
[2] *Parl. Hist.*, xviii, 299. Pownall and Knox drew up this Bill. Wedderburn made the main revisions, but Jenkinson, Grey Cooper, Welbore Ellis, Cornwall, North, Dartmouth and Hutchinson all made suggestions for alterations. Hutchinson, *op. cit.*, i, 375-7, 392-3.
[3] *Parl. Hist.*, xviii, 298-305, especially 299. North to King, 11 February 1775. Fortescue, *op. cit.*, iii, 1592. *Commons Journals*, xxxv, 112.

would be necessary to repress any factious colonists. On the evening of the 15th the King wrote happily to North that

> where violence is with resolution repelled it commonly yields, and I owne though a thorough friend to holding out the Olive Branch I have not the smallest doubt that if it does not succeed that when once vigorous measures appear to be the only means left of bringing the Americans to a due submission to the Mother Country that the colonies will submit.[1]

The offer of the 'olive branch' was the third part of the American plan devised by the Ministry in January. Then it had been decided that the offer to the Americans to desist from raising taxes should be included in the Address of Parliament to the King. But some time between the Cabinet meeting on 21 January and the presentation of the Address on 2 February this decision was changed, and the Address became in effect a declaration of rebellion and an authorisation to the Ministry to coerce the colonists. In the middle of February, the 'olive branch', in the form of the tax concession, and a royal pardon to the Massachusetts patriots, was considered again.

In the background of these proposals for conciliation were the negotiations between Franklin, Barclay and Fothergill which have been described above.[2] These had run into serious difficulties on 4 February, when Franklin had pointed out the impossibility of dropping the colonial demands for the repeal of the 1774 Coercive Acts, for the limitation of the Admiralty Courts, for the amendment of the Navigation Acts, and for the withdrawal of British troops. On 6 February Fothergill wrote to Dartmouth announcing the failure of their efforts:

> I wish it had been in my power to have informed my noble friend that our negotiations had been successful. But it is not . . . our difficulties arose from the American Acts. . . . As a concession to pay a tax was the *sine qua non* on this side; so a rescinding of those acts, or rather repealing them in the terms of reconciliation on the other.

Was the whole of Administration as cordially disposed to

---

[1] King to North, 15 February 1775. Fortescue, *op. cit.*, iii, 1595.
[2] See Chapters IX pp. 214-15, Chapter X, pp. 221-2.

peace and as sensible of its advantages as Lord Dartmouth, I think there would be very little difficulty in accomplishing it. But I see and perceive so strong a current another way, that I despair with it the interposition of Omnipotence of any reconciliation. . . . Should the King's servants happily coincide in adopting the simple plan of pacification which our noble friends so generously conceived, and *include the repeal of the acts above mentioned*, we have not the least doubt but America would immediately return to every just expression of duty both in language and in conduct. Dr. Franklin, should this be tacitly consented to, would have not the least objection to petition for the restoration of peace; to offer on the part of Boston to pay the East Company for the tea . . . and endeavour *bona fide* to concert every means of a lasting and reciprocally beneficial union.[1]

Barclay, however, refused to despair. He called another meeting on 16 February, and then himself produced a paper entitled 'A Plan which, it is believed, would produce a *permanent* union between Great Britain and her Colonies'.[2] It was vague and conciliatory on the main points in dispute. The crux of his scheme lay in the first clause, which, because the Ministry insisted that the Americans should make the first conciliatory gesture, suggested that the colonial agents should petition the King promising to pay for the tea destroyed at Boston. Franklin said he had no authority from his American employers to do so, but he was prepared to risk petitioning if he was assured in return that all the recent offensive legislation relating to Massachusetts would be repealed.[3] The next day, 17 February, he returned to Fothergill's house with a draft of a petition to this effect. But Barclay and Fothergill told him there was no hope of securing the repeal of any but the Boston Port Act. Their negotiations came to an end on this point.

It is not clear how seriously the negotiations between Barclay, Fothergill and Franklin were taken by their contacts in the Government. Perhaps the two Quakers exaggerated the

[1] Printed in R. Hingston Fox, *Dr. John Fothergill and his Friends*, pp. 332-3.
[2] Printed in *ibid.*, Appendix A, pp. 398-400.
[3] *Franklin Complete Works*, v, 507-8.

encouragement they received [1] and interpreted it as meaning that there was more support in the Ministry for this point than existed in fact. But it does seem possible that the negotiations in Harpur Street had some influence on, and in turn directly reflected, developments in the Cabinet. For the production of Barclay's plan on 16 February, and Franklin's promise to petition the King, coincided with — and perhaps inspired — the sudden raising in Cabinet that evening of the idea which had lain fallow since North suggested it to the Cabinet in January, that of putting a conciliatory proposition to Parliament.[2] According to Israel Mauduit it was Dartmouth who this time persuaded the rest of the Cabinet to agree that the American Assemblies should make requisitions and in return Parliament should give up 'its right to taxation'.[3] Mauduit may have received a garbled account of what happened in Cabinet, yet it is clear that ways of reconciling the Americans were again under consideration. But Franklin's insistence on the repeal of all the Coercive Acts presumably dashed any hopes which Dartmouth may have held of going beyond North's original proposition. Certainly the final motion scarcely differed from that drawn up in January.[4] The wording had been rearranged, and where formerly it had merely required 'the Colonies' to make financial provisions, it now said 'the Governor, council, and assembly or general court' should do so, but there were no other changes.[5]

As the Ministry refused to make further concessions the negotiations with Franklin were then brought to an end. Hyde told Franklin on 1 March that several of his final propositions had proved unacceptable. That evening Fothergill wrote to him that there was now no hope of reconciliation and that he must inform the Americans that, 'whatever specious pretences

---

[1] Hyde's role is particularly ambiguous. See his letters to Howe, 10 February 1775, *HMC*, 14, X, *Dartmouth MSS.*, ii, 269, and to Dartmouth, 4 July 1775. *Ibid.*, 325.

[2] North to King, 19 February 1775. Fortescue, *op. cit.*, iii, 1599. The suddenness of this development is referred to in Dartmouth to Hardwicke, 19 February 1775. BM. Add. MS. 35612, f. 184. See also Hardwicke's reply to Dartmouth, 19 February 1775 : Dartmouth MS. D 1778, II, 1153.

[3] So Mauduit told Hutchinson on 17 February. Hutchinson, *op. cit.*, i, 379, 381. On Mauduit see above, p. 28.

[4] See above, p. 223.　　　　　　　　　[5] *Parl. Hist.*, xviii, 320.

are offered, they are all hollow'.[1] Franklin sailed from Portsmouth the next day, 2 March, and by the time he landed in America war had begun.

The Cabinet also decided on 16 February to offer a pardon to all those in the Bay Colony who had aided and abetted the treasonable offences, on condition that within one month they surrendered to the Chief Justice and subscribed to the following declaration:

> I . . . do profess, testify and declare that I will obey the laws and statutes which the King's Majesty by and with the advice and consent of the Lords spiritual and temporal and Commons of Great Britain in Parliament assembled hath made, or shall make, to bind the colonies of America.[2]

Next day a draft was sent to the Law Officers and they were asked to prepare a Bill for this purpose to be put through Parliament.

In one sense this pardon, like the attempt early in 1774 to prosecute the leaders of the Boston Tea Party, was a moderate measure. In as much as it attempted to deal only with certain guilty persons, and then made provision to pardon them, it was much less extreme than the other coercive measures which had punished all colonists indiscriminately. Had it been possible from the beginning to deal with a few individuals on purely legal grounds then the extent of the political crisis in the Colonies might have been limited. But the likelihood of this, even early in 1774, had been remote. Now in February 1775 it seemed virtually impossible. Moreover there was a political sting in the tail of the proposed pardon which reveals that the mood of the Ministry was far from conciliatory. The wording of the declaration which was required from the penitent traitors constituted a blunt statement of Britain's legislative supremacy. The colonists were expected to acknowledge this explicitly — something which many British politicians had already admitted was unnecessary — and to submit both to the past coercive measures, which they had clearly found repugnant, and to any future policies that the Ministry might devise. Therefore,

---

[1] *Franklin Complete Works*, v, 531.   [2] PRO. CO. 5/159, f. 50.

taken as a whole, the pardon must be judged as uncompromising to the colonists. Yet this proposal, together with Lord North's conciliatory plan in respect of taxation, constituted the maximum of concessions by means of which the Government, in February 1775, proposed, and presumably hoped for, reconciliation with the Colonies. The declarations of loyalty and obedience which were required might still, perhaps, be obtained from a few Colonies. But it is hard to believe that the abject submission demanded from the individual patriots in the Colonies was ever likely to take place.[1]

When North introduced his Conciliatory Proposition to the Commons on 20 February,[2] he emphasised that it was in no way a detached and independent proposal. He said that it arose naturally from the Address (which was true in as much as it was an integral part of the policy devised in January and was originally intended to be part of the Address). He claimed that it answered the need to state clearly 'the ground on which negotiation may take place. It is explicit, and defines the terms, and specifies the persons from whom the proposals must come, and to whom they must me made.' If the Americans rejected it, he thought that would put the responsibility for bloodshed squarely

---

[1] A Cabinet on 30 March 1775 officially decided to issue the pardon. The Ministry proposed to apply it to eleven Colonies (Georgia and Delaware were omitted) and in time extended it to cover many more acts and meetings than those originally declared treasonable. Cabinet Minute, 30 March 1775. Dartmouth MS. D 1778, II, 1197. Law Officers to Dartmouth, 26 February 1775. PRO. CO. 5/160, f. 52. Same to same, 14 April 1775. PRO. CO. 5/159, f. 52. Dartmouth to Law Officers, 28 March 1775. PRO. CO. 5/159, f. 52.

[2] 'That it is the opinion of this Committee, that when the governor, council, and assembly, or general court, of any of his Majesty's provinces or colonies in America, shall propose to make provision, according to the condition, circumstances, and situation of such province or colony, for contributing their proportion to the common defence (such proportion to be raised under the authority of the general court, or general assembly of such province or colony, and disposable by Parliament) and shall engage to make provision also for the support of the civil government, and the administration of justice, in such province or colony, it will be proper, if such proposal shall be approved by his Majesty and the two Houses of Parliament, and for so long as such provision shall be made accordingly, to forbear, in respect of such province or colony, to levy any duty, tax, or assessment, or to impose any further duty, tax or assessment, except only such duties as it may be expedient to continue to levy or to impose for the regulation of commerce ; the net produce of the duties last mentioned to be carried to the account of such province or colony respectively.' Parl. Hist., xviii, 320.

upon their shoulders. But he hoped that the Resolution would in fact induce some of the moderate Americans, maybe whole Colonies, to dissociate themselves from their extreme colleagues.[1]

It is difficult to determine the Ministry's true motives in pursuing this offer, and the precise benefits they believed would arise from it. In the Commons North argued that it might bring peace, or at least divide the colonial ranks. Yet, the day before, he explained to the King that he hoped

> for great utility (if not in America, at least on this side of the water) to arise to the public from this motion ; he is confident it gives up no right, and that it contains precisely the plan which ought to be adopted by Great Britain, even if all America were subdued. He has reason to think it would give general satisfaction here, and that it will greatly facilitate the passing the Bill now in the House for restraining the Trade of New England.[2]

Most probably North wanted every possible advantage and he wanted to please everyone. He genuinely believed some concession on taxation was necessary. He knew that the grounds for a possible reconciliation must be drawn in general terms. He also hoped to split the Americans.[3] And he wanted to placate those in England who were disturbed at the repressive nature of the Government's policy.[4] These were sufficient reasons to justify the motion. But it is worth repeating that this Resolution was not a separate and last-minute gesture to moderates in Britain and America. Whatever particular advantages North discovered in the Resolution, it was part of the general policy which had been decided upon from the beginning of the year.

[1] *Ibid.*, 320-1.

[2] North to King, 19 February 1775. Fortescue, *op. cit.*, iii, 1599.

[3] Richard Champion wrote that good news from Virginia had persuaded the Ministry that a conciliatory offer might divide some Southern States from the rebels. To Messrs. Willing Morris & Co., 6 March 1775. G. H. Guttridge, ed., *Letters of Richard Champion*, pp. 45-6. Richard Oswald was offering advice of this kind to Lord North. E. Robson, *The American Revolution, 1763–1783*, p. 90.

[4] He took care to inform the Opposition beforehand and asked them to attend. See North to Burke, 19 February 1775. W.W.M. Bk., *CEB*, iii, 115. According to Jenkinson, this step upset many people, 'it not being usual to notify any but the friends of Government on such occasions'. Hutchinson, *op. cit.*, i, 399-400.

That policy was based upon the Ministerial belief, certainly justified, that the whole Empire was at stake, and that the dispute in America was not about revenue or the payment of a tea tax but about the whole basis of colonial subordination to Britain. Its object was to restore obedience in the Colonies.

The King highly approved the Resolution, not because it appeared to be conciliatory, but because it would satisfy Parliament. He was also happy because it avoided any recognition of Congress as a body competent to vote taxation in America.[1] The House of Commons gave it a more mixed reception. At first several supporters of the Administration rose in deep shock to attack it.[2] Welbore Ellis, William Adam, John Acland and Henry Dundas declared it was contrary to the Government's previous policy and opened the door to the abandonment of British sovereignty. But Sir Gilbert Elliot rallied the Government ranks by assuring them that it abandoned nothing at all and was quite consistent with what had gone before.[3] The Opposition spokesmen, Burke, Dunning, Barré and Fox, denounced the proposal as both contradictory, because it seemed to differ from previous proposals, and as treacherous, because in reality it did not. When the debate continued on the 27th some Members were still puzzled. Acland doubted if the Americans would accept the proposition, and General Burgoyne thought such a refusal was to be desired because it would prove what rogues the Americans were. In the end the Government was sustained by its usual large majority, the Resolution being

---

[1] King to North, 19 February 1775. Fortescue, *op. cit.*, iii, 1600.

[2] 'In the first part of the day an idea struck several gentlemen that it was too great a concession, we were likely to lose several friends, but their wavering was a strong proof that the disposition of the House independent of any ministerial connection is to maintain the authority of Great Britain over America.' North to King, 20 February 1775. *Ibid.*, 1601.

[3] Gibbon reported : 'We went into the House in confusion every moment expecting that the Bedfords would fly into rebellion against those measures. Lord North rose six times to appease the storm ; all in vain, till at length Sir Gilbert declared for Administration, and the troops all rallied to their proper standards.' To J. B. Holroyd, 25 February 1775. *Letters of Edward Gibbon*, ii, 61. Elliot had a copy of the motion at his house on the morning before the debate when Hutchinson visited him. Hutchinson, *op. cit.*, i, 380.

approved by 274-88 in Committee, and without a division when reported back to the House.[1]

Not surprisingly North's motion found no welcome among friends of the rebellious colonists. Benjamin Franklin reported to an American moderate :

> Those in administration, who are for violent measures, are said to dislike it. The others rely upon it as a means of *dividing*, and by that means subduing us. But I cannot conceive that any colony will undertake to grant a revenue to a government that holds a sword over their heads with a threat to strike the moment they cease to give or do not give so much as it is pleased to expect. . . . It seems to me the language of a highwayman.[2]

Richard Champion wrote in a similar vein : 'The motion of Lord North falsely termed conciliatory only shews his weakness. He knew it could not be adopted, and had no other hope than that it would delude, and divide, if not the Colonies, at least the few friends the Americans had at home.' [3] Since there seemed little hope that this motion would mollify the Americans it could not be a basis for future colonial peace.[4] When it reached America, events had already by-passed it at Lexington and Concord. The time for olive branches was past, and the sword had become the sole instrument of policy.

The Bill to restrain the commerce and fishery of New England was next taken through the Commons.[5] It was delayed a little on 28 February while a petition was presented against it by the Quakers, and again later that day in the Committee stage, when David Barclay, agent for the London merchants interested in North American trade, was called in to speak against it. Barclay pointed out that the operation of the Bill would reduce many Colonies to a state of famine, that it

---

[1] *Parl. Hist.*, xviii, 322-58. King to North, 21 February 1775. Fortescue, *op. cit.*, iii, 1602.

[2] Franklin to Joseph Galloway, 25 February 1775. *Franklin Complete Works*, v, 438-9.

[3] Champion to Messrs. Willing Morris & Co., 13 March 1775. *Letters of Richard Champion*, pp. 51-2.

[4] It was rejected by the Continental Congress at Philadelphia in August 1775. J. C. Miller, *Origins of the American Revolution*, p. 459.

[5] Leave had been given to introduce it on 10 February.

would punish the innocent with the guilty and that it would prevent the colonists from repaying their debts to England. But these arguments seem to have had very little effect. On 6 March, when the Bill was reported back from Committee to the House, Charles Jenkinson described the measure as merciful considering that the colonists had aimed at rebellion and independence from the beginning. Henry Dundas admitted it was coercive and insisted that this was essential since only strong coercion could end the dispute. George Rice recognised that it was harsh, but claimed there was no alternative since the Americans clearly aimed to cut their ties with England.[1] Charles Fox led for the Opposition and asserted that 'the Bill was meant for nothing else but to exasperate the Colonies into open and direct rebellion'. Lord John Cavendish was shocked by the ease and unconcern with which the Commons voted famine on a whole people. Edmund Burke closed the debate by ridiculing a scheme 'to preserve your authority by destroying your dominions'. He also predicted that just as the Boston Port Bill had begotten this New England Bill, so the New England Bill would beget Bills for Virginia, Carolina and Pennsylvania. But the House was unmoved by the prospect of such a proliferation of coercive measures, and it voted 215-61 that the Bill should be engrossed.[2] Two days later, after an abortive attempt by David Hartley to amend the Bill so that food might be carried from one American Colony to another, it was passed through its third reading with little debate and without a division.[3]

Rockingham tried to organise his followers for an attack on the Bill when it went up to the Lords. But the Duke of Richmond declined to come to London for a meeting beforehand. Lord John Cavendish was staying with him at Goodwood and

---

[1] Hutchinson objected strongly to the Bill since it would punish friends of Government as well as enemies. He persuaded Dartmouth, Suffolk, Pownall and Grey Cooper to agree with him on this point, but the proposed amendments were rejected in Cabinet. Hutchinson, *op. cit.*, i, 403, 405, 407.

[2] For this debate, *Parl. Hist.*, xviii, 379-92, especially 380-99. *Commons Journals*, xxxv, 152, 163, 166 and 174. North to King, 6 March 1775. Fortescue, *op. cit.*, iii, 1611.

[3] 15, George III, c. 10. *Parl. Hist.*, xviii, 393-9. *Commons Journals*, xxxv, 182. The vote against Hartley's motion was 188-58. North to King, 8 March 1775. Fortescue, *op. cit.*, iii, 1613.

Richmond wrote that they wanted to enjoy a good day's hunting.[1] This was not the first time Richmond had proved reluctant to join in the Parliamentary battle. In September 1774 he
wrote to Burke: 'Indeed, the more I live, the more I grow to
think, that few things are worth making one's self enemies for,
after all, we can do no good and why should we toil and labour
so much in vain ? I grow very sick of Politics, but not one jot
less affectionate to my friends.'[2] Again in the New Year he
told Rockingham that he returned to London much against his
inclinations.[3] With morale so low, it is not surprising that the
Opposition made little impression on the Lords debates. Rockingham spoke on both 15 and 16 March, attacking the Bill as
oppressive and tyrannical throughout. Lord Camden, Shelburne and the Duke of Manchester supported him. But the
most interesting discussion came from the Government benches
on the 16th. First the Earl of Sandwich rose to reply to Camden's statement that it was impracticable for Britain to try to
conquer America. 'I cannot think the noble lord can be serious
on this matter', he said.

> Suppose the colonies do abound in men, what does that
> signify ? They are raw, undisciplined, cowardly men. I
> wish instead of 40 or 50,000 of these brave fellows, they
> would produce in the field at least 200,000, the more the
> better, the easier would be the conquest; if they did not run
> away, they would starve themselves into compliance with our
> measures.

Sandwich then went on to claim that the Bill under discussion
'was not, nor ought to be, a Bill of intimidation or experiment,
but a perpetual law of commercial regulation, operating to
extend our trade, to increase our seamen, and strengthen our
naval power'.

Each of these statements revealed Sandwich as an extreme
advocate of colonial subordination. His interpretation of the
new Bill as a permanent regulation which would deprive the
colonists of vital commercial rights was original and quite

---

[1] Richmond to Rockingham, 12 March 1775. W.W.M. R1-1559.
[2] Richmond to Burke, 26 September 1774. W.W.M. Bk., *CEB*, iii, 37.
[3] Richmond to Rockingham, 12 January 1775. W.W.M. R1-1538.

inexplicable. Nothing that was said in the Commons debates or in the original Cabinet Minutes suggested that this was the Government's intention. The Earl of Suffolk, his colleague in the Cabinet, promptly sprang up to oppose Sandwich. He denied that any of the King's subjects, American or British, lacked courage, and he denied that the Bill before them was intended to be a permanent commercial regulation. 'It was intended', he said, 'as a Bill of coercion, to oblige the people of New England to submit to the legal and just power of the mother country, and that the faith of parliament would be pledged to them, to restore the fishery, as soon as it should appear that they had returned to their former obedience.' It was an odd episode, revealing how independent, even irresponsible, a member of an eighteenth-century Cabinet could be. But neither the Opposition peers nor the colonists could draw much comfort from it, since the Bill was committed by 104 against 29 and passed the third reading, with certain amendments, by 73-21.[1]

As the news from America grew worse, and more Colonies declared their support for the decisions taken at the Philadelphia Congress, it became apparent that the Ministry would not confine its revenge to New England. On 19 February, before he introduced his Conciliatory Motion, Lord North referred to another restraining Bill 'which must, he fears, be soon brought into the House for subjecting Virginia, Maryland and other provinces to the same restrictions'.[2] It was a delicate question whether to punish all the remaining Colonies, or whether to omit certain ones and so try to divide the colonial cause. New York was at first an obvious candidate for special treatment. On 28 February a letter arrived from Lieutenant-Governor Colden informing Dartmouth that the New York Assembly had voted not to take into consideration the resolutions of the Continental Congress. The Assembly's address to the Governor also asked

---

[1] *Parl. Hist.*, xviii, 421-58, especially 446, 448, 450. The Bill was sent back to the Commons with the Lords amendments on 23 March. The Commons rejected some of these amendments, so a conference was held with the Lords on 27 May and the Lords agreed not to insist on them. *Commons Journals*, xxxv, 220, 225, 226, 230-1.

[2] North to King, 19 February 1775. Fortescue, *op. cit.*, iii, 1599.

that some method of reconciliation be found. Colden pointed out that this proved the loyalty of New York to the Crown and he hoped that the Ministry would encourage it.[1] George III, probably reflecting Ministerial opinions, took this as a good augury. 'I am', he wrote to Dartmouth, 'infinitely happy at the receipt of the very comfortable appearance of temper in the Assembly of New York, which if it continues must greatly tend to bring the other provinces to their senses.'[2]

Leave was asked to bring in this additional Bill on 9 March. It extended the restraint of trade and commerce to New Jersey, Pennsylvania, Maryland, Virginia and South Carolina.[3] The two Colonies excluded were New York and North Carolina. The treatment of New York is explained by the tenor of Colden's dispatch;[4] the Ministry still hoped to win it over to the British side. North Carolina was omitted for similar reasons. The Colony's agents, Elmsley and Barker, had not joined in the general petition from Congress to the King but had sent a separate petition in more moderate terms.[5] This Bill went through its second reading on 17 March, through Committee on the 20th, was reported on 30 March and was approved, 192-46, at its third reading on 5 April.[6] It then went rapidly through its stages in the Lords and was passed into law on 12 April without an amendment and 'without debate'.[7]

While the two Bills blockading American trade and fishery were in the Lords and the Commons respectively, the Opposition made its last attack of this session on the Government's

[1] Colden to Dartmouth, 1 February 1775. PRO. CO. 5/1139, ff. 205-8.
[2] King to Dartmouth, 28 February 1775. Dartmouth MS. D 1778, Supplementary George III. Quoted in HMC, 13, IV, Dartmouth MSS., iv, 501.
[3] Parl. Hist., xviii, 411-12. Burke to Richard Champion, 9 March 1775. W.W.M. Bk., CEB, iii, 131-2. Commons Journals, xxxv, 187.
[4] New York also at first declined to send delegates to the next Congress, scheduled for May 1775. But it later decided by a large majority to send delegates. J. C. Miller, op. cit., pp. 402-7.
[5] Ella Lorn, The Colonial Agents of the Southern Colonies, p. 210. Also Franklin to Charles Thomson, 13 March 1775. The Writings of Benjamin Franklin, ed., A. H. Smyth, vi, 316.
[6] For a description of the debate on the Third Reading see James Harris to Earl Hardwicke, 6 April 1775. BM. Add. MS. 35612, f. 201. Also Parl. Hist., xviii, 593-606. Commons Journals, xxxv, 204, 206, 241 and 250.
[7] 15, George III, c. 18. Lords Journals, xxxiv, 392, 393, 398 and 407.

colonial policy. On 22 March Edmund Burke introduced his Resolutions for making peace with the Americans. These had been under discussion for some weeks. A meeting of the Rockingham group was called on 7 March to examine them.[1] On 12 March Richmond wrote to Rockingham:

> As to Burke's Resolutions I have not seen them, but from what I hear from Lord John, I like them, and so far from fearing to lose English popularity, or to appear to run a race with Lord Chatham for American popularity, I would be very explicit in disclaiming any wish for a revenue, as an unwise measure, not only from the difficulty in obtaining it, but as not founded in sound policy, or indeed in justice while we cramp their trade. We must be satisfied with one or t'other and the advantages of commerce are far the more preferable.[2]

They were due to be brought in on Friday, 17 March, but at the last moment they were put off until the 22nd. This was fortunate for Burke, since he had been in ill health for some time, and his proposed mammoth speech would impose considerable physical strain on him.[3] It also allowed more time to circulate the propositions among Rockingham's friends.

Burke spoke for two and a half hours on 22 March.[4] He said straight away that

> the proposition is peace. Not peace through the medium of war ; not peace to be hunted through the labyrinth of intricate and endless negotiations ; not peace to arise out of universal discord, fomented from principle in all parts of the empire ; ... It is simple peace ; sought in its natural course, and in its ordinary haunts. It is peace sought in the spirit of peace ; and laid in principles purely pacific.

He acknowledged that Lord North's conciliatory motion a month earlier had paved the way for his own. It had made the idea of conciliation admissible and it had also admitted that reforms were necessary in the mode of raising taxation in the Colonies. Now there were two questions which had to be

---

[1] Sir G. Savile to Rockingham, 7 March 1775. W.W.M. R1-1557.
[2] Richmond to Rockingham, 12 March 1775. W.W.M. R1-1559.
[3] Burke to James Delancey, 14 March 1775. *CEB*, iii, 137.
[4] For the whole speech see *Parl. Hist.*, xviii, 478-538.

decided: 'first, whether you ought to concede; and secondly, what your concession ought to be'. Before answering them, Burke reminded the House that it must deal with the realities of the American situation. For when we governed America in future we should have to govern according to those realities 'and not according to our own imaginations; not according to abstract ideas of right; by no means according to mere general theories of government, the resort to which appears to me, in our present situation, no better than arrant trifling'. He listed six characteristics of America which had bred such a spirit of liberty there: ethnic origins; religious background; the social framework in the South; widespread education in law; democratic forms of government; and the remoteness of the Colonies from Great Britain. 'The question is', he asserted, 'not whether their spirit deserves praise or blame; — what, in the name of God, shall we do with it?' He saw only three conceivable ways of dealing with this rebellious spirit in the Colonies: to change it, to prosecute it as criminal, or to comply with it. He dismissed the first, because it is not possible to change the temper of a people. He attacked the policy of criminal prosecution, which the Government had so far followed, as both inexpedient and impractical. He said disputes would always arise in an Empire such as ours. But

in such unfortunate quarrels, among the component parts of a great political union of communities, I can scarcely conceive any thing more completely imprudent, than for the head of the Empire to insist, that, if any privilege is pleaded against his will, or his acts, that his whole authority is denied; instantly to proclaim rebellion, to beat to arms, and to put the offending provinces under the ban. Will not this, Sir, soon teach the provinces to make no distinctions on their part? Will it not teach them that the government, against which a claim of liberty is tantamount to high treason, is a government to which submission is equivalent to slavery? It will not always be quite convenient to impress dependent communities with such an idea.

He went on to point out that although the Government had made a Proclamation of rebellion, it had not been able to start any proceedings on those grounds; and that although other coercive measures had been passed, and military reinforcements sent out, no progress had been made towards reducing the rebellious spirit in the Colonies. 'When I see things in this situation', he said, 'after such confident hopes, bold promises, and active exertions, I cannot, for my life, avoid a suspicion, that the plan itself is not correctly right.'

This left only one means of dealing with the colonists — 'to comply with the American spirit'. Burke explained that the Americans' main complaint was that they were taxed by a Parliament in which they were not represented, and satisfaction would have to be given on this point. He refused to treat the question of the right of taxation — that 'great Serbonian bog . . . where armies whole have sunk'. He said:

> I do not intend to be overwhelmed in that bog, though in such respectable company. The question with me is, not whether you have a right to render your people miserable; but whether it is not your interest to make them happy. It is not, what a lawyer tells me, I may do; but what humanity, reason, and justice, tell me, I ought to do.

He was concerned with the exercise of taxation. Therefore he suggested that Parliamentary taxation should be abandoned in favour of a system of grants by the colonial Assemblies. Such a system had worked efficiently in previous times of war; now it would remove the colonists' main complaint against British sovereignty and make possible a restoration of peace. He also made other subsidiary proposals, all designed to pacify the Americans — to repeal the coercive legislation, to reform the Admiralty courts and to make judges in the Colonies hold office during good behaviour, removable only after official complaint from the Colony to the King in Council.

Burke took the trouble to meet at least one expected criticism in advance. He claimed that the argument that the colonists would not be contented with taxation concessions, but would press for others, was mere speculation. He asked the House to consider 'whether it be prudent to form a rule for punishing people, not on their own acts, but on your conjec-

tures ? . . . It is not justifying your anger by their misconduct ;
but it is converting your ill-will into their delinquency.' He
insisted that taxation was the public cause of the dispute.
'Unless you consent to remove this cause of difference, it is
impossible, with decency, to assert that the dispute is not upon
what it is avowed to be.'

Burke concluded with a great invocation to Empire, even, in
fact, to a British Commonwealth as yet unborn. He put his
trust in

> the close affection which grows from common names, from
> kindred blood, from similar privileges, and equal protection.
> These are ties, which, though light as air, are as strong as
> links of iron. Let the colonies always keep the idea of their
> civil rights associated with your government ; they will cling
> and grapple to you ; and no force under heaven will be of
> power to tear them from their allegiance.

He pointed out that Britain alone could give the Colonies
freedom.

> Deny them this participation of freedom, and you break the
> sole bond, which originally made, and must still preserve,
> the unity of the Empire. Do not entertain so weak an imagina-
> tion, as that your registers and your bonds, your affidavits and
> your sufferances, your cockets and your clearances, are what
> form the great securities of your commerce. Do not dream
> that your letters of commerce, and your instructions, and your
> suspending clauses, are the things that hold together the great
> contexture of this mysterious whole. These things do not
> make your government. Dead instruments, passive tools as
> they are, it is the spirit of the English communion, that gives
> all their life and efficacy to them. It is the spirit of the
> English constitution, which, infused through the mighty
> mass, pervades, feeds, unites, invigorates, vivifies every part
> of the empire, even down to the minutist member. . . .
> All this, I know well enough, will sound wild and chimeri-
> cal to the profane herd of those vulgar and mechanical politi-
> cians, who have no place among us ; a sort of people who
> think that nothing exists but what is gross and material ; and
> who therefore, far from being qualified to be directors of the
> great movement of empire, are not fit to turn a wheel in the

machine. . . . Magnanimity in politics is not seldom the truest wisdom ; and a great Empire and little minds go ill together. . . . We ought to elevate our minds to the greatness of that trust to which the order of Providence has called us. By advertising to the dignity of this high calling, our ancestors have turned a savage wilderness into a glorious empire ; and have made the most extensive, and the only honorable conquests ; not by destroying, but by promoting, the wealth, the number, the happiness of the human race. Let us get an American revenue as we have got an American empire. English privileges have made it all that it is ; English privileges alone will make it all it can be.

Burke's speech was a remarkable exhibition of sustained argument and impassioned oratory. It was received with praise on most sides.[1] Richard Burke (senior), who was waiting in the Commons lobby at six o'clock when Edmund finished, described how 'from a torrent of members rushing from the house when he sat down, I could hear the loudest, the most unanimous and the highest strains of applause. That such a performance even from him was never before heard in that house.' [2] Late that night, Rockingham wrote to Burke : 'I never felt a more complete satisfaction on hearing any speech than I did on hearing yours this day. The matter and the manner were equally perfect, and in spite of envy and malice and in spite of all politics, I will venture to prognosticate, that there will be but one opinion, in regard to the wonderful ability of the performance.' [3] A similar opinion also came from a more independent source. James Harris wrote to Lord Hardwicke that Burke had never spoken better 'nor with more force and eloquence' though Harris did not feel his propositions for peace were worthy of his speech introducing them.[4] Edmund himself said later, with a little pride, that 'I have the pleasure of assuring you,

---

[1] For a discussion of Dean Josiah Tucker's attacks on Burke's proposals see G. H. Guttridge, *English Whiggism and the American Revolution*, pp. 81-3. Tucker advocated separation as the only possible solution.

[2] Richard Burke (senior) to Richard Champion, 22 March 1775. *CEB*, iii, 139.

[3] Rockingham to Burke, 22 March 1775. W.W.M. R1-1560, *CEB*, iii, 139.

[4] James Harris (unsigned but in Harris's handwriting) to Hardwicke, 23 March 1775. BM. Add. MS. 35612, f. 191.

that the grounds of pacification were far from being ill-received by the House. I never had stronger marks of their favour and indulgence.' [1]

Despite this warm reception for Burke's performance, his specific proposals were decisively rejected in the Commons.[2] Speakers for the Ministry did not come to grips with his arguments or respond to his plea that the need for peace must override all considerations of pride or theories of government. They maintained that he had artfully avoided the crucial issue of the right to taxation and accused him of implicitly abandoning that right. These criticisms may have been true; but they alone did not justify dismissing Burke's whole scheme out of hand. One must ask what were the virtues, and the defects, of his propositions, given the situation in America at that time ?

The first virtue of Burke's speech was his attempt to be practical and pragmatic. Burke was himself a theorist of British Party and Empire. But here he tried to detach his argument from the prevailing theories about how to rule Colonies and to rid it of the dominant metaphors about Mother Countries and colonial children. He tried to deal with the reality of America, as an already powerful nation. He considered how to keep the allegiance of the American Colonies, rebellious spirit and all, rather than just making useless judgments condemning that spirit. He properly reminded a House accustomed to look on issues of policy from a legalistic point of view that there was little compensation in Britain being constitutionally in the right if in fact she lost her Empire. There was no appeal to equity in high politics.

In this practical vein he suggested that Britain ought to make the first gesture, to take the first step towards peace. The nature of the colonial crisis since the Boston Tea Party had been that each side waited for the other to submit, administering a few vicious kicks in the groin while waiting in the belief that

---

[1] Burke to Richard Champion, 24 March 1775. *CEB*, iii, 143.

[2] His proposals were split into thirteen motions, some of which were negatived and some were voted on the Previous Question. When the motion for the Previous Question was put on the first resolution, the Government majority was 270-78. North to King, 22 March 1775. Fortescue, *op. cit.*, iii, 1619.

this would hurry the process of submission. In fact, neither would submit first, and each kick — whether it was a coercive Bill or an act of sedition in Massachusetts — pushed the other side closer to open hostilities. Burke argued that this remorseless slide into war should be halted. He suggested that Britain should make the first magnanimous gesture because she was the senior member; he also pointed out that it was politic for Britain to do so because her primary interest lay in getting a reconciliation.

Burke was in some ways speaking common sense. But his propositions also contained serious defects. Although he was commendably pragmatic when discussing the American people, when he talked about the spirit of the Empire he was full of nebulous theories. The traditional concept of Empire was of a Mother Country surrounded by her dependent brood. This was already blurred by 1775 and, as Burke realised, definitely did not convey the reality of the Anglo-American relationship. But the old conception had certainly not yet been replaced by an image of a brotherhood of peoples in which the sovereignty lay benevolently and silently with one older member; or at least it had not been so replaced other than in Burke's mind. The imperial relationship as it was reflected in Statute up to 1775 contained many tangible economic advantages to Britain and many consequent restraints on the colonists. It also left the Home Country able to exercise considerable political power in the Colonies, even to take away certain political rights which were very dear to the colonists. This was the reality of the imperial connexion to the colonists, not Burke's magical portrait, prescient and brilliant though it was. The Ministers were more practical in their appreciation that there was as yet no person or institution or spirit which could represent the whole Empire apart from particular British Governments. In 1774 and 1775, when the colonists defied Lord North's Ministry, refused to obey its laws and attacked its officers, they were putting themselves in rebellion against the Empire. They could only be brought back by accepting British sovereignty, which meant obeying the British Government.

Of course, it was open to Britain to modify the terms of the imperial relationship so that the Americans would willingly accept them. It was with this possibility in mind that Burke suggested that Britain should take certain first steps to mollify the colonists. But here one must ask whether his suggested modifications would have been adequate. The Ministers were certain that only the abandonment of the right to legislate would satisfy the Americans. They believed, and Burke had always agreed with them on this point, that this would mean the end of the Empire because Britain would then no longer exercise sovereignty over it. But Burke said that he did not agree that the Americans were as extreme in their demands as this. Anyway, he refused to discuss the question of right to tax and he confined himself to suggesting a reform of the mode of collecting taxes. In partial defence of himself, he rightly pointed out that Britain should first find out whether this concession would satisfy the Americans. However, Burke's propositions must still be judged on the likelihood that the Americans would accept his taxation suggestion; if it was not acceptable then the proposition was little use as an instrument of peace.

No final judgment is possible, since the offer was never made to the Americans. But there are strong grounds for doubting its success. The colonists had said 'it is not merely the mode of raising, but the freedom of granting our money, for which we have contended'.[1] The Continental Congress, with its avowed aim to repeal all colonial legislation passed since 1763, had raised the Americans' ambitions beyond a mere revision of tax collecting methods. Lord North's conciliatory proposals were rejected outright by the colonists, although that was after the battle of Concord had put an end to compromise. There was not, of course, a complete unanimity of opinion in America, and many conservatives there might have been won over by Burke's offer. But the balance of probability suggests that the Americans, though certainly open to conciliatory gestures, would not have been prepared to make peace on Burke's terms. The question of sovereign rights, on which Burke had always previously been adamant, and which he had sidestepped

---

[1] Quoted in J. C. Miller, *op. cit.*, p. 407.

in the Commons, was the key to the colonial problem. It was possible to omit it in a speech to the House. But it is difficult to imagine serious peace negotiations which were not centrally concerned with it.

Burke had not produced an elixir of peace. His most important immediate contribution was to remind the House that unless Britain made the first gesture she would almost certainly find a war on her hands. He had also drawn up for posterity the formula for a commonwealth of nations. But this peculiar mixture of practicality and philosophy, of predictions of doom and golden visions of Empire, did not win the Government or the Commons.[1]

David Hartley, a talented Rockinghamite just come into Parliament, suffered a similar rebuff when he proposed on 27 March that the Ministry should repeal the coercive legislation and should in future raise money by free requisitions in the Colonies. This was the end of the Opposition's suggestions for solving the American problem in peace-time. Throughout the crisis it had been impotent. Now it lost all hope. 'I believe our meridian is past', wrote Richmond to Burke, 'and we must submit to our political as to our natural old age, weakness, and infirmity . . . we must patiently submit.'[2]

One final protest was made on 10 April when the Lord Mayor, Alderman and Livery of the City of London presented a Remonstrance to the King against the American measures. George III replied that it was

> with the utmost astonishment that I find any of my subjects capable of encouraging the rebellious disposition which unhappily exists in some of my colonies in North America. Having entire confidence in the wisdom of my Parliament, the great Council of the nation, I will steadily pursue those measures which they have recommended for the support of the Constitutional rights of Great Britain, and the protection of the commercial rights of my Kingdom.[3]

[1] North to King, 22 March 1775. Fortescue, *op. cit.*, iii, 1619.
[2] Richmond to Burke, 16 June 1775. W.W.M. Bk., *CEB*, iii, 170.
[3] 10 April 1775. PRO. S.P. Dom. George III, 37/11, f. 287. Also Sir John Fielding to the Lord Mayor, and Rochford to Sir John Hawkins, 9 April 1775. PRO. S.P. Dom. George III, 37/11, ff. 88/5a and 5b, 88/6.

Three days later Parliament adjourned for the Easter recess and when it reassembled on the 25th the civil war, which Burke and others in Opposition had long foretold, had broken out in America.

During this spring session of 1775, Parliament for the last time debated the colonial problem while Britain was still at peace with America. The Ministry's new policies were presented. These — composed of Bills to restrain the Trade and Fishery of the Colonies and Lord North's offer not to exercise the right of taxation, backed up by a declaration of rebellion in Massachusetts and the dispatch of military reinforcements across the Atlantic — seemed designed to produce submission rather than conciliation. The various Colonies were required to make declarations of loyalty and obedience in return for Parliament's promise not to exercise its unquestioned supremacy. The individual rebels were expected to submit and make explicit acknowledgment of British sovereignty in return for the royal pardon. The Commons debates revealed a widespread awareness among the politicians that the country was on the brink of war. The King, Suffolk, Gower, and Sandwich rejected all suggestions of compromise and talked openly of the possibility of using military force. The position in the Cabinet of Dartmouth, divided in mind between his desire to punish and to conciliate, was becoming increasingly difficult.

On the Opposition side, two major attempts were made to grapple with the situation. Chatham's sweeping proposals to restore peace and vitality to the British Empire were defeated from the beginning by his failure to inform or to try to convince any other British politicians, in the Ministry or the Opposition. Burke's conciliatory proposals revealed all that was sound in the political position of his group — the appreciation of American strength, the recognition that England must make the first gesture if war was to be avoided. But their weaknesses, their failure to come to grips with the problem of sovereignty, their refusal to admit the extremity of the ambitions of many Americans, was equally clear. The Opposition vote rose a little, and Chatham and Rockingham at least began to write to one another again, but their two parties continued to act without unity or coordination and with no hope of securing office and power.

CHAPTER XII

WAR

THE persistent flow of bad news in the New Year and early spring of 1775 confirmed the Ministry in the need for the firm measures which it had proposed to Parliament. Riots continued throughout New England. The colonists were collecting ammunition and openly training their militia. General Gage received no cooperation in barracking his troops. The coercive legislation remained a dead letter, in striking contrast to Congress's non-importation agreement, which had taken almost total effect.[1]

In response to this increasingly grave situation, attempts were made to hurry on the arrangements for sending military reinforcements to the Colonies. Dartmouth assured Gage on 22 February that the troops and the newly appointed Generals would soon be dispatched.[2] Four days later the Admiralty was ordered to prepare transports to collect the 22nd, 40th, 44th and 45th Foot Regiments from Ireland.[3] However, it was found that they could not be embarked for another month, by when it had been decided to send them to New York rather than to

[1] Admiralty to Dartmouth, 21 February 1775. PRO. CO. 5/121, f. 39. Same to same, 27 March 1775. PRO. CO. 5/247, f. 120. Commissioners of Rhode Island customs to Boston customs, December 1774 (forwarded and received in London on 12 March 1775). PRO. Treasury Papers, T. 1/505. From New York alone came reassuring news to the effect that the Assembly there still refused to join the Continental Congress. Colden to Dartmouth, 1 March 1775. PRO. CO. 5/1139, ff. 220-5, especially 220-1. On the deteriorating American situation see J. C. Miller, *Origins of the American Revolution*, pp. 398-402.

[2] Dartmouth to Gage, 22 February 1775. PRO. CO. 5/765, ff. 368-73, especially 368-71. See also Rochford to Admiralty, 23 January 1775. PRO. State Papers Naval, 42/49, f. 12.

[3] Rochford to Admiralty, 26 February 1775. PRO. S.P. Naval, 42/49, f. 19. Also King to Rochford (undated). J. W. Fortescue, ed., *The Correspondence of King George III, 1760–1783*, iii, 1591. There was some dissention in the Cabinet about how many men should be raised in Ireland. See Rochford to King, 13, 14, 15, 20 March 1775. *Ibid.*, 1614, 1615, 1617, 1618.

Boston in order to prevent 'any attempt to send succour to the New England people from the middle colonies'.[1] These four regiments totalled nearly two thousand men and would bring the force under Gage's command to around five thousand five hundred men.[2] Generals Howe, Clinton and Burgoyne also prepared to embark for America to strengthen Gage's resolution.[3]

The stage was now set for major military operations in America. Dartmouth's letter of 27 January reached Boston on 16 April,[4] and another in the same vein, written on 22 February,[5] arrived on 14 April. These told Gage to take the offensive against the Massachusetts patriots, who were now declared to be traitors in rebellion against the Crown, to prevent the training of militiamen, and to confiscate arms and ammunition in the hands of the colonists.

One problem remained to be dealt with by the Government at home. On 24 February Barrington had again raised the question of whether the troops in America could take action without direction from the civil magistrate.[6] This was put to the Law Officers, but apparently no satisfaction was obtained from them, since on 1 April Barrington was forced to repeat his request.[7] Governor Tryon of New York now also raised the same question.[8] He was in some hurry for a reply since he was about to return to his duties in New York.[9] Consequently, on

[1] Dartmouth to Gage, 15 April 1775. PRO. CO. 5/765, ff. 376-99, especially 387. See also Dartmouth to Rochford, 28 March 1775. PRO. CO. 5/138 (part 1), f. 34. Same to Barrington, 28 March 1775. PRO. CO. 5/250, f. 96. Rochford to Admiralty, 30 March 1775. S.P. Naval, 42/49, f. 20. The troops were eventually taken to Boston as originally planned.

[2] Gage to Barrington, 1 November 1774. PRO. CO. 5/167, ff. 148-50.

[3] They sailed in the frigate Cerberus on 20 April — at about the same time that the troop transports, which had been delayed by the strong westerly winds in the Atlantic, finally left for America. Dartmouth to Admiralty, 2 March 1774. PRO. CO. 5/250, f. 95. Admiralty to Dartmouth, 4, 13, 20 April 1775. PRO. CO. 5/247, ff. 120, 122, 124. G. R. Barnes and J. H. Owen, eds., The Private Papers of John, Earl of Sandwich, First Lord of the Admiralty 1771-1782, i, 124. Hutchinson, Diary and Letters, i, 436.

[4] See above, p. 226.

[5] Dartmouth to Gage, 22 February 1774. PRO. CO. 5/765, ff. 368-73.

[6] See above, p. 92.

[7] Barrington to Dartmouth, 1 April 1775. Dartmouth MS. D 1778, 11, 1203.

[8] Tryon to Dartmouth, 29 March 1775. PRO. CO. 5/1139, ff. 211-12.

[9] Tryon to Dartmouth, 12 April 1775. PRO. CO. 5/1139, ff. 216. Tryon had returned to England in April 1774.

15 April, Dartmouth issued a circular to all Governors in America which stated that the orders of the Commander-in-Chief, General Gage, were supreme in all cases relating to the use of troops and he might take whatever action with them that he deemed necessary.[1]

In addition to sending this circular on 15 April, Dartmouth also took the opportunity to write a letter to Gage in which he emphasised that nothing had happened to weaken the determination of the Ministry to stamp out sedition, and that the orders contained in Dartmouth's previous letters still held. He told Gage to capture any rebel fortresses, to seize all stores of arms, and to imprison any persons who committed acts of treason and rebellion. On the use of troops Dartmouth said that 'the authority of Government must be maintained, let the consequence be what it may'. He authorised Gage to issue to anyone who made a proper submission the royal pardon which had been discussed and agreed in Cabinet on 16 February and 30 March.[2] But it was 'to the exertion of the Fleet and Army, in support of the vigorous measures which have been adopted by His Majesty and the two Houses of Parliament, that we are to trust for putting an end to the present troubles and disorders'.[3] No one reading this letter can seriously doubt that by April the Ministry was committed to severe military measures against the Americans and was prepared to risk the consequences, though they might be war. The changing emphasis in British policy, away from expressing Parliamentary sovereignty through legislation, towards enforcing colonial subordination by military repression, was now almost complete. Three days later, long before this letter and circular reached America, Gage marched on Lexington and Concord and the consequence was war.

During March Gage had begun to send his troops out of Boston in search of arms. He had to prevent the colonials from equipping and training a private army. Dartmouth's instructions encouraged him in this policy; the latest reached him on

---

[1] Dartmouth MS. D 1778, I, ii, 1113.
[2] See above, p. 247.
[3] Dartmouth to Gage, 15 April 1775. PRO. CO. 5/765, ff. 376-99. It was sent on the *Cerberus* with Howe, Clinton and Burgoyne.

16 April. On the night of the 18th he sent some 800 soldiers from Boston across the Charles river and out towards the small town of Concord, some eighteen miles away, where there was reported to be a munitions store. The road passed through the village of Lexington, and there on the green at dawn on the 19th the British found themselves confronted by a group of armed militiamen. Someone opened fire and after a brief exchange of shots the militiamen dispersed, having suffered some casualties. The British then continued to Concord, where they destroyed various stores and arms. But the alarm was given throughout the New England countryside. Groups of militia converged on Concord and attacked the British. As the King's troops retreated to Boston, they were continually harassed by the colonists. When they recrossed the Charles to safety late on the 19th, they had suffered nearly three hundred casualties, and Boston was ringed by the camp fires of the Americans.

Throughout the Colonies the effect was climactic. The Massachusetts Provincial Congress at Watertown declared that it no longer felt any obligation to obey General Gage and that it now considered him as an enemy. On 10 May the Continental Congress met at Philadelphia and during the first few weeks it passed Resolutions to raise an army, to issue a currency, and to set up a separate Post Office. It declared that the compact between the Crown and the people of Massachusetts Bay was dissolved by the violation of the charter of William and Mary. It decided that the Congress members should be designated the 'United Colonies'. In August Lord North's conciliatory motion was rejected [1] — a fate it also received in the separate Provincial Assemblies.

Generals Howe, Clinton and Burgoyne arrived at Boston with the troop reinforcements on 25 May. On 12 June Gage issued the royal pardon, making exceptions only of John Hancock and Samuel Adams; he also proclaimed martial law. It was announced that any who refused the pardon were to be treated as rebels and traitors. Five days later heavy fighting broke out on the heights overlooking Boston harbour. In this

---

[1] J. C. Miller, *op. cit.*, p. 459.

engagement, known, inaccurately, as the battle of Bunker Hill, the British suffered over 1,000 casualties. The siege of Boston, now led by George Washington, continued for the rest of 1775. Meanwhile the colonials sent an expedition to the Great Lakes. It surprised Ticonderoga, Crown-Point and other fortresses commanding the gateway to Canada — an entry their troops shortly forced.

As with the Boston Tea Party sixteen months earlier, the British Government remained long in ignorance of the sudden and serious turn of events in Massachusetts. The breadth of the Atlantic left Dartmouth and North another seven weeks in which they believed England was still technically at peace, if not at ease, with her Colonies, when in fact New England was in rebellion and the British army was beleaguered in Boston. The Americans were in no doubt from the start about the significance of the skirmishes on 19 April. From New York John Cruger wrote that

> the melancholy situation that this city and colony is in is beyond expression since the receival of the account from Boston of the engagement between the King's troops and the provincials. The cause is now become general throughout the whole continent of America, and almost every man determined to make it our general cause. . . .[1]

But there could be no such immediate quickening in the English political scene. A packet arrived from America precisely on 19 April, with the report that in the previous month Gage had marched on Salem in an unsuccessful search for cannon. This expedition, a dress rehearsal for Lexington and Concord, gave some satisfaction in London because it proved that Gage was not being idle.[2] But otherwise there was little news of interest. Gage's next dispatch, dated 28 March, arrived on 4 May, but again there was nothing significant to report. It stated that the Provincial Congress in Massachusetts was still in session, and that trouble continued to brew without actually boiling over into a major incident — though Gage felt 'some convulsion' must

[1] Cruger to Edmund Burke, 4 May 1775. Transcript in Sheffield Central Library taken from an incomplete MS. copy in the possession of the Earl of Dartmouth.   [2] Hutchinson, *op. cit.*, i, 432.

happen before long.[1] A packet also arrived from New York on 4 May with the good news that the Colony still remained loyal and refused to send delegates to the second Continental Congress which was due to open in Philadelphia on 10 May.[2]

When Parliament reassembled after the Easter recess there was little American business of any importance remaining to be considered. The main new colonial discussion arose over the Remonstrance from the New York Assembly. This arrived early in May, but there was some delay in presenting it to Parliament, partly because many of the Opposition were out of Town, partly because the Ministry was divided over whether it should be accepted.[3] When put to the Commons by Burke on 15 May the Remonstrance evoked little interest. Burke himself was sick, 'said little, and scarce did anything more, save reading the remonstrance'.[4] Fox made a spirited attack on the Government but he could provoke little response. Edward Gibbon reported afterwards: 'The House tired and languid. In this season and on America the Archangel Gabriel would not be heard . . . and for myself having supported the British I must destroy the Roman Empire.'[5] On the 19th, the Commons discussed Sir George Savile's motion to repeal the Quebec Act

[1] Gage to Dartmouth, 28 March 1775. Printed in C. E. Carter, ed., *The Correspondence of General Thomas Gage, 1765–1775*, i, 394-5.

[2] Colden to Dartmouth, 5 April 1775. PRO. CO. 5/1139, ff. 230-6, especially 230-1.

[3] Dartmouth and North were apparently for receiving it, and Thurlow and Wedderburn against. Hutchinson, *op. cit.*, i, 44-5. On the Remonstrance see Dartmouth to Tryon, 23 May. PRO. CO. 5/1141, ff. 149-50.

[4] James Harris to Hardwicke, 15 May 1775. BM. Add. MS. 35612, f. 221. The vote was 186-67. Burke afterwards told his New York employers that the Commons rejected the Remonstrance because the Government 'could not so much as receive any paper which tended to call in question the Right of Parliament to make laws to bind the subjects of this Empire in all cases whatsoever. That in this point the Declaratory Act had only stated the ancient constitution. That if this Remonstrance were admitted, it would be tacitly to abandon Legislative Authority in its most essential particular privileges and dignity of the House of Commons.' The Rockingham dilemma in presenting a Remonstrance which was rejected on the grounds of the Rockingham Declaratory Act is made clear in this incident. Burke to New York Committee of Correspondence, 7 June 1775. *CEB*, iii, 165.

[5] Gibbon to J. C. Holroyd, 15 May 1775. *The Letters of Edward Gibbon*, ed., J. E. Norton, ii, 69.

and the Opposition increased its minority to 86.[1] Parliament
then rose on 26 May — the day before the first news of Lexington and Concord reached England.

This news arrived in a most curious fashion and created
great confusion in London. Gage had sent his reports on 24
April, but there had since been no sign of his packet. The ship
which reached Southampton on 27 May, under a Captain
Derby, had been dispatched by the rebels at Salem. It carried
copies of the *Essex Gazette*, dated 25 April, in which were
printed accounts of the Concord battle. These reached London
on 28 May. They came into Hutchinson's hands, and he
promptly took the news to Dartmouth, who 'was much struck
with it'.[2] Next day the London newspapers carried the full
story.

The Government was at first surprised, but soon began to
take heart from the fact that this was an American report and
therefore certainly unreliable. The King wrote to Dartmouth :

> It is not improbable but some detachment sent by Lieut.
> General Gage may have not been strong enough to disperse
> the provincials assembled at Concord ; but no great reliance
> can be given to the manner in which it will understandably be
> exaggerated in American newspapers, or when related by an
> American trader.[3]

Hutchinson was another who assured the American Secretary that the report was biased, and added that Captain Derby
'belongs to one of the most incendiary families' in the Colonies.[4]
This balm seems to have worked. When Hutchinson called
next day upon Suffolk, Cornwall, Jenkinson, Lord George
Germain and Hillsborough, he found that 'the alarm of yester-
day' was 'much abated' and there was 'great expectation of
Gage's account'. And on the 31st Dartmouth read to Hutchinson a note from Lord North which admitted that 'the beginning
of action in America was rather inauspicious' but which ex-

---

[1] Harris to Hardwicke, 19 May 1775. BM. Add. MS. 35612, f. 227.
[2] Hutchinson, *op. cit.*, i, 455.
[3] King to Dartmouth, 29 May 1775. Dartmouth MS. D 1778, Supplementary George III. Quoted in *HMC*, 11, V, *Dartmouth MSS.*, i, 440.
[4] Hutchinson to Dartmouth, 29 May 1775. Dartmouth MS. D 1778,
11, 1278. Quoted in *HMC*, 14, X, *Dartmouth MSS.*, ii, 304.

pressed the Prime Minister's hope that the American reports were exaggerated.[1]

On 1 June Dartmouth wrote to tell Gage that Captain Derby had arrived with a report 'which is plainly made up for the purpose of conveying every possible prejudice and mis-representation of the truth'. Consequently he dismissed the affair at Concord as unimportant, but he felt it was 'very much to be lamented that we have not heard some account from you of the transaction . . .'.[2]

Not everyone was as complacent as the leading Ministers. John Pownall wrote to Knox that now 'the dye is cast, and more mischief will follow'.[3] Gibbon's view was that 'this looks serious and is indeed so'.[4] But the situation was complicated, and final opinions made impossible, by the lack of official news. Furthermore, Captain Derby had disappeared before anyone could interview him seriously.[5] As a result the Ministry and the public were able to slip back briefly into complacency and optimism. 'Your American news seemed for almost two days to draw some attention,' reported Richard Burke, 'but people are returned to that happy tranquility of mind, which cannot, I fancy, be much interrupted, unless the Regatta day should prove wet and cold.'[6]

But on 10 June the official reports finally arrived and dashed any grounds for optimism.[7] Gage bluntly announced that hostilities were commenced and that he had suffered 244 casualties.[8] The only real difference from the newspaper accounts brought by Captain Derby was that Gage claimed that the Americans had fired first. At the same time a letter arrived

---

[1] Hutchinson, *op. cit.*, i, 460.
[2] Dartmouth to Gage, 1 June 1775. PRO. CO. 5/765, ff. 405-6.
[3] *HMC, Various*, vi, *Knox MSS.*, p. 118.
[4] Gibbon to J. B. Holroyd, 30 May 1775. *Letters of Edward Gibbon*, ii, 70-2.
[5] Gibbon to J. B. Holroyd, 3 June 1775, and 7 June 1775. *Ibid.*, 73-4.
[6] To Richard Champion, 3 June 1775. *CEB*, iii, 163.
[7] Burgoyne later said the ship carrying Gage's reports was a poor one, and was driven to the West Indies by adverse winds. To [?], 10 August 1775. Fortescue, *op. cit.*, iii, 1693.
[8] Gage to Dartmouth, 22 April 1775. Printed in *The Correspondence of General Thomas Gage, 1763–1775*, i, 396-7. Also Admiral Graves to the Admiralty, 22 April 1775. PRO. CO. 5/121, ff. 137-8.

from Governor Colden stating that civil government had collapsed in New York, that an assembly of the people had decided to join the Continental Congress, and that the Colony was almost entirely cut off by rebel forces.[1]

Hardly any of the Ministers were in Town when the official news arrived that England was at civil war with the colonists. Even by 12 June the only ones in London were Dartmouth and Gower. These two met with various Secretaries — Pownall, Eden,[2] Jenkinson, and Brummell — at the American office to discuss the situation, which seemed 'dark and discouraging'. But as nothing could be done while Lord North and his other colleagues were still in the country, Dartmouth cancelled the Cabinet which had been provisionally called for the 12th.[3]

The news depressed some junior members of the Ministry. John Pownall said that the colonists 'ruin all our measures and disconcert our whole plan'.[4] Grey Cooper and Wedderburn were in despair, and William Eden wrote to Suffolk describing the Government as 'tottering'. But the senior Cabinet Ministers rallied behind the King. Suffolk wrote to Eden:

> For God's sake don't let Wedderburn despond or be slack to act. Now is the time for men of real talent, spirit and honour to appear gloriously. . . . This American business makes lambs of us all. By the by, I have been thinking about these 20,000 Russians. They will be charming visitors at New York and civilise that part of America wonderfully . . . no more of your tottering, or of anything Cooperian . . . i.e. desponding . . .'.[5]

Rochford wrote to the King in a similar vein, assuring him that he did 'not a bit despair of the news from America. The

[1] Colden to Dartmouth, 3 May 1775. PRO. CO. 5/1139, ff. 237-42.
[2] Eden later commented: 'We certainly are victorious in this engagement of the 17th, but if we have eight more such victories there will be nobody left to bring the news of them'. In this same letter Eden described himself as having been 'a croaker throughout the whole of the American History'. Eden to Suffolk, June 1775. BM. Add. MS., 34, 412, f. 340.
[3] Hutchinson, *op. cit.*, i, 466-8.
[4] Pownall to W. Knox, 13 June 1775. *HMC, Various*, vi, *Knox MSS.*, p. 118.
[5] Suffolk to W. Eden, 20 June 1775. BM. Add. MS., 34, 412, f. 339. The mention of 20,000 Russians refers to proposals to recruit Russian troops to serve in America.

Rubicon is passed, and if pursued we must get the better.' [1]
The King himself was as firm as ever :

> I am not apt to be over sanguine, but I cannot help being
> of opinion that with firmness and perseverance America will
> be brought to submission : if not, old England will though
> perhaps not appear so formidable in the eyes of Europe as at
> other periods, but yet will be able to make her rebellious
> children rue the hour they cast off obedience : America must
> be a colony of England or treated as an enemy. Distant
> possessions standing upon an equality with the superior state
> is more ruinous than being deprived of such connections. [2]

Dartmouth, the Minister with whom the responsibility lay,
was at first unwilling to admit that the Rubicon had indeed been
crossed, and he tried to place the most moderate construction
on the news. [3] This optimism soon passed. At the beginning of
July when he wrote to Gage his tone was sharp. He reprimanded
him for not sending more detailed reports by faster boats, and
he presumed, with some sarcasm, that the Concord expedition
'was taken up on the fullest consideration of the advantages on
one hand and the hazard on the other . . . and of all the probable
consequences that would result from it'. Some of the inferences
here seem a little unfair in view of Dartmouth's letters to Gage
demanding more vigorous military action against the rebels.
But his conclusions were realistic.

> From the moment this blow was struck and the town of
> Boston was invested by the rebels, there was no longer any
> room to doubt of the intention of the people of Massachusetts
> Bay, to commit themselves in open rebellion. . . . In this
> situation every effort must be made both by sea and land to
> subdue rebellion should the people persist in the rash mea-
> sures they have adopted. [4]

Dartmouth was clearly aware that the time for arguing about
constitutional rights, for drawing fine academic distinctions

---

[1] Rochford to King, 11 June 1775. Fortescue, *op. cit.*, iii, 1661.
[2] King to Dartmouth, 10 June 1775. Dartmouth MS. D 1778, Supplementary George III. Quoted in *HMC*, 13, IV, *Dartmouth MSS.*, iv, 501-2.
[3] Hutchinson, *op. cit.*, i, 467-8.
[4] Dartmouth to Gage, 1 July 1775. PRO. CO. 5/765, ff. 407-16,
especially ff. 409-10.

between forms of sovereignty, was passed. He wrote on the same day to Governor Tryon that

> . . . however desirable a reconciliation with America may be, it must not be sought for on the ground of a submission of the authority of Great Britain to their pretensions, but can only be found in their submission to that authority . . . obedience to it is, and must be, that bond of peace and unity upon which the dignity and security of the Empire are to depend.[1]

To the Admiralty he wrote:

> The King having received advices that not only the New England governments are in open and actual rebellion . . . but also that the flame has extended itself to most of the other colonies, in which the greatest violences have been committed, the constitutional authority trampled upon, and the people armed and arrayed with a vowed intention of resistence by force . . . it is His Majesty's firm resolution . . . that every measure be pursued for suppressing by the most vigorous efforts, by sea and land, this unnatural rebellion, which menaces the subversion of the present happy constitution.[2]

From the other side of the Atlantic the approach was equally uncompromising. Gage reported: 'I see no prospect of an offer of accomodation . . .'.[3] Burgoyne wrote: 'America is to be subdued by arms or to be given up . . .'.[4] Benjamin Franklin, who was a leading protagonist at the very beginning of this phase of Britain's struggle with her American Colonies, also wrote its conclusion:

> You are a member of Parliament, and one of that majority which has doomed my country to destruction. You have begun to burn our towns, and murder our people. Look upon your hands; they are stained with the blood of your relations. You and I were long friends; you are now my enemy.[5]

---

[1] Dartmouth to Tryon, 1 July 1775. PRO. CO. 5/1141, ff. 150-2, especially 152.
[2] Dartmouth to Admiralty, 1 July 1775. PRO. CO. 5/250, ff. 106-7.
[3] Gage to [?], 12 June 1775. Fortescue, *op. cit.*, iii, 1662.
[4] Burgoyne to [?], 25 June 1775. *Ibid.*, 1670.
[5] Franklin to William Strahan, M.P., 5 July 1775. *The Complete Works of Benjamin Franklin*, ed. J. Bigelow, v, 534. This is the whole of the letter.

When the full Cabinet met at Lord North's on 15 June to discuss Lexington and Concord it was a Cabinet of War, devoting its time to considering ways of raising the vast forces which would be needed to defeat the Americans.[1] At another meeting on the 21st it decided to recruit a regiment of Canadians.[2] On 26 July it was agreed that England must have twenty thousand troops by April 1776 [3] — a number which Gage had long ago requested but had been denied.

The scale of the colonial crisis was not underestimated in London. On 26 July, by which date news had arrived of the capture by the rebels of the Ticonderoga and Crown-Point forts on the Great Lakes, the Prime Minister wrote to the King that 'the war is now grown to such a height, that it must be treated as a foreign war, and that every expedient which would be used in the latter case should be applied in the former'.[4] This serious view was confirmed when the news of Bunker Hill arrived in the middle of August. The problems of supporting such a war engrossed the Government in the weeks ahead.

The Secretary of War, Barrington, was convinced that it would prove impossible to raise the twenty thousand regular troops by next spring. Moreover, he believed no attempt should or need be made. He felt that a land war was impracticable and that the best strategy was to use the navy.[5] Lord North at first agreed with Barrington, particularly since recruiting was going badly. But the King insisted that they should press ahead with the existing plan to recruit in England and Ireland.[6] He was reassured by the fact that recruiting was going better elsewhere. At the beginning of August an agreement was concluded making available 2,355 Hanoverian troops with officers. They were to be ready for embarkation in

[1] Cabinet Minute, 15 June 1775. PRO. S.P. Dom. George III, 37/11, F. 88/15a.
[2] Cabinet Minute, 21 June 1775. *Ibid.*, f. 88/15b. Sandwich was absent from this meeting.
[3] Cabinet Minute, 26 July 1775. *Ibid.*, f. 88/15c. Sandwich and Suffolk were absent from this meeting.
[4] North to King, 26 July 1775. Fortescue, *op. cit.*, iii, 1682.
[5] Barrington to Dartmouth, 31 July 1775, and to King, 31 July 1775. Quoted in Shute Barrington, *Life of Viscount Barrington*, pp. 148-50.
[6] King to North, 26 August 1775. Fortescue, *op. cit.*, iii, 1702. Memorandum from the King, 5 August 1775. *Ibid.*, 1690.

September — three battalions to Gibraltar and two to Minorca. This would release an equivalent number of British troops, who would be brought back to Ireland, so that troops stationed there could go on American service.[1]

The King was confident in the face of so many problems. He believed that 'the difficulties many of the Colonies will suffer the next winter, and the force that will act the next campaign will I trust bring them to soberer thoughts'.[2] He never suffered any doubts about the rectitude of his policies. 'I am clear as to one point', he wrote to North, 'that we must persist and not be dismayed by any difficulties that may arise on either side of the Atlantick; I know I am doing my Duty, and I can never wish to retract.'[3] This smugness and self-righteousness was an unattractive side of George III's character. Yet it was allied with a concern for his true duty as Monarch, and with the courage to carry out that duty as he saw it. Responsibility, loyalty, courage, complacency and priggishness were probably the five main ingredients of George III's character. None of them, separately or in combination, caused him to lose his American Colonies. The forces at work there were much wider than a King or Government could master. But these royal qualities were certainly factors influencing the manner in which Britain faced up to the colonial crisis.

By the end of the summer Britain was harnessing herself for full-scale civil war, though nobody suspected how long and exhausting and fruitless the struggle was to prove. Preparations were well under way to reinforce the hard-pressed troops in North America. During September Lord North began discussions with a merchant shipping agency to arrange regular freighting of provisions in convoys across the Atlantic.[4] In October the last monthly mail packet sailed to New York. All that remained to be done to seal the final non-military phase

[1] See King to North, 1 August 1775. Fortescue, op. cit., iii, 1687; Rochford to Admiralty, 31 July 1775. PRO. S.P. Naval, 42/49, f. 28.
[2] King to Dartmouth, 21 July 1775. Dartmouth MS. D 1778, Supplementary George III. Quoted in HMC, 11, V, Dartmouth MSS., i, 440-1.
[3] King to North, 26 July 1775. Fortescue, op. cit., iii, 1683.
[4] For the fascinating history of the Government's arrangements to supply the American war see the relevant documents in the Liverpool papers. BM. Add. MSS. 38343.

of Britain's dispute with her American colonists was for the officials who were most associated with recent policies to be replaced by men more suited to direct a war. By Christmas this had been achieved: General Gage was recalled from Boston in August,[1] and in November Dartmouth resigned from the American Department in favour of Lord George Germain. This latter change caused considerable turmoil and embarrassment in the Government.[2] Once it was effected the Ministry was better able to settle down to wage war.[3]

[1] See Dartmouth to Gage, 2 August 1775. PRO. CO. 5/765, ff. 424-30, especially 428. Also King to North, 28 July 1775. Fortescue, *op. cit.*, iii, 1685.

[2] On the circumstances of Dartmouth's resignation see : W. R. Anson, ed., *Autobiography and Political Correspondence of Augustus Henry, third Duke of Grafton*, pp. 271-2. HMC, *Various*, vi, *Knox MSS.*, p. 256. Germain to Suffolk, 16 or 17 June 1775. HMC, *Stopford-Sackville MSS.*, ii, 2-3. Germain to Irwin, 26 July, 13 September and 4 November 1775. *Ibid.*, i, 136-8. Eden to Germain, 3 October and 21 October 1775. *Ibid.*, ii, 10-12. Also see the large correspondence between the King and Lord North at the beginning of November : Fortescue, *op. cit.*, iii, 1740, 1741, 1742, 1743, 1744, 1745, 1748, 1749, 1750.

[3] On the conduct of the war see Piers Mackesy's excellent study, *The War for America, 1775-83.*

CHAPTER XIII

CONCLUSION: POLICIES AND POLITICIANS

THE Boston Tea Party raised, for what proved to be the last and most crucial time, the problems of imperial authority which had troubled Britain's relations with the American colonists since the end of the Seven Years' War. It proved to be the conclusive challenge because the home Government chose to make it so. Previous Administrations, weakened by the instability of domestic politics and uncertain of the nature and depth of colonial discontent, had invariably compromised in a crisis. Lord North's Ministry was in a stronger position. It had by 1773 absorbed many of the former leaders of the Parliamentary Opposition and was perfectly acceptable to the King and Commons. The political complexion of the Government was also changed by the introduction of Ministers and advisors who were known to favour a more strict assertion of British supremacy over the American Colonies. In 1773, even before the Tea Party, it had considered taking action against the malcontents in Massachusetts, but it then agreed to wait until a full Parliament met in the New Year. At the same time in 1773, it decided to introduce the cheap tea into America, and there is some evidence that the Ministry was aware of the possible consequences. This was not, however, just a wilfully provocative action. It can be fully understood only within the context both of the urgent need to restore the finances of the East India Company and of an already existing policy of granting duty concessions on tea re-exported to America. Even so it was a policy fraught with danger and consciously undertaken which rapidly led to violence and disorder in the Bay Colony.

After the Tea Party the Government believed that only by publicly exercising its authority in Massachusetts could British sovereignty be restored there, and the measures decided in

Cabinet were meant to make a demonstration of this authority. The first intention was to work through the prerogative, issuing decrees to close the port of Boston, to move the Bay Colony Government out of the capital, and to start proceedings for treason against the rioters. This was a conservative approach, since it was hoped to act within existing law. It was also moderate in that the intention was to confine the inconvenience to Boston and the punishment to those who had offended — though such executive action was bound to raise again the hoary question of royal prerogative. But these processes were abandoned during the second half of February 1774. Instead, it was decided to lay the main features of the Government's policies before Parliament and have them embodied in legislation, thus placing the Boston troubles on a plane of high imperial politics and involving broad principles which concerned the inhabitants of every American Colony.

The measures which were passed through Parliament in the spring of 1774 and early in 1775 were not stupidly irrational. On the contrary, they seemed perfectly logical at the time, for each was an automatic response to the situation developing in the Colonies. When the Bostonians destroyed the English tea in Boston Harbour, the Government closed the harbour, and tried to punish the offenders and to indemnify the victims. Because near-anarchy existed in Massachusetts, troops were sent to help the executive to restore order. Provision was also made to garrison these troops and to protect them from prosecution in the local courts for carrying out their duties. With the Massachusetts Administration virtually at a standstill, the King and his Ministers took certain steps, which had been for some time under consideration, to change the Constitution of the Colony in an attempt to strengthen the executive. And in 1775, after the home Government learned of the colonial ban on imports from Britain, it passed a Bill preventing trade with anyone else. These were pragmatic and obvious ways to deal with the various aspects of the crisis as it developed. They also followed logically from the fundamental premise on which the Government worked throughout the period under review. Every Minister believed that the Empire could be preserved intact only if the Americans accepted the principle of total subordination. Having once taken the decision not to let the Empire disintegrate by default, they saw no alternative to demonstrating the supremacy of Britain and enforcing the submission of the colonists. They could not conceive of any constitutional compromise which could be offered to the colonial radicals while still maintaining the imperial relationship; and in any case they were quite convinced that the American patriot leaders would not be prepared to accept one. The whole list of coercive legislation during 1774 and 1775 reflects these beliefs.

But the very logic and consistency with which the British Government applied its premises about the colonial situation explains the seemingly inevitable slide into war from the Boston Tea Party to the events on Lexington Green and the bridge at Concord. Faced by continuing sedition and disorder in Massachusetts, the Government applied ever stiffer doses of coercion, culminating in the Declaration of Treason and Rebellion in February 1775. The Americans refused to be coerced, and were instead provoked into organised resistance. Each act of refusal and resistance on their part was another denial of Britain's right to legislate for the Colonies, thus sharpening the issue of sovereignty into a test of strength. Not for the last time in British colonial history there seemed to be no alternative to the use of troops to restore law and order; not for the last time a military initiative produced a military response that made a return to law and order even more distant.

The question which naturally arises here is whether, had the Government acted upon different premises, and applied different policies, there would have been a less tragic outcome to the colonial problem. What if the Ministry had tried from the beginning to compromise? Had some of their past complaints been met, would the colonists, many of whom were certainly not yet bent on independence, have acknowledged British authority in the future? If so, then the Government itself was partly responsible for driving the Americans more rapidly to extreme measures; for treating all colonists as rebels was bound to force even moderates closer to actual rebellion. But this view cannot be put with any certainty. It does not follow that because the coercive measures failed, others more conciliatory would have succeeded. Many forces in America — in finance, in industry, in trade, and among settlers and land speculators west of the Alleghenies — stood to gain from breaking the imperial bonds. Many colonists genuinely desired greater freedom and the dignity of independent nationhood. It is also seriously open to doubt whether there was any acceptable constitutional compromise which the Ministry could have offered to the colonial leaders. It is impossible to decide finally whether the Ministry was right or wrong in the general lines of its policies during 1774 and early 1775. It is only possible to present the alternative assumptions which had to be made. If the Government was wrong in the assumptions it made about American intentions and the nature of the imperial relationship, then it was wrong in the measures which followed from this. If it was right, then no Government which wished to keep the Empire intact could have adopted any policies other than coercive ones.

The 1774 Quebec Act, passed at the same time as the early coercive measures, was to some extent connected with recent developments in the Old Colonies. The crisis there almost certainly precipitated its introduction, and the new boundary provisions for Quebec were a convenient way of sealing the western frontier. There is also no doubt that the anger and tension in the Colonies was increased by the Act, and both the Americans and the Parliamentary Opposition treated it as part of the Ministry's coercive plan. But it was in fact very different from the legislation directed at Massachusetts. Its chief provisions were concerned with long-standing Canadian and Indian problems, had been determined some time before the Tea Party crisis, and reflected credit on the Ministry which piloted them through the most hostile Parliamentary debates of this period.

The attitudes, the hopes, and the morale of the individual members of the British Government emerge clearly from their conduct during the crisis. Gower, Suffolk and Sandwich were temperamentally inclined to coercion and never once seem to have doubted the rectitude of the Government's measures. Lord North was of a different, less confident, personality, but there is no indication that he tried to modify the policies adopted until his curiously ambiguous Resolution in February 1775. At times he gave the impression of preferring conciliatory policies, but at others he expressed himself with great passion and animosity against the Americans. Rochford and Apsley were of much less political significance and were apparently happy to support their fellow Ministers. The King was an extremely active force in Administration, repeatedly pressing North and Dartmouth to be resolute in their approach to the colonists, and vigorously defending the premises on which the coercive policies were based. In the first half of 1774 he and his Ministers seemed to nurse high hopes that the measures adopted would achieve their objectives. During the period from October 1774 to January 1775, when the news from America grew worse, one or two members of the Government expressed disappointment and some doubt at the future outcome, but these reactions quickly disappeared and the Ministers put their confident trust in more coercion. Abandoning initial misgivings about the use of troops, they placed increasing dependence upon the force under General Gage. Their resentment against the Americans for refusing to submit, and their contempt for the potential strength of the colonists, made most of the Ministers psychologically prepared for war some months before it broke out. Indeed, the prospect of military conflict seemed at times almost to appeal to them as refreshingly simple in comparison with the political and constitutional complexities in which they were involved after the Tea Party. The boisterous reactions of the King, Suffolk and Rochford to the news of Lexington and Concord support this impression.

The only man among the Ministers whose views did not conform to this general pattern was Dartmouth. In the autumn of 1774, after Gage reported that the coercive measures were failing to restore the colonies to obedience, he became very depressed and pessimistic. Between December 1774 and February 1775 he was involved in the negotiations with Benjamin Franklin to find a basis for a colonial reconciliation. He also proposed, unsuccessfully, to the Cabinet that Peace Commissioners should be sent to America to settle grievances on the spot. This was the only unequivocal conciliatory proposal put before the Ministry by one of its members during this period. But it would be rash to deduce that Dartmouth disagreed seriously with the Government's American policies. He was as fierce as anyone in his reactions to the Tea Party and in his annoyance with Franklin for his role in the affair of the Hutchinson-Oliver correspondence. He believed completely in British supremacy over the Colonies. In February 1774 he pressed urgently for the prosecution of the Bostonians and he took an active role in drawing up the coercive measures. During the summer he told Hutchinson that British authority must be enforced and he looked with optimism to General Gage's achieving this by means of the Coercive Acts. In the autumn he made it clear that the Mother Country could not compromise, and early in 1775, even while considering ways of reaching a peaceful reconciliation, he wrote to Gage insisting that the troops should be used aggressively and arguing that it might be better to provoke hostilities then rather than at a later stage when the Americans would be better prepared. The American Secretary was at this time obviously suffering from divided feelings. He was annoyed by the Massachusetts outrages, and he believed that British sovereignty must be restored, and could only be restored, by asserting British authority. Yet he was also a man of deeply pacific temperament who wanted a settlement, preferably without bloodshed. This latter instinct influenced his behaviour late in 1774, when the Government's initial measures had clearly failed and when the prospect of war was suddenly much closer. Even then the desire to punish and enforce submission prevailed over his desire for peace. As the least single-minded member of the Ministry it is not surprising that he left the American Department shortly after war broke out, but it would be misleading to overestimate the degree of difference between him and his colleagues, particularly during the first nine months of 1774, when there seems to have been no serious differences over policies at all.

As a policy-making body the Government worked better

during this period than would be expected from the later conduct of the war. The Ministers appreciated the gravity of the colonial situation and it absorbed a good deal of their political energies. Before Hutchinson's official reports of the Tea Party reached London, Dartmouth had begun to collect information, and within fourteen weeks the four Coercive Acts had been drafted and passed through the Commons. The three measures of January 1775 were agreed in Cabinet within the space of eight days and were approved by Parliament before Easter. Delays did occur for a variety of reasons — because North took so much informal advice, because the amount of official assistance available was small compared to the problems and work in hand, because the Law Officers had to be consulted on most proposals and, on one occasion at least, proved slow and obstinate — but never because of serious disunity or lack of purpose in the Cabinet.

One insurmountable difficulty for the Government was the question of communication with America. It took a minimum of four weeks for correspondence to cross the Atlantic, and usually more on the westbound crossing. Consequently it was impossible to consult fully with the executive officers in the Colonies on any proposed policies. For instance, Dartmouth wrote to Hutchinson on 5 February 1774 telling him that the Ministry intended to take punitive action against Boston ; the Governor's reply and comments did not reach England until 1 June, by which time all the coercive legislation of that year had been enacted. The Massachusetts Regulating Act and the Impartial Administration of Justice Act received the royal assent on 20 May. They did not reach America until 6 August, and Gage's description of the colonial reaction to them only arrived in London on 1 October — on which day the Parliament which had passed them was dissolved. Consequently the Government was always either sitting tight waiting for news, or else was forced to take steps though still ignorant of the effects of its previous measures.

But if the North Ministry displayed more competence and sense of purpose on the eve of the war than is often realised, and if it laboured under difficulties beyond its control, its deficiencies were also already apparent. It lacked vision, magnanimity, and the statesmanship which these two qualities make possible. Certain Ministers repeatedly denigrated the potential strength, courage and resolution of the Americans. At times their public and private statements revealed a great deal of vindictiveness, as if they were more concerned to punish the colonists for bringing the colonial problem to a head than they were to solve the problem. It is very arguable that the Ministry was realistic in believing that, constitutionally, the only possible imperial relationship was the traditional one of total supremacy on the one side and subordination on the other, and that, politically, this could now be restored and maintained only by force. But it is most certainly true that the Government gave little thought to any alternative solutions which took more account of the maturity of colonial society in the 1770's. Ministers did not seem to look beyond the latest outrage, and their collective responses rarely rose above the personal emotions of pride, resentment, anger and revenge, which it should be the task of Government to control and to channel into constructive policies.

Their treatment of General Gage was also open to reproach. They ordered him to be both more judicious and more aggressive. In the situation which had developed in Massachusetts, disorder continued whether he was judicious or not ; and the Government did not provide him with the military strength necessary to quell it by force. Gage was not a great soldier. He had also encouraged excessive optimism in the King and his Ministers before leaving London, and had failed to keep them adequately informed after reaching America. His recall was probably wise and necessary. But it does seem that the Ministry did not appreciate his difficulties and, when the coercive policies collapsed, criticised him excessively and made him something of a scapegoat for their own failures.

The Government could have been deterred from its coercive policies only if the balance of forces making up the British political system had swung against it. In fact it is evident from the preceding chapters that the weight of effective opinion was strongly behind the Administration and that the Americans could expect little assistance at this stage from the potential political opposition in the Mother Country. The Opposition in Parliament was fatally divided, and Rockingham and Chatham, the leaders of the main groups, made no attempts to work together until the end of January 1775. Even then Chatham gave only a last-minute indication of his intention to introduce proposals to save the Empire and revealed no detail whatsoever of their sweeping provisions. This division between the two parties was to some extent personal, but it was perpetuated during the American crisis by their differences over colonial policy. The Rockinghams believed in Britain's absolute supremacy over the Colonies. Their policy was rooted in the events of 1766. It took little account of the fact that the colonists were in virtual rebellion and that the problem was not to maintain British supremacy without exercising it, but to prove that it existed at all now that it had been resisted and apparently denied. Chatham, in contrast, believed that his country's supremacy over the colonists was qualified by certain natural rights, and he considered that the repeal of the Rockinghams' Declaratory Act was essential to the restoration of imperial harmony. This disagreement was fundamental and constantly weakened the Opposition in debate. But in any case the Opposition was numerically too weak to make much impression on the Ministry's majorities in Parliament. The Rockingham confederation in the Commons numbered less than forty and Chatham's followers no more than a dozen. Their morale was equally low. After over seven years in the political wilderness the purity of the Rockinghams' principles may have been increased, but the squadron's hopes of office were sorely diminished ; their attendance in Parliament was poor and several of Rockingham's colleagues considered total secession. These weaknesses were apparent during the Parliamentary discussions of the Government's colonial measures. Burke excepted, scarcely an Opposition voice was raised against the Boston Port Bill and several followers of both Rockingham and Chatham supported the measure. More decided opposition was shown during the later stages of the Massachusetts Regulating Bill and the Impartial Administration of Justice Bill, when the Chatham group seems finally to have become engaged, but in terms of votes it amounted to very little, never rising above sixty-four and falling as low as twenty. An analysis of the only known list of the minority in the divisions on the coercive legislation of 1774 shows that only four members of the Rockingham confederation and two supporters of Chatham voted against the Government. During the debates of early 1775 they raised their numbers a little, but never enough to worry the Administration, and it is a reflection of Opposition morale that throughout most of the crisis the political groups in Opposition were not deploying anything near their full potential vote. Of equal significance was the attitude of the independent Members, who made up the majority of the Commons. Some spoke against the Ministry's policies, and twelve of the minority list were from their numbers, but the reported debates show the vehemence with which a great number of representatives of 'country' opinion demanded the punishment of the Americans, and there is no evidence that any substantial number of them considered withdrawing their support from the Administration on colonial questions. Until that happened, North's majority in the Commons was safe, and in the Lords the hard core of Opposition peers were as ineffective as their followers in the Lower House.

During the 1760's the Parliamentary friends of America had received valuable support 'without doors'. The mercantile interests, in London and the provinces, and the City politicians had worked with the colonial agents for the repeal of the Stamp Act and of Townshend's duties. By 1774 certain important developments had eroded this alliance. Firstly, the City had grown more radical and many of those most active in its civic affairs were no longer able to work harmoniously with the traditional political interests in Opposition at Westminster. Secondly, British merchants were looking increasingly to markets other than in America. Thirdly, the growing extremism of the colonists alienated many of the Parliamentary and mercantile forces which had previously defended them. Mainly because of this absence of support from substantial sections of the community in the Mother Country, but partly also because of their own weaknesses and divisions, the American colonial agents were rendered almost impotent during this period of crisis and their efforts to stir up a campaign of petitions against the Government were a dismal failure.

The 1774 elections were only to a very small extent a barometer of opinion on the American question. Much the most interesting contests were the dozen or so which involved radicals, for in at least half of these the popular candidate took an oath to work for the repeal of the coercive measures. But elsewhere there was no question of choosing between alternative party policies. The large majority of contests were purely local affairs in which the several interests concerned strove to maintain or extend their electoral positions. Yet even had the elections been a true test of political opinion there is little reason to suppose that the Government would have suffered badly at the hands of the electors. It was not the initial direction of the North Ministry's American policies in the early 'seventies, but its later inability to implement them, which gave rise to widespread public criticism and discontent. That discontent was to find voice in Parliament only very slowly in the years ahead.

OPPOSITION PERSONNEL IN THE
HOUSE OF COMMONS, 1774–1775

THE members in this first list composed, as far as can be ascertained, the central core of the Rockingham squadron :

William Baker (Plymton Earl), Charles Barrow (Gloucester), Edmund Burke (Wendover), Sir William Codrington (Tewkesbury), George Dempster (Perth Burghs), William Dowdeswell (Worcestershire), Savile Finch (Malton), Sir Harbord Harbord (Norwich), Augustus Keppel (New Windsor), William Keppel (Chichester), Frederick Montagu (Higham Ferrers), William Plumer (Herts), Sir Charles Saunders (Hedon), Sir George Savile (Yorks),[1] James Scawen (St. Michael), Beilby Thompson (Hedon), Earl Verney (Bucks), William Weddell (Hull), Sir Robert Clayton (Bletchingley), and Lord Ludlow (Hunts) sat throughout the period 1773–75. Nathaniel Cholmley (Boroughbridge) and William Burke (Great Bedwin) were in the squadron until the 1774 elections. George Saunderson, Lord Lumley (Lincoln) came into Parliament at those elections.

The groups in the following list accepted the general leadership of Rockingham and so can be included, for voting purposes, in the Rockingham confederation :

There were four members of the Cavendish family : Frederick Cavendish (Derby), George Cavendish (Derbyshire), Lord John Cavendish (York), Richard Cavendish (Lancaster). Sir Anthony Abdy (Knaresborough) was closely connected and acted with them. Lord Edward Bentinck (Carlisle), Sir Henry Bridgeman (Wenlock), George Byng (Wigan), Henry Fletcher (Cumberland), Booth Grey (Leicester) and Beaumont Hotham (Wigan), had varying degrees of attachment to the Duke of Portland. Thomas Conolly (Chichester) and George Lennox (Sussex) followed Richmond. Edward Foley (Droitwich), Thomas Foley senior (Herefordshire), Thomas Foley junior (Herefordshire) formed the

[1] Sir George Savile was always an independent county gentleman, yet he was in such close consultation with Rockingham that it is permissible to include him in this group.

Foley connection, and were joined after the 1774 elections by Andrew Foley (Droitwich). Charles Fox (Midhurst) began to give some support to the Rockingham confederation early in 1774. Samuel Salt (Liskeard), a friend of Portland, supported Rockingham regularly, though the nature and degree of his attachment is not clear.

The following list contains the supporters of Chatham and Shelburne :

John Aubrey (Wallingford), Isaac Barré (Chipping Wycombe), Sir Piercy Brett (Queensborough), Thomas Calcraft (Poole), John Dunning (Calne), Thomas Fitzmaurice (Calne), Robert Pratt (Horsham), James Townsend (West Looe, a City radical who was close enough in sympathy with Shelburne to be included here), and Sir George Yonge (Honiton). Brett, Calcraft and Pratt left Parliament in 1774. Also among the Chatham supporters might be included the Rutland Group, containing Lord George Sutton (Grantham), Earl Tyrconnel (Scarborough), John Manners (Newark until 1774), and Charles Manners (Cambridge University) and George Sutton (Newark) after 1774.

The following tended to vote against the Ministry but were not regular members of the above Opposition groups. Being independent, they voted differently on different issues, and their opposition tendencies might not extend to colonial policies.

Benjamin Allen (Bridgwater), George Anson (Lichfield), Sir Edward Astley (Norfolk), Nathaniel Bayley (Abingdon), Frederick Bull (London), Joseph Bullock (Wendover), Godfrey Clarke (Derbyshire), Wenman Coke (Derby), Thomas Coventry (Bridport), Richard Hippesley Coxe (Somerset), John Damer (Dorchester), Sir Charles Davers (Weymouth), Thomas Duncombe (Downton), Henry Dawkins (Chippenham), Paul Feilde (Hertford), Jacob Bouverie, Lord Folkestone (Salisbury), Sir Thomas Frankland (Thirsk), Rose Fuller (Rye), John Glynn (Middlesex), Ambrose Goddard (Wiltshire), Robert Gregory (Maidstone), James Grenville (Buckingham), Sir John Griffin (Andover), Sir William Guise (Gloucestershire), Thomas Halsey (Herts), John Hanbury (Monmouth), Thomas Hay (Lewes), Noel Hill (Shrewsbury), George Hunt (Bodmin), William Hussey (Hindon), George Johnstone (Cockermouth), John Luther (Essex), Thomas Lister (Clitheroe), Charles Marsham (Maidstone), Joseph Martin (Gatton), Joshua Mauger (Poole), Sir Joseph Mawbey (Southwark), Crisp Molineux (Castle Rising), Will Nedham (Winchelsea),

Richard Oliver (London), John Parker (Devon), Richard Pennant (Liverpool), Sir James Pennyman (Scarborough), Charles Penruddock (Wiltshire), Alex Popham (Taunton), William Pulteney (Cromartyshire), John Radcliffe (St. Albans), John Sawbridge (Hythe), John Scudamore (Hereford), Henry Seymour (Huntingdon), Thomas Skipwith (Warwickshire), Frederick Standert (Bletchingley), Humphrey Sturt (Dorset), John Tempest (Durham), Thomas Townshend (Whitchurch), Charles Turner (York), Gerard Vanneck (Dunwich), Philip Lord Wenman (Oxfordshire), Thomas Whitmore (Bridgnorth), Watkin Williams (Montgomery), Sir Cecil Wray (East Retford), Sir Watkin Williams-Wynn (Shropshire).

These lists are not necessarily complete ; finality of classification is as impossible now as it was in the eighteenth century.

OPPOSITION TO THE AMERICAN MEASURES IN THE HOUSE OF LORDS, 11 MAY AND 18 MAY 1774

ROCKINGHAM'S papers include a list of the twelve Peers who opposed the Impartial Administration of Justice Bill on 18 May 1774; they were Rockingham himself, Richmond, Portland, Leinster, Manchester, Scarborough, Bessborough, FitzWilliam, Shelburne, Torrington, Craven and the Bishop of St. Asaph.[1] It is less easy to establish the complete composition of the minority of twenty against the Regulating Bill on 11 May, but most of them can be identified with some degree of confidence. After the division on the 11th the Rockinghams put down a Protest in the *Lords Journals*,[2] and the eleven Peers who signed the Protest presumably also voted in the minority on that day; Rockingham, Richmond, Portland, Leinster, Bessborough, FitzWilliam, Craven, Effingham, Abingdon, King and Abergavenny. A further five can be taken from a published list of Peers who voted against one or other or both of the two measures:[3] Camden, Ravensworth, Sondes, Spencer and Stamford did not vote on the 18th and so, if the list is accurate, must have voted on the 11th. Shelburne, Torrington and the Bishop of St. Asaph were present in the Chamber on the 11th and may well have joined the minority then as they did on the 18th. This would cover nineteen out of the twenty dissenters.

[1] Richmond to Rockingham, 18 May 1774. W.W.M. R1-1490.
[2] *Lords Journals*, xxxiv, 182-4. *Parl. Hist.*, xvii, 1321-5.
[3] *Jackson's Oxford Journal*, 21 May 1774.

BIBLIOGRAPHY

Note on the Bibliography.—The numbers which precede the descriptions of the manuscripts in the Public Record Office are those in use at that repository. In the case of Printed Sources and Secondary Works the books are listed in the alphabetical order of authors and editors except when a volume or series is usually known by its title. In Printed Sources volumes have been listed under the name of the editor, in Secondary Works under the name of the author.

BIBLIOGRAPHICAL GUIDES

ADAMS, R. G., ed., *The Papers of Lord George Germain; a Brief Description of the Stopford-Sackville Papers now in the William L. Clements Library*, University of Michigan, William Clements Library Bulletin, No. 18, Ann Arbor, 1928.

ANDREWS, C. M., and DAVENPORT, F. G., *Guide to the Manuscript Materials for the History of the United States to 1783, in the British Museum, in Minor London Archives and in the libraries of Oxford and Cambridge*, 2 vols., Washington, D.C., 1908.

BEERS, H. P., *Bibliographies in American History. Guide to Materials for Research*, New York, 1942.

BESLER, R., MUGRIDGE, D., and McCRUM, B., eds., *A guide to the Study of the United States of America*, Library of Congress, 1960.

CRANE, R. S., and KAYE, F. B., *A Census of British Newspapers and Periodicals, 1620–1800*, Chapel Hill, North Carolina, 1927.

CRICK, B. R., and ALMAN, M., *A Guide to Manuscripts relating to America in Great Britain and Ireland*, British Association of American Studies, London, 1961.

CUTHBERT, N. B., *American Manuscript Collections in the Huntingdon Library for the History of the Seventeenth and Eighteenth Centuries*, San Marino, California, 1941.

EWING, W. S., *Guide to the Manuscript Collections in the William L. Clements Library*, Ann Arbor, Michigan, 1953.

EWING, W. S., *Supplement to the Guide to the Manuscript Collections in the William L. Clements Library*, Ann Arbor, Michigan, 1959.

GIUSSEPPI, M. S., *A Guide to the Manuscripts Preserved in the Public Record Office*, 2 vols., London, 1923–24.

HALL, H., ed., *A Repertory of British Archives, Part I, England*, Royal Historical Society, London, 1920.

HAMER, P. M., ed., *A Guide to Archives and Manuscripts in the United States*, Yale, 1961.

MILFORD, R. T., and SUTHERLAND, D. M., *A Catalogue of English*

Newspapers and Periodicals in the Bodleian Library, 1622–1800, Bibliographical Society, Oxford, 1936.

PARGELLIS, S., and MEDLEY, D. J., *Bibliography of British History. The Eighteenth Century, 1714–1789*, Oxford, 1951.

MANUSCRIPTS

(a) *Manuscripts in the Public Record Office*

CO. 5, 42, 43, 47, 323	Colonial Office.
PRO. 30/8	Pitt MSS., Chatham Papers.
PRO. 30/29	Granville Papers.
SP. 37, 47	State Paper Office, Domestic.
TI. 29	Treasury.

(b) *Manuscripts in the British Museum*

Additional MSS. :

29476, 34412	Auckland Papers.
35370, 35371, 35375, 35427, 35502, 35611, 35612, 35613, 35614, 35693, 35912	Hardwicke Papers.
37833, 37836	Papers of John Robinson.
38207, 38208, 38342, 38358, 38470, 38567, 38570, 38577, 38580	Liverpool Papers.
41354	Martin Papers.
41851, 41855	Thomas Grenville Papers.
42071	Hamilton and Greville Papers.

Egerton MSS. :

253–262	Reports of the Debates of the House of Commons from 10 May 1768 to 13 June 1774, partly written in shorthand by Sir Henry Cavendish, M.P.

MS. Facs. :

340 (1–4)	Robinson Papers in the possession of the Marquess of Abergavenny at Eridge Castle.

(c) *Manuscripts in other Collections*

Oxford, Bodleian Library

The North Papers, from Wroxton Abbey, near Banbury : the papers of Francis North, 3rd Baron, afterwards 1st Earl of Guilford (1704–90), and the papers of Frederick, Baron North, afterwards 2nd Earl of Guilford (1732–92).

Nottingham, University of Nottingham Library

Mellish Manuscripts: the papers of Charles Mellish (1737–96), M.P. for Pontefract 1774–80, and for Aldborough 1780–84.

Newcastle Manuscripts: the papers of Henry Fiennes Clinton, 2nd Duke of Newcastle (1720–94).

Portland Manuscripts: the papers of William Henry Cavendish Bentink, 3rd Duke of Portland (1738–1809).

Sheffield, Sheffield City Libraries

Wentworth Woodhouse Muniments:

(a) the letters and papers of Charles Watson-Wentworth, 2nd Marquess of Rockingham (1730–82).

(b) the letters and papers of Edmund Burke (1729–97).

Transcripts of:

Burke correspondence in Brown University Library, Rhode Island, U.S.A.

Burke correspondence in Champion Letter Books, at Denbigh and at New York.

Burke correspondence in Fitzwilliam MSS., Northampton County Record Office.

Burke correspondence in National Library of Ireland.

Burke correspondence in O'Hara MSS., Annaghmore, Sligo.

Stafford, County Record Office

Sutherland Manuscripts: letters and papers of the Gower family from Trentham, Staffordshire.

William Salt Library

Dartmouth Manuscripts: the letters and papers of William Legge, 2nd Earl of Dartmouth (1731–1801), First Lord of Trade, Secretary for the Colonies 1772–75.

Transcripts from Various Collections

Baker Manuscripts: transcripts from Hertfordshire County Record Office.

Dowdeswell Manuscripts: transcripts from William L. Clements Library, Ann Arbor, Michigan.

Griffin Manuscripts: transcripts from Essex County Record Office.

Verney Manuscripts: transcripts from Claydon House, Bletchley, Bucks.

PRINTED SOURCES

(a) *Calendars and Collections of Documents*

Acts of the Privy Council of England. Colonial Series, v, A.D. 1766–1783, 6 vols., ed., W. L. GRANT and J. MUNRO, London, 1912.

BAILEY, K. P., ed., *The Ohio Company Papers, 1753–1817*, Calif. Society of the Sons of the Revolution, Los Angeles, 1947.

BELOFF, M., ed., *The Debate on the American Revolution, 1761–1783*, London, 1949.

BOYD, J. P., ed., *The Susquehannah Company Papers, 1750–1772*, Sheldon Reynolds Memorial Publications, Wyoming Historical and Geological Society, Wilkes-Barré, Pennsylvania, 2 vols., 1930–33.

COSTIN, W. C., and WATSON, J. S., *The Law and Working of the Constitution: Documents, 1660–1914*, 2 vols., London, 1952.

FORCE, P., ed., *American Archives: Fourth Series*, i, ii, Washington, 1837, 1839.

HARLOW, V. T., and MADDEN, F., eds., *British Colonial Developments, 1774–1834. Select Documents*, Oxford, 1953.

HISTORICAL MANUSCRIPTS COMMISSION :

Fifth Report, Appendix, Part I, Manuscripts of the Duke of Sutherland at Trentham, Staffs., ed., A. J. Horwood, London, 1876.

Tenth Report, Appendix, Part VI, Manuscripts of the Marquis of Abergavenny, ed., H. C. Maxwell Lyte, London, 1887.

Eleventh Report, Appendix, Part V, The Manuscripts of the Earl of Dartmouth, i, ed., W. O. Hewlett, London, 1887.

Thirteenth Report, Appendix, Part IV, The Manuscripts of the Earl of Dartmouth, Supplementary Report, iv, ed., W. O. Hewlett, London, 1892.

Fourteenth Report, Appendix, Part X, The Manuscripts of the Earl of Dartmouth, American Papers, ii, ed., B. F. Stevens, London, 1895.

Fifteenth Report, Appendix, Part I, The Manuscripts of the Earl of Dartmouth, iii, ed., W. Page, 1896.

Fifteenth Report, Appendix, Part VI, The Manuscripts of the Earl of Carlisle, Preserved at Castle Howard, ed., R. E. G. Kirk, London, 1897.

Report on the Manuscripts of Mrs. Stopford-Sackville, of Drayton House, Northamptonshire, i, ed., R. B. Knowles, W. O. Hewlett and Mrs. S. C. Lomas, London, 1904.

Report on the Manuscripts of the Marquess of Lothian Preserved at Blickling Hall, Norfolk, ed., D'A. B. Colyer and W. D. Macray, London, 1905.

Report on Manuscripts in Various Collections, vol. VI. The Manuscripts of Captain Howard Vicente Knox, ed., Mrs. S. C. Lomas, Dublin, 1909.

HORNE, D. B., and RANSOME, M., eds., *English Historical Documents, 1714–1783*, x, general editor, D. C. Douglas, London, 1957.

JENSEN, M., ed., *American Colonial Documents to 1776*, ix, general editor, D. C. Douglas, London, 1955.

Journal of the Commissioners for Trade and Plantations . . . 1704 . . . 1782 . . . in the Public Record Office, 14 vols., 1920–38.

Massachusetts Historical Society. Collections, 79 vols., Cambridge, Massachusetts, 1792–1941.

MORISON, S. E., ed., *Sources and Documents illustrating the American Revolution, 1764–1788, and the foundation of the Federal Constitution,* Oxford, 1929.

New York Historical Society. Collections, Publication Funds Series, New York, 1868.

SHORTT, A., and DOUGHTY, A. G., eds., *Documents relating to the Constitutional History of Canada, 1759–1791,* Canadian Archives, The Historical Documents Publication Board, Ottawa, 1918.

WILLIAMS, E. N., ed., *The Eighteenth Century Constitution: Documents and Commentary,* Cambridge, 1960.

(b) *Contemporary Correspondence, Memoirs and Histories*

ALBEMARLE, GEORGE, EARL OF, ed., *Memoirs of the Marquis of Rockingham and His Contemporaries,* 2 vols., London, 1852.

ANSON, W. R., ed., *Autobiography and Political Correspondence of Augustus Henry, third Duke of Grafton, K.G.,* London, 1898.

BALLAGH, J. C., ed., *The Letters of Richard Henry Lee,* 2 vols., New York, 1911.

BARNES, G. R., and OWEN, J. H., eds., *The Private Papers of John, Earl of Sandwich, First Lord of the Admiralty, 1771–1782,* Navy Records Society, 4 vols., London, 1932–38.

BIGELOW, J., ed., *The Complete Works of Benjamin Franklin,* 10 vols., New York and London, 1887.

BONNER-SMITH, D., ed., *The Barrington Papers,* Navy Records Society, 2 vols., London, 1937–41.

BROWNING, O., ed., *The Political Memoranda of Francis, fifth Duke of Leeds,* Camden Society, New Series, xxxv, London, 1884.

CARTER, C. E., ed., *The Correspondence of General Thomas Gage with the Secretaries of State, 1763–1775,* Yale Historical Publications, Manuscripts, and Printed Texts, xi, 2 vols., New Haven, 1931–33.

COPELAND, W., SUTHERLAND, L. S., and GUTTRIDGE, G. H., eds., *The Correspondence of Edmund Burke,* i, *April 1744–June 1768,* ii, *July 1768–June 1774,* iii, *July 1774–June 1778,* Cambridge, 1958–1961.

FERGUSSON, J., ed., *Letters of George Dempster to Sir Adam Fergusson, 1756–1813. With Some Account of his Life,* London, 1934.

FITZMAURICE, E., *Life of William, Earl of Shelburne, afterwards first Marquess of Lansdowne,* 3 vols., London, 1875–76.

FLICK, A. C., ed., *The Papers of Sir William Johnson,* University of the State of New York, Division of Archives and History, vii, Albany, 1931.

FORD, W. C., ed., *The Letters of William Lee, Sheriff and Alderman of London, 1766–1783,* New York, 1891.

FORTESCUE, SIR J. W., ed., *The Correspondence of King George III. From 1760 to December 1783,* 6 vols., London, 1927–28.

FRANKLIN, W. T., ed., *Memoirs of the Life and Writings of Benjamin Franklin, . . .* 3rd edition, 6 vols., London, 1818–19.

GRANVILLE, C., ed., *Lord Granville Leveson-Gower (first Earl Granville), Private Correspondence, 1781–1821*, 2 vols., London, 1916.

GUTTRIDGE, G. H., ed., *The American Correspondence of a Bristol Merchant, 1766–1776. Letters of Richard Champion*, University of California Publications in History, xxii, no. 1, Berkeley, California, 1934.

HOFFMAN, R. J. S., ed., *Edmund Burke, New York Agent.* The American Philosophical Society, Philadelphia, 1956.

HUTCHINSON, J., ed., *The History of the Province of Massachusetts Bay from 1749–1774, by Thomas Hutchinson*, London, 1828.

HUTCHINSON, P. O., ed., *The Diary and Letters of his Excellency Thomas Hutchinson, Esq.*, 2 vols., London, 1883, 1886.

JAMES, J. A., ed., *George Rogers Clark Papers, 1771–1781.* Collections of the Illinois State Historical Library, viii, Virginia Series, iii, Springfield, Illinois, 1912.

LAPRADE, W. T., ed., *Parliamentary Papers of John Robinson, 1774–1784*, Royal Historical Society, Camden Third Series, xxxiii, London, 1922.

LETTSOM, J. C., ed., *The Works of John Fothergill, M.D.* . . . 2 vols., London, 1783.

MACDONALD, W., ed., *The Autobiography of Benjamin Franklin*, London, 1905.

MAYO, L. S., ed., *The History of the Colony and Province of Massachusetts Bay, by Thomas Hutchinson*, Cambridge, Mass., 1936.

MINTO, COUNTESS OF, *Life and Letters of Sir Gilbert Elliot, first Earl of Minto, from 1751–1806*, 3 vols., London, 1874.

MULKEARN, L., ed., *George Mercer Papers Relating to the Ohio Company of Virginia*, Pittsburgh, 1954.

NORTON, J. E., ed., *The Letters of Edward Gibbon*, 3 vols., London, 1956.

RUSSELL BARKER, G. F., ed., *Horace Walpole Memoirs of the Reign of King George the Third*, 4 vols., London, 1894.

RUSSELL, LORD JOHN, ed., *Memorials and Correspondence of Charles James Fox*, 2 vols., London, 1853.

SMITH, W. J., ed., *The Grenville Papers: Being the Correspondence of Richard Grenville Earl Temple, K.G., and the Right Hon. George Grenville, Their Friends and Contemporaries*, 4 vols., London, 1852–53.

SMYTH, A. H., ed., *The Writings of Benjamin Franklin*, 10 vols., New York, 1907.

STEUART, A. F., ed., *The Last Journals of Horace Walpole During the Reign of George III From 1771–1783*, 2 vols., London, 1910.

TAYLER, A., and H., eds., *Lord Fife and his Factor, the correspondence of James, 2nd Lord Fife, 1729–1809*, London, 1925.

TAYLOR, W. S., and Pringle, J. H., eds., *Correspondence of William Pitt, Earl of Chatham*, 4 vols., London, 1838–40.

TOYNBEE, MRS. P., ed., *The Letters of Horace Walpole, fourth Earl of Orford*, 16 vols., Oxford, 1903–25.

VAN DOREN, C., ed., *Letters and Papers of Benjamin Franklin and Richard Jackson, 1753–1785*, 1947.

VAUGHAN, B., ed., *Political, Miscellaneous, and Philosophical Pieces. . . . Written by Benj. Franklin*, London, 1779.

WRAXALL, SIR N., *Historical Memoirs of My Own Time . . . from 1772 to . . . 1784*, London, 1904.

WRIGHT, J., ed., *Debates of the House of Commons in the year 1774, on the Bill for making more effectual provision for the Government of the Province of Quebec. Drawn up from the notes of the Rt. Hon. Sir Henry Cavendish, Bart.*, London, 1839.

YORKE, P. C., *The Life and Correspondence of Philip Yorke, Earl of Hardwicke*, 3 vols., Cambridge, 1913.

(c) *Selected Contemporary Pamphlets*

ANON., *The Expediency of Securing our American Colonies by Settling the Country adjoining the River Mississippi and the Country upon the Ohio*, Edinburgh, 1776.

CARTWRIGHT, J., *American independence the interest and glory of Great Britain*, London, 1774.

JOHNSON, S., *Taxation no tyranny; an answer to the resolutions and address of the American Congress*, London, 1775.

(KNOX, W.), *Extra Official State Papers. . . . By a Late Under Secretary of State*, London, 1789.

(KNOX, W.), *Thoughts on the Act For making more Effectual Provision for the Government of the Province of Quebec*, London, 1774.

(KNOX, W.), *The Justice and Policy of the late Act of Parliament, For Making more Effectual Provision for the Government of the Province of Quebec, Asserted and Proved; . . .* London, 1774.

PRICE, R., *Observations on the nature of civil liberty, the principles of government, and the justice and policy of the war with America*, London, 1776.

PRIESTLEY, J., *An Essay on the first principles of government, and on the nature of political, civil, and religious liberty*, 2nd edition, London, 1771.

PULTENEY, W., *Thoughts on the Present State of Affairs with America and the Means of Conciliation*, London, 1778.

TUCKER, JOSIAH, *The True Interest of Great Britain set Forth*, London, 1774.

(d) *Other Printed Sources*

The Annual Register . . ., London, 1774, 1775.

COBBETT, W., ed., *The Parliamentary History of England*, xvii, xviii, London, 1813.

DEBRETT, J., ed., *The History, Debates and Proceedings of both Houses of Parliament . . . 1743 to . . . 1774*, vii, London, 1792.

The Journals of the House of Commons, xxxiv, xxxv, London, 1804.
The Journals of the House of Lords, xxxiv, xxxv, London, 1804.
Public General Acts, A.R. George III, London, 1774, 1775.
Votes of the House of Commons, London, 1774, 1775.

(e) *Selected Newspapers and Periodicals*

Edinburgh Magazine and Review, Edinburgh ; *The Freemen's Magazine*, Newcastle ; *Gentleman's Magazine*, London ; *Jackson's Oxford Journal*, Oxford ; *London Chronicle*, London ; *London Gazette*, London ; *London Magazine*, London ; *Monthly Review*, London ; *Morning Chronicle*, London ; *Oxford Magazine*, Oxford ; *Public Advertiser*, London ; *St. James's Chronicle*, London ; *St. James's Magazine*, London ; *Town and Country Magazine*, London.

SELECTED SECONDARY WORKS

(a) *Printed*

ABERNETHY, T. P., *Western Lands and the American Revolution*, University of Virginia Institute for Research in the Social Sciences, Institute Monograph no. 25, New York, 1937.

ADAMS, R. G., *Political Ideas of the American Revolution*, Durham, North Carolina, 1922.

ADOLPHUS, J., *The History of England from the Accession of King George the Third to . . . 1783*, 3 vols., London, 1802.

ALBERY, W., *A Parliamentary History of Horsham, 1295–1885*, London, 1927.

ALVORD, C. W., *The Mississippi Valley in British Politics*, 2 vols., Cleveland, 1917.

ALVORD, C. W., 'The Genesis of the Proclamation of 1763', *Collections and Researches made by the Michigan Pioneer and Historical Society*, Lansing, Michigan, xxxvi, 1908, pp. 20-52.

ALVORD, C. W., *Lord Shelburne and the Founding of British-American Goodwill*. Raleigh Lecture on History, British Academy, London, 1925.

ALVORD, C. W., and CARTER, C. E., *The Critical Period, 1763–1765*, Collections of the Illinois State Historical Library, x, British Series, i, Springfield, 1915.

ALVORD, C. W., and CARTER, C. E., *The New Regime, 1765–1767*, Collections of the Illinois State Historical Library, xi, British Series, ii, Springfield, 1916.

ALVORD, C. W., and CARTER, C. E., *Trade and Politics, 1767–1769*, Collections of the Illinois State Historical Library, xvi, Springfield, 1921.

ANDREWS, C. M., *The Colonial Background of the American Revolution*, New Haven, 1923.

APPLETON, M., 'The Agents of the New England Colonies in the Revolutionary Period', *The New England Quarterly*, vi (2), Portland, Maine, 1933, pp. 371-87.

BAILEY, K., *The Ohio Company of Virginia and the Westward Movement, 1748–1792*, Glendale, California, 1939.

BARNWELL, J. W., 'The Hon. Charles Garth, M.P., The Last Colonial Agent of South Carolina in England, and some of his work', *South Carolina Historical and Genealogical Magazine*, Charleston, South Carolina, xxvi, 1925, pp. 67-92, xxviii, 1927, pp. 33 *seq.*

BARRINGTON, S., *The Political Life of William Wildman, Viscount Barrington*, London, 1814.

BARROW, J., *The Life of Richard Earl Howe, K.G.*, London, 1839.

BASYE, A. H., *The Lords Commissioners of Trade and Plantations Commonly Known as the Board of Trade, 1748–1782*, Yale Historical Publications, Miscellany, xiv, New Haven, 1925.

BASYE, A. H., 'The Secretary of State for the Colonies, 1766–1782', *American Historical Review*, xxviii, 1922, London and New York, pp. 13-23.

BEAN, W. W., *The Parliamentary Representation of the Six Northern Counties of England*, Hull, 1890.

BEATSON, R., *A Political Index To The Histories of Great Britain and Ireland, or A Complete Register of The Hereditary Honours, Public Offices, and Persons in Office*, 2 vols., London, 1788.

BEER, C. L., *The Old Colonial System*, 2 vols., reprint, New York, 1933.

BEER, C. L., *The Commercial Policy of England towards the American Colonies*, 2 vols., New York, reprint 1948.

BEMIS, S. F., *The Diplomacy of the American Revolution, 1775–1823*, The American Historical Association, New York, 1935.

BILLINGTON, R. A., *Westward Expansion, A History of the American Frontier*, New York, 1949.

BINNEY, J. E. D., *British Public Finance and Administration, 1774–92*, Oxford, 1958.

BOND, B. W., 'The Colonial Agent as a popular representative', *Political Science Quarterly*, xxxv, New York, 1920, pp. 372-92.

BONSALL, B., *Sir James Lowther and Cumberland and Westmorland Elections*, Manchester, 1960.

BOYD, J. P., *The Susquehannah Company: Connecticut's Experiment in Expansion*, Tercentenary Commission of the State of Connecticut, Historical Publication xxxiv, New Haven, 1935.

BOYD, J. P., *Anglo-American Union. Joseph Galloway's Plans to preserve the British Empire, 1774–1788*, Philadelphia, 1941.

BRINTON, C., *The Anatomy of Revolution*, London, 1953.

BROOKE, J., *The Chatham Administration, 1766–1768*, London, 1956.

BROUGHAM, H. P., *Historical Sketches of Statesmen who flourished in the time of George III*, 3 parts, London, 1839–43.

BROWN, W. A., *Empire or Independence: A Study in the Failure of Reconciliation, 1774–1783*, Louisiana State University Press, 1941.

BURNS, J. J., *The Colonial Agents of New England*, Washington, 1935.

BURT, A. L., *The Old Province of Quebec*, Toronto, 1933.

BURT, A. L., *The United States, Great Britain and British North America From the Revolution to the Establishment of Peace after the War of 1812*, New Haven, 1940.

BUTTERFIELD, H., *George III, Lord North, and the People, 1779–1780*, London, 1949.

BUTTERFIELD, H., *George III and the Historians*, London, 1957.

CARTER, C. E., *Great Britain and the Illinois Country, 1763–1774*, American Historical Association, Washington, 1910.

CARTER, C. E., 'The significance of the Military Office in America', *American Historical Review*, xxviii, London and New York, 1923, pp. 475-88.

CHRISTIE, I. R., *The End of North's Ministry, 1780–1782*, London, 1958.

CLARK, D. M., *British Opinion and the American Revolution*, Yale Historical Publications, Miscellany, xx, New Haven, 1930.

CLARKE, M. P., *Parliamentary Privilege in the American Colonies*, Yale Historical Publications, Miscellany, xliv, New Haven, 1943.

COFFIN, V., *The Province of Quebec and the Early American Revolution*, Bulletin of the University of Wisconsin, Political Science and History Series, Madison, Wisconsin, I (iii), 1896, pp. 275-562.

COLLYER, C., 'The Rockinghams and Yorkshire Politics, 1742–1761', *The Publications of the Thoresby Society*, xli (4, no. 99), *The Thoresby Miscellany*, xii (4), Leeds, 1954, pp. 352-82.

COPELAND, T. W., *Edmund Burke, Six Essays*, London, 1959.

COUPLAND, R., *The Quebec Act a Study in Statesmanship*, Oxford, 1925.

COURTENEY, W. P., *The Parliamentary Representation of Cornwall to 1832*, London, 1889.

DICEY, A. V., *Lectures introductory to the study of the law of the constitution*, London, 4th edition, 1893.

DICKERSON, O. M., *The Navigation Acts and the American Revolution*, Philadelphia, 1951.

Dictionary of National Biography.

DOBSON, W., *History of the Parliamentary Representation of Preston during the last hundred years*, Preston, 1856.

DOUGLAS, S., *The History of the Cases of Controverted Elections which were tried and determined during the . . . Fourteenth Parliament of Great Britain*, 3 vols., London, 1775-77.

FARRAND, M., 'The Taxation of Tea, 1767-1773', *American Historical Review*, iii, January 1898, pp. 226-9.

FEILING, K. G., *The Second Tory Party, 1714–1832*, London, 1938.

FITZMAURICE, E., *The Life of Granville George Leveson-Gower, second Earl Granville, K.G., 1815–1891*, London, 1905.

FOORD, A. S., 'The Waning of the influence of the Crown', *English Historical Review*, lxii, London, 1947.

FOORD, A. S., *His Majesty's Opposition, 1714–1830*, Oxford, 1964.

FOX, R. H., *Dr. John Fothergill and his Friends*, London, 1919.

GIPSON, L. H., *The Coming of the American Revolution, 1763–1775*, The New American Nation Series, New York, 1954.

GOODER, A., *The Parliamentary representation of the county of York, 1258–1832*, 2 vols., Wakefield, 1935–38.

GORE-BROWNE, R., *Chancellor Thurlow*, London, 1953.

GUTTRIDGE, G. H., *English Whiggism and the American Revolution*, University of California Publications in History, xxviii, Berkeley, California, 1942.

HARBIN, S., *Members of Parliament for Somerset*, Somersetshire Archaeological and Natural Historical Society, 1939.

HARLOW, V. T., *The Founding of the Second British Empire, 1763–1793*, London, 1952.

HARPER, L. A., *The English Navigation Laws*, New York, 1939.

HENDERSON, A., 'A Pre-Revolutionary Revolt in the Old Southwest', *The Mississippi Valley Historical Review*, xvii (2), Lincoln, Nebraska, 1930, pp. 191-212.

HINKHOUSE, F. J., *The Preliminaries of the American Revolution as seen in the English Press, 1763–1775*, Columbia University Studies in History, Economics and Public Law, no. 276, New York, 1926.

HINSDALE, B. A., 'The Western Land Policy of the British Government from 1763 to 1775', *Ohio Archæological and Historical Quarterly*, i, 1887, Columbus, Ohio, pp. 207-29.

HOLDSWORTH, SIR W. S., *A History of English Law*, x, London, 1938.

HOTBLACK, K., *Chatham's Colonial Policy*, London, 1917.

HUGHES, E. R., 'Lord North's Correspondence, 1766–83', *English Historical Review*, lxii, London, 1947, pp. 218-38.

HUMPHREYS, R. A., 'Lord Shelburne and the Proclamation of 1763', *English Historical Review*, xlix, London, 1934, pp. 241-64.

HUMPHREYS, R. A., 'Lord Shelburne and British Colonial Policy, 1766–1768', *English Historical Review*, l, London, 1935, pp. 257-277.

HUMPHREYS, R. A., and SCOTT, S. M., 'Lord Northington and the Laws of Canada', *The Canadian Historical Review*, xiv, Toronto, 1933, pp. 42-61.

HUNT, W., *The History of England . . . (1760–1801)*, The Political History of England, x, London, 1905.

HUTCHINS, J., *The History and Antiquities of the County of Dorset . . .*, ed., W. Shipp and J. W. Hodson, iv, London, 1873.

INNIS, H. A., *The Fur Trade in Canada*, Toronto, 1956.

JUDD, G. P., *Members of Parliament 1734–1832*, Yale Historical Publications, Miscellany lxi, New Haven, 1955.

KEIR, SIR D. L., *The Constitutional History of Modern Britain since 1485*, 6th edition, London, 1960.

KEMP, B., *The King and Commons, 1660–1832*, London, 1957.

LASKI, H. J., *Political thought in England from Locke to Bentham*, London, 1932.

LECKY, W. E. H., *A History of England in the Eighteenth Century*, 8 vols., London, 1879–90.

LEYLAND, H. T., 'The Ohio Company A Colonial Corporation',

Quarterly Publication of the Historical and Philosophical Society of Ohio, xvi (1), Cincinnati, Ohio, 1921, pp. 1-19.

LILLY, E., *The Colonial Agents of New York and New Jersey*, Washington, D.C., 1936.

LONN, E., *The Colonial Agents of the Southern Colonies*, Chapel Hill, North Carolina, 1945.

LUCAS, R., *Lord North, second Earl of Guilford, K.G., 1732–1792*, London, 1913.

MACCOBY, S., *English Radicalism, 1762–1785. The Origins*, London, 1955.

MACKESY, P., *The War for America, 1775–1783*, London, 1964.

MAHONEY, T. H. D., *Edmund Burke and Ireland*, Cambridge, Mass., 1960.

MARSHALL, D., *Eighteenth-Century England*, London, 1962.

MARTELLI, G., *Jemmy Twitcher. A Life of John Montagu, 4th Earl of Sandwich, 1718–1792*, London, 1962.

MARTIN, C., *Empire and Commonwealth Studies in Governance and Self-Government in Canada*, Oxford, 1929.

MATTHEWS, A., *Notes on the Massachusetts Royal Commissions, 1681–1775*, Publications of the Colonial Society of Massachusetts, xxxvii, Cambridge, Mass., 1913.

METZGER, C. H., *The Quebec Act*, U.S. Catholic Historical Society, xvi, New York, 1936.

MILLER, J. C., *Origins of the American Revolution*, Stanford, California, 1959.

MORGAN, E. S., and MORGAN, H. M., *The Stamp Act Crisis*, Chapel Hill, North Carolina, 1953.

MORRIS, R. B., ed., *The Era of the American Revolution. Studies Inscribed to Evarts Boutell Greene*, New York, 1939.

MORRIS, R. B., *The American Revolution*, New York, 1955.

MUMBY, F. A., *George III and the American Revolution*, London, 1924.

NAMIER, SIR LEWIS B., *England in the Age of the American Revolution*, 2nd edition, London, 1961.

NAMIER, SIR LEWIS B., *Personalities and Powers*, London, 1955.

NAMIER, SIR LEWIS B., *The Structure of Politics at the Accession of George III*, 2nd edition, London, 1957.

NAMIER, L. B., 'Charles Garth and his Connections', *English Historical Review*, liv, London, 1939, pp. 443-70, 632-52.

NAMIER, SIR LEWIS B., and Brooke, J., *The History of Parliament: The House of Commons, 1754–1790*, London, 1964.

Notes and Queries.

OLDFIELD, T. H. B., *The representative history of Great Britain and Ireland . . .*, 6 vols., London, 1816.

OLSON, A., *The Radical Duke*, Oxford, 1961.

OWEN, J. B., *The Rise of the Pelhams*, London, 1957.

PARES, R., *King George III and the Politicians. The Ford Lectures delivered in the University of Oxford, 1951–1952*, Oxford, 1953.

PARES, R., and TAYLOR, A. J. P., eds., *Essays Presented to Sir Lewis Namier*, London, 1956.

PEMBERTON, W. B., *Lord North*, London, 1938.

PENSON, L. M., *The Colonial Agents of the British West Indies*, London, 1924.

PHILLIPS, P., *The West in the Diplomacy of the American Revolution*, University of Illinois Studies in the Social Sciences, xi, Urbana, Illinois, 1913.

PINK, W., and BEAVON, A., *The Parliamentary Representation of Lancashire (County and Borough), 1258–1885*, London, 1889.

PORRITT, E. and A. G., *The unreformed House of Commons*, 2 vols., Cambridge, 1903, 1909.

POSTGATE, R. W., *That Devil Wilkes*, London, 1930.

RITCHESON, C. R., *British Politics and the American Revolution, 1763–83*, Norman, Oklahoma, 1954.

ROBSON, E., *The American Revolution in its Political and Military Aspects, 1763–1783*, London, 1955.

ROSE, J. H., and others, eds., *The Cambridge History of the British Empire*, i, Cambridge, 1929.

ROWLAND, K. M., *The Life of George Mason, 1725–1792*, London, 1892.

SCHLESINGER, A. M., *The Colonial Merchants and the American Revolution, 1763–1776*, New York, 1917.

SCHUMPETER, E. B., *English Overseas Trade Statistics, 1697–1808*, Oxford, 1960.

SCHUYLER, R. L., *The Fall of the Old Colonial System*, Oxford, 1945.

SHARP, C., *A List of the Knights and Burgesses who have represented the County and City of Durham in Parliament*, Durham, 1831.

SHARPLES, I., *The Quakers in the Revolution*, Philadelphia, 1899.

SHERRARD, O. A., *Lord Chatham and America*, London, 1958.

SIOUSSAT, ST. G. L., 'The Breakdown of the Royal Management of Lands in the Southern Provinces, 1773–5', *Agricultural History*, iii, Urbana, Illinois, 1929, pp. 67-98.

SMITH, F. F., *Rochester in Parliament*, London, 1933.

SMITH, J. E., *The Parliamentary Representation of Surrey, 1290–1924*, London, 1927.

SPECTOR, M. M., *The American Department of the British Government, 1768–1782*, Faculty of Political Science, Columbia University Number 466, New York, 1940.

STANHOPE, P. H., Viscount MAHON, *The History of England . . . (1713–1783)*, 7 vols., London, 1836–54.

STEVENS, W. E., *The Northwest Fur Trade, 1763–1800*, University of Illinois Studies in the Social Sciences, xiv (3), Urbana, 1926.

STOOKS SMITH, H., *The Register of Parliamentary Contested Elections*, 3 vols., London, 1842–50.

SUTHERLAND, L. S., *The East India Company in Eighteenth-Century Politics*, Oxford, 1952.

SUTHERLAND, L. S., *The City of London and the Opposition to Government, 1768–1774*, The Creighton Lecture in History 1958, London, 1959.

SUTHERLAND, L. S., 'Edmund Burke and the First Rockingham Ministry', *English Historical Review*, xlvii, London, 1932, pp. 46-72.

TANNER, E. P., 'Colonial Agencies in England during the Eighteenth Century', *Political Science Quarterly*, xvi, New York, 1920, pp. 24-49.

TEMPERLEY, H. W. V., 'Inner and outer cabinet and Privy Council, 1679–1783', *English Historical Review*, xxvii, London, 1912, pp. 682-99.

TEMPERLEY, H. W. V., 'A note on inner and outer cabinets ; their development and relations in the eighteenth century', *English Historical Review*, xxxi, London, 1916, pp. 291-6.

THOMSON, M., *The Secretaries of State, 1681–1782*, Oxford, 1932.

THOMSON, M., *A Constitutional History of England, 1642–1801*, London, 1938.

TREVELYAN, G. O., *The American Revolution*, 4 vols., London, 1928.

TURBERVILLE, A. S., *The House of Lords in the XVIIIth Century*, Oxford, 1927.

TURNER, E. R., *The Cabinet Council of England in the Seventeenth and Eighteenth Centuries, 1622–1784*, Oxford, 2 vols., 1930–32.

UNDERDOWN, P. T., 'Henry Cruger and Edmund Burke : Colleagues and Rivals at the Bristol Election of 1774', *The William and Mary Quarterly*, Third Series, xv (1), Williamsburg, Virginia, 1958, pp. 14-34.

VAN DOREN, C., *Benjamin Franklin*, London, 1939.

VAUGHN, C. E., *Studies in the history of political philosophy before and after Rousseau* (ed. A. G. Little), 2 vols., Manchester, 1925.

WASHBURNE, G. A., *Imperial control of the administration of justice in the thirteen American colonies, 1684–1776*, New York, 1923.

WATSON, J. S., *The Reign of George III, 1760–1815*, The Oxford History of England, xii, Oxford, 1960.

WECTER, D., *Edmund Burke and his Kinsmen*, University of Colorado Studies, Series B, I (i), Boulder, Colorado, 1939.

WEYMAN, H. T., 'The Members of Parliament for Bridgnorth', *Transactions of the Shropshire Archæological and Natural History Society*, 4th Series, v, Shrewsbury, 1915, pp. 1-76.

WHITLEY, T. W., *The Parliamentary Representation of the City of Coventry*, Coventry, 1894.

WILLIAMS, B., *The Life of William Pitt, Earl of Chatham*, 2 vols., London, 1913.

WILLIAMS, E. T., 'The Cabinet in the eighteenth century', *History*, n.s. xxii, London, 1937, pp. 240-52.

WILLIAMS, W. R., *The Parliamentary History of the County of Gloucester, 1213–1898*, Hereford, 1898.

WILLIAMS, W. R., *The Parliamentary History of the County of Hereford and the Boroughs of Leominster, Weobley, Bromyard, Ledbury and Ross*, Brecknock, 1896.

WILLIAMS, W. R., *The Parliamentary History of the County of Oxford, 1213–1899*, Brecknock, 1899.

WILLIAMS, W. R., *The Parliamentary History of the Principality of Wales, 1541–1895*, Brecknock, 1895.

WILLIAMS, W. R., *The Parliamentary History of the County of Worcester, 1213–1897*, Hereford, 1897.

WINSTANLEY, D. A., *Personal and Party Government: . . . 1760–1766.* Oxford, 1910.

WINSTANLEY, D. A., *Lord Chatham and the Whig Opposition*, Oxford, 1912.

(b) *Unprinted*

REID, M., 'Canada in British Politics from 1763–1783', D.Phil. thesis in the University of Oxford, 1929.

SHAW, H. L., 'British Administration of the Southern Indians, 1756–1783', Ph.D. thesis presented at Bryn Mawr College, deposited in the University of Harvard, 1931.

INDEX

INDEX

Mills, Sir Thomas, 125 n.
Ministry, British: morale of, 83, 103-4, 167, 175, 209, 274-6, 283-7. *See also,* American Colonies, Cabinet, *and individual members of, under separate names*
Minorca, 278
Mississippi river, 106, 108, 118-19
Mississippi Company, 114 n.
Molasses Act (1733), 5 n.
Molineux, Crisp (1731–92), 140, 292
Molleson, William, 155 n.
Monson, Lewis, Lord Sondes (d. 1795), 294
Montagu, Lord Charles, 185, 187, 197
Montagu, Edward, 157 n.
Montagu, Frederick (1733–1800), 90, 136, 291
Montagu, George, 4th Duke of Manchester (1737–88), 83, 100 n., 101-102, 233-4, 253, 294
Montagu, John, 4th Earl of Sandwich (1718–92), 40-1, 213, 223, 242, 253-4; joins Ministry, 15-16; American policy of, 44, 70, 283-4; and 1774 Elections, 179, 183; sends reinforcements, 203-205; and Chatham's motion to withdraw troops, 237; use of troops, 265
Montagu, Admiral John, 25, 63 n., 64-5, 93 n.
Morant, Edward (1730–91), 88 n.
Morgann, Maurice, 120
Morice, Humphrey (1723–85), 184-185, 191 n.
Morning Chronicle, 185
Mountmorres, Lord, 186 n.
Murray, Governor, 109, 123
Murray, William, 1st Earl of Mansfield (1705–93), Lord Chief Justice, 46-7, 59, 87, 120, 166, 175, 177 n., 242

Namier, Sir Lewis, 132 n., 140
Navy, British, 25, 40, 93 n.; Marines, 204-5, 221, 223-4; and America, 204-5, 206-7, 223-4, 277
Nedham, William (*c.* 1740–1806), 292
Neville, George, 15th Baron, later 1st Earl Abergavenny (*c.* 1727–85), 294
Neville, Richard Neville (1717–93), 184 n.

New Hampshire, 1 n.; Assembly, 4 n.
New Jersey, 1 n., 255
New Woodstock, 140 n.
New York, 1 n., 4, 114, 118, 122, 124, 156, 207-8, 220, 254-5, 266-7, 270-1, 274; disorders at, 52; mail packet, 216-17, 271, 278; Assembly, 254-5, 266 n.; Assembly Remembrance 1775, 271
Newark, 137 n.
Newcastle, Duke of, *see* Pelham Clinton
Newcastle-on-Tyne, 196 n., 197
Newcastle-under-Lyme, 195
Newport, Cornwall, 191 n.
Newspapers, 33, 179, 272-3
Noel, Thomas (1705–88), 11 n.
Non-Importation Campaigns, 6, 152-153, 159 n., 175, 209, 219 n. *See also* Continental Congress, Continental Associations
North, Brownlow, Bishop of Litchfield (1741–1820), 99 n., 100, 176 n.
North Carolina, 1 n., 252, 255; Assembly, 4 n.
North, Frederick, Lord North (1732–1792), 10, 13, 39, 45, 47, 66-7, 68, 132 n., 172, 205 n., 216, 242, 244, 271 n.; and Tea Duty, 6, 21 n., 22-4; American policy of, 9, 16, 38, 44, 166, 171-2, 203, 209-10, 230; as Prime Minister, 14-15, 36-7, 83, 84-5, 286, 289-90; and petition to dismiss Hutchinson, 33; and sending General Gage, 49; and Boston Port Act, 50-1, 64-5, 68-9, 76-81, 83; and prosecuting Boston rioters, 60-2; and Massachusetts Regulating Act, 69-71, 87-8; debates on America, 73, 238-40; and Impartial Administration of Justice Act, 95; and Quebec Act, 110-11, 120-4; and Continental Congress, 175; and 1774 Elections, 177-88, 200; and dismissal of Gage, 210-12, 217; and use of troops, 213, 218; and Franklin, 221, 225; his Conciliatory Proposition, 223, 225, 248-51, 256, 269, 284; and Act to restrain New England trade, 243; Lexington and Concord, 272-4; and sending reinforcements, 277-8
North, George (1757–1802), 182 n.

THE END

PRINTED BY R. & R. CLARK, LTD., EDINBURGH